The Independence of Judges in China and Germany

# European University Studies

Europäische Hochschulschriften
Publications Universitaires Européennes

**Series II**
**Law**

Reihe II Série II
Rechtswissenschaft
Law

**Vol./Bd. 5171**

PETER LANG
Frankfurt am Main · Berlin · Bern · Bruxelles · New York · Oxford · Wien

Yuanyuan Wang

# The Independence of Judges in China and Germany

PETER LANG
Internationaler Verlag der Wissenschaften

**Bibliographic Information published by the Deutsche Nationalbibliothek**
The Deutsche Nationalbibliothek lists this publication in the Deutsche Nationalbibliografie; detailed bibliographic data is available in the internet at http://dnb.d-nb.de.

Zugl.: Berlin, Humboldt-Univ., Diss., 2010

11
ISSN 0531-7312
ISBN 978-3-631-61532-4



www.peterlang.de

# Vorwort

Ein besonderes Wort des Dankes möchte ich an meinen Doktorvater Prof. Dr. Ingolf Pernice richten, ohne den ich niemals ein Licht am Ende der Doktorarbeit gesehen hätte. Er hat nicht nur in fachspezifischen, sondern auch in privaten Gesprächen immer dafür gesorgt, dass ich meinen Geist anstrenge.

Für die Übernahme des Zweitgutachtens bin ich Prof. Dr. Ulrich Battis dankbar.

Mein Dank gilt auch den Kolleginnen und Kollegen von Graduiertenkolleg „Verfassung jenseits Staats: Von der europäischen zur globalen Rechtsgemeinschaft?". Sie gaben mir mit ihrem fundierten Fachwissen viele Anregungen für meine wissenschaftliche Arbeit. Ohne ihr Wissen, ohne ihre Ideen und ihre Kritik wäre mein Forschungsprojekt niemals soweit gekommen.

Auch möchte ich mich bei meinen Freunden Terry Stickland und Toni Li bedanken, die mich nicht nur tatkräftig unterstützt haben, sondern mich stets aufbauten und für die erforderliche Abwechslung sorgten. Meinen Freunden Ragnar Amsel und Li Yang schulde ich auch großen Dank für ihre Unterstützung während meines Studienaufenthaltes in Deutschland.

Von ganzem Herzen bedanke ich mich bei meinen Eltern, meinem Bruder und meinem Freund, die alle auf ihre Weise zum Gelingen dieser Arbeit beigetragen haben.

# Contents

# Introduction

## I. Why China?

Since the 1980s, a contemporary global movement has arisen and developed which may be described as the third wave of globalisation. In the course of these modern developments, different market players have been drawn into a "market without borders" by revolutionary changes in global information and communications technology and the gradual formation of a global network. Given this tide of globalisation in investment and trade, it is also clear that the State is unable to deal on its own with global challenges such as poverty, the environment, terrorism, etc. Without communication and integration, there can be no supranational co-operation between different peoples across the world, no mechanisms such as the EU, the Asian Union and the African Union which are more open and inclusive, nor the requisite share and balance of global rights, and so-called globalisation would be some monstrous many-headed colossus with countless different hearts and minds, forever trapped in self-dispute and self-harm.

The inherent motive of economic globalisation as characterised by the globalisation of trade and finance is the operation of the market economy, which has the expanded feature of market relationships and the accumulation of capital. Objectively, it seeks its developing space in the global arena, and the technological revolution provides the technological support for expansion of the market economy. In the course of this process, the economies of many countries are opened up, and economic co-operation and association become closer and more integrated. The global economy as a whole has become more interdependent and integrated, such that it significantly affects the development of the market economy in many countries. As an emerging dominant power in an intricate and rapidly changing global situation, China is constantly developing its vibrancy and energy. Its huge economic achievements since the beginning of reform and opening-up have also attracted the attention of the world. In the modern world in which multi-polarisation and economic globalisation have developed so deeply, what position will China have when it emerges onto the world stage? What is the "real China"? This is a topic which has attracted general interest. The future and destiny of China are increasingly linked to that of the world at large. China's development cannot avoid the outside world, and global prosperity and stability likewise cannot ignore China. However, it is regrettable that the world's knowledge of China does not compare to China's knowledge of the world.

In 2001, China finally joined the WTO thanks to its tireless efforts and so took a first step in its formal return to the world stage. China thus formally undertook to adopt an active participating role in the process of economic globalisation. The refined market economy has strict requirements regarding the distinction and specialisation of market behaviour, the unity of market rules and the distinction and specialisation of social management functions. As unified international economic laws, the fundamental rules of the WTO have had a deep influence on the content and application of domestic economic law in China. The unified principles of transparency, impartiality and judicial unity established by the WTO rules require judicial activities in China to be independent, just, public and effective. This dissertation aims to introduce the judicial system in China in order to inform a wider audience of the efforts being expended in order to develop a better legal framework and organisation in China, and of the problems which still have to be solved. This essay shall also endeavour, by analysing various relevant topics, to assist in a global understanding of the current state of the law in China, so that China may be allowed in due time to develop its legal environment and to make more and better suggestions for developments in the law in China.

Some readers may ask whether it is of general relevance to research questions of modern China. In this author's opinion, it is of general relevance, since whether certain knowledge is of general relevance or not does not depend on the subjective intention or aims of the author but rather on whether it is applicable to other areas and/or may be usefully referenced by a wider audience. The origin of knowledge or intellectual resources does not influence the ultimate quality and/or effect of such knowledge or resources. This point applies equally to the provision of knowledge and the provision of other, for example commercial products. For example, television sets made in Japan can be sold around the world. From the point of view of the current sum of development knowledge and experience in the developed Western countries, it may be that the problems in China are specific to their locale. But if modernisation is not regarded as a one-track evolution, and the rule of law is not regarded as having only one model, then the experience and knowledge of any country will always once have been localised (for example, the Anglo-American legal system arose from the circuit judges dispatched by the British monarchy, who settled disputes in accordance with local customs and traditions, as was also the local practice). In this respect, there is never a distinct boundary between what is local and what is general.

Modernisation in China is different from the modernisation of Western countries. The process of modernisation in China does not merely involve adapting and transforming so as to adopt Western theories. If it may be said that issues in China, which has a fifth of the world's population, have a certain degree of relevance, then practical problems in China must have both practical and theoretical value.

## II. Why the Independence of Judges?

The tide of globalisation with which we are confronted not only promotes the integration of the global economy and to some extent of society, but also leads to the remodelling of global laws and the development of judicial procedure. China is also experiencing this historical process of remodelling laws and the judicial system.

Since the Chinese Constitution was amended for the third time and the management of state affairs under the rule of law was introduced into the Constitution in 1999, the rule of law in the management of state affairs has become a fundamental national guideline. The "management of state affairs under the rule of law" means that the law becomes the final principle and standard for distinguishing between right and wrong; no-one can limit or reduce the authority of the legal system or the dignity of the law at any time, let alone place himself above the law. However, laws cannot be effective by themselves. In order to realise the management of state affairs under the rule of law, it is necessary to safeguard judicial fairness, since the vitality of the law lies in its execution. Only if judicial fairness is guaranteed can the authority of the law be established and the dignity of the law maintained. Unfortunately, judicial fairness in China currently falls far short of the required standard. The judiciary cannot provide the relief that should be provided, and the difficulties of execution make judges' decisions into hollow words on a sheet of paper. Moreover, corruption in the judiciary is far more serious than in other institutions. Accordingly, the issues of promoting judicial reform and guaranteeing judicial fairness were explicitly raised at the 15$^{th}$ and 16$^{th}$ Congresses of the Chinese Communist Party. The 16$^{th}$ Congress of the Chinese Communist Party further stressed to need to guarantee that judicial and procuratorial organs exercised their jurisdiction and procuratorial authority independently within the system. As an indispensable precondition of judicial fairness, the problem of the need for judges to adjudicate independently has become the subject of close and unprecedented attention by Chinese society at large.

The beginnings of the reform of Chinese courts are to be found in the mid-1980s. In the 1990s, the reform of Chinese courts began to develop against a gradually more extensive background and across a wider scope, the most significant expression of which was the Judges Law of the People's Republic of China, approved at the 12$^{th}$ meeting of the Standing Committee of the 8$^{th}$ National People's Congress on 28$^{th}$ February 1995. Based on the aim of guaranteeing that courts execute their jurisdiction legally and independently and that judges execute their duties in accordance with the law, the Judges Law offers provisions on such issues as the duties, obligations and rights of judges, and detailed conditions for their appointment and removal, thus opening the door to the professionalisation of contemporary Chinese judges. At the 15$^{th}$ Party Congress held in October 1997, one issue raised was that of the historical mission to manage state affairs under the rule of law and to establish a socialist state under the rule of law. Reforms to the system of court staffing began in the early 1990s, but the most significant milestones were when the Judges Law was amended in June 2001 and when a meeting to establish a nationwide system of courts was held in July 2002. The amended Judges Law not only raised the entry requirements for judges but also established a unified state examination for judicial qualification. It then stipulates that those who pass the unified state examination for judicial qualification are qualified to serve as judges. At the meeting to establish a nationwide system of courts, the stated aims were to further the professionalisation of judges, emphasise the strict professional admittance of judges, strengthen the professional awareness of judges, cultivate a professional philosophy among judges, enhance the professional skills of judges, reinforce the professional protection of judges, refine the professional supervision of judges, implement a system for the allocation of judges, reform the system of judicial selection and review the system of assistant judges. All these plans are intended to achieve a core purpose, namely the independence of judges, since the history of legal development across the globe shows that judicial independence is an essential element in establishing an impartial court system.

As the last protective shield safeguarding personal rights, the judiciary is not only about realising the rights of citizens as endowed by the law but also about safeguarding the people's concept of the same, in order to realise it. The judicial process is also a process of seeking the rationality of what exactly "justice" is. Although there is no such thing is immutable justice, specific norms of justice that are generally accepted by everyone can be embodied in an institution or organ which everyone can acknowledge, and this organ is the judiciary. The most important factor here is the independence of judges. The independence of judges is the one essential precondition for judicial fairness. If there is impartiality, but no independence of judges, the judiciary still has no safeguards. Adjudication has to be an independent occupation, and a judge has to be independent as an individual, so the most important quality of judges is their independence. Why do judges have to be independent? Because the way in which judges exercise their powers is different from the way in which administrative officials exercise their powers. Judges exercise their jurisdiction and adjudicate in specific courts and specific cases. It is necessary for judges to have good observation and judgment skills when exercising their powers in court and adjudicating cases. The judicial process has an aspect of personal interaction to it, for example when a witness testifies or when a party makes a statement, and judges must be able to observe and consider whether the witness or party is making a false statement and what is their expression. In ancient China, people called this "listening to statements in courts according to the five looks". This means that when judges make a decision in a case, they need to consider what a witness or party said, but also for instance their breath and why it was a little short and rapid when they spoke, or why they suddenly stuttered, or blushed, or why they were shaking. All of these are closely connected with the case. In the presence of witnesses and/or parties, judges have to observe and interpret their faces.[1] Therefore, judicial independence needs to establish the independence of individual judges. The system of selecting and appointing chief judges as recently implemented in China aims to establish a system which ensures the independence of individual judges. However, a careful examination of the internal methodology at courts reveals that some systems still prevail which do not meet the necessary requirements for the independence of individual judges. This dissertation will analyse these critical aspects of the current systems and the reasons why they exist, in order to find improved methods which are compatible with the current state of the Chinese nation and which would contribute to gradually establishing a genuinely independent judicial system.

## III. Why Germany?

This dissertation will look into ways of resolving the various problems in the Chinese system by comparing and analysing the systems of China and Germany, both of which employ Civil Law. As China's largest trading partner in Europe, Germany signed the Sino-German Agreement on Legal Exchanges and Co-operation on 30th June 2000 and established the precedent of equitable dialogue

1 He Weifang, Eight Major Issues of Judicial Reform in China, from a speech by He Weifang delivered at the Intermediate People's Court of Haikou on 21st December 2001, entitled "Talk on the Length and Breadth of Judicial Reform", http://article.chinalawinfo.com/article_print.asp?articleid=19684

and friendly communication on aspects of establishing a state under the rule of law between countries which have a different social system and cultural tradition. China and Germany have so far maintained the system of "dialogue between countries under the rule of law" for ten years. The incumbent German co-ordinator and Federal Minister of Justice Brigitte Zypries has said: "what connects Germany and China is not only their ever closer economic co-operation but also their continuing convergence in terms of politics and culture. China is a partner moving in the direction of the state under the rule of law."[2] The two countries exchange experiences and problems with each other and look for suitable solutions in view of the current circumstances in the respective countries. This dialogue also allows the two countries a thorough understanding of each other's legal system, culture, traditions und social values, which in turn undoubtedly serves to create a broader scope for co-operation and exchanges.

China's use of Germany's judicial experiences did not however begin with the dialogue on the rule of law between the two countries. As early as the late Qing dynasty, China referred to the Civil Law of Germany when drafting its own Civil Code. Due to previous periods of study in Germany, this author is familiar with the history and current state of the system of judicial independence in Germany and believes there are many similarities with China in the German process of realising the independence of judges and establishing the existing system. As compared to say Great Britain or the United States, it would thus appear more useful to draw on the German experience.

## 1. Tradition

In reviewing the history of judicial independence in Germany, it may be said that Germany has not always had a tradition of judicial independence but rather progressed through the development stages from absolutism to liberalism, the Weimar Republic and state socialism, and ultimately established the principle of judicial independence. This process is accompanied by the judiciary being independent of the legislative and executive, the judiciary becoming a state power with its own character and gradually being endowed with the legal task of examining the executive and the legislative. Of these, the American idea of the separation of powers served in particular to strengthen the German judiciary, and a powerful judiciary is undoubtedly an indispensable condition of realising judicial independence.

As is clear from China's lengthy legal history, there are some similarities between China and Germany in the progress of their development. Although

2 http://npc.people.com.cn/GB/42168/9211229.html

there were judges at the time of the slave-holding society in China,[3] the period from a slave-holding society up until the feudalist society saw China in the same situation as the absolutism in Germany up until the 14$^{th}$ century. Judges in China were completely under the command of the king and the ranks of judges were set by administrative organs. Generally speaking, the local judges were also the local chief executives. Only at the centralised level were the specialised functions of each duty separated. In the modern era, Western science was introduced and China learned from Western legal theories and established comparable systems, but since gunsmoke was flying all over China and society was unstable, many legal systems could not be effectively applied and were completely overturned once New China was founded. This is astonishingly similar to the historical developments in Germany, in which the principle of judicial independence was initially established at the time of the Weimar Republic, but the Weimar Republic was only short-lived and the principles were not implemented and utilised but rather distorted into State Socialism. When the Basic Law was established in West Germany, this principle was recovered and was gradually ingrained into people's hearts and minds.

## 2. The Qualifications of Judges

As in Germany, those who serve as judges in China are not required to have years of employment and experience as a lawyer, unlike the way in which judges are chosen from lawyers in Great Britain or the United States. In accordance with Article 5 of the German Judges Act, those who are to become judges in Germany must take the first state examination after completing a university degree majoring in law, and must then take the second state examination after two years' preparatory service.[4]

In China, those who wish to become judges also have to have a university educational background and must pass the unified state examination for judicial qualification. But the qualification for Chinese judges is not limited to majoring in law at a university. In accordance with the provisions of Paragraph 2 of Article 34 of the Organic Law of the People's Court of the People's Republic of

3 The occupation of judge existed during the Western Zhou dynasty (1046 to 771 BC), the special title of which was Sikou, and involved being in charge of such matters as criminal punishment and maintaining public order. See Zhang Zhaokai, A History of the Judiciary in Ancient China, Yuelu Press, Changsha 2005, pp. 3-4

4 Jörg Zätzsch, Richterliche Unabhängigkeit und Richterauswahl in den USA und Deutschland, Baden-Baden 2000, p. 36

China, judges who have not majored in law must be trained in the specifics of the law.

## 3. The Selection and Appointment of Judges

The pattern of the selection and appointment of judges in China is almost the same as that in Germany. In Germany, the general process of selecting and appointing judges is that judges are initially appointed as probationary judges for three years. The personal ability and professional capability of the probationary judge is decided in the course of the probationary period. During this period, the probationary judge may be dismissed and cannot then enjoy the independence of judges as stipulated by the Constitution.[5] The Organic Law of the People's Courts of the People's Republic of China has similarly been supplemented through negotiations with new provisions on newly qualified judges which are almost identical to those in Germany. He Weifang, commissioned by the Supreme People's Court to compile the draft for the Organic Law, believes that the standard for admittance to court as a judge will be raised. In the draft, he suggests implementeing a system for newly qualified judges. After a five-year probationary period, those deemed eligible could be made duly appointed judges. Newly qualified judges are not entitled to adjudicate cases independently. They are charged with matters such as legal examination, researching legal issues and drafting documents for trial. Those who are not deemed eligible following their probationary period must come off probation.[6]

In Germany, judges are not directly elected, and even the election of judges by representatives of the people is extremely limited (for example, the selection of judges at the Federal Constitutional Court; also, Paragraph 2 of Article 82 of the Berlin Constitution and Article 2 of the German Judges Act stipulate that the presidents of Berlin state (*Land*) courts shall also be elected by representatives of the people). In China, as in Germany, judges are also not directly elected. Only a limited number of judges are elected by delegates of the people, such as for example the president of the Supreme People's Court who is elected by the National People's Congress, and the presidents of the Local People's Courts at all levels who are elected by the local people's delegates at all levels.

---

5 Günter Schmidt-Räntsch, Jürgen Schmidt-Räntsch, Deutsches Richtergesetz (DRiG), Kommentar (*Commentary on the German Judges Act*), 6th edition, Munich 2008, Article 12, margin number 4, p. 321

6 See He Weifang, Amendments to the Organic Law of the Courts Should Emphasise the Independence of Judges, in answer to a question from the Beijing News, http://article.chinalawinfo.com/Article_Detail.asp?ArticleId=33872

Judges in Germany are traditionally selected and appointed by the administrative departments, and the head of the department answers to parliament. At the federal level, all the judges of federal courts at lower levels are selected by the administrative department.[7] In Baden-Württemberg, Bavaria, Mecklenburg-West Pomerania, Lower Saxony, North Rhine-Westphalia, the Rhineland Palatinate, Saxony und Saxony-Anhalt, the *Land* judges are also selected by the administrative departments.[8] In China, judges are ostensibly selected and appointed by delegated electing organs. In reality, however, the power to appoint judges is held by the organisational department of the Party committee at the same level and by the organisational departments of the courts, and the appointment of judges is also decided by the organisational department by way of the executive. In accordance with Article 35 of the Organic Law of the People's Courts of the People's Republic of China, the judges of courts at all levels are appointed by the Standing Committee of the People's Congress at the same level. In practice, however, candidate judges are examined and accepted or rejected by the organisation department of the courts and the Party committee, and the People's Congress and its Standing Committee never question their decisions regarding candidates, hence the selection and appointment of judges is essentially handled by the administrative departments.

## 4. The Status of Judges

In both China and Germany, judges count as civil servants. In order to take account of the particularities of judges' work, against the background of universally applying the law regarding civil servants, the Judges Law of China is additionally applied in order to regulate those aspects by which judges differ from other civil servants because of the nature of their work. Many scholars in China heavily criticise the administrative management of judges, feeling that this leads judges to become little more than common administrative clerks, always under the command of their superior. Also, the system of promotion, rewards and punishments has strict rankings, so if judges wish to be promoted and/or attain a position of importance, they must follow the wishes of the president or presiding judge of their court. If they contradict the wishes of their superiors and insist on deciding cases according to the law, they will have little hope of being promoted and may even risk dismissal. The administrative management of judges may

7 Ernst Teubner, Die Bestellung zum Berufsrichter in Bund und Ländern, Entwicklung, Modelle, Analysen, Köln 1984, pp. 34 f

8 Jörg Zätzsch, Richterliche Unabhängigkeit und Richterauswahl in den USA und Deutschland, Baden-Baden 2000, p. 49

thus cause judges to lose their independence, such that an independent trial cannot be realised.[9]

The similarities mentioned above are the reason why this dissertation has chosen Germany as the object of comparison with China. Moreover, many systems which are denounced by Chinese scholars, such as the provisions on the qualifications of judges, the method of selection and administrative management, are able to operate well in Germany. It is therefore worth considering in-depth how and why the same system can protect judicial independence within the legal environment in Germany but prevent it in China. For precisely these reasons, this dissertation shall attempt to compare the systems in the two countries on the basis of their similarities, isolate their differences and identify what aspects need to be improved.

## IV. Purpose, Methodology and Main Conclusions

This dissertation shall compare the systems of judicial independence in China and Germany, with the aim of drawing lessons from the experience of Germany which may be used to improve the judicial system in China. The review of the German system of judicial independence will not only discuss the system of judicial independence itself but will also analyse its corresponding social and constitutional set-up in order to identify the social and constitutional and/or governmental foundations necessitated by the system of judicial independence in Germany and to decide which experiences by the German system of judicial independence the Chinese system could draw on, which aspects would have to be adapted to certain particularities of the Chinese system, and which problems of execution or social context might arise because a system which operates well in Germany is not suitable for China against the background of present-day Chinese society and constitutional government. It could perhaps also be said that the problems in modern China are such that a chain of fundamental changes in the current Chinese social system as a whole are required in order to realise judicial independence. However this would depart from the intention of this dissertation, hence it is necessary to make some assumptions.

Judicial independence is a precondition for the independence and impartiality of the courts. The greatest difference between China and for example Germany or the United States is that the Communist Party of China exercises comprehensive control over social life, including the judiciary. Generally speak-

9 Han Xu, New Ideas on Chinese Judges in the 21st Century, in: Yunnan University Journal of Jurisprudence, 2001, Volume 1, pp. 19-24

ing, the judiciary cannot be independent under such a system, since one person cannot credibly be both player and referee. Society cannot therefore be just. Judicial independence need not, however, conflict with the leadership of the Communist Party as such. On the contrary, the overall control of the legislative, executive and judiciary by the Communist Party can even advance efficiency, reduce the political cost and prevent in-fighting between state powers. In China, judicial independence must be respected by the administrative power of the executive, because the Constitution stipulates that the Party must implement all aspects of the Constitution. The Constitution is also the starting point for all work by the courts. If the activities of the Party are limited by the Constitution, then it is clear that the Party cannot interfere with the judiciary without violating the Constitution. It is therefore this author's opinion that it is still possible for Chinese courts to be independent. It is not the case that the independence of courts and judges can only be realised under a political system comprising the separation of powers, because these powers always come from the people, and the separation of powers is merely a political mode of operation.

What is most important is that the concept of judicial independence should gradually pervade all of society, and the relevant provisions of the Constitution and laws should be amended, not only so that judicial independence has a theoretical basis but also so that the conditions are created in order to draw lessons from the German experience in practice.

This dissertation primarily uses a comparitive method. First, it compares the different concepts of judicial independence. By analysing the formation and development of the systems of judicial independence in the two countries, this dissertation posits that it was easier for the German legal system to merge well with Roman Law and absorb the ideas of natural law from Roman Law and to accept the ideas of liberalism and the separation of powers by Locke and Montesquieu which come down in one continuous line. Influenced by the idea of liberalism, German citizens themselves gradually awoke to the notion of judicial independence and embarked on a fight for judicial independence in order to secure more rights for themselves, whereas in the process of the legal modernisation in China, a trained specialist group of legal professionals was not created when Western laws were simply transplanted, so there was no such group to provide an impetus to actively analyse and select the laws to be transplanted, hence this transplantation of laws to China was merely similar in appearance but not ultimately in spirit, and the idea of the independence of judges and the courts had difficulty taking root in society. Another difference with respect to Germany is that China has been situated in a natural economy pattern for a long time, and the characteristics of traditional penalty-orientated legal culture in China have been the spirit of the rule of man and the concentration of power under its direction. Whether China can realise a genuine independence of judges depends largely on developing those aspects of traditional legal culture which are still useful, abandoning those which are not, and realising a modernising transformation of traditional legal culture which continues to renew the legal system and to reform concepts of the law.

This dissertation shall then compare the systems of judicial independence in each of the two countries in detail, first in comparing the respective systems for the substantial independence of judges, including selecting judges, supervising judges' posts, the examining powers of judges, and the administration and organisation of courts.

By comparing the qualifications of judges and the procedures for appointing judges in the two respective countries, this dissertation shall establish that although China is similar to Germany in its provisions regarding nationality and the principle of upholding the Constitution, there are many differences in other provisions such as those relating to age, educational background, the judicial examination, practical experience and even candidates' physical constitution. Moreover, the provisions on the qualifications of judges in China are unified, and there is no obvious difference in the qualifications of judges serving in courts at different levels, but different standards are permitted in different areas. By comparing the selection procedures, this dissertation shall establish that there are many shortcomings and defects in the procedure for selecting judges in China, such that the independence of judges is seriously threatened. There are for example no clear provisions on the procedure for selecting and appointing judges, nor any unified standards pertaining to selection and appointment, one upshot of which is that most newly qualified judges are employed and appointed as judges for life by their court presidents. In addition, the standard and the procedure of selecting newly qualified judges are the same as for general civil servants, i.e. there is no special organisation or procedure, as in Germany. In addition, judges in China are not promoted progressively as they are in Germany, but are rather assigned in parallel to courts at higher and/or lower levels. Promotion from courts at lower levels to courts at higher levels occurs by means of administrative transfer and not reselection. One of the most important aspects in China is that all positions of court presidents are filled by promoting cadres and not by selecting judges, and that candidates are decided by the local Party committee. In this dissertation, the view will be advanced that the legislation in China needs to be reinforced, the methods and standards of judicial selection have to be unified nationwide, a separate organisation and procedure specifically for selecting judges, such as exists in Germany, needs to be established, the system of selecting judges needs to be improved, and selected judges should be required to have adequate and pertinent personal and professional qualities. Only then it is possible for there to be a feasible basis for the independence of judges, on which other related systems can then be subsequently established.

It is generally agreed that the selection of judges and the service supervision of judges represent the areas in which the executive most severely infringes upon judicial independence. Following a comparison of the respective systems for the service supervision of judges in the two countries under consideration here, this dissertation shall establish that because the Chinese Constitution does not make explicit provisions in this regard, there are no clear boundaries restricting the service supervision of judges in China as there are in Germany, where these are intended to prevent the independence of judges from being infringed. In German law, the supervisors of posts and the methods of supervision are restricted, and an independent organisation and the so-called service courts which examine whether a particular method of supervision is appropriate are established in order to guarantee judicial independence. In Chinese law, there are no such considerations at all. The relevant provisions are all muddled and lack a unifying system; the power to examine and punish judges in particular is entrusted entirely to court presidents, so judges are not independent of their court presidents. Furthermore, the power of the People's Congress and its Standing Committee to recall presidents by way of investigation is heavily mitigated by the structure of the system and its crude and vague procedures, such that the supervision of presidents exists in name only. Some means of supervision are not provided for in law and have no legal force but are still in fact means of service supervising of judges, such as supervision by the disciplinary department of the Party and supervision by the news media. It may be said that it is impossible for the independence of judges in China to exist under these numerous sources of service supervision of them. It is thus time to change the current situation in China, in which judges are supervised from numerous sides and supervision is largely unrestricted. It may be seen from German law that limits placed on supervisors, a strict regulation of the power of supervision, and a separately organised system of punishment specifically for judges can serve to protect the independence of judges.

Where political forces can utilise their power to supervise the judicial system to cause the judiciary to develop in line with their regulations, the independence of judges is again threathened. Generally speaking, every country in the world limits the legislative supervision of the judiciary on the basis of its Constitution. The judiciary can itself be an important means of balancing state powers by examining the constitutionality of rules and regulations and declaring them invalid where appropriate. At present, the Constitution and the law in China do not give judges this right of examination, although the latitude to presume that a regulation is inapplicable has already been extensively used in practice. However, judges have no power to declare a regulation invalid, but can merely refuse to apply it. A judge who suspects that a certain regulation is invalid must submit it to the executive, who decides whether it is valid or invalid, which clearly cannot involve a supervisory effect. Following a comparison of the systems of judicial examination in the two countries, this dissertation shall assert that at present, the design of the system of judicial examination in China has certain obvious flaws which are open to abuse and need to be developed so as to pre-empt this. In this dissertation, the opinion shall be advanced that China should draw on the experience of Germany and differentiate the power to examine regulations according to a "power to presume" and a "power to refuse to apply", thus clarifying the scope within which judges may refuse to apply regulations within legislative law and broadening the scope for administrative litigation, in order to prevent the possibility of different decisions being reached when one judge applies different regulations, which would destroy the unity of the national legal system. Lastly, an organ which is independent of the National People's Congress needs to be established in order to examine the validity of laws and regulations, thus fulfilling a similar function to the Constitutional Court in Germany. This examination of laws, rules and/or regulations should not be left to the National People's Congress or its Standing Committee itself.

Another potential threat which is not currently addressed but which may affect the independence of judges is the judiciary itself. In theory, the organisation and administration of courts do not have the purpose of deciding court cases, but if certain material and/or logistical conditions are not met, the court cannot perform its function. It may be said that the purpose of the organisation and administration of courts is to ensure that judges are able to decide cases objectively and justly, free of any influence or interference from external parties. There are clear differences between China and Germany in this respect. In China, the internal administrative management function of courts is performed mainly by the Supreme People's Court and the court presidents, whereas in Germany, it is shared between ministers of justice and court presidents. The organisation and administration of courts in China is different than in Germany. In Germany, the law provides on all matters, and any factors which prevent judges from deciding cases independently are considered illegal. In China, however, there are many inconsistencies in this respect: on the one hand, courts are controlled by the administrative organs in terms of their funds and personnel; and on the other hand, the powers of the courts sometimes extend far beyond what is actually provided for in law. Additionally, the dependency on other court at higher levels is far more marked in China than it is in Germany. Judges in Germany are bound only by the law, whereas in China, judges always have to request instructions from their presiding judge and/or president, and courts at lower levels have to request instructions from courts at higher levels. The pressure which judges in Germany suffer from within the court itself or from courts at higher levels is slight, but in China, this pressure is a well-known phenomenon, since judges in China are not only restricted by presidents and chief judges in their selection and appointment, supervision and assessment, but are also guided by them in other administrative matters. Accordingly, this dissertation shall address this burning issue and conclude that the following reforms are needed: 1) reform of the management system for court funding, in order for courts to be independent in their funding, so as to reduce the potential for administrative organs to interfere with the judiciary by this route; 2) reform of the internal administrative organs at courts, to the effect that the powers of the court president need to be regulated, and judicial committees such as those which exist in Germany need to be established in order to discuss and decide the administrative affairs of court; 3) reforms to strengthen the powers of collegial panels, abolish the system of examining and approving cases, and revoke the system whereby courts at lower levels request instructions from courts at higher levels, such that the courts at higher levels effectively direct the court at lower levels.

Substantive independence is the independence of trial adjudication, which prohibits judges from being directed, but it is still insufficient to guarantee the independence of judges. In order to make judges truly secure from the danger of any loss of status as a result of disobeying instructions from superiors or forming their own independent judgments, it is necessary to ensure the independence of the status of judges. The theory of the independence of status is clearly and directly related to substantive independence, such that the independence of status provides a factual premise for the independence of trial adjudication, in order for the independence of trial adjudication by judges to be more adequately realised. Following a discussion of the systems for guaranteeing the substantive independence of judges, this dissertation shall compare the systems for the independence of the status of judges in the two countries, mainly comprising the aspects of dismissal, suspension, transfer, retirement and salary. By comparing and analysing, this dissertation shall establish that there are clear legal grounds and detailed procedural protection in Germany with regard to the dismissal, suspension, transfer and retirement of judges, whereas in China, there are no provisions with regard to either the grounds for dismissing judges or procedural protection. In China, judges are subject to the retirement system for civil servants. There are no specific provisions on a retirement system for judges. In accordance with the provisions of the Law of the People's Republic of China on Public Servants, the age of retirement for judges is different between males and females, which has no scientific basis and violates the principle of sexual equality. The most striking problem is that of judges' salaries. The salaries and conditions for judges in

China are even lower than those for general civil servants. In search of a higher standard of living, judges are often tempted to break the law and/or rules of discipline, leading to constant judicial corruption in practice. In this dissertation, it shall be stated that China should be the same as Germany in this respect, separately stipulating the salaries of judges due to their special status as judges and determining a feasible standard according to which local government can allocate judges' salaries. This dissertation shall also discuss the problems that need to be resolved and feasible ways of realising a higher level of salaries for judges in China. Only if judges have this degree of economic protection can they diligently study and concentrate on their judicial skills, without having to worry about their financial security, and can thus pursue justice.

Finally, this dissertation shall analyse the internal independence of judges. The most significant influences on Chinese judges are social influences and the influence of the Party. Germany specifically allows judges to engage in political activities. After analysing and comparing these two aspects, this dissertation shall find that the posts occupied by judges in China are different in nature to those in Germany. In addition to the function of trial adjudication, Chinese judges also bear many social functions. When judges in Germany deal with disputes, they consider only the merits of that particular case, apply the law, and pursue a just outcome in the particular case accordingly. They do not undertake voluntary action with respect to social problems in order to demonstrate their vocational influence. Chinese society, however, applies much more diverse standards and criteria for evaluating the adjudicative decisions of judges, so Chinese judges have to consider many factors in addition to the law and perform a great deal of extrajudicial work within the scope of their jobs in order to achieve the greatest degree of justice and resolve disputes as conclusively as possible. In addition, neither Germany nor China strictly requires judges to join a party or to be engaged in political activities. In this respect, German law emphasises that judges have to moderate their political activities, whereas Chinese law emphasises the development in judicial practice of the augmented influence which members of the Communist Party have. Courts in China even have to arrange for judges who are members of the Communist Party to learn all the ideas and policies of the Party. However, this dissertation finds that whether in China or Germany, the influence of parties is realised in the process of appointment and promotion. The mere fact that there are many political parties in Germany means that this procedure is contained and restricted by the different parties among each other, thus reaching a balance. But in China, the supreme power to select judges is held almost exclusively by the Party Committee, so from the outset, judges cannot be independent either of the Party or of the court presidents. Hence in order to truly realise the independence of judges in China, it is necessary to begin with the appointment of judges, by establishing independent selection organs and preventing the Party from influencing and monopolising this power.

# Part 1 Basic Principles

## Chapter I Principles of the Independence of Judges

### Section I Necessity for the Independence of Judges

In a modern state under the rule of law, independent adjudication by judges according to the law and free of outside intervention is usually expressed in the constitution, in order to be able to strictly apply the rule of law, guarantee human rights and justify the verdicts of courts. Some scholars have said: "Only when there are independent judges can there be justice."[10] The English judge Edward Coke also emphasised that: "The safeguarding of personal rights rests with the independence of the courts."[11]

Why is it necessary for judges to be independent? In a democratic society, laws reflect the normal will of society with regard to how conflicts are resolved and the rules which members of society must generally comply with, and judicial judgement is the process whereby judges interpret and apply the law in the pursuit of justice in a case. This process is not just the direct and rigid application of legal provisions, but rather also involves judges applying their knowledge, experience and wisdom and making decisions based on values by recognising and taking into account people's social circumstances and attitudes to the law, and then considering the various circumstances of a specific case. In order to enable judges to apply themselves fully to this process and to have an appreciation of the significance and honour of the responsibility which they bear, the judge's right to independent judgement has to be guaranteed beyond question. Only if they are free of internal and external intervention can judges establish a contemplative judging environment in which they may fully comprehend the essence of laws and make appropriate and reasoned judgements in the pursuit of a just outcome.[12] But in order to achieve justice in the judiciary, judges

---

10 Klaus Louven, Inhalt und Grenzen richterlicher Unabhängigkeit, German Judges Journal (*Deutsche Richterzeitung* = *DRiZ*) 1981, pp. 299

11 Lin Chaorong, Research on Democratisation of the Prosecution System, doctorial dissertation in the legal research institute of the political science university, June 1993, p. 303

12 Piero Calamendrei, Procedure and Democracy, translated by John Clarke Adams and Helen Adams, Washington Square: New York University Press, 1956, pp. 35, 36

must exempt from retaliation or inappropriate influence from parties with a vested interest in the judgement, hence the independence of judges is necessary.[13]

## (1) The Principle of the Independence of Judges and the Separation of Powers

The principle of the independence of judges derives from the principle of the separation of powers,[14] i.e. that the state judiciary should be independent of the legislature and the executive. The principle of the separation of powers is a system designed such that state powers are separated into different government agencies so as to avoid the concentration of powers, prevent autocracy, restrict the discretionary use of powers and achieve a balance of power between the various authorities vested with state powers. In order for judges to perform the duty of legally settling disputes between different people and between people and the government, they must be independent. If judges are answerable to other government agencies, then the state powers assigned to judges actually belong to these other government agencies and the purpose of the separation of powers is not met.[15] As stated by the French political thinker Charles de Secondat, Baron de Montesquieu: "If judicial power is not independent of legislative power and executive power, people cannot enjoy freedom. For if judicial power is combined with legislative power, judges are also legislators, and the survival and freedom of people will be trampled on by the law. If judicial power is combined with executive power, judges are also executive officers, who may easily use violence to oppress people. If any one person or organisation has all three powers simultaneously, whether the person holding the powers is born of a noble family or is a commoner, freedom will not exist."[16] It is thus clear that legislative power, executive power and judicial power should be separated; each of them is different from the others and they should monitor and balance each other. Judges shall objectively and neutrally perform the duty of settling disputes between different citizens or between citizens and the state, according to the law, and shall be independent. Otherwise, if judges are answerable to other government agencies, then the state powers assigned to judges actually belong to

---

13 See also John Henry Merryman, Judicial Responsibility in the United States, The Rabel Journal of Comparative and International Private Law (*Rabelszeitschrift für Ausländisches und Internationales Privatrecht = RabelsZ*) 41, pp. 332, 337

14 Zhang Wenyu, Evaluating Judges and the Independence of Judges, Constitutional Government Times, Volume 26, July 2000, p. 5

15 Günther Schmidt-Räntsch, Deutsches Richtergesetz, 3rd edition, Munich, p. 218, Article 25, margin number 3

16 Li Hongxi, Constitutionalism and the Judicial System, China Forum, Volume 5, October 1977, p. 22

these other government agencies and the purpose of the separation of powers is not met.

Judges shall abide by the law, which does not conflict with the principle of the separation of powers but is rather the positive result of the even separation of powers. If other government agencies did not abide by the law, legal provisions would just be a piece of paper, state legislation would not be carried out effectively by the legislative authorities and legislation would lose its meaning completely.[17] Restricting the application of the law to judges is a balancing force away from the legislative authorities in favour of the judicial authorities, and a requirement for the principle of the separation of powers. Thus, it may be said that the separation of powers is a prerequisite for the independence of judges. It allows judges to perform their duties fearlessly, effectively and independently[18] and requires judges to concentrate only on the law.[19]

### (2) The Independence of Judges and the Principle of the State under the Rule of Law

The idea of the independence of judges is inextricably linked to the concept of the state under the rule of law. "In all the institutions belonging to our existence under the rule of law, the independent judgements by judges are the ultimate triumph in the idea of the state under the rule of law"[20]. The independence of judges is one of the means for guaranteeing that judgements are substantively and legally correct, the instrumental value of which relates to "the identification of the state under the rule of law with a substantive law which is objectively correct and fulfilled by courts and science"[21]. As the ultimate safeguard for independent discussion by judges, it must also be conceived of in the first place and forever striven for.[22]

The principle of the state under the rule of law is always understood to have a formal meaning and a substantive meaning. The formal meaning of the principle of the state under the rule of law emphasises that state public powers are to be appropriately limited. The methods of limitation include the separation of

---

17 Ruth Schmidt-Räntsch, Dienstaufsicht über Richter, Bielefeld 1985, p. 14

18 See Kurt Rudolf, Die Unabhängigkeit des Richters, DRiZ 1984, pp. 135, 136

19 E. Schunck & H. De Clerck, Allgemeines Staatsrecht und Staatsrecht des Bundes und der Länder, 3rd edition, Siegburg 1970, p. 264

20 Max Grünhut, Die Unabhängigkeit der richterlichen Entscheidung, Monatszeitschrift für Kriminalpsychologie und Strafrechtsreform, Supplement No. 3 , Heidelberg 1930, p. 1

21 Fritz Scharpf, Die politischen Kosten des Rechtsstaats, Tübingen 1970, p. 56

22 Dieter Simon, Die Unabhängigkeit des Richters, Darmstadt 1975, pp. 2 ff

powers, laws to ensure that people can predict the action of a public authority in exercising state public powers, and the independence of adjudication by judges. By contrast, the substantive meaning of the principle of the state under the rule of law emphasises the safeguarding of people's basic rights.[23] However, both the formal meaning and the substantive meaning of the principle of the state under the rule of law emphasise the significance of the independence of judges.

The principle of the state under the rule of law is originally a phrase from German law, the essence of which is similar to the "Rule of Law" in Anglo-American law.[24] The Rule of Law rejects the rule of man and aims to realise the goal of guaranteeing human rights in accordance with the law in order to enhance personal happiness. The substantive Rule of Law does not permit any one person or power to establish the law or to rule others by law. Legislation, administration and judicature according to the rule of law are paramount.[25] As a result, if judicial power is not independent and is influenced by legislative power or executive power, then it cannot effectively perform its function and cannot guarantee that the principle of the state under the rule of law is implemented effectively. In particular where the state is one of the interested parties, it is even more important that judicial power be independent and free of intervention from executive power, otherwise a judgement can hardly be just.[26]

For legal purposes, the law itself provides an objective standard of conduct which people are to observe, in order to avoid or at least resolve disputes. As arbitrators of disputes who are appointed by the state, judges cannot be chosen arbitrarily by interested parties, and must have the right of independent judgement in order for them to be able to avoid any kind of intervention, to adjudicate absolutely on the merits of the law and to apply the same standard to everyone. Only then can the parties involved in a lawsuit be confident that the judge represents a just, independent and unbiased third party.[27]

---

23 Li Jianliang, Introduction to Administrative Law, Yue Dan Express, Taiwan, January 1988, pp. 168, 169

24 Chen Xinmin, The Principle of the State under the Rule of Law, the Concept of the Rule of Law in Britain and the State under the Rule of Law in Germany, Taiwan University Essays, Volume 28, October 1998, p. 93

25 Li Zhenshan, Independent Adjudication by Judges According to the Law, in: Law and Justice, Wunan Press, Taiwan 2000, p. 74.

26 Ruth Schmidt-Räntsch, Dienstaufsicht über Richter, Bielefeld 1985, p.14

27 Martin Shapiro, Courts, paperback edition, University of Chicago Press, 1986, p. 65

## Section II Material Aspects of the Independence of Judges

Because of the importance of the independence of judges, the realisation of the independence of judges has been a major goal of judicial reform in China since 1999. However, the fact remains that the independence of judges is not mentioned in the Constitution or laws of China, there is no one consensus within juristic theory regarding the material aspects of the independence of judges, and the relationships between the numerous systems intended to guarantee the independence of judges, such as the appointment, promotion, supervision, disciplining and remuneration of judges has been not worked out in detail. In Germany, however, these aspects have already been refined. Accordingly, an introduction to German theory may offer a good starting point in establishing a theoretical basis for the independence of judges in China.

In accordance with the provisions of Article 97 of the Basic Law (*Grundgesetz = GG*) in Germany, the independence of judges is traditionally divided into the substantive independence and the independence of status of judges,[28] wherein these two aspects of independence interact with each other. If judges have the freedom to work without intervention, but there are no safeguards against being removed and/or dismissed, then the judges are not truly independent, since they may be afraid of being removed and/or dismissed if they make an "unacceptable" judgement. Conversely, if there are safeguards against judges being removed and/or dismissed, but judges do not have the freedom to work without intervention, then they are still not independent.[29]

### (1) Substantive Independence

Substantive independence is a safeguard intended to ensure that judges can make judgement independently. When passing judgements, judges should be free from illegitimate interference, in particular interference from other state powers.[30] Substantive independence is therefore considered to be a fundamental

---

28 Helmut Grimm, Richterliche Unabhängigkeit und Dienstaufsicht in der Rechtsprechung des Bundesgerichtshofs, Cologne 1972, p. 56

29 Günther Schmidt-Räntsch, Deutsches Richtergesetz, 3rd edition, Munich, Article 25, margin number 4

30 Cf. Rudolf Wassermann, Alternative Commentary on the Basic Law (*Grundgesetz-Alternativkommentar = GG-AK*), Luchterhand, Neuwied 1984, Article 97, margin numbers 21 ff; Kissel/Mayer, Gerichtsverfassungsgesetz (GVG): Kommentar (*Commentary on the Court Constitution Act*), 4th edition, Munich 2005, Article 1, margin numbers 39 f

aspect of the independence of judges.[31] Independence of status is a prerequisite for realising substantive independence.[32]

The primary aspect of substantive independence is protection against influence from the executive.[33] Historically, this can be traced back to the judges' struggle against the sovereign for directive freedom. Directive freedom is now ensured, yet there is still the risk of other interference from the executive. This applies above all to legal disputes, which are mainly disputes governed by public law, in which the executive has an immediate interest in the outcome of the proceedings, which may lead to increased influence on the judges.[34] In Germany, this kind of threat is mainly posed by the supervising function exercised by the executive – regular assessments by the supervisory authority are for example a requirement for promotion.[35] Such supervision is however almost unknown in Chinese law. The introduction of variously composed supervisory commissions has only recently been called for in China.[36] The issues associated with such supervision will be discussed in more detail below.[37]

In China, the incidence of executive power interfering with the judiciary and the independence of judges is greater than in Germany. This is partly because at present, courts are established by the local administrative district division, hence the local executive authorities not only control the courts' funds but are also in charge of appointing the important courts personnel.[38] How best to reform the

---

31 Eichenberger, Kurt, Die richterliche Unabhängigkeit als staatsrechtliches Problem, p. 54. See also Article 1 (c) of the International Bar Association Code of Minimum Standards of Judicial Independence: "Substantive independence means that in the discharge of his judicial function, a judge is subject to nothing but the law and the commands of his conscience."

32 Jörg Zätzsch, Richterliche Unabhängigkeit und Richterauswahl in den USA und Deutschland, Baden-Baden 2000, p. 63

33 Herzog, in: Maunz/Dürig, Grundgesetz: Kommentar, Munich 2009, Article 97, margin number 23 calls this the central element in the independence of judges.

34 This aspect is recognised in Bettermann, Die Unabhängigkeit der Gerichte und der gesetzliche Richter, p. 529, and in Oppermann, Richterberufung und richterliche Unabhängigkeit, Marburg 1966, pp. 46 ff

35 Günther Schmidt-Räntsch, Deutsches Richtergesetz, 3rd edition, Munich, Article 26, margin numbers 30 ff. This assessment is often criticised. See the discussions in: Arndt, DRiZ 1971, pp. 254, 418; Arntz, DRiZ 1972, p. 199; Bluhm, DRiZ 1971, pp. 330, 331, and also Vultejus, DRiZ 1993, pp. 177, 183 f

36 Composition of the System of Chinese Judges, p. 210

37 Discussed in detail in Part 2, Chapter 2

38 See Han Bo, Research on Reform of the Court System, People's Court Press, Beijing, May 2003, Volume 1, p. 240

process of establishing courts in China is also one of the issues discussed in this dissertation and will be treated in Part 2, Chapter III.

The independence of judges with respect to the legislature is much less firmly guaranteed than with respect to the executive. Rather, in relation to the legislature, the principle of being bound by the law is applied, which is highly emphasised in German law[39] and even articulated in the wording of Paragraph 1 of Article 97 and in Article 20 of the Basic Law. Being bound by the law is often regarded as a basic premise for the independence of judges,[40] and is also mentioned in discussions in China regarding the independence of judges. In Germany, however, this dependency on the legislature was relaxed after 1945 by the right of judicial review, although not all judges can declare a law to be unconstitutional.[41] China, by contrast, does not at present have an established system of judicial review. According to the provisions of the constitution and laws of the People's Republic of China (PRC), issues of constitutionality can only be handled and decided by the National People's Congress (NPC) and the Standing Committee of the NPC.[42] Under this system, judicial authorities are obliged to faithfully implement the laws legislated by the organs of state power and have no right of constitutional review, hence it is difficult for judicial authorities and judges to achieve real independence.[43] Whether judges should have the right of constitutional review is also one of the central issues being discussed in educated circles in China today. This dissertation will discuss this aspect in Part 2, Chapter II.

The independence of judges primarily protects judges against influence from the state. However, the independence of judges also includes protecting against illegal private and/or social influence on judges in specific proceedings.[44] This principle is applied in both Chinese and German law.[45] In German law, this is

---

39 Rudolf Wassermann, GG-AK, Luchterhand, Neuwied 1984, Article 97, margin number 43; Kissel/Mayer, Gerichtsverfassungsgesetz (GVG): Kommentar, 4th edition, Munich 2005, Article 1, margin number 110

40 Rudolf Wassermann, GG-AK, Luchterhand, Neuwied 1984, Article 97, margin number 43

41 Decisions by the Federal Constitutional Court (*Entscheidungen des Bundesverfassungsgerichts = BVerfGE*) 2, 124

42 Paragraph 2 of Article 62 and Paragraph 1 of Article 67 of the Constitution of the PRC

43 Pan Jiaming, The System and Chosen Method of Judicial Review of Constitutionality, in: Journal of Literature, History and Philosophy, March 2004, pp. 144-149

44 See Schlosser, Zivilprozeßrecht I: Erkenntnisverfahren, Munich 1991, p. 56, which discusses social independence.

45 Kissel/Mayer, Gerichtsverfassungsgesetz (GVG): Kommentar, 4th edition, Munich 2005, Article 1, margin number 109; similarly: Manfred Wolf, Eduard Kern, Gerichtsverfassungsrecht, Beck, 5th edition, Munich 1975, p. 215; see also DRiZ 1996, pp. 246,

expressed in Paragraph 1 of Article 97 of GG. According to this provision, judges are subject only to the law.[46] Thus, if individual social groups were to protest and/or strike in order to influence the content of a judgement issued, this would be an example of an improper influence on the independence of the judge and on the proceedings.[47] If, for example, evidence in a high-profile case is discussed in advance by the press, this can also damage the independence of judges and proceedings under the rule of law. In both countries, however, there are few ways of defending against such damage.[48] Moreover, unlike the Basic Law in

---

248, which considers the live broadcasting of court proceedings on television to be a threat to the independence of judges. This is countered by Rudolf Wassermann, GG-AK, Luchterhand, Neuwied 1984, Article 97, margin number 85 (independence not protected from the influences of social organisations) and margin number 89 (public crusades are detrimental to impartial judicature); for a consideration of the balance between judicial independence and private freedom of opinion which threatens it, and thus in favour of the validity in principle of judicial independence even over private parties, see Detterbeck in: Sachs, Michael, Grundgesetz, Kommentar 5th edition, Munich 2009, Article 97, margin number 11

46 Herzog, in: Maunz/Dürig, Grundgesetz: Kommentar, Munich 2009, Article 97, margin number 40. The validity of judicial independence over non-governmental influences is particularly evident in Germany, for example in the Decisions by the Federal Court of Justice in Criminal Cases (Entscheidungen des Bundesgerichtshofes in Strafsachen = BGHSt) 41, pp. 119, 121 f, according to which the protection of judicial independence does not allow students to participate in court deliberations within the framework of their practical training. Article 193 of GVG, which governs the presence at deliberations of persons being trained and does not include students, protects – in accordance with the prevailing interpretation in terms of the parties involved – the right of the statutory judge who is solely qualified to deliberate on the one hand, and the confidentiality of deliberation and therefore judicial independence on the other. See BGHSt 41, pp. 119, 121 f; also Seifert, in: German Law Monthly (Monatsschrift für Deutsches Recht = MDR) 1996, pp. 125, 127 with additional references, which criticises the decision on the grounds that judicial independence is hardly impaired by this; this is also hinted at in Bayreuther, Legal Instruction (Juristische Schulung = JuS) 1996, pp. 686, 687, in which the conclusion that the reference by the Federal Court of Justice to the threat to judicial independence posed by trainees does not lack "a certain smugness" remains unclear.

47 See Manfred Wolf, Eduard Kern, Gerichtsverfassungsrecht, Beck, 5th edition, Munich 1975, p. 213, or more critically Rudolf Wassermann, GG-AK, Luchterhand, Neuwied 1984, Article 97, margin number 89. Another issue is that of how the judge can be protected against such actions.

48 The regional state or *Land* press laws often allow an option for the public prosecutor's office or the police to refuse to give information, in order to prevent indictments from being published before they have been discussed at trial, cf. Bornkamm, Pressefreiheit und Fairneß des Strafverfahrens, p. 224. Is this seen as protecting the independence of judges, or rather proceedings in accordance with the rule of law, from the influences of

Germany, the Constitution of the PRC stipulates that the People's Courts shall adjudicate according to the law and shall be free of interference from any executive authorities, social groups and/or individuals. These provisions clearly leave judicial proceedings open to interference from the Communist Party. How to deal with the relationship between the independence of judges and the Communist Party is thus also an important and unavoidable issue when considering Chinese judges, and will be discussed in Part 2, Chapter VI.

### (2) Independence of status

Independence of status is the safeguarding of the position of judges, i.e. judges are in principle to be protected from arbitrary dismissal and/or transfer to other posts.[49] It ensures that judges are free to judge without fear of personal detriment due to their judgement.50 Basic prerequisites for this are in particular an appropriate and irreducible salary and a guaranteed period of tenure. Without sufficient financial security, judges cannot be truly independent. The Federal Remuneration Act specifically stipulates judges' salaries.[51] Under federal regulations, each regional state or *Land* can also legislate on the salary of its judges[52] in order to guarantee the economic independence of its judges. In China, there is no specific salary law, and the salary of judges is usually determined according to their administrative grade and seniority.[53]

---

the media? See specifically Manfred Wolf, Eduard Kern, Gerichtsverfassungsrecht, Beck, 5th edition, Munich 1975, p. 213. By contrast, Hassemer in the New Judicial Weekly (*Neue Juristische Wochenschrift* = *NJW*) 1985, pp. 1921, 1926, finds that protection against pre-trial prejudice is rightly intended primarily to ensure proceedings in accordance with the rule of law, although even he also has to admit that this also therefore protects judicial independence, albeit – in accordance with his interpretation – only indirectly. Lastly, since it is not always possible to exclude the possibility of the judge being influenced by news coverage, judicial independence and impartiality should also be protected at least in order to ensure fair proceedings, see also Bornkamm, Pressefreiheit und Fairneß des Strafverfahrens, pp. 217 f and 212 ff, cf. also German Judges Association (*Deutscher Richterbund* = *DRB*), DRiZ 1996, pp. 246, 248, which opposes the transmission of court proceedings on television on the grounds that it threatens judicial independence.

49 Cf. Paragraph 2 of Article 97 of GG

50 See Rudolf Wassermann, GG-AK, Luchterhand, Neuwied 1984, Article 97, margin numbers 60 ff

51 Article 37 of the Federal Remuneration Act (*Bundesbesoldungsgesetz* = *BBesG*); Appendix III of the Federal Remuneration Ordinance (*Bundesbesoldungsordnung*) R, Federal Law Gazette (*Bundesgesetzblatt* = *BGBl.*) I 2002, pp. 3065–3067

52 Paragraph 4 of Article 1 of BBesG

53 From a discussion with a judge of the First Court of Beijing, held on 29th March 2007

The foremost aspect of independence of status, however, is that judges be protected against being dismissed before their period of tenure has expired. In accordance with the Judges Law of the People's Republic of China (PRC), judges – once appointed – cannot be removed or demoted from their post or dismissed or given a sanction without statutory basis and without going through statutory procedures.[54] The "statutory basis" for dismissal refers to the eight circumstances specified in Article 13 of the Judges Law of the PRC.[55] Because all Chinese judges are appointed by the People's Congress or the Standing Committee of the People's Congress at various levels, the statutory procedures for dismissal are also carried out by the People's Congress or the Standing Committee of the People's Congress at the respective levels.

In Germany, Paragraph 2 of Article 97 of GG guarantees that judges cannot be unduly dismissed or transferred. This protection is so important that if it were absent, the panel would be denied the nature and status of a court.[56] However, it is only enjoyed by the judges who are permanently appointed to full-time positions. Judges who do not have this status,[57] such as for example probationary judges, also however enjoy a certain degree of protection.[58] The dismissal, impeachment or removal of a judge without his consent is only permitted in principle in a few cases expressly provided for by law.[59] In accordance with Article 24 of DRiG, that status of being a judge can only be terminated if the judge has been convicted of particular crimes. For an impeachment, it is for example required in accordance with Paragraph 1 of Article 30 of DRiG that impeachment proceedings in accordance with Paragraph 4 of Article 98 of GG or disciplinary

---

54 Article 8 of the Judges Law of the PRC

55 Article 13 of the Judges Law of the PRC

56 BVerfGE Volume 4, pp. 331, 345 f

57 Such as judges appointed for a fixed term (*Richter auf Zeit*; Article 11 of the German Judges Act (*Deutsches Richtergesetz = DRiG*)), probationary judges (*Richter auf Probe*; Article 12 of DRiG), judges on commission (*Richter kraft Auftrags*; Article 14 of DRiG), judges appointed in a subsidiary capacity (*im Nebenamt*) and honorary and deputy judges. See *inter alia* Jarass/Pieroth, Grundgesetz für die Bundesrepublik Deutschland, 7th edition, Munich, Article 97, margin number 6

58 See Rudolf Wassermann, GG-AK, Luchterhand, Neuwied 1984, Article 97, margin numbers 67 ff for more details.

59 "Dismissal" means removal from office in conjunction with termination of one's status as a judge (see Article 21 of DRiG). If only removed from office, the status as a judge is retained, the judge simply being removed from his specific office without being transferred to a new one. "Transfer" means a judge is transferred to a new office at another court or is retired (see Article 30 of DRiG). With respect to the terminology in general, cf. Manfred Wolf, Eduard Kern, Gerichtsverfassungsrecht, Beck, 5th edition, Munich 1975, pp. 205 f

proceedings be brought against a judge. A legally valid judicial decision is generally a prerequisite of any transfer or impeachment (Paragraph 2 of Article 30 of DRiG).

An issue closely linked to independence of status is that of the period of tenure.[60] A very long tenure or even a tenure for life is particularly significant in ensuring the independence of judges, and a short tenure may endanger it, since the judge may fear that he will not be re-appointed for a new tenure after the end of his current tenure of office.[61] Regarding the duration of tenure, the guiding principle in German law is that of judges appointed for life.[62] This is not required by the Constitution, as indicated in the second sentence in Paragraph 2 of Article 97 of GG by the possibility of setting age limits,[63] but the ordinary legislator has opted for this in accordance with German legal tradition[64] in Article 28 of DRiG.[65]

The Constitution and laws of the People's Republic of China do not provide limits for the term of office of an ordinary judge.[66] The retirement age of a judge is always in accordance with the provisions of the retirement system for Party and government personnel.[67] The Judges Law of the PRC considers the nature of the occupation of judge to be different from that of other state government occupations and clearly stipulates that the retirement system for judges is to be provided for by separate regulations, although a separate retirement system for judges has not yet been specified by the state.[68]

---

60 Herzog, in: Maunz/Dürig, Grundgesetz: Kommentar, Munich 2009, Article 97, margin numbers 63 ff

61 See Eichenberger, Kurt, Die richterliche Unabhängigkeit als staatsrechtliches Problem, p. 219

62 But there are exceptions to this, see Günther Schmidt-Räntsch, Deutsches Richtergesetz, 3rd edition, Munich, Article 28, margin numbers 6 ff

63 BVerfGE Volume 3, pp. 213, 224

64 Günther Schmidt-Räntsch, Deutsches Richtergesetz, 3rd edition, Munich, Article 28, margin number 3

65 Though note the retirement age in Paragraph 1 of Article 48 of DRiG

66 Although the Constitution does stipulate that the term of office of the President of the Supreme People's Court shall be the same as that of the NPC and that the President shall serve no more than two consecutive terms, see the second paragraph of Article 124 of the Constitution of the PRC.

67 Zhao Xiaosuo, Structure of the Chinese System of Judges, People's Court Press, Beijing, April 2003, p. 178; Ma Jianhua, Research on the Professionalisation of Judges, p. 69

68 Ma Jianhua, Research on the Professionalisation of Judges, p. 69

The specific system of personal safeguards, i.e. that judges cannot be arbitrarily removed, demoted or dismissed, and the retirement system and system of salaries for judges will be dealt with in Part 2, Chapter V of this dissertation.

# Chapter II Historical Aspects of the Independence of Judges

## Section I Development

### (1) The Feudal Period

The term "judge" emerged very early in Chinese history. The earliest established use of the term "judge" or "law officer" appears in the Book of Lord Shang, a legal tract written during the Warring States Period (475 to 221 BC). In Chapter 5, Paragraph 26 "Fixing of Rights and Duties" of the Book of Lord Shang, it is said: "The Son of Heaven [the emperor] shall set up three law officers, one in the palace, one in the office of the Yu-shi, together with a government official, and one in the chancery of the Cheng-Xiang. In the various prefectures and sub-prefectures of the feudal lords shall be instituted one law officer, together with government officials, all of whom shall be similar to the law officers in Qin." In this text, however, judges are not officials who adjudicate legal cases, but rather merely give legal advice to officials and other individuals. According to legend, the earliest judge in the modern sense of the term was Gao Yao (皋陶 Gāo Yáo) who served as chief judicial officer for the legendary ruler Shun (舜 Shùn) in the ancient Yao and Shun period. Many different terms for judges have been used in the course of Chinese history, such as Tingwei (廷尉 tíngwèi), Tuishi (推事 tuīshì), Panguan (判官 pànguān), Sifa (司法 sīfǎ), Facao (法曹 fǎcáo), Shenpanyuan (审判员 shěnpànyuán), Peishenyuan (陪审员 péishěnyuán), etc. Only when the Judges Law of the People's Republic of China was issued on 28th February 1995 was the term "judge" (法官 fǎguān) officially confirmed in law.

During the thousands of years of slavery and feudalism in Chinese society, a form of government combining the judiciary and the executive was maintained. In practice, the judiciary was subject to the executive, and supreme judicial power was held and exercised by the feudal emperor.[69] From the Qing Dynasty onwards, the local judiciary was controlled by local magistracies at various levels such as the prefecture official, the governor, and the county magistrate. The

---

69 Research by some scholars has suggested that the judiciary and executive were once separated in the Zhou Dynasty. In the Zhou Dynasty, local magistrates such as the Shidafu (师大夫 shīdàfū), Zhouzhang (州长 zhōuzhǎng) and Dangzheng (党正 dǎngzhèng) took charge of administrative affairs. Qiuguan (秋官 qiūguān) included Fensui (分遂 fēnsuì) and Xianfangyazhutu (县方讶诸土 xiànfāngyàzhūtǔ) who handled adjudicative affairs. They had jurisdiction over the same geographical areas, but administrative affairs and adjudicative affairs were separate. Shen Jiaben thought this very similar to the separation-of-powers principle in Europe. See also Wang Liming, Research on Judicial Reform, Legal Press, Beijing 2000, p. 98

so-called "judicial officers" in local government (such as the Sifa Canjun (司法参军 sīfăcānjūn), Sifa Zuo (司法佐 sīfăzuŏ), etc. in the Tang dynasty) were merely minor officials who assisted magistrates in adjudicating cases and had no independent judicial power. Although special judicial authorities did exist at the province level, their judgements had to be approved by provincial magistracies.[70] In central government, there were special judicial authorities in all previous dynasties, such as the Dali (大理 dàlǐ) and the Sikou (司寇 sīkòu) in the Qing Dynasty, or the so-called Tingwei (廷尉 tíngwèi), Dalisi (大理寺 dàlǐsì) and the Ministry of Criminal Prosecutions after the Qing Dynasty, all of which however were controlled by central government authorities such as the Zhongzai (冢宰 zhŏngzăi), the Chengxiang (丞相 chéngxiàng, prime minister), the Sansheng (三省 sānshěng, the "three departments"), the Cabinet, etc. and ultimately had to obey the orders of the emperor or monarch. The traditional system in which the judiciary and the executive were linked continued until the judicial reforms at the end of the Qing Dynasty.

Because the judiciary could not break away from the executive and stand alone, this allowed the executive to dominate and prevent judges from making judgements solely in accordance with the law, hence just and fair judgements were difficult to implement. In the feudal Chinese society in which "the emperor is the state", the independence of judges depended on whether the emperor and senior officers could mentor themselves and on the extent and determination with which they pursued a "policy of benevolence". Thus, the independence of judges could not in fact be affirmed and/or guaranteed.[71]

Unlike in Germany, there were no professional legists in the Western sense at any time in China's feudal history. In previous dynasties, none of the Tingwei, Dali, Tuiguan (推官 tuīguān) or Panguan were special judicial officers but rather merely administrators. A judge was merely a subject of those in authority, functioning as an agent of executive power. In Chinese history, there was no hierarchy of legal practitioners or any specific form of legal training. A French scholar, Jean Escarra,[72] argued that the examination system in China ruined those of particular talent and hindered the emergence of professional legists. This is not without merit. In China, those who had studied literature, passed the imperial examinations at the provincial level and secured an official position could adjudicate cases, while others taught themselves the laws and statutes in order to

70 See Zhang Jinfan, China's Legal Tradition and its Modern Transformation, Legal Press, Beijing 1997, pp. 42, 427

71 Kong Qingyu, How Ancient Judges "Rivalled" the Emperor, People's Court Weekly, 28th July 2006

72 Escarra was a legal counsellor at the law revision department when Western laws were introduced in China at the end of the Qing Dynasty.

serve as a Shuli (书吏 shūlì), Xingmingmuyou (刑名幕友 xíngmíngmùyǒu, a private advisor or assistant attending to legal, fiscal or secretarial duties in a local Yamen (衙门 yámén) or government office) or private legal practitioner. Shuli in the Qing Dynasty received no salary and derived their income mainly from corruption and fraudulent practices. They did not study the law, but merely made themselves superficially aware of the articles of law. Although Xingmingmuyou received a favourable salary, they only learnt law in order to assist the Dongweng (东翁 dōngwēng) in adjudicating cases, and did not systemically study the law. Private legal practitioners tricked citizens into bringing lawsuits in order to make ill-gotten profit, fabricating cases, making up extended or mitigated penalties and/or bringing false charges against other parties. They worked in the shadows, neither signing the legal cases nor presenting arguments in court.[73] They had no ethical basis, no public recognition, no economic status and no political future. Therefore, reading law was not encouraged but rather looked down upon.

## (2) Modern Times

From the Opium War in 1840 onwards, due to the invasion of imperialist powers and the enervation of China, the intelligentsia began to explore Western culture and gradually introduced Western science, technology and learning to the East. At this time, Western legal culture such as the system of judicial independence also caught the attention of some scholars. In particular after the Sino-Japanese War of 1894-95, the Wu Hsu Reform movement broke out in 1898. The Chinese Reformists advocated a "system of the separation of powers" as the substance of political reform. After translating the works of Montesquieu, for example, Yan Fu strongly advocated the principle of the "separation of powers" as advanced by Montesquieu. He considered that the key to implementing such a new legal system was to put the separation-of-powers principle into practice.[74] The leader of the Reformists, Kang Youwei, proposed a political reform package which included the separation of the judiciary and the executive as well as independent trials and decisions.[75] He proposed that the political system should comprise "the system of separation of powers" in order to realise political reform and a strong

73 See Qu Tongzu, Essays on Law by Qu Tongzu, China University of Political Science and Law Press, 1998, p. 413

74 Yan Fu, The Essence of the Law, Volume 19, Chapter 26, authors' comments, Commercial Press, Shanghai 1909

75 Kang Youwei, Comment on Politics, in: The Kang Youwei Collection, Volume 1, Shanghai Chinese Classics Publishing House, 1987

state.[76] The progressive Reformers not only advocated these reforms but also put forward a very specific program and plan for their implementation, hence this stance spread throughout China. At the same time, some progressive bourgeois democrats were also strongly advocating the Western system of separation of powers and judicial independence. With respect to the implementation of the separation of powers and judicial independence, the position of the progressive Reformers and the bourgeois democrats were essentially the same.[77]

In 1903, beset with difficulties both at home and abroad, the government of the late Qing Dynasty accepted the proposals for political reform, and in the same year, amended laws of government were established, with Shen Jiaben and Wu Tingfang serving as reform ministers. Shen Jiaben advocated a combination of West German and Chinese law, wide-ranging improvements to the law and constitutionalism. While presiding over the formulation of the Qing Code of Criminal and Civil Law and the Organisational Law of the Courts, he strongly advocated following the Western system of separation of powers and establishing a litigation system, wherein the judiciary and the executive would be separated. He repeatedly emphasised that: "The roots of constitutional government in all Eastern and Western countries depend on judicial independence" and publically stated that: "Judicial independence is the basis for future constitutional government."[78] Shen Jiaben strongly advocated reforming the official appointment system so as to bring about the separation of the judiciary and the executive. Due to his efforts, the Ministry of Criminal Prosecutions was changed in 1906 to the Ministry of Law, which no longer adjudicated legal cases, and the Dalisi was changed to the Daliyuan (大理院 dàlǐyuàn) which handles the highest-level legal cases and has the right to interpret laws and review any local judgements. Under the direction of Shen Jiaben, the Provisional Regulations on Courts at various levels were issued in 1907. In 1910, the first countrywide organic law of the courts – the Law on the Structure of the Courts – was formulated, in which Article 164 stipulated that administrators and prosecutors "are not allowed to interfere in the adjudications made by Tuishi." This was the first time a system of judicial independence was confirmed in law. This regulation made specific provisions on the organisation, establishment and range of authority of courts and on the internal responsibilities regarding trial procedures, thus safeguarding the independence of judges within the system. When the Qing

76 Kang Youwei, Sixth Letter to the Qing Emperor, Wu Hsu Reforms, in: The Kang Youwei Collection, Volume 2, Shanghai Chinese Classics Publishing House, 1990

77 See the representative bourgeois democrat Zhang Taiyan, Criminal Officer, in: Zhang Clan Series, Volume 7, People's Press, Shanghai 1980

78 Historical Records of the Preparations for Constitutionality in the late Qing dynasty, Volume 2

government finally collapsed, it was forced to take a constitutionalist stance in order to head off the increasing upsurge in the bourgeois revolution. The Qing government issued the Guiding Principles for an Imposed Constitution in 1908 and re-issued the Grand Tenets in 1911 which had the character of a constitution. Both of these laws applied the principle of the separation of powers and affirmed the system of judicial independence, however these laws were unfortunately never implemented.

In the wake of the destruction of the Qing government, the Qing judicial system also came to an end. But the stance on judicial independence advocated by Shen Jiaben during the process of political reform was in tune with that of the leader of the bourgeois-democratic revolution, Sun Zhongshan, hence judicial independence also became an outcome of the bourgeois revolution.[79] In 1911, the Nanjing provisional government issued the Provisional Constitution of the Republic of China which constitutionally provided for the independent status of judges' judgements for the first time, and Article 51 of which stipulated that: "Judges shall adjudicate cases independently and free of intervention from more senior government offices," thus establishing a reasonable basis for a system of independent judgement by judges. In order to guarantee that judges adjudicate cases independently, the Provisional Constitution also established the status of judges, a mandatory standard of pay and a ban on arbitrary removal. Article 52, for example, stipulated that: "Judges in office cannot be transferred or have their salary decreased unless they have been convicted by law, or if disciplined, cannot be dismissed. The disciplinary measures shall be in accordance with the law." Judges are therefore not only materially but also personally independent.

The organic law of the courts at the time of the Republic of China also carried on the notion and system of judicial independence, and made more elaborate provisions than those of the late Qing Dynasty regarding the status and salaries of judges. In the twenty-first year of the Republic of China, the central government conference adopted the 12 articles of the Legislative Principles on the Organic Law of the Courts, Article 11 of which definitively stipulated that: "Current Tuishi cannot be suspended from duty or transferred or have their salary decreased without statutory basis and without going through statutory procedures". On the basis of this, the Organic Law of the Courts issued and implemented in the twenty-fourth year of the Republic of China further stipulated that: "Current Tuishi cannot be suspended from duty, removed, transferred or have their salary decreased without statutory basis and without going through statutory procedures" (Article 40); and that: "Tuishi and prosecutors who have been in service for more than 15 years and who can no longer cope may retire

79 Wang Liming, Research on Judicial Reform, Legal Press, Beijing 2000, p. 100

and receive retirement benefits" (Article 43). In the twenty-fifth year of the Republic of China, and in the same vein as the Organic Law of the Courts, the judicial and executive departments copied the German and French models and approved the Regulations on Retirement Benefits for Judges which stipulated among other things that those who have served in office for more than 15 years and retire themselves because they can no longer cope, and those who are required to retire by the state because they are over 60, shall receive retirement benefits from the state. By way of these legal provisions, the notion of the independence of judges was implemented.[80]

In the meantime, legal education had also developed greatly. In 1904, in order to foster the talents of those familiar with Chinese and foreign law and so meet the urgent needs of diplomacy and legislation, the Qing government established the first specialist legal education institute in Chinese history, being Zhili Law and Politics University. In September 1905, the Qing government declared an end to the imperial examination, established a number of universities, and allowed private universities to teach law and political science. Public and private law and political science universities thus spread all over China and greatly advanced the development of modern legal education and the cultivation of those with a talent for law.[81],[82] The Republic of China further improved on this basis, and following the late Qing dynasty, a well-rounded professional group of legists was created, taking overseas students as its nucleus.[83] They actively participated in the modernisation of the Chinese legal system and developed Chinese modern law.

## (3) From the Founding of New China to the Cultural Revolution

After the founding of New China, the old legal system of the Kuomintang government was completely abolished.[84] In order to draw a clear distinction with respect to the old legal system, the Interim Organic Regulations on the People's

---

80 He Qinhua, Choosing the Western Model and Modernisation of the Chinese Judiciary in: Huadong Law Issues, Beijing Legal Press, 2002, Volume 1, p. 3

81 Zhang Jinfan, Summary of a Hundred Years of Law and China under the Rule of Law, in: China Legal Science, 2005, Volume 5, pp. 185-192

82 According to three statistical records on education from the general service department of the Qing government, there were 127 institutions of higher education in China in 1909 comprising 23735 students, including 47 law and political science universities comprising 12282 students, i.e. 37% of the total number of institutions and 32% of the total number of students.

83 Zhang Jinfan, Summary of a Hundred Years of Law and China under the Rule of Law, in: China Legal Science, 2005, Volume 5, pp. 185-192

84 Wang Liming, Research on Judicial Reform, Legal Press, Beijing 2000, p. 102

Courts of the People's Republic of China passed in 1951 abolished the title of Faguan ("judge"), using the term "Shenpanyuan" (审判员 shěnpànyuán, judge or trior)[85] instead.[86] In 1952, a nine-month campaign for judicial reform was in full swing.[87] During this period, the point of view of judicial independence was uniformly denied, and a policy whereby cases were examined and approved by the Party committee working jointly with the judicial and political institutions was advocated.[88] When the Constitution of 1954 was drawn up, it confirmed the principle of judicial independence in legal form for the first time in the history of New China. Article 78 of the Constitution stipulated that the People's Court shall exercise judicial power independently and shall be subject only to the law. According to the 1954 Constitution, the first National People's Congress adopted the Organic Law of the People's Courts of the People's Republic of China,[89] which recapitulates the provisions of the 1954 Constitution[90] and provides for the election and appointment of judicial professionals, thus to a certain degree guaranteeing the independence of judges by law.

The construction of a judicial system and legal institutions in New China begins to enter a period of sound development. However, the Anti-Rightist Campaign of 1957 interrupted this process. During this campaign, judicial independence was criticised as an anti-party sentiment, and the correct political

85 The term Shenpanyuan has been used continuously since then until the present day. Although the Judges Law of 1995 uses the term Faguan, the term Shenpanyuan is still widely used in all kinds of standard administrative documents and in judicial practice.

86 Hu Xiabing, edited by Feng Rengqiang, Summary of Research on Judicial Fairness and Judicial Reform, Tsinghua University Press, Beijing 2001, p. 164

87 This was a campaign, based on the success of the "Movement Against the Three Evils" and the "Movement Against the Five Evils", which criticised old judicial opinion, old judicial methods and judicial authority reform, and the aim of which was to draw a clear distinction between the new and old legal boundaries, to politically, organisationally and ideologically reorganise the people's judicial authorities at various levels and to progressively establish and improve a people's judicial system. The campaign for judicial reform lasted nine months, marking the initial completion of the founding of the New China cadres. But there was some problems with this campaign, in that many personnel with no special training in legal disciplines were allowed into the ranks of the judicial cadre, professional qualifications and standards severely declined, and misjudged cases often resulted because judicial actions overemphasised directly serving campaigns and politics. Some judges, ignorant of law, handled cases according to class conscience and politics, leading to illegal phenomena such as extorting confessions by torture.

88 Wang Renbo, On the Rule of Law, People's Press, Shandong 1989, p. 325

89 Adopted by the first National People's Congress on 21st September 1954

90 Article 4 of the Organic Law of the People's Courts of the People's Republic of China of 1954

statement regarding the independent adjudication of cases according to the Constitution was to say that "the Rightists fight the Party leadership under the pretext of judicial independence." Many legal professionals who advocated improving judicial independence were therefore wrongly labelled as "Rightists". The criticism of the principle of judicial independence enshrined in the Constitution damaged the Constitution and the rule of law, leading to a prevalence of legal nihilism. At the same time, an emphasis that the Party committee should "take a direct interest in the judgements made by courts" made the Party committee into the executive office of specific judicial affairs, wherein the head of a local Party committee directly decided judgements and the extent of punishments, and the fundamental procedure and system of trial were dismissed as bourgeois affairs.[91] In November 1960, after the Chinese Communist Party (CCP) Central Committee gave an official response to a report by the Central Political Sub-Committee on simplifying executive structures and changing the management system of the political and judicial organs, the Supreme People's Court, the Supreme People's Procuratorate and the Ministry of Public Security of the State Council handled official affairs jointly, under the unified leadership of the Party Organisation of the Ministry of Public Security, which denied the principle of judicial independence in the judicial system established by the Constitution, hence the independence of judges was set adrift on the tide.

During the ten-year internal chaos from 1966 to 1976, the system of judicial independence suffered universal criticism. In many local authorities, Party leaders and government concentrated all authorities and openly considered judicial authorities as their instruments. In many instances, leaders of provinces, cities and counties issued arrest orders and instructed courts on how to adjudicate cases. The directives and reviews of the Party organisations and their leaders often became the law outside the law, affecting judiciary proceedings and even directly influencing the outcome of judgements.[92] Many kinds of mass organisations and "study classes" had the right to arrest people at random, search houses and confiscate possessions, parade people through the streets under escort and extort confessions by torture, so that miscarriages of justice spread throughout the country, society became a dog-eat-dog world, and the country and the people fell into the deepest of catastrophes. The Constitution enacted in 1975

91 Wang Renbo, On the Rule of Law, People's Press, Shandong 1989, p. 340
92 Chen Xiaofeng, Research on Chinese Legal Culture, Henan People's Press, p. 491

even revoked the principle of judicial independence,[93] leading to a serious reversal of the development of an established legal system.

Legal education also disappeared in this political campaign. All political science and law universities were disbanded during the Cultural Revolution, and many legal experts, including law professors and judicial officers, also disappeared. Adjudication increasingly depended on political factors and not legal provisions.[94]

### (4) After the Third Plenum of the 11th Central Committee of the CCP

After experiencing ten years of calamitous disaster, the Chinese people reawakened to the importance of judicial independence. In 1978, the Third Plenum of the 11th Central Committee of the Chinese Communist Party brought order to the chaos and made an important decision which strengthened the socialist democracy and the legal system. At the same time, it declared in an official communiqué that: "The independence of procuratorial and judicial authorities is to be safeguarded, laws and the legal system are to be observed, the interests and benefits of the people are to be respected, equality before the law is to be guaranteed, and no-one is to have privileges above the law".[95] This affirmation in an official communiqué of the principle of judicial independence was just a consequence of the bitter lesson from the ten years of inner chaos when judicial independence has been denied. The official communiqué of the Third Plenum of the 11th Central Committee recognised judicial independence as an important element in perfecting a Socialist legal system, indicating the extreme importance of this system.[96]

The Organic Law of the People's Courts approved at the Second Session of the Fifth NPC in 1979 reinstated the provision from the 1954 Constitution that: "The People's Courts shall adjudicate cases independently and shall be subject only to the law". The 1982 Constitution again identified the principle of judicial independence, Article 126 of which stipulated that: "The People's Courts shall, in accordance with the law, exercise judicial power independently and are not

---

93 The 1975 Constitution reduced the 106 articles of the 1954 Constitution to 30 articles, deleting Article 78 on the principle of judicial independence and maintaining only the provision of the right to trial by court.

94 Xu Chunzhi, Judicial Fairness and the Qualities of Judges, http://www.law-lib.com/lw/lw_view.asp?no=3824

95 See the Third Plenum of the 11th Central Committee of the CCP (issued on 22nd December 1979)

96 Wang Liming, Research on Judicial Reform, Legal Press, Beijing 2000, p. 104

subject to interference by administrative organs, public organisations or individuals", thus providing a strong safeguard for independent adjudication by judges. The Judges Law passed in 1995 further clarified the provisions in the Constitution, and not only officially designated adjudicating officers as "Faguan" (judges) but also defined the meaning of Faguan.[97] The Judges Law also systemically stipulates the duties, obligations and rights of judges, the specifics of their qualification, appointment and dismissal, and withdrawal from public office, the examination and grading of judges, their training, remuneration, disciplinary measures, salary, insurance and welfare, resignation and retirement, etc. Its promulgation and enactment was a sign that the system of Chinese judges was making initial strides towards modernisation.[98]

Between 1978 and 1995, legal education was also resumed and continually expanded. By 1995, there were 140 universities with an established department of law (School of Law), and about 80,000 students and 6,000 teachers.[99] However, all the judicial authorities which in 1978 were also beginning to be rebuilt were confronted with a lack of personnel; the legal education system which was only just re-emerging could not meet the demand for personnel in the judicial authorities. Therefore, judicial authorities had to recruit a large number of court personnel who were ignorant of the law, by drawing on cadres transfers from the military, cadres who had taken the social examination and cadres enrolled from among the workers. The Judges Law as amended in 2001 enhanced the qualification of judges to that of "obtaining a bachelor of law degree from an institution of higher education or obtaining a non-law bachelor degree yet having expertise in law"[100] and "passing the unified state examination for judicial qualification";[101] however, "judges" already appointed for historical reasons maintained their status as judges. Accordingly, the current cache of judges in China[102]

97 Article 2 of this law stipulates that: "Judges are the judicial personnel who exercise the judicial authority of the State according to law, including presidents, vice presidents, members of judicial committees, chief judges and associate chief judges of divisions, judges and assistant judges of the Supreme People's Court, local People's Courts at various levels and special People's Courts such as military courts."

98 Hu Xiabing, edited by Feng Renqiang, Summary of Research on Judicial Fairness and Judicial Reform, Tsinghua University Press, Beijing 2001, p. 167

99 Xu Chunzhi, Judicial Fairness and the Qualities of Judges, http://www.lawlib.com/lw/lw_view.asp?no=3824

100 Judges Law of China, Chapter 4: Qualifications for a Judge, Article 9, Paragraph 1, Section 6

101 Judges Law of China, Chapter 5: Appointment and Removal, Article 12, Paragraph 1

102 By 2005, the number of judges with a bachelor degree or higher had increased nationwide from 10,000 to more than 90,000 (see Wu Jing, In the Ten Years Since Implementation of the Judges Law, the Overall Quality of Chinese Judges Has Continuously In-

has an unreasonable structure of knowledge and an irregular level of theory, and exhibits an overall low quality.[103] Therefore, there is cause to be suspicious of their ability to make correct judgements in cases and to question whether they are entirely independent.

In addition to the factors mentioned above, there are many other factors influencing the independence of judges in the performance of their duties in China today.[104] The most prominent is that the guiding ideology that the Party directs judicial work destroyed the principle of judicial independence.[105] Some local party and government leaders often inappropriately or even unlawfully interfered in judgements by judicial authorities, such as intervening in the extent of punishments, requesting that the benefits of one party be considered in civil and economic cases, issuing directions on the procedures by which cases were to be heard and processed, and other interventions which influenced the natural course of adjudication to varying degrees. This method whereby the Party directed the judiciary had a strong sense of the Rule of Man, and clearly went against judicial independence. The question of how to dispel this aspect of the Rule of Man and rationalise the relationship between the Party and the independence of judges will be discussed later in this dissertation.[106]

Moreover, both the Constitution and the Organic Law of the People's Courts of the PRC have so far provided only for the independence of courts and have not mentioned the independence of judges. The independence of judges is even considered to be a falsity of a bourgeois judiciary, and the independence of courts as a whole is considered the advantage of a socialist judiciary. The reason for this is that many feel that the independence of judges represents bourgeois individualism and liberalism, whereas China implements collectivism and state authorities execute democratic centralism, hence the People's Courts should also employ democratic centralism and not the independence of judges.[107]

---

creased, People's Court website), but this only represents 40% of the total number of judges (about 220,000, see Tian Yu and Li Shufeng, A View on the Professionalisation of Chinese Judges, People's Court Gazette, 21st December 2002).

103 See He Weifang, The Course of Chinese Legal Education, China University of Political Science and Law Press, Beijing, 1997 edition, pp. 9-30

104 Specific factors come from all aspects of the system of judicial independence, such as judicial selection, supervision and safeguarding of status, to be introduced in detail in the following chapter of this dissertation.

105 Tan Shigui, Research on Issues of Judicial Independence, pp. 121-127; Ma Jianhua, Research on the Professionalisation of Judges, p. 109

106 See the detailed statements in Part 2, Chapter VI, the Party Leadership and the Independence of Judges

107 Tan Shigui, Research on Issues of Judicial Independence, p. 116

However, the shortcomings in the independence of the courts are becoming more and more obvious as the process of the rule of law advances. Firstly, in the adjudicative procedures of the People's Courts, a collegial panel or single-judge bench first hears a case and makes proposals or other comments of advice and then reports to the presiding judge or president of a court for examination and approval, which leads to uncertainty in the principal part of judgement. However, judicial certainty, consistency and stability have to have certainty in the principal part of judgement as their central premise. Secondly, this leads to a lack of unity between the actions and obligations of judges. All the final outcomes of judgements made in cases by judges are decided by the president of the court, the presiding judge or a judicial committee. Accordingly, cases are decided by a collective decision of the court, such that it is not possible to ascertain who is responsible in the event of a miscarriage of justice. Therefore, the independence of judges is increasingly considered to be a necessary requirement for social development. He Weifang, a jurist entrusted with amending the Organic Law of the People's Courts[108] has clearly pointed out that the new Organic Law has to give prominence to the independence of judges.[109] Paragraph 2 of Article 3 of the most recent Administrative Procedure Law of the People's Republic of China in a proposed amended version stipulates that: "Judges shall hear and adjudicate administrative cases independently by law, free of any intervention."[110] This was the first breakthrough past the principle of the independence of trial and decision, i.e. the independence of courts existing in the three major procedure laws in China, realising a systematic transition from the "independence of courts" to the "independence of judges". However, whether this can be approved by the legislature is still uncertain.[111]

Although the independence of judges has not yet been officially confirmed in any Chinese laws, many measures and programs of judicial reform indicate an approach towards establishing a system of judicial independence. The Second

---

108 In early 2004, an amendment to the Organic Law of the People's Courts was listed in the calendar of the five-year legislation plan of the Standing Committee of the National People's Congress, but so far, the amendment to this law is still at the internal confirmation stage at the Supreme People's Court.

109 He Weifang, Amendments to the Organic Law of the People's Courts of the People's Republic of China and Judicial Independence, a speech given at the "Seminar on the Rule of Law in China" at the Carnegie Foundation

110 Fu Dalin, Proposed Amendment to the Administrative Procedure Law – a Breakthrough in the Adjudicative Administration "Bottleneck" , in: China Youth News, 9th November 2005

111 The proposed amended version of the Administrative Procedure Law was put forward in 2005, but there is so far still no news regarding its approval.

Outline for Reform of the People's Courts (2004-2008) issued by the Supreme People's Court in October of 2005 clearly proposed that in future, the direction of court reforms shall include establishing and perfecting the system of judicial selection, training, examination and supervision, and progressively improving the system of court personnel, finance and materials, in order to achieve genuinely independent judgement by judges.[112] In short, the establishment and perfection of the system of judicial independence is regarded as a top priority for Chinese judicial reforms and has already become an inexorable trend.

## Section II Historical Development of the Independence of Judges in Germany

Germany also does not have a long tradition of judicial independence. Even in the 16th and 17th centuries, the judges of absolutist states were counsellors and ministers appointed by the state who were completely dependent on their sovereign. From the end of the 18th century, the theories of Montesquieu caused sovereigns in Germany to opt to refrain from amending or repealing decisions made by the courts,[113] and at the beginning of the 19th century, the ideas of the Enlightenment and the American and French revolutions found their way to Germany and invoked a political liberalism which aimed to guarantee rights of freedom to individuals. In order to achieve this freedom, courts had to be able to guarantee the substantive independence of judges.[114] The idea of judicial independence was gradually accepted, but the status of courts within the state was still weak, and was not strengthened until the Weimar period. State jurisdiction was introduced, forms of standard judicial review were developed and administrative jurisdiction was established.[115] Using the wording of the Prussian Constitution of 1850 and Article 1 of the GVG of 1877, the independence of judges was constitutionally guaranteed in Article 102 of the Weimar Constitution (*Weimarer Reichsverfassung = WRV*) and safeguarded by Article 104 WRV which

112 See Section 6 of the Second Five-year Reform Plan of the People's Courts (2004-2006), Reform and Perfection of the Court Personnel Management System, http://www.dffy.com/faguixiazai/xf/200512/20051214221735-2.htm

113 Günther Schmidt-Räntsch, Deutsches Richtergesetz, 3rd edition, Munich, Introduction, margin number 3

114 Von Hodenberg, Die Partei der Unparteiischen, pp. 163 ff, describes the idea of judicial independence as a political weapon of the early liberals.

115 Ernst Rudolf Huber, Die Verfassungsgeschichte seit 1789, Band VI: Die Weimarer Reichsverfassung, Stuttgart/Berlin/Cologne 1993, p. 90

protected judges from being removed.[116] In the age of National Socialism, the independence of judges was abolished, returning it to the age of absolutism. Not until the establishment of the Basic Law was the independence of judges continuously developed. The separation of powers, independence of status and substantive independence are fixed in constitutional law.[117]

## Section III Comparison

From the historical development of the independence of judges in China and Germany, it may be said that neither of the two countries has had a long tradition of judicial independence and that both countries have struggled in their efforts to recognise and then realise the independence of judges. Both countries also experienced periods of building up such independence from scratch and of falling back to square one. The final turning point came only once the Basic Law was established in Germany in 1945, and the system was fundamentally stabilised and could be gradually perfected. China, by contrast, is still at the stage of exploration and learning. In my opinion, the two countries differ for the following reasons:

### (1) The Transplantation of Laws and Legal Education

Influenced by the movement at Bologna University for the revival of Roman law, all German universities began to teach Roman law from the 13$^{th}$ century onwards.[118] In ecclesiastical institutions and executive authorities, the body of those specially trained in Roman law gradually took the form of a specific hierarchy.[119] Around the end of the 15th century, German judges began to hold official posts as persons educated in the law.[120] By the end of the Thirty Years' War (1648), almost all courts were entirely or mostly composed of academically educated jurists. Initially, the doctorate degree in civil law and church law (*doctor iuris utriusque*) acquired at university was sufficient for qualification as a judge.

---

116 Ernst Rudolf Huber, Die Verfassungsgeschichte seit 1789, Band VI: Die Weimarer Reichsverfassung, Stuttgart/Berlin/Cologne 1993, p. 90

117 Jörg Zätzsch, Richterliche Unabhängigkeit und Richterauswahl in den USA und Deutschland, Baden-Baden 2000, p. 80

118 He Qinhua, A History of Western Jurisprudence, China University of Political Science and Law Press, Beijing 1996, p. 191

119 Su Yanxin, Influence of Roman Law in Mediaeval Western Europe, in: CASS Journal of Foreign Law, 1997, Volume 4, pp. 35-51

120 Albrecht Wagner, Der Richter: Geschichte, aktuelle Fragen, Reformprobleme, Karlsruhe 1959, pp. 51 ff

Later, the courts also subjected candidates for judgeships to a special examination; general state examinations were introduced from the beginning of the 18$^{th}$ century.

In China, by contrast, specialist legal education institutions did not come into being until the latter years of the Qing Dynasty. Establishing law and political science universities was one of the legal transplantation measures which the Qing government was compelled to take under pressure from foreign powers. In the Renewed Treaty of Commerce between Britain and China of 1902, the Qing government stated that: "China is deeply desirous of consolidating its laws so as to bring them in line with the laws of other countries." Within a few years of this, the Qing government hastily launched a comprehensive legal transplantation. The substance of legal education against this background was not to cultivate legal experts but rather to train officials in active service, and studying at law and political science universities merely satisfied the common degree requirements for going into politics.[121]

The motivating force for China to implement this legal transplant was not a pressure or considered choice for reform from within the country, but rather as a condition for the Western powers to give up their extraterritorial claims and the expected benefits of meeting this condition.[122] This was clearly different from Germany's initiative in accordance with its economic development situation and continuance with Roman law. And in Germany, legal education and legal transplantation complemented each other. As Wagner has said, Roman law entered the courtrooms through the educated judges.[123] China has not always attached importance to legal education, and only with the amendment of laws in the late Qing dynasty did a system of legal education begin to be established. But by the fall of the Qing Dynasty, there were only five political science and law universities such as the Imperial Capital University and about 4,000 graduates in China. The vehicles pushing for Chinese legal transplantation were usually government-run legal education institutions, but due to excessive disregard for inherent Chinese tradition, hasty abandonment of unwritten customary law and a lack of

---

121 In the five years after this, Beijing and the other provinces successively established 25 law and political science universities, and law departments were established at six "major universities" comparable to "multiversities" or comprehensive universities.

122 Fang Liufang, Observations on Legal Education in China, in: Research on Comparative Law, 1996, Volume 2

123 Albrecht Wagner, Der Richter: Geschichte, aktuelle Fragen, Reformprobleme, Karlsruhe 1959, pp. 51 ff

considered inspection of foreign laws, the foreign laws taught in the classroom often metamorphosed into a doctrine which was divorced from reality.[124]

From the course of development of the independence of judges in Germany, it can be seen how the German legal system merged well with Roman law and assimilated the natural law philosophy of Roman law, making it easier to adopt the liberalism and idea of the separation of powers of Locke and Montesquieu which came down in one continuous line. Under the influence of the idea of liberalism, German citizens gradually awoke to the idea of fighting more for their rights and for judicial independence and the independence of judges. But the Chinese legal transplantation could not create a trained specialist group of legal professionals, and there was a lack of active analysis of this law transplantation or of a driving force of choice. Finally, the Chinese law transplantation was only similar in form and not in essence, and the notion of judicial independence and the independence of judges struggled to take root in society.

## (2) Establishment of the Idea of the Rule of Law

As mentioned above, the independence of judges is inseparable from the establishment of the idea of the rule of law. Civil law, which has commercial economic relationships as its subject, is usually taken as the origin of the rule of law. The human rights, ownership rights and rights of equality in civil law are the prototype of modern citizens' rights. Civil law sufficiently embodied the value of the rule of law. The spirit of the sanctity of rights and freedom of contract in civil law tradition is the origin of the culture of constitutionalism and the rule of law.[125] In 18th century Prussia, Friedrich II issued civil codes in 1751 and launched a campaign to implement a "codification" of all laws. This campaign rapidly expanded and was hugely successful, such that many Napoleonic Codes were issued between 1800 and 1810. The campaign of legal codification as a whole determined to a large degree the general characteristics and direction of development of the movement for the rule of law in continental Europe, and is regarded as one of most important aspects of efforts in continental Europe to establish the rule of law.[126]

124 Fang Liufang, Observations on Legal Education in China, in: Research on Comparative Law, 1996, Volume 2

125 Zhang Zhongqiu, Comparative Research on Chinese and Western Legal Culture, Nanjing University Press, 1999, Volume 2, p. 348

126 F. A. Hayek, translated by Deng Zhenglai, The Constitution of Liberty, Part 2, Freedom and the Law, Chapter 13, Liberalism and Administration: The State Under the Rule of Law

Unlike Germany, China has been situated in a natural economy pattern for a very long time, and the characteristics of traditional penalty-orientated legal culture in China have been the spirit of the rule of man and the concentration of power under its direction. This basic structural pattern of legal culture lasted for over 2000 years in China and influenced and restricted the historical process of modernisation of Chinese legal culture at every turn.[127] Whether China can realise a genuine independence of judges depends largely on developing and/or abandoning aspects of traditional legal culture and realising a modernising transformation of traditional legal culture, i.e. specifically, continuously renewing the legal system and continuously amending legal concepts.

In China today, 20 years of economic reform have provided a certain economic basis and legal order for this, and these times call for a nation to mature politically. If China can seize the opportunity to promote the establishment and perfection of civil society by state authorities and really push for a free market economic order and a system of judicial independence, then the state under the rule of law which safeguards civil society in the sense of the later Hegel and the "state under the rule of common law"[128] in the sense of the later Hayek is not impossible.[129]

---

127 Liu Zuoxiang, Legal Culture Theory, Commercial Press, Beijing, 1999 edition, p. 301

128 With respect to the philosophical thinking on law of the later Hegel and the theory of a new mode of constitution of the later Hayek; in addition to their respective major works "Elements of the Philosophy of Right" and "Law, Legislation and Liberty", see also Gao Quanxi, Legal Order and Liberalism: Hayek's Law and Constitutionalist Thought, and On the Mutual Recognition of Legal Rights: Research on the Phenomenology of Mind, Beijing University Press, 2003 and 2004 editions. In the latter book, the author elucidates the secret relationships between the constitutionalist thought of Hayek and Hegel's theories of state law and considers both of them to fall within the spectrum of conservative liberalist thought or authoritative liberalist thought.

129 Gao Quanxi, On Constitutional Politics. This text was presented at the "Theory Seminar to Commemorate the Semi-Centennial of the "May Fourth" Promulgation of the Constitution and Founding of the National People's Congress" hosted by the Chinese Academy of Social Sciences Research Institute on 5th September 2004; it is also the introductory section to the short document "Essay on Constitutional Politics" which the author has recently been in the process of writing.

# Chapter III The Court System and the Independence of Judges

In order to understand the system of judges, it is first necessary to explain the court system in China. The most important differences between the Chinese and German court systems will then be described.

## Section I The Situation in Chinese Courts

### (1) The Relationship between Courts and Legislative Authorities

China employs the system of the People's Congress. Article 57 and Article 96 of the Constitution separately stipulate that "The National People's Congress of the People's Republic of China is the supreme organ of state power" and that "local People's Congresses at various levels are local organs of state power." The system of the People's Congress is commonly considered to employ a system of combined legislative and executive powers, i.e. the National People's Congress executes a centralised and consolidated national sovereignty and has sovereign authority.[130] In state organs, such as law courts serving as state judicial authorities, their position is below the People's Congress, so there is no constraining relationship between the courts and the People's Congress. However, aside from the judicial and legislative relationship, there are two other connections between the courts and the People's Congress. Article 3 of the Constitution stipulates that: "All administrative, judicial and procuratorial organs of the State are created by the People's Congresses, to which they are responsible and by which they are supervised." On the one hand, judicial authorities at the various levels are created by the People's Congress. The President of the Supreme People's Court is elected and installed by the National People's Congress; vice-presidents, presiding judges, assistant presiding judges and judges are appointed by the National People's Congress; presidents of the local People's Courts at the various levels are elected and installed by the local People's Congress at the various levels; and vice-presidents, presiding judges, assistant presiding judges and judges are also appointed by the local People's Congress at the various levels. If judges violate the law or commit dereliction of duty, they may be removed, dismissed or demoted by the People's Congress or the People's Congress may accept their resignation. On the other hand, courts have to accept supervision by the People's Congress. This supervision is commonly considered to be democra-

130 He Huahui, Theory and Practice of the System of the People's Congress, Wuhan University Press, 1992, p. 55

tic supervision and not executive supervision by a superior of a subordinate.[131] This supervision may be divided into general work supervision and the supervision of specific cases.

The general work supervision is where the People's Congress reports on the work of the courts through hearings and deliberations, reviews the validity of judicial interpretation, inspects how courts deal with the motions assigned by the Standing Committee of the National People's Congress and the proposals of the representatives of the National People's Congress, and supervises the manner in which judges who violate the law or commit dereliction of duty are removed, dismissed, etc. Because such supervision is carried out within the framework of constitutional government and outside of judicial practice in individual cases, there are few objections.[132]

The supervision of specific cases, however, is where an investigation committee for specific issues, composed by the People's Congress and its Standing Committee above county level, supervise the handling of serious criminal cases by judicial authorities.[133] Because this supervision directly affects judicial practice and influences the result of how individual cases are handled, and thus potentially violates judicial independence and obstructs justice, the pros and cons of this type of supervision are the subject of heated discussion in Chinese academic circles.

In 2004, a case which became famous as the second in which the People's Congress exercised the rights of the investigation committee for specific issues made some scholars even more resolute in their determination to affirm this manner of supervision. As reported in the Chinese Youth Daily on 21st January, the court at Xingcheng in Liaoning province entrusted an accounting firm to evaluate 100 tons of corn at a state-owned grain depot and approximately 5,000 square metres of land and buildings so as to be lower than the practical value price of 400,000 RMB, and issued a ruling. The Xingcheng Standing Committee of the People's Congress then launched an investigation procedure for specific issues, specifically established an investigation committee for specific issues for the grain depot case, and drafted a resolution regarding the handling and ruling

131 Xu Yang, Research on Issues within the Subject of Criminal Adjudication, master's thesis at Renmin University of China, June 2004, p. 27

132 Xu Yang, Research on Issues within the Subject of Criminal Adjudication, master's thesis at Renmin University of China, June 2004, p. 27

133 Article 71 of the Constitution stipulates that: "The National People's Congress and its Standing Committee may, when they deem it necessary, appoint committees of inquiry into specific questions and adopt relevant resolutions in the light of their reports. All organs of State, public organisations and citizens concerned are obliged to furnish the necessary information to the committees of inquiry when they conduct investigations."

by the court at Xingcheng, in which the court at Xingcheng was ordered to repeal its original ruling, review the legal procedures and its handling of the case, and deal severely with the principal staff involved and the senior officer in charge.[134]

Many scholars consider that in the current situation, in which the adjudication at some courts is not up to standard, the supervision by the People's Congress in specific cases is to a certain extent propitious to guaranteeing strict enforcement of the law and fair judgements from the courts. At present, judicial inequality and judicial corruption are quite serious in some local courts. Judgements based on friendships, relationships and money are relatively prominent. Supervision by the People's Congress in specific cases can help to strengthen restrictions and prevent judicial corruption. Moreover, the organisation of the special investigation committee of the People's Congress has a legal basis[135] and helps to implement the provisions of the Constitution.[136]

In this author's opinion, the supervision by the People's Congress in specific cases has its limitations and may lead to some malpractice, and inadvertently interfere with the judiciary, as manifested mainly by the following:

Firstly, destabilisation of judicial independence. In China, the People's Congress exercises legislative rights and the courts exercise judicial and adjudicative rights. The People's Congress has no judicial rights or potential judicial rights. Therefore, too much supervision by the People's Congress blurs the division of labour between the functions and powers of the state and forfeit judicial independence and judicial authority.

Secondly, if supervision by the People's Congress in specific cases is too extensive, this is tantamount to establishing another level of adjudication above that of the courts. Parties who do not accept the judgement of a court could seek the "supervision" of the People's Congress without going through any procedures, which will impact on the legal procedure and render courts unable to make final judgements.

---

134 Related articles include: "Court at Xingcheng in Liaoning Province Gets Red Card from the NPC" at http://www.people.com.cn/GB/14576/14528/2471307.html; "How the 'Heavy Weapon' of NPC Supervision Should be Used" at http://www.people.com.cn/GB/14576/28320/30714/31443/2329901.html

135 See Article 45 of the Discussion Regulation of the NPC: when it is considered necessary, the NPC may organise the investigation committee on special problems; Article 31 of the Organic Law of the Local People's Congresses and Local People's Governments of the PRC stipulates that a Local People's Congresses above county level can organise an investigation committee on special problems.

136 Fang Baoguo, Supervision of Specific Cases by the National People's Congress Must be Approached with Caution, in: New Beijing News, 27th April 2004

Thirdly, the level of legal education of deputies of the People's Congress is unequal. Supervision by the People's Congress in specific cases could lead to a layman instructing an expert. Furthermore, deputies of the People's Congress do not participate in the court proceedings or adjudicate cases themselves, and do not hear the deliberations or the testimony, cross-examination, opinions expressed, etc. They usually review the written records after the case has been processed. Therefore, the result is not necessarily "correct".

Fourthly, there is no comprehensive legal procedure for supervision by the People's Congress in specific cases. The three major procedure laws in China have already enacted some relief measures for parties, such as an appeals system and a retrial system, but these procedures do not include any provisions regarding the People's Congress correcting judgements made by the courts. Moreover, if the supervision by the People's Congress in specific cases is in error, it is difficult to remedy this through legal procedures. Must we then "re-supervise" the supervision by the People's Congress in specific cases?

Consequently, supervision by the People's Congress in specific court cases should not become widespread, and the People's Congress should not criticise court judgements indiscriminately. Modes of supervision by the People's Congress regarding court judgements should be restricted to the following aspects: firstly, that the People's Congress examines the work reports of the courts every year, i.e. a collective and macroscopic supervision which can be exercised continuously; and secondly, that the supervision by the People's Congress focuses on whether judges are involved in corruption, bribery, favouritism or other fraudulent during trial proceedings, and on supervising legality and discipline.

### (2) The Relationship Between the Courts and Executive Authorities

Executive power is the most distensible and invasive of the state powers and is thus the core of the "controlling power" under the political structure of the separation of powers.[137] When considering the relationship between the courts and executive authorities, the most important aspect is that of how to safeguard the independence of the courts from restrictions by executive authorities. On the other hand, it is not possible to completely isolate the courts from executive authorities, since these two state authorities always retain a connection within the system. In Germany, the Ministry of Justice is also the judicial and executive authority in charge, albeit with limited powers.

As is well known, only courts which have full powers and can standardise and restrict the execution of government powers can break away from the control of the executive authority and achieve independence. Every country usually

137 Zhuo Zeyuan, The State under the Rule of Law, Legal Press, Beijing 2001, p. 64

establishes a series of safeguarding systems to help courts realise their independence from the executive authorities.

Firstly, the organisational framework of the system of courts is established across administrative divisions. The court structure is an organisation system independent of administrative divisions. This system of establishing courts is mainly aimed at preventing regional protectionism. Secondly, the courts' expenditure must be independent. If the courts' expenditure is allocated by the executive authority, then the courts will be financially dependent on the executive authority. Therefore, the independence of courts' expenditure is a fundamental basis and safeguard for judicial independence. Lastly, court personnel management must be independent. If executive authorities can influence the promotion, appointment and dismissal of judges, then clearly judges cannot make independent judgements.

At present in China, there are many problems in the relationship between the courts and executive authorities. It is largely possible for executive authorities to interfere in the activities of courts.

According to the Organic Law of the People's Courts of the People's Republic of China, the organisational structure of Chinese courts corresponds exactly to administrative divisions (for a related introduction, please see the next section). Accordingly, the court fiscal budget and appointment and dismissal of court personnel are subject to local government. To break the influence of the administrative division on the court system, Chinese scholars expound a variety of proposals for re-establishing the court system, which shall be discussed in detail in Part 2, Chapter III.

## Section II Establishment and Authority of Chinese Courts

Courts in China are divided into local People's Courts at various levels, special People's Courts and the Supreme People's Court,[138] and operate a four-level system (three local levels and one Supreme Court level) in which the second instance is the final instance. By the end of 2004, there were 3,548 People's Courts and special People's Courts at various levels and 190,627 judges.[139] Local People's Courts at various levels exercise jurisdiction within their area of jurisdiction. Special People's Courts include the maritime courts, military courts and railway transport courts which have jurisdiction over the cases which they are responsible for hearing and judging. The Supreme People's Court has juris-

138 Article 2 of the Organic Law of the People's Courts

139 See the white paper of 19th October 2005 on Building of Political Democracy in China

diction over all cases throughout the country. The difference as compared to Germany, aside from the many special courts in addition to ordinary courts, is that Chinese courts have different panels for judging all kinds of cases, instead of transferring particular kinds of cases to different courts for judging the same kind of cases. The First Intermediate Court of Beijing, for example, has twelve established courts including two criminal courts and five civil courts in addition to the administrative courts,[140] of which the third and fourth civil courts adjudicate economic cases and the fifth civil court adjudicates intellectual property cases.[141] All the cases which in Germany are adjudicated by labour courts, social courts and finance courts are adjudicated in China by the civil courts.[142] The organisation and authority of the courts at various levels is outlined below:

---

140 Furthermore, there are adjudication supervisory courts, case-filing courts and executive courts. The adjudication supervisory courts are responsible for hearing retrial cases (with respect to retrial procedures, see Section IV of this chapter on the System of Adjudication Supervision); the case-filing courts are responsible for receiving and examining all kinds of cases in the first instance and second instance and other cases which are to be accepted and heard under the jurisdiction of that court, re-examining adjudication supervisory cases, enforcing conservatory measures in litigation at the court, serving prosecution bills in criminal cases of the court in the first instance, managing trial procedures, monitoring time limits, supervising the conclusion of trials, transferring special judicial missives, etc.; executive courts are responsible for executing payment-related judgements, written verdicts, reconciliation papers and civil sanction orders coming into legal effect, and the share of property in criminal-law judgements, written verdicts and judgements, and executing the legal provisions of the court and other legal documents coming into effect.

141 With respect to how the First Intermediate Court of Beijing is set-up, see http://bj1zy.chinacourt.org/public/detail.php?id=183

142 See Articles 2 to 3 of the Labour Court Act (*Arbeitsgerichtsgesetz = ArbGG*), Article 51 of the Social Court Act (*Sozialgerichtsgesetz = SGG*) and Articles 33 to 36 of the Finance Court Code (*Finanzgerichtsordnung = FGO*)

## (1) The Organisation and Authority of the Local People's Courts at various levels[143]

### *(a) Basic People's Courts*

The Basic People's Courts are established in counties, autonomous counties, municipalities without district divisions and in municipal districts.[144] According to the Organic Law of the People's Courts[145] and Procedure Law,[146] the tasks of the Basic People's Courts are:

- To adjudicate criminal, civil and administrative cases of the first instance, unless otherwise stipulated in law. If a Basic People's Court considers that a criminal or civil case it is handling is of major importance and requires trial by the People's Court at a higher level, it may request that the case be transferred to that court for trial.
- To settle civil disputes and handle minor criminal cases which do not need to be decided by trial.
- To direct the work of people's mediation committees. A Basic People's Court may set up a number of people's tribunals according to the conditions of the locality, population and cases.[147] A people's tribunal is a component part of the Basic People's Court. Its tasks include adjudicating ordinary civil cases and minor criminal cases, directing the work of people's mediation committees, propagandising legal system, dealing with letters from people, and re-

143 According to the provisions of Article 30 of the Constitution of the People's Republic of China, the administrative division of the People's Republic of China is as follows: 1. the country is divided into provinces, autonomous regions and municipalities directly under the Central Government; 2. provinces and autonomous regions are divided into autonomous prefectures, counties, autonomous counties and cities; 3. counties and autonomous counties are divided into townships, nationality townships (autonomous townships of ethnic minorities) and towns. Municipalities directly under the Central Government and other large cities are divided into districts and counties. Autonomous prefectures are divided into counties, autonomous counties and cities. As well as the level of townships, there are comparable local People's Courts at all other levels.

144 Article 18 of the Organic Law of the People's Courts

145 Articles 21 and 22 of the Organic Law of the People's Courts

146 See Article 16 of the Civil Procedure Law of the People's Republic of China, Article 19 of the Criminal Procedure Law of the People's Republic of China, and Article 13 of the Administrative Procedure Law of the People's Republic of China

147 Article 20 of the Organic Law of the People's Courts

ceiving people's visits.[148] Their judgements and orders are the judgements and orders of the Basic People's Court.[149]

*(b) Intermediate People's Courts*

The Intermediate People's Courts are established in prefectures of a province or autonomous region, municipalities directly under the Central Government, municipalities directly under the jurisdiction of a province or autonomous region and in autonomous prefectures.[150] According to the Organic Law of the People's Courts[151] and Procedure Law, the tasks of the Intermediate People's Courts are:

(i) To adjudicate the following cases:

1. Cases of the first instance assigned by laws and decrees to their jurisdiction.

- According to Criminal Procedure Law,[152] criminal cases of the first instance which come under the jurisdiction of the Intermediate People's Courts are:
  - counter-revolutionary cases and cases jeopardising State security;
  - ordinary criminal cases punishable by life imprisonment or the death sentence;
  - criminal cases in which the offenders are foreigners or in which Chinese citizens have infringed the legal rights and interests of foreigners.
- According to the Civil Procedure Law,[153] civil cases which come under the jurisdiction of the Intermediate People's Courts are cases involving foreign interests, cases which have a major impact on the area under their jurisdiction, and cases which the Supreme People's Court directs the Intermediate People's Court to have jurisdiction over.
- According to the Administrative Procedure Law,[154] the administrative cases of the first instance which come under the jurisdiction of the Intermediate People's Courts are:
  - cases of confirming patent rights of an invention and cases handled by Customs;
  - actions initiated against specific administrative acts taken by departments under the State Council or by the people's governments of provinces, au-

148 Xiong Xianjue, The Judicial System and Judicial Reform, p. 67
149 Article 20 of the Organic Law of the People's Courts
150 Article 23 of the Organic Law of the People's Courts
151 Article 25 of the Organic Law of the People's Courts
152 Article 20 of the Criminal Procedure Law
153 Article 17 of the Civil Procedure Law
154 Article 14 of the Administrative Procedure Law

tonomous regions or municipalities directly under the Central Government;
- grave and complicated cases in areas under their jurisdiction.

2. Cases of the first instance transferred by the Basic People's Courts.

3. Cases of appeals and of protests lodged against judgements and orders of the Basic People's Courts.

4. Cases of protests lodged by the people's procutatorates in accordance with the procedures of judicial supervision.

If an Intermediate People's Court considers that a criminal or civil case which it is handling is of major importance and requires trial by the People's Court at a higher level, it may request that the case be transferred to that court for trial.

(ii) To supervise the adjudication of the Basic People's Courts in the area under their jurisdiction. If the Intermediate People's Courts find some definite error in a legally effective judgement or order, they have the right to remove the case for trial or to order the Basic People's Courts to rehear the case.[155]

*(c) Higher People's Courts*

The Higher People's Courts are established in provinces, autonomous regions and municipalities directly under the Central Government.[156] According to the Organic Law of the People's Courts[157] and related laws and regulations, their tasks are:

- To adjudicate the following cases:
  - Major criminal cases which are of significance to their entire jurisdiction,[158] civil cases having a major impact on the areas under their jurisdiction159 and grave and complicated administrative cases in areas under their jurisdiction[160].
  - Cases of the first instance transferred from People's Courts at lower levels.
  - Cases of appeals and of protests lodged against judgements and orders of People's Courts at lower levels. The Higher People's Court in the locality

155 Paragraph 2 of Article 12 of the Organic Law of the People's Courts
156 Article 26 of the Organic Law of the People's Courts
157 Article 28 of the Organic Law of the People's Courts
158 Article 21 of the Criminal Procedure Law
159 Article 20 of the Civil Procedure Law
160 Article 15 of the Administrative Procedure Law

where a maritime court is located shall have jurisdiction over appeals against the judgements and orders of the maritime court.161
  - Cases of protests lodged by people's procuratorates in accordance with the procedures of judicial supervision.
- In cases of the first instance in which an Intermediate People's Court has passed a death sentence and the defendant does not appeal, to examine the sentence and report it to the Supreme People's Court for approval. If the Higher People's Court does not agree with the death sentence, it may bring the case up for trial or remand the case for a retrial.[162]
- To review cases in which the Intermediate People's Court has passed a death sentence with a two-year suspension of execution.[163]
- To supervise the adjudication of the People's Courts at lower levels in the area under their jurisdiction. If the Higher People's Courts find error in a legally effective judgement or order, they have the right to remove the case for trial or to order the People's Courts at lower levels to rehear the case.

The former Organic Law of the People's Courts even stipulated that Higher People's Courts could approve death penalties if authorised to do so by the Supreme People's Court,[164] but this provision has since been deleted.

---

161 Paragraph 3 of Article 3 of the Decision of the Standing Committee of the National People's Congress on the Establishment of Maritime Courts in Coastal Port Cities

162 Article 200 of the Criminal Procedure Law

163 Article 73 of the Constitution of 1954

164 The Decision Concerning the Revision of the Organic Law of the People's Courts of the People's Republic of China, adopted at the Second Session of the Sixth Standing Committee of the National People's Congress, stipulates that: "The Supreme People's Court may, when it deems it necessary, authorise Higher People's Courts of provinces, autonomous regions and municipalities directly under the Central Government to exercise the power to approve cases involving the imposition of death sentences for homicide, rape, robbery, causing explosions and others gravely endangering public security and disrupting social order." The Supreme People's Court issued a notice on 7th September 1983 conferring this right to approve such cases to the Higher People's Courts and military courts of provinces, autonomous regions and municipalities directly under Central Government. In fact, this authorisation merely confused appeals and approvals and had no effect on the review of death sentences. See Xiong Xianjue, The Judicial System and Judicial Reform, pp. 68 ff. In order to guarantee human rights and more rigidly control the application of death sentences, China amended the Organic Law of the People's Courts on 31st October 2006, removing the right of Higher People's Courts to approve death sentences and reserving this right for the Supreme People's Court (Article 13 of the Organic Law of the People's Courts; Article 199 of the Criminal Procedure Law; Article 48, paragraph 2, first sentence of the Criminal Law of the People's Republic of China)

## (2) Organisation and Authority of the Special People's Courts

The Special People's Courts are a particular part of the organisation of Chinese People's Courts and judicial authorities which have their own special character. They are established by specific departments and for specific cases. They adjudicate cases relevant to them or specific cases.[165] According to the provisions of the Organic Law of the People's Courts, the People's Republic of China establishes special People's Courts such as military courts.[166] In practice, the Special People's Courts of the People's Republic of China currently include military courts, maritime courts and railway transport courts. These will be dealt with individually below.

### *(a) Military Courts*

The establishment of military courts in the People's Republic of China has been altered many times. In January 1954, the Military Commission of the Central Committee of the Communist Party of China (CPC) approved the establishment of People's Liberation Army (PLA) military tribunals and judge advocate departments at various levels. In November of the same year, in accordance with the Constitution[167] and the Organic Law of the People's Courts,[168] military judicial authorities at various levels were changed to military courts and brought into the state judicial system. The highest judicial organ in the army is the People's Liberation Army Military Court. In December 1956, the People's Liberation Army Military Court was changed to the Military Tribunal of the Supreme People's Court of the People's Republic of China. From January 1961 to September 1962, the security departments of the Army, the prosecutor's office and the courts handled official affairs jointly. In May 1965, the Central Committee of the Chinese Communist Party approved the resumption of the People's Liberation Army Military Court. In December 1969, the system of military courts was again cancelled. In January 1979, the Central Committee of the Chinese Communist Party decided to resume the People's Liberation Army Military Court of China and military courts for the military, navy, air force and the PLA. In November of the same year, the Central Committee of the Chinese Communist Party again resumed the military courts for the naval fleet, air command and units of the army land force at the corps level. Then, a system of three-level mi-

---

165 Xiong Xianjue, The Judicial System and Judicial Reform, pp. 69 ff

166 Paragraph 1 of Article 124 of the Constitution; Article 2, paragraph 1, Section 2 of the Organic Law of the People's Courts

167 Article 73 of the Constitution of 1954

168 Article 26 of the Organic Law of the People's Courts of 1954

litary courts headed by the Chinese People's Liberation Army Military Court came into being. The final instance for military courts in China is the Supreme People's Court of the People's Republic of China. The establishment and authority of the three levels of military courts in the army are as follows:[169]

- The Chinese People's Liberation Army Military Court. This is the supreme military court and its tasks include:
  - adjudicating cases of the first instance committed by individuals above the division commander level;
  - adjudicating foreign-related criminal cases;
  - adjudicating cases which the Supreme People's Court authorises or directs it to adjudicate and other criminal cases of the first instance which it considers it should adjudicate;
  - adjudicating cases of the second instance and reviewing death sentences.
- Great Military Region and Services and Arms Courts. These include military courts of the Great Military Regions, military courts of the navy and air force, and the general military court of the People's Liberation Army, and are intermediate military courts whose tasks include:
  - adjudicating cases of the first instance committed by individuals at the deputy division commander and regiment level;
  - adjudicating cases which may involve a death sentence and cases which they are authorised or directed to adjudicate by a higher military court;
  - adjudicating cases of appeals and of protests lodged against judgements and orders.
- Corps military courts. These include military courts for units of the army land force at the corps level, military courts of provincial military regions, military courts of the naval fleet, military courts of the air force within the Great Military Regions and military courts in army units deployed in Beijing directly under the headquarters, and are basic military courts whose tasks include:
  - adjudicating criminal cases of the first instance committed by individuals under the battalion commander level and cases of the first instance which may involve a penalty of up to life imprisonment;
  - adjudicating cases which they are authorised or directed to adjudicate by a higher military court.

---

169 Since this area may involve state secrets, it is difficult to find information on the related military laws, and this introduction refers to the details published on the official network of the Xinhua news agency, see http://news.xinhuanet.com/ziliao/2004-07/22/content_1626588.htm

After the reform and opening-up policy was implemented, military courts also began to accept and hear civil cases within the army.[170]

### (b) *Maritime Courts*

Maritime courts are special People's Courts which specifically adjudicate maritime and maritime trade cases of the first instance for the purpose of exercising judicial jurisdiction over maritime affairs. The special Water Transport Courts established in Tianjin, Shanghai and Wuhan from 1954 were removed in 1957. On 14th November 1984, the eighth session of the Sixth Standing Committee of the National People's Congress issued the Decision on the Establishment of Maritime Courts in Coastal Port Cities, stipulating that maritime courts shall only specifically hear maritime and maritime trade cases of the first instance and not criminal cases or other civil cases.[171] Accordingly, the Supreme People's Court decided on 28th November of the same year to establish maritime courts in coastal port cities such as Guangzhou, Shanghai, Wuhan, Qingdao, Tianjin and Dalian, the organisational system of which corresponds to that of local Intermediate People's Courts.[172] The Supreme People's Court prescribed the scope within which the maritime courts may accept cases in 1984 and 1989. After the Maritime Action Special Procedure Law was put into force in 2000, the Supreme People's Court again issued the Regulation by the Supreme People's Court on the scope within which maritime courts may accept cases on 11th September 2001, in accordance with the Civil Procedure Law, the Maritime Action Special Procedure Law, the Administrative Procedure Law and related international treaties which China is party to and which are in accordance with international custom. The scope within which maritime courts may accept cases was regulated to include ten kinds of maritime tort disputes, 22 kinds of maritime contract disputes, 26 kinds of other maritime trade and maritime cases and 5 kinds of maritime implementation cases, i.e. a total of 63 kinds of cases.[173] On 11th August 2003, the General Office of the Supreme People's Court again issued a Notice

170 The Supreme People's Court of China issued a judicial interpretation in response to questions concerning military courts hearing civil cases within the army, which stipulated that military courts may accept and hear only civil cases in which the two parties are active or retired army officers, armed forces staff or legal persons in the army, cases concerning servicemen declared missing or dead and cases referred to the military court.

171 Article 3 of the Decision of the Standing Committee of the National People's Congress on the Establishment of Maritime Courts in Coastal Port Cities

172 Article 5 of the Decision of the Supreme People's Court of China concerning some questions regarding the establishment of maritime courts

173 See Articles 1 to 63 of the Regulations by the Supreme People's Court on the Scope within which Maritime Court may Hear Cases of 9th August 2001

on the Jurisdiction of Maritime Administrative Cases.[174] According to this Notice, maritime courts do not adjudicate administrative cases or administrative compensation cases and do not examine or implement cases in which executive authorities are applied to execute their specific administrative acts. Therefore, maritime administrative cases no longer fell within the scope of cases which maritime courts could accept.

When maritime courts were first established, the maritime board had jurisdiction over them. By 1999, the Supreme People's Court had reformed the management system of maritime courts and sorted them into the supervisory sequence of the People's Courts.[175] Maritime courts then became relatively independent special judicial organs and had the same status as local intermediate courts. There are currently ten maritime courts in China.[176] Their establishment breaches the boundaries of administrative divisions. Presidents, chief judges and judges of maritime courts are essentially nominated by the organising departments of the provinces and municipalities and appointed and removed by the Standing Committee of the National People's Congress of the provinces and municipalities. Their finances are also guaranteed by provincial finance.[177]

### *(c) Railway Transport Courts*

Railway Transport Courts are special People's Courts established along railways. From 1953 to 1954, 16 Railway Transport Courts were successively established at the sites of national railway authorities and 39 detached tribunals were established at the sites of railway administration sub-offices and heard criminal cases relating to railway transport. All of the Railway Transport Courts has been disbanded by late 1957, and related cases were accepted by the Basic People's Courts or Intermediate People's Courts within whose jurisdiction the cases had occurred. The Railway Transport Courts were then re-established between March 1980 and May 1982. Basic Railway Transport Courts were established at the sites of railway administration sub-offices, Intermediate Railway Transport Courts were established at the sites of railway administration main offices, a

174 http://www.law-lib.com/law/law_view.asp?id=81508

175 See the speech by Xiao Yang, President of the Supreme People's Court: Course and Outlook of Reform of the People's Courts, http://www.hflib.gov.cn/law/law/falvfagui2/CXF/LWJ/1019.htm

176 These ten courts are established separately at Dalian, Tianjin, Qingdao, Shanghai, Guangzhou, Wuhan, Haikou, Xiamen, Ningbo and Beihai.

177 See the 21st Century Economic Report of 14th June 2004, the Logic of Central Enterprises Breaking Away From Public Security Organisations, Prosecutorial Organisations and People's Courts

Higher Railway Transport Court was established in Beijing and a Transport and Communications Tribunal was established at the Supreme People's Court. In March 1987, the Higher Railway Transport Court in Beijing was abolished, but the Intermediate and Basic Railway Transport Courts were retained. Cases of appeals and of protests lodged against judgements and orders by the Intermediate Railway Transport Courts are heard by the Higher People's Courts of the provinces, autonomous regions and municipalities directly under the Central Government in which they are located. This system is been maintained to date.

The task of the Railway Transport Courts is to adjudicate the following criminal and economic cases in accordance with the law:

- criminal cases occurring along railways which are investigated by railway public security authorities and filed by railway prosecutors;
- cases involving economic disputes. In accordance with rulings by the Supreme People's Court, these cases fall into 12 categories,[178] including:
  - disputes over railway cargo transport contracts;
  - disputes over railway passenger and luggage transport contracts;
  - disputes over collaboration transport contracts handled by the railway;
  - disputes over the execution of international railway collaboration contracts;
  - disputes over railway cargo transport insurance contracts;
  - disputes over railway transport extended service contracts including consignment, packing, warehousing and delivery;
  - disputes over building, managing and transport contracts between national railways and local railways, accessed railways and leased lines;
  - disputes over outsourcing labour service contracts with respect to railway cargo operations and line maintenance;
  - economic disputes within the railway system;
  - disputes over torts which have resulted in damages to railways in violation of railway safety regulations;
  - disputes over torts involving human and property losses caused by railway operations and dispatch operations, in which the party chooses to bring an action before the Transport and Communications Tribunal;[179]

178 See the Joint Notice of the Supreme People's Court, the Supreme People's Prosecutors' Office, the Ministry of Public Security, the Ministry of Justice and the Railway Department on relevant issues in the adjudication by Railway Transport Courts and the Prosecutors' Office

179 See the Regulation on the Jurisdiction of Railway Transport Courts with Respect to Economic Disputes issued by the Supreme People's Court on 16th June 1990

- other economic disputes which the Higher People's Courts refers to the Railway Transport Courts.

Although the Railway Transport Courts are directed in their operations by the local Higher Courts, from the point of view of administration they are subject to the railway administration main office and the railway administration main sub-office, i.e. they are financially supported by the railway administration main office or sub-office; the appointment and dismissal of judicial staff is approved by the relevant Railway Transport Party Committee in accordance with the regulations Central Government, and the procedure of executive appointment and dismissal is handled by the courts; the court staff are treated the same as the railway staff according to current railway regulations.[180] Railway Transport Courts were established by introducing the special court system of the former Soviet Union,[181] and they are a product of the period of the planned economy. In that period, there were no independent private enterprises, and in all walks of life there was little contact with the outside or generation of profits, hence Railway Transport Courts were established mainly in order to settle internal disputes within the railway system. Once the market economy system was established, not only did independent enterprises quickly emerge as business entities, but railway transport corporations also became enterprises and business entities, each being one of a number of market players. Given these circumstances, preserving the Railway Transport Courts would appear to breach the Constitution and basic principles of law and to oppose the market economy. Therefore, many scholars have recently suggested that Railway Transport Courts should be abolished.[182]

In early 2001, the relevant departments of Central Government had in fact brought up the issue of progressively abolishing the management system of special courts such as the Railway Transport Courts and incorporating them into the state judicial system under a unified administration.[183] The Supreme People's

180 The plaintiff can also bring a case to the local courts where torts occurred, see Article 30 of the Civil Procedure Law

181 Xiong Xianjue, The Judicial System and Judicial Reform, p. 73

182 Yan Yang, Railway Courts Should Be Allowed to Die a Natural Death, Kaidi Weekly of 7th October 2007. Some scholars suggest preserving the existence of Railway Transport Courts but reforming them, see Liao Shunjiang, Zhang Weirong, Thoughts on the Authority of Railway Transport Courts and on Reform of the Railway Transport Court System, Contemporary Legal Forum, Volume 2, 2006

183 Document No. 9 of the Central Committee of the Chinese Communist Party identifies: "progressively regulating the management system of the People's Court s along railways, forests and farms, reasonably adjusting the composition of institutions, rectifying

Court also listed regulation of the system of special People's Courts as one of the reforms of the People's Courts in 2005.[184] Now, several years on, the Railway Transport Courts are however still an independent court system. If and when the Railway Transport Courts can either go completely "entrepreneurial" or die a natural death still depends on judicial reform.

## (3) Organisation and Authority of the Supreme People's Court

The Supreme People's Court is based in Beijing. It is the supreme judicial authority. In the 1950s, it consisted only of a review committee, a criminal court, a civil court, a supervision department, a laboratory, a reception room and a general office. By the 1980s, it had added an administrative court, an economic court, a transport court, an appeal court, a personnel services office, a supervision office, a judicial administrative office and an education office, and judgement collection and judicial administration. Now in the 21st century, the economic court and transport court have been incorporated into the civil court, forming the structure of a criminal court, a civil court and an administrative court. Each court separately establishes tribunals; the civil court for example establishes four tribunals, and the criminal court establishes two.[185]

The tasks of the Supreme People's Court include:

*(a) Supervising the adjudication of the local People's Courts at various levels and special People's Courts.*[186]

If the Supreme People's Court finds some definite error in a legally effective judgement or order by local People's Courts at various levels, it has the authority to try the case itself or to order the lower court to rehear the case.

*(b) Handling three kinds of cases which it adjudicates:*

- Cases of the first instance assigned by laws and decrees to its jurisdiction and/or those which it considers it should adjudicate itself.[187] The Criminal

---

the assignment of personnel and bringing the workforce within the state judicial system under a unified management."

184 The Second 5-year Reform Program of the People's Courts by the Supreme People's Court in October 2005 again identified: "Reforming the current court management system of the railway transport, forestry, petroleum, farming and mining departments in terms of personnel, financing and assets".

185 The set-up of the Supreme People's Court can be seen in the introduction on the main page of the website of the Supreme People's Court, http://www.court.gov.cn/about/

186 Paragraph 2 of Article 30 of the Organic Law of the People's Courts

187 Paragraph 1 of Article 32 of the Organic Law of the People's Courts

Procedure Law stipulates that the Supreme People's Court shall have jurisdiction as the court of the first instance over major criminal cases which are of significance to the whole country.[188] The Civil Procedure Law stipulates that the Supreme People's Court shall have jurisdiction as the court of the first instance over cases which have a major impact on the whole country and cases which it deems it should try.[189] The Administrative Procedure Law stipulates that the Supreme People's Court shall have jurisdiction as a court of the first instance over grave and complicated administrative cases in the whole country.[190]

- Cases of appeals and of protests lodged against judgements and orders of the Higher People's Courts and the Special People's Courts.[191]
- Cases of protests lodged by the Supreme People's Procuratorate in accordance with the procedures of judicial supervision.[192]

*(c) Examining and approving death sentences.*[193]

According to Article 13 of the Organic Law of the People's Courts of 1979, Article 199 of the Criminal Procedure Law, and Article 48, paragraph 2, first sentence of the Criminal Law, a death sentence is examined and approved by the Supreme People's Court. At the same time, the Decision Concerning the Revision of the Organic Law of the People's Courts of the People's Republic of China, adopted at the Second Session of the Sixth Standing Committee of the National People's Congress, stipulates that: "The Supreme People's Court may, when it deems it necessary, authorise Higher People's Courts of provinces, autonomous regions and municipalities directly under the Central Government to exercise the power to approve cases involving the imposition of death sentences for homicide, rape, robbery, causing explosions and others gravely endangering public security and disrupting social order." According to the revised Organic Law of the People's Courts of 1983, the Supreme People's Court may devolve the competence to examine and approve death sentences for ordinary criminal cases involving homicide, rape, etc. to Higher People's Courts of provinces, while it examines and approves mainly serious economic criminal cases involving corruption. Devolving the competence to examine and approve death sentences to lower courts makes if difficult to guarantee the prudence and justice of death sen-

188 Article 22 of the Criminal Procedure Law

189 Article 19 of the Civil Procedure Law

190 Article 16 of the Administrative Procedure Law

191 Paragraph 2 of Article 32 of the Organic Law of the People's Courts

192 Paragraph 3 of Article 32 of the Organic Law of the People's Courts

193 See Footnote 161

tences within the system. After the denounced execution of Dong Wei in Shaanxi in 2002,[194] all quarters of Chinese society strongly appealed to the Supreme People's Court to withdraw the devolved competence to examine and approve death sentences. During the "two conferences" of 2003 (the National People's Congress and the Chinese Political Consultative Conference), the NPC delegate and professor of Southwest University of Political Science and Law, Chen Zhonglin, was the first to suggest that the Supreme People's Court should withdraw the devolved competence to examine and approve death sentences. By 2005, miscarriages of justice such as the approved death sentence carried out on Nie Shubin in Hebei,[195] and the incarcerations of She Xianglin in Hubei[196] and Xu Jingxiang in Henan[197] had increasingly exposed the problem of devolved competence to examine and approve death sentences and brought the issue to the forefront. At the end of 2005, the Supreme People's Court issued a notice that from 1st July onwards, a hearing would have to be held in all cases of the second instance involving a death sentence. Prior to this, however, hearings had not been held in 80% of all cases of the second instance involving a death sen-

194 Dong, a 26-year-old peasant, was sentenced to death on 21st December 2001 after killing a man in a fight outside a dance hall in Yan'an, Shaanxi province, though he pleaded self-defence. His lawyer appealed on these grounds. The Higher People's Court of Shaanxi province reviewed its own decision and rejected the appeal, issuing an order on 22nd April 2002 for an execution on 29th April 2002. Dong's lawyer was not informed, but found out by chance on 27th April 2002. He was initially refused entry to the Supreme People's Court in Beijing but snuck in and convinced a judge to issue a stay of execution, which was hastily communicated to the executioner by mobile phone four minutes before the execution was due to take place. The Supreme People's Court ordered the Shaanxi Higher People's Court to review its decision again. Under this review, the Higher People's Court again rejected the appeal and Dong Wei was executed on 5th September 2002.

195 Nie Shubin was executed in 1995 by a bullet to the back of the neck after confessing, likely under duress, to a rape and murder. His parents were not informed in advance. Ten years later, a man arrested on another matter additionally confessed to the same crime and was able to provide convincing details from the scene.

196 She Xianglin was arrested for murder after his wife Zhang Zaiyu went missing and a woman's body was later found in a nearby pond and identified by Zhang's family. He confessed to the crime under police torture. He was sentenced to 15 years and served 11 years before his wife suddenly reappeared, having left the marriage due to boredom and secretly remarried in Shandong. She Xianglin has received State compensation for loss of earnings.

197 Xu Jingxiang served 13 years for robbery before being acquitted.

tence, which was widely criticised.[198] Following a round of preparatory work, the Standing Committee of the NPC amended the Organic Law of the People's Courts on 31st October 2006, abolishing the last vestiges in law of the devolved competence to examine and approve death sentences to lower courts. Up until then, the process of withdrawing the competence to examine and approve death sentences has been in the state of revision. The Decision of the Supreme People's Court on a Unified Exercise of the Competence to Examine and Approve Death Sentences was approved and issued on 28th December 2006. It abolished the Notice on Devolving the Competence to Examine and Approve Death Sentences to Higher People's Courts and Military Courts of the PLA enacted by the former Article 13 of the Organic Law of the People's Courts. As of 1st January 2007, the Supreme People's Court has formally withdrawn the competence to examine and approve death sentences and implemented this accordingly.[199]

### *(d) Judicial Interpretation*

The Supreme People's Court gives interpretation on questions concerning the specific application of laws and decrees in judicial proceedings before the People's Courts.[200] According to the regulations on judicial interpretation by the Supreme People's Court, judicial interpretation by the Supreme People's Court is divided into four forms: "interpretations", "provisions", "written replies" and "decisions". "Interpretations" means judicial interpretation on how to apply a certain law when adjudicating or how to apply laws when handling a certain case or problem; "provisions" means providing criteria and opinions for adjudicating in accordance with the spirit of the law; "written replies" means judicial interpretation on how to apply laws when adjudicating at the Higher People's Courts and the Military Courts of the PLA; and "decisions" means judicial interpretation of amendments and abolitions.[201]

---

198 See "Looking Back at 27 Years of Devolved Competence to Examine and Approve Death Sentences to Lower Courts: From the Rule of Man to the Rule of Law", China Newsweek, 29th December 2006

199 With respect to the process of withdrawing the competence to examine and approve death sentences, see the special topic in the Prosecutors' Daily, "Focus on the Withdrawal by the Supreme People's Court of the Devolved Competence to Examine and Approve Death Sentences", http://www.jcrb.com/zyw/sxfh/index.htm

200 Article 33 of the Organic Law of the People's Courts; Article 2 of the Decision of the Standing Committee of the NPC on Strengthening Judicial Interpretation

201 Article 6 of the Regulations of the Supreme People's Court on Work Relating to Judicial Interpretation (2007)

## Section III Judicial Organisation of Chinese Courts

Judicial organisation is the organisation of adjudication in courts. According to the Organic Law of the People's Courts of the People's Republic of China[202] and Procedure Law, there are three forms of judicial organisation of the People's Courts, as follows:

### (1) Single-judge Bench

The single-judge bench is the form of judicial organisation whereby one judge adjudicates simple cases, including:

- criminal cases of private prosecution of the first instance and other minor criminal cases, and lawsuits of public prosecution in which a fixed-term imprisonment not exceeding three years, criminal detention, confinement or exclusive fines could be meted out, for which the facts of the cases are clear and evidence is sufficient, and to which the People's Procuratorate suggests or approves the application of summary procedure;[203]
- simple civil cases adjudicated by the Basic People's Courts and the People's Tribunals dispatched by them;[204]
- cases adjudicated by special procedure. Except for cases concerning a roll of voters and other important and complicated cases which are adjudicated by a collegial panel of judges, special procedure cases are adjudicated by one judge.[205]

### (2) Collegial Panel

The collegial panel is the form of judicial organisation whereby more than three judges or judges and People's Assessors adjudicate cases collectively. Accord-

---

202 Article 10, paragraph 2 of the Organic Law of the People's Courts

203 See Zhang Yongquan, On the System of Collegial Panels, http://www.dffy.com/faxuejieti/ss/200404/20040405212454-3.htm; Bai Shanyun, Thoughts on Strengthening the Authority of Collegial Panels, http://www.law-lib.com/LW/lw_view.asp?no=498; "Supreme People's Court Wishes to Establish a System of Authority for Collegial Panels", reported on Xinhua Net on 6th January 2007, http://news.xinhuanet.com/legal/2007-01/06/content_5573359.htm; Article 174 of the Criminal Procedure Law

204 Articles 40 and 42 of the Civil Procedure Law

205 Article 161 of the Civil Procedure Law. According to Article 128 of the Civil Procedure Law, the cases for which the special procedure applies include cases concerning a roll of voters, the proclamation of death of a missing person, the determination of a citizen as incompetent or partially incompetent for civil acts, and the determination of a property as ownerless.

ing to the Organic Law of the People's Courts and the Criminal, Civil and Administrative Procedure Law,[206] criminal and civil cases of the first instance – except for a few simple cases which are adjudicated by a single judge – and all administrative cases of the first instance[207] are adjudicated by a collegial panel composed of an odd number of three or more judges or a combination of judges and People's Assessors; all cases of the second instance, retrial cases and judicial reviews of death sentences are adjudicated by a collegial panel.[208]

In legal principle, a collegial panel is the basic form of judicial organisation for adjudication by courts and its members are not permanent but are appointed temporarily. The president of a court or the chief judge of a division appoints one of the judges to act as the presiding judge of the collegial panel; when the president of the court or the chief judge of a division participates in the judicial proceedings, he or she acts as the presiding judge.[209] In practice, however, the members of a collegial panel are fixed. For example, there are six collegial panels in the first civil court of the Second Intermediate People's Court of Beijing, each collegial panel comprising 4 or 5 members including one or two clerks. For each new case, the chief judge of the division confirms one judge as commissioner who directs the adjudication of the case. Other members of the collegial panel take part in adjudicating the case, and the clerk serve to record the minutes. In most cases, the collegial panel adjudicates the case in theory, but in practice, it is the commissioner who mainly serves to provide the facts and laws of the case. From the preparation of a hearing, through the investigation of the evidence up to the judgement of the case, all the opinions are provided solely by the commissioner. Other members of the collegial panel do not directly take part in adjudication, but merely provide comments on the case at the end by stating their opinions on the judgement of the commissioner by reading the documents and listening to the commissioner's reports. Thus, the collegial system essentially becomes a single-judge system, and the supposed function of the system of collegial panels is not implemented.[210]

---

206 Paragraph 2 of Article 10 of the Organic Law of the People's Courts

207 Article 46 of the Administrative Procedure Law

208 Paragraph 3 of Article 10 of the Organic Law of the People's Courts; Paragraph 4 of Article 147 of the Criminal Procedure Law; Articles 187, 205 and 206 of the Criminal Procedure Law

209 Paragraph 4 of Article 10 of the Organic Law of the People's Courts

210 See Zhang Yongquan, On the System of Collegial Panels, http://www.dffy.com/faxuejieti/ss/200404/20040405212454-3.htm; Bai Yunshan, Thoughts on Strengthening the Authority of Collegial Panels, http://www.law-lib.com/LW/lw_view.asp?no=498

In order to change this situation, former vice-president of the Supreme People's Court, Cao Jianming, indicated clearly at the Seventh Conference on National Civil Judicial Work that the situation whereby collegial panels meet but do not function collegially must change, such that all the members of a collegial panel take part in a court trial, become involved in the facts of cases and apply laws collectively, review and sign off on judgement documents collectively and take collective responsibility. After a court trial, members of a collegial panel should meet, form a consensus and forge a common direction of adjudication with constant collective responsibility, so as to progressively realise a system which strengthens the authority of collegial panels.[211]

## (3) Judicial Committee

According to the Organic Law of the People's Courts, the People's Courts at various levels establish judicial committees.[212] Members of judicial committees of local People's Courts at various levels are appointed and removed by the Standing Committees of the People's Congresses at the corresponding levels, upon the recommendation of the presidents of these courts.[213] The presidents of the People's Courts preside over meetings of judicial committees of the People's Courts at various levels,[214] and their tasks include the following three aspects:[215]

### *(a) Discussing important or difficult cases*

Judicial committee does not adjudicate cases directly, but rather discusses important or difficult cases adjudicated by collegial panels and makes decisions. Judgements and orders are still signed by the members of the collegial panels. In accordance with adjudicating practice, cases which may need to be submitted to the judicial committee for discussion include difficult, complex or major cases,[216] cases involving death sentences, cases which need to be reheard and/or arraigned,[217] and foreign cases.

---

211 "Supreme People's Court Wishes to Establish a System of Authority for Collegial Panels", reported on Xinhua Net on 6th January 2007, http://news.xinhuanet.com/legal/2007-01/06/content_5573359.htm

212 Article 11, Paragraph 1, first sentence of the Organic Law of the People's Courts

213 Paragraph 2 of Article 11 of the Organic Law of the People's Courts

214 Article 11, Paragraph 3 of the Organic Law of the People's Courts

215 Article 11, Paragraph 1, second sentence of the Organic Law of the People's Courts

216 Article 149 of the Criminal Procedure Law

217 As stipulated in the Organic Law of the People's Courts, if the president of a People's Court finds, in a legally effective judgement or order of his court, some definite error in

### (b) Summarising judicial experience

Judicial committee summarises the judicial experience acquired from adjudicating work undertaken within a certain period, with respect to particular types of cases, in particular important cases, and the methods and approaches used in adjudicating.

### (c) Discussing other issues relating to adjudication

The judicial interpretations of the Supreme People's Court, for example, have to be discussed and approved by judicial committee.[218]

Judicial committee is a creation of the organisation of the courts in China. Previously, the legal system in China had not been sound, as there was no law for judges to abide by when adjudicating cases, hence judicial committee could have the effect of ensuring that adjudication was just. However, this form of organisation itself has serious defects, because it is a judicial organisation but not an executive organisation. As a judicial organisation, it only makes judgement and does not hear cases, hence hearing and judgement are separated, such that areas of authority and responsibility are confused, interfering with independent judgement by judges. Therefore, whether it should exist is currently a topic of urgent discussion, which this dissertation shall discuss in the section on judges' independence and related systems.[219]

---

the determination of facts or application of law, he or she must submit the judgement or order to the judicial committee for disposal.

218 Such as the judicial interpretation approved at the 1414th congress of the judicial committee of the Supreme People's Court on 22nd January 2007, being the "Provisions of the Supreme People's Court on Some Issues Relating to the Judicial Review of Death Sentences"

219 Discussed in detail on page 70

## Section IV Basic System of Adjudicative Work

### (1) Public Trial System

The Constitution, the Organic Law of the People's Courts and the Civil, Criminal and Administrative Procedure Laws of China all stipulate that the People's Courts shall hear cases publicly, except as otherwise specified by law.[220]

"Publicly" means that the entire proceedings before a court in session – except for the discussions of the collegial panel – are published in the public domain, allowing citizens to assess a trial and journalists to report on it. If a case is to be tried in public in accordance with the law, courts publish the details of the case, such as the names of the parties and the time and place of a court session, on a notice board before each session. If the case is not to be tried in public, courts still have to publicly pronounce a judgement or sentence.[221]

In accordance with the law,[222] the following three types of cases shall not be tried publicly:

- cases involving state secrets;
- cases involving the private affairs of individuals;
- cases involving of the commission of crimes by minors.

The Criminal Procedure Law stipulates that all cases involving crimes committed by minors between fourteen and sixteen years of age shall not be tried publicly.[223] Cases involving crimes committed by minors between sixteen and eighteen years of age shall generally[224] not be tried publicly.[225] This is to prevent minors from being traumatised and becoming bad influences in society, and to better the chances of educating and rehabilitating juvenile delinquents.

---

220 Article 125 of the Constitution; Article 7 of the Organic Law of the People's Courts; Articles 8 and 103 of the Civil Procedure Law; Articles 11 and 152 of the Criminal Procedure Law; Articles 6 and 45 of the Administrative Procedure Law

221 Article 115 of the Civil Procedure Law stipulates that: "The People's Courts shall publicly pronounce its judgement in all cases."

222 Article 125 of the Constitution; Article 7 of the Organic Law of the People's Courts; Article 103 of the Civil Procedure Law; Article 152 of the Criminal Procedure Law; Article 45 of the Administrative Procedure Law

223 In absolutely non-public trials, the judges have no discretion and the case must not be tried publicly.

224 In generally non-public trials, the judges has some discretion and can decide whether or not to hear the case publicly, depending on the circumstances of the case, wherein there are specific requirements for making a trial public.

225 Article 152 of the Criminal Procedure Law

In accordance with the Civil Procedure Law, divorce cases and cases involving commercial secrets may[226] also be heard in private if a party so requests.[227] The reason for not hearing the case in public must be announced in court.

## (2) System in which the Second Instance is the Final Instance[228]

China implements a four-level system in which the second instance is the final instance, wherein the four levels are four levels of People's Courts and trial levels and jurisdiction are divided according to the character and difficulty of cases. The system in which the second instance is the final instance means that a judgement pronounced following a trial before a court of the second instance is final. A party contesting a judgement[229] or order[230] of the first instance can appeal to the People's Court at the next higher level in a legal time limit;[231] the People's Procuratorate considering a judgement or order of the first instance mistaken firmly can protest to the People's Court at the next higher level in a legal time

226 Second sentence in Article 120 of the Civil Procedure Law, http://news.sina.com.cn/c/l/2007-10-29/012314183634.shtml (original Chinese text)

227 Either of the parties can apply for a non-public trial in these types of case, but the decision rests with the judge.

228 Article 12 of the Organic Law of the People's Courts stipulates that: "In the administration of justice, the People's Courts adopt a system whereby the second instance is the final instance."

229 Judgements are generally the decision made by People's Courts on material issues at the end of adjudication.

230 Orders are generally determinations made by People's Courts in order to resolve procedural issues while adjudicating cases.

231 Article 144 of the Civil Procedure Law stipulates that if a party refuses to accept a judgement or order of the first instance made by a local People's Court at any level, he or she shall have the right to file an appeal with the People's Court at the next higher level. Article 145 of the Civil Procedure Law stipulates that the time limit for an appeal against a judgement shall be 15 days, and the time limit for an appeal against an order shall be 10 days, from the date on which the court verdict was delivered. Article 183 of the Criminal Procedure Law stipulates that the time limit for making an appeal or a protest for not accepting a judgement shall be 10 days, and the time limit for making an appeal or a protest for not accepting a ruling shall be five days, computed from the second day from the day on which the written judgement or ruling is received. Article 58 of the Administrative Procedure Law stipulates the if a party refuses to accept a judgement of the first instance made by a People's Court, the party shall have the right to file an appeal with the People's Court at the next higher level within 15 days after the service of the written judgement; if a party refuses to accept a ruling of the first instance made by a People's Court, the party shall have the right to file an appeal with the People's Courts at the next higher level within 10 days after the service of the written ruling.

limit.[232] If the party does not appeal and the People's Procuratorate does not lodge a protest within the appeal time limit, the judgement or order of the first instance comes into force. The judgement or order made by the People's Court at the next higher level after adjudicating a case of appeal or of protest in accordance with the procedures of the second instance is then a final judgement or order. Except for the cases involving death sentences which have to be examined by law, cases come into force immediately.

According to the relevant laws, some special cases employ a system whereby the first instance is the final instance, mainly including the following:

- cases of the first instance heard by the Supreme People's Court;[233]
- cases concerning a roll of voters, the proclamation of death of a missing person, the determination of a citizen as incompetent or partially incompetent for civil acts, and the determination of a property as ownerless, which are adjudicated by Basic People's Courts in accordance with special procedure.[234] Generally, these cases are not disputes between parties, but merely require the re-

232 Paragraph 2 of Article 12 of the Organic Law of the People's Courts stipulates that: from a judgement or orders of the first instance made by a local People's Court, a party may bring an appeal to the People's Court at the next higher level in accordance with the procedure prescribed by law, and the People's Procuratorate may present a protest to the People's Court at the next higher level in accordance with the procedure prescribed by law, wherein protests in China are divided into two kinds: one is to raise a protest by appeal proceedings, which only exists in criminal litigation when the prosecutorial organ is the public prosecutor's office, i.e. a protest lodged by a local People's Procuratorate at various levels with the People's Court at the next higher level within the legal time limit for protesting if it considers that criminal judgements or orders made by the People's Court at the same level are in error; the other kind is a protest raised in accordance with judicial supervision procedures, i.e. a protest lodged in accordance with judicial supervision procedures when the Supreme People's Procuratorate considers effective judgements and orders made by the People's Courts at various levels to be in error, and when Higher People's Procuratorates consider effective judgements or orders made by lower People's Courts to be in error. This protest is not limited by time. The protest mentioned here is the first protest. According to Article 185 of the Criminal Procedure Law, a protest to be lodged by the local People's Procuratorate at any level against the judgement or ruling of the first instance of the People's Court of the same level shall be presented through the People's Court which originally tried the cases, and the copies of the written protest shall be sent to the People's Procuratorate at the next higher level. The People's Court which originally tried the case shall transfer the written protest, together with the case files and evidence, to the People's Court at the next higher level and shall deliver duplicates of the written protest to the parties.

233 Article 123 of the Civil Procedure Law

234 Article 128 of the Civil Procedure Law

cognition of facts, some of which may need to be heard and settled quickly, hence the application of a system in which the first instance is the final instance.

## (3) System of Judicial Review of Death Sentences

The competence to examine and approve death sentences and the procedure of the judicial review for death sentences covers both death sentences for immediate execution and death sentences with a two-year suspension of execution. The former is then referred to as the competence to examine and approve death sentences, and the latter as the competence to examine and approve suspended death sentences. China's Criminal Procedure Law of both 1979 and 1996 stipulated that the Supreme People's Court has the competence to examine and approve suspended death sentences, which is also implemented in practice. Given the special nature of the system of suspended death sentences, and with a view to reducing the work pressure on the Supreme People's Court, it may be feasible for Higher People's Courts to have the competence to examine and approve suspended death sentences. On this at least, theoretical and practical circles are agreed.[235]

The competence to examine and approve death sentences has, however, been a bone of contention. As the severest criminal penalty, death sentences deprive criminals of their lives. But the wrongly condemned cannot then be brought back, hence it is imperative to make doubly sure before death sentences are carried out. In ancient China, the competence to examine and approve death sentences always rested with the central government and was strictly controlled by the Sanfuzou system (三复奏 sān fù zòu, a written statement of report submitted to the throne three times) and the Wufuzou system (五复奏 wǔ fù zòu, a written statement of report submitted to the throne five times). In Chinese judicial practice, the competence to examine and approve death sentences has been withdrawn and transferred to lower courts several times.[236] In 2006, the Supreme People's Court withdrew the competence to examine and approve death sentences from other courts. The competence to examine and approve death sentences is now exercised by the Supreme People's Court only, reflecting the serious attitude of the state government regarding circumspect use of the death sentence. Indeed, the government aims to correct irregularities and errors in death sentencing, uni-

235 See Chen Weidong, Liu Jihua, Thoughts on the Current Situation and the Preservation or Abolition of the Procedure of Judicial Review of Death Sentences, in: Chinese Legal Science, 1998, Volume 5, p. 98

236 See the discussion of the authority of the Supreme People's Court in Section II of this chapter

fy the standard for the application of death sentences, guarantee the quality of adjudication in death sentence cases and effectively control the number of death sentences approved. This is highly significant for preventing wrongful executions, successively reducing the number of executions and approaching the issue of executions with caution.[237]

## (4) System of Trial Supervision

### *(a) Brief Introduction*

The system of trial supervision is also known as the rehearing or retrial system and refers to a special judicial system in which a People's Court rehears a case in which an effective judgement or order has already been made. The precondition for initiating a trial supervision procedure is that some definite error is discovered in the determination of facts or application of law in a legally effective judgement or order.[238] Those having the right to initiate a trial supervision procedure are the president and judicial committee of a People's Court, the Supreme People's Court and the Higher People's Courts, and the Supreme People's Procuratorate and the Higher People's Procuratorates. The appeal or application for retrial lodged by a party to an effective judgement or order is just the main material catalyst for a trial supervision procedure, and an appeal or application for retrial in no way ensures that a trial supervision procedure will be initiated. This will be discussed in detail below.

### *(b) Rehearing or Retrial Lodged by a People's Court*[239]

The modes of rehearing or retrial when lodged by a People's Court are:

- if the president of a People's Court at any level finds some definite error in a legally effective judgement or order of his court and deems it necessary to have the case retried, he or she shall refer it to the judicial committee for discussion and decision;
- if the Supreme People's Court finds some definite error in a legally effective judgement or order by a local People's Court, it has the right to arraign[240] or instruct the lower People's Court to rehear the case;[241]

237 See Li Yunlong, Shen Deyong, Comparative Study of the System of Death Sentences, China People's Public Security University Press, Beijing 1992, p. 248

238 This does not however apply to the effective judgement in divorce cases. Article 183 of the Civil Procedure Law; Article 3 of the Temporary Regulations of the Supreme People's Procuratorate on Protests by Civil Trial Supervision Procedure of 1992

239 Article 205 of the Criminal Procedure Law; Article 157 of the Civil Procedure Law

- if a higher People's Court finds some definite error in a legally effective judgement or order by a lower People's Court, it has the right to arraign or instruct the lower People's Court to rehear the case.

### *(c) Rehearing or Retrial Lodged by the People's Procuratorate*[242]

The modes of rehearing or retrial when lodged by a People's Procuratorate are:

- if the Supreme People's Procuratorate finds some definite error in a legally effective judgement or order by a local People's Court, or if a higher People's Procuratorate finds some definite error in a legally effective judgement or order by a lower People's Court, I has the right to protest to the People's Court at the same level in accordance with the judicial supervision procedure;
- if a local People's Procuratorate finds some definite error in a legally effective judgement or order by a People's Court at the same level, it has the right to submit a protest to a higher People's Procuratorate in accordance with the judicial supervision procedure;
- the People's Courts shall rehear cases protested by the People's Procuratorates; when a People's Court rehears such a case, it shall notify the People's Procuratorate which protested to appoint prosecutors to appear in court.[243]

### *(d) Rehearing or Retrial Lodged by a Party*

A party can apply to have an effective judgement or order reviewed, amended or withdrawn. If the application meets any of the follows conditions,[244] the People's Courts shall lodge an application for a rehearing or retrial:

- there is new evidence which would reverse the original judgement or order;
- crucial evidence in the original judgement or order is found to be insufficient;

240 Arraignment is when the higher People's Court considers that the People's Court which originally adjudicated a case committed some definite error in the determination of facts or application of law and is not suitable to rehear the case, and decides to hear to case.

241 An instruction to retry a case is when the higher People's Court instructs the lower People's Court to retry a case which the lower People's Court has already concluded, in accordance with the judicial supervision procedure.

242 Article 205 of the Criminal Procedure Law; Articles 10 and 64 of the Administrative Procedure Law

243 Article 190 of the Civil Procedure Law

244 Article 204 of the Criminal Procedure Law

- the application of law in the original judgement or order is found to be erroneous;
- the People's Court violated legal procedure in a way which may have prejudiced the passing of a correct judgement or order;
- the judge is found to have taken bribes, committed malpractice for personal gain, and/or bent the law in rendering judgement when trying the case.[245]

### *(e) Trial Procedure of Rehearing Cases*

When a decision is made to retry a case in accordance with the procedure for trial supervision, the original People's Court first issues an order to suspend the execution of the original judgement.[246] If the Supreme People's Court or a higher People's Court arraigns the cases, it can issue an order to suspend the execution of the original judgement and notifies the original People's Court accordingly.

In the retrial of a case in accordance with the procedure for trial supervision, if the case was originally one of the first instance, it shall be tried in accordance with the procedure of the first instance, and the parties may appeal against the new judgement or order; if the case was originally one of the second instance or was brought up for trial by a People's Court at a higher level, it shall be tried in accordance with the procedure of the second instance, and the new judgement or order rendered shall be legally effective and final.[247]

Moreover, the People's Court which is to adjudicate a case to be retried shall form a new collegial panel[248] and shall settle the case within three months from the day on which the decision to retry the case or to bring the case up for trial itself is made; if the time limit needs to be extended, the maximum time limit may not exceed six months.[249]

## Section V Comparing the Court Systems

### (1) German Federal Court System

The German court system is complicated due to the two principles contained within it, namely the principle of specialisation and the principle of decentralis-

245 Article 179 of the Civil Procedure Law stipulates 13 situations in which a civil party can apply to have a case reheard.

246 Article 159 of the Civil Procedure Law

247 Article 206 of the Criminal Procedure Law; Article 160 of the Civil Procedure Law

248 Article 206 of the Criminal Procedure Law; Article 36 of the Civil Procedure Law

249 Article 207 of the Criminal Procedure Law

ing rights. Rights are decentralised by being distributed between the federal courts and *Land* courts. As the highest court within each court system, the federal court – as the court of final appeal for judgments by *Land* courts – is responsible for ensuring that German law is interpreted uniformly and developed in a co-ordinated way. Nevertheless, the German judicial system is more unified than for example that of the USA, which also operates a federal system. As a country with a typical federal judicial system, the USA establishes courts at federal and state level, respectively. The structure of federal courts is such that they are divided into the court of the first instance, the court of appeal and the supreme court of appeal; the same court structure is employed at state level. State courts exercise jurisdiction over cases concerning state law, while the federal court only exercises jurisdiction over cases concerning federal law. Unlike this absolute federal court system, Germany has a unitary court system from the court of the first instance to the supreme court of appeal. Courts are established differently at the federal level and within the *Länder*. From the federal level to the *Länder*, the German court system exhibits a unified adjudicative structure from the court of the first instance to the supreme court of appeal. The federal court is the highest arbitrator and also the court of final appeal within the scope of its jurisdiction. Except for some special tribunals established in German ordinary courts which may hear cases as a court of the first instance, all other federal courts hear cases as the court of final appeal for *Land* courts. In Germany, a case is usually tried by a *Land* court in the first instance and by the federal court in the final instance, if appealed. Therefore, German *Land* courts apply not only *Land* law but also federal law, just like the federal courts.

In the German judicial system of *Bund* (federation) and *Land* (federal state), only the relationship between the constitutional courts is similar to the American federal model. There are essential differences in the scope of jurisdiction between the federal constitutional court and *Land* constitutional courts: the federal constitutional court deals with cases concerning the Basic Law and federal law, whereas *Land* constitutional courts deal with cases concerning the respective *Land* constitution. Each constitutional court is independent, and a *Land* constitutional court is not a court of the first instance with respect to the federal constitutional court. The judgments made by all constitutional courts are final judgments and cannot be appealed. Their structure, constitutions, judgments and the legal status of judges are also governed by different laws: the federal constitutional court is governed by the Basic Law and federal law, whereas *Land* constitutional courts are governed by the respective *Land* constitution and *Land* law.

In practice, more than 95% of *Land* matters brought before *Land* courts in Germany are governed by federal law. Correspondingly, the responsibility of *Land* governments for *Land* courts in Germany is limited as compared to the

USA; the majority of *Länder* governments are limited in their involvement with financial support, budgetary decisions and the appointment of judges and judicial staff.[250]

"Specialisation" means that German courts are highly specialised in the cases with which they deal. There are five different court systems, namely ordinary courts, administrative courts, labour courts, social courts and finance courts. Each court system has its own scope of jurisdiction and is independent. Such a division means that a specific dispute and related matters are tried by the court specifically established for that purpose. Because judges therefore have specialist knowledge and experience in the relevant matters, the individual can demonstrate a higher quality in their application of the law. Many scholars believe that the efficiency of German courts is due to this division into specialised fields.[251]

In recent years, however, the abuses of this specific division of German courts have gradually begun to manifest themselves. There are many courts of the first instance that individuals do not know which court they should bring a particular case before. A dispute may also involve legal problems which fall within the jurisdictions of more than one special court, causing further difficulty for parties in choosing the correct court of jurisdiction. Moreover, different special courts have devised complicated and differing rules of court. Lastly, it is possible that various rules of court may differ or even conflict, thus influencing the unity of the law.[252]

After the Second World War, a legal reform was initiated in Germany in order to solve the problems mentioned above. In accordance with this reform, a party may bring a dispute to any court that he/she thinks has jurisdiction over it. If the court accepts the case, this decision has a constraining effect, i.e. the party cannot then bring the same dispute before other court. If the court finds that the dispute does not fall within its jurisdiction, it is obliged to indicate to the party in question the correct court of jurisdiction. This system of bringing cases is very convenient and ensures that cases are dealt with by the correct courts.

---

250 Daniel J. Meador, German Appellate Judges: Career Patterns and Anglo-American Comparisons, 67 Judicature No. 1, June-July 1983, pp. 29-30

251 Daniel J. Meador, German Appellate Judges: Career Patterns and Anglo-American Comparisons, 67 Judicature No. 1, June-July 1983, pp. 27-29; Anke Freckmann and Thomas Wegerich, The German Legal System, Sweet & Maxwell, 1999, pp. 129-131; Nigel G. Foster and Satish Sule, German Legal System & Laws, 3rd edition, Oxford University Press, 2003, pp. 67-68

252 Donald P. Kommers, Autonomy versus Accountability: The German Judiciary, in: Peter H. Russell / David M. O'Brien (eds.), Judicial Independence in the Age of Democracy, University Press of Virginia, 2001, pp. 140-141

Secondly, in order to guarantee that all special courts – in particular all supreme federal courts – apply laws uniformly, there are provisions in the Basic Law which establish a special institution, the Common Senate of the Federal Supreme Courts of Justice (*Gemeinsamer Senat der obersten Gerichtshöfe des Bundes*), for this purpose. This is a specifically established institution consisting of delegates from all the supreme federal courts. Where the possibility exists that a judgment made by a supreme federal court conflicts with former judgments made by other supreme federal courts, the case needs to be submitted to this institution.

## (2) Comparing the Court Systems of China and Germany

### *(a) The Position of the Courts within the Organisation of the State*

The Basic Law explicitly stipulates that the essential constitutional principle is the separation and restriction of powers, the acknowledgement of judicial independence and guarantees regarding the special status of courts within the system of restrictions. In this respect, the German court system differs fundamentally from the Chinese court system. In China, the status of courts is below that of the People's Congresses as the legislature, and courts do not restrict the People's Congresses but are rather supervised by them.

The independence of German judges from the legislature is seen mainly in their power to review constitutionality. In a legal system which pursues the ideal that the Constitution is paramount, judges are in principle bound only by constitutional laws and regulations. If justice needs to be strengthened, and if judges are independent of the legislature, courts should be able to review the laws drafted by legislators and have the power to question the constitutionality of laws and declare unconstitutional laws void, depending on the circumstances. In a state which employs constitutional government and pursues the ideal of the rule by law, it is necessary to supervise the legislative state power. In Germany, special constitutional courts are established which exercise the power to review constitutionality. In a federal system such as in Germany, the federal constitutional court has the same status as the *Bundestag*, the *Bundesrat*, the Federal President and the federal government. Its constitutional status is reflected in its independence from the executive and the legislature. By applying and interpreting the Constitution, it can restrict other constitutional institutions. In China, however, there is still no relatively independent institution for reviewing constitutionality. In accordance with the provisions of the Chinese Constitution and administrative law, only the legislature – i.e. the National People's Congress and its Standing Committee – has the power to review constitutionality. As the court of the final instance, the Supreme People's Court only has the power to interpret laws and regulations, but not the additional power to interpret the Constitution. In addition, even the Supreme People's Court is to be supervised by the National People's Congress and its Standing Committee. This system of constitutional government means that Chinese courts cannot be independent of the legislature, and independent judgments by judges also cannot therefore be truly realised.

### *(b) The Configuration of Courts*

The configuration of courts in China is a unitary system, whereas in Germany it is a plural system. A unitary system means that judicial power is exercised uniformly by the ordinary courts, and the supreme judicial decision-making power is exercised by – for example in the case of China – the Supreme People's Court. A plural system means that judicial power is respectively exercised by various courts, and the supreme judicial decision-making power is likewise respectively exercised by various institutions. In China, the Supreme People's Court and the three levels of local courts deal with all civil, criminal and administrative cases, operating a system in which the second instance is the final instance. The Supreme People's Court is the highest court of appeal.[253] In Germany, by contrast, there are – in addition to the ordinary courts from the federal level to *Land* level – four special courts, namely the administrative court, the labour court, the finance court and the social court, which operate a system of four levels in which the third instance is the final instance. Each federal supreme court has supreme jurisdiction over the cases which is governs. Their judgments cannot be interfered with by other courts. This arrangement whereby various courts exercise supreme jurisdiction in parallel shows how the German court system is a plural system.

Both countries have also established special military courts charged with cases concerning military affairs and soldiers. Unlike China, however, the German court system has no special maritime courts or railway transport courts. A civil division and commercial division are respectively established in German ordinary courts at the *Land* level. Disputes over maritime affairs are governed by the commercial division.[254]

In China, there have been many serious discussions about whether or not to abolish railway transport courts. The majority of scholars believe that railway transport courts should be abolished.[255] From the point of view of the jurisdiction

253 Zhu Fuhui, Shao Zihong, Comparison of the Court Systems in the USA and Germany, Modern Jurisprudence, December 2001, Volume 23, Issue 6, p. 16

254 Section 4 f) of Paragraph 1 of Article 95 of GVG

255 On 4th July 2009, the Research Centre for Applied law at the China University of Political Science and Law convened a special seminar on the question of retaining or abol-

of railway transport courts, although such cases concern railway transportation, they are not substantially different in nature to other ordinary cases. If the railway transport courts were abolished, the cases in question would be transferred to the jurisdiction of the local courts, which have the capacity to deal with such cases. Abolishing railway transport courts is also necessary in order to promote judicial reform and streamline the judicial system, to establish a sound and unified judicial system, and to guarantee judicial fairness and impartiality.

### *(c) Forms of Adjudicative Organisation*

The forms of adjudicative organisation in both countries include single-judge benches and collegial panels. In addition, China also has a special form of adjudicative organisation, the so-called judicial committee.

As a product of specific historic and judicial circumstances, judicial committee has played an active role in the period of the planned economy in which the quality of judges has been low.[256] But given the progress in the quality of Chinese judges, the gradual establishment of a market economy system, the reform of the judicial system as promoted and required by the market economy system, the continuous penetration of reform in the Chinese political system, the constant development of democracy and the legal system, and the more democratic, scientific, fair, open, standardised and complete judicial organisation and judicial procedure required by judicial modernisation, it is time to abolish the system of judicial committee,[257] since the system of judicial committee essentially makes collegial panels and single-judge benches into a mere figurehead in terms of legal jurisdiction and ultimately influences the realisation of judicial independence. The level of reasoning incorporated into trial proceedings by collegial panels and single-judge benches is disturbed by the involvement of judicial committees. In judicial practice, it is clear that the judicial committee makes the final decision, but this decision is issued in the name of the collegial panel. In addition, the judicial committee sets the direction in advance, and the start of the actual trial by the collegial panel is then a mere formality. In some cases, a

---

ishing railway transport courts. Professors and scholars from Beijing University, the People's University, the University of Political Science and Law and the National Judges College held discussions and expressed their own opinions. Most of the scholars expressed the view that the railway transport courts should be abolished.

256 Xiao Jianguo, Xiao Jianguang, Examining the System of Judicial Committee and the Factual Basis for Abolishing the System of Judicial Committee, Journal of Beijing University of Science and Technology (Social Sciences Edition), 2002, Volume 3

257 Yu Weiqing, It is Time to Abolish Judicial Committees, Journal of Fuyang Normal College (Social Sciences Edition), 2002, Volume 2

single-judge bench has adjudicated but reached a decision which the court president in charge has not agreed with, who has then ordered the case to be transferred from the single-judge bench to a collegial panel for retrial, so that the case can be submitted to the judicial committee for discussion. Quite aside from the negative effect that this is severely wasteful of judicial resources and seriously obstructs judicial efficiency, this also negatively influences the independence of judges and critically obstructs the initiative of judges.

Judicial practice has shown that in terms of external interference, the most important factor is that the People's Courts are not be able to exercise jurisdiction independently, but within the courts, there is no guaranteed way of protecting the independence of judges in the course of adjudication, which greatly disrupts the principle of judicial independence. Many examples show that external interference on adjudicative activities is usually realised by specific leaders in the court putting pressure on the form of adjudicative organisation and especially on judges. Because of a lack of clarity in the courts regarding duties and division of labour, some non-statutory forms of adjudicative organisation, such as for example judicial committee, exercise actual jurisdiction and fulfil the adjudicative role. In practice, for example, presiding judges and court presidents have to be consulted on and approve every case, which has become an almost insurmoutable procedure. The judicial committee enjoys essential jurisdiction, such that collegial panels and judges have become dependent on it.

One scholar has said: "If the independence of judges in trying cases is not strengthened and substantive and independence of status in trying cases is not recognised as an organic and indivisible part of the principle of judicial independence, then it will be essentially impossible to establish and promote the principle of judicial independence."[258] Under the existing judicial system, by contrast, a series of "super-judicial organisations" such as the judicial committee mean that judges' capacity for independent judgement cannot obtain the respect it deserves, and their subjective initiative cannot develop either. As time passes, some judges grow to depend more and more on the judicial committee and lose their sense of responsibility. In judicial practice, when judges meet difficult and/or complicated problems in the course of trying cases, such as when determining the nature of a criminal, weighing the severity of a punishment, applying laws and interpreting facts and evidence, some do not always try every means of investigating and researching but hit upon the idea of simply "submitting to the judicial committee for discussion." This mindset of "contradictory submission" not only means that members of the judicial committee are hard put to it to deal

---

258 Wang Qiguo, Zhang Diqiu, On the Dual Nature of Adjudicative Independence, Legal Science, 1989, Volume 3, pp. 67-69

with considering "approvals" for all kinds of cases, but also causes the subjective initiative of judges to be weakened and their dependency to be instead reinforced. Moreover, irrespective of whether the decision made by the judicial committee is the same as that made by the collegial panel or not, the collegial panel has to execute it unconditionally and "make" said decision in its own name. If the opinion of the collegial panel is turned down by the judicial committee, this puts the collegial panel in a very awkward position. Lastly, the collegial panel will then inevitably take the view that since the decision is not really made by them, any problems arising from it are "nothing to do with us".[259]

In short, the system of judicial committee causes judges' sense of responsibility and honour to disappear completely, prevents the quality of Chinese judges from being improved, hinders the realisation of personal judicial independence, and ultimately allows the principle of judicial independence to simply become a slogan. This system has gradually become a significant obstacle to realising judicial independence and procedural fairness and impartiality in modern judicial practice. The conflict between the system of judicial committee and modern concepts of the rule by law and of the judiciary has been increasingly aggravated. Reform alone has failed to resolve this conflict. Therefore, abolishing the system of judicial committee is imperative under the circumstances.

259 Peng Dongfang, On the Feasibility of Abolishing the System of Judicial Committees, Western Legal Review, 2009, Volume 1, p. 118

# Part 2 Elements of the Independence of Judges

# A Substantive Independence

## (A) Independence from the Executive

## Chapter 1 Selection of Judges

The system of judicial selection is an introductive system, which is important in order to achieve the independence of judges. The system of judicial selection primarily assures that all the selected judges are well qualified to be judges. All countries with an advanced legal system attach importance to establishing and perfecting the system of judicial selection, and stipulate quite rigid conditions and procedures of judicial selection, in order to assure the good character and image of domestic judges. The German legal framework for judicial selection and the design of the system of judicial service may be regarded as being near-perfect, helping to improve public order and the quality of judges against the background of German culture, while corresponding systems have yet to be established and perfected in China. In this Chapter, I will introduce the existing system of judicial selection in these two countries, analyse and compare their differences and present ideas on how to perfect the Chinese system of judicial selection.

The system of judicial selection comprises two aspects, namely regulations concerning the conditions for judicial selection, i.e. who can be selected or appointed as a judge, and regulations concerning the procedures of judicial selection, i.e. what procedures should form the basis of judicial selection. Because judges have powers to adjudicate and conclusively settle disputes, the conditions and procedures of judicial selection are much more rigid than for other occupations. Enforcing the adjudicating powers of judges affects not only the common interest of others' property, but also people's personal liberties and even their lives. Hence, greater demands are made on judges' character and capabilities, and their capacity to exercise their adjudicating powers correctly and justly. Otherwise, people's rights of property, liberties and lives would be too easily threatened, and they may be treated unjustly.[260] On the other hand, the question of who selects judges and decides the conditions for judicial selection needs to be considered within the wider context of separation of powers. Also, the question of how to avoid negative influences of the institution and conditions for selection should lead to conclusions concerning the system of judicial selecti-

260 Ma Jianhua, Research on the Professionalisation of Judges, p. 33

on.[261] In Germany, there are rigid conditions for judicial selection. Although an apparent administrative mandate is included in the conditions for judicial selection, whether at federal level or federal state (*Land*) level, this does not compromise the independence of judges.[262] In China, by contrast, the law clearly stipulates the conditions for judicial selection, but they are comparatively too relaxed. Furthermore, court presidents who have a strong influence on judges do not have to meet the conditions for judges, which leads people to doubt the judges' character and the justness of judgements handed down by such judges. Also, whether formally or in practice, the question of assuring the independence of judges is not taken into consideration in China when establishing the system of judicial selection. Court presidents have extensive powers to decide who will be judges, which threaten the independence of judges from the outset, let alone court presidents deciding the future promotion and supervision of judges.

## Section I Selection Criteria for Judges in China

### (1) Posts and Grades of Judges

Judges in China differ from those in Germany. Formally, there is only one kind of judge, similar to the kind of judge appointed for life in German law.[263] Generally speaking, those appointed as judges can be judges for life, until retirement. In China, the law explicitly provides for a number of posts for judges, including: Assistant Judge; Judge; Associate Chief Judge of a Division; Chief Judge of a Division; Vice-President; and President. Moreover, because the judicial commit-

---

261 See Gerhard Schmid, Richterauswahl und Richterwahl im Kanton Basel-Landschaft: Auslegeordnung des Status quo und der Reformvorschläge, in: Aspekte der richterlichen Unabhängigkeit und Richter(aus)wahl, Liestahl 2000, p. 111

262 Van-Hoa To, Judicial Independence: Legal Research on its Theoretical Aspects, Practices from Germany, the United States of America, France and Vietnam, and Recommendations for Vietnam, Lund 2006, p. 179

263 But in practice, there are also judges – similar to junior judges in Germany – in Chinese courts, who are candidate judges still not appointed as assistant judges and merely recruited in courts. Generally, they start out dealing with assistant affairs of judges or the affairs of clerks of the court, work for a certain period of years (the law does not provide for a specific period of years, hence this varies depending on the circumstances in each court), are appointed as assistant judges and later become judges, enjoying the rights and assuming the obligations of a judge. Unlike in Germany, it is normally the case that they can all be appointed as assistant judges and need not be dismissed. If, for example, the working capacity of a candidate judge has not been recognised within four years, it merely means that he still needs more time to be recognised, and he would not be obliged to be dismissed.

tee system is still being implemented in China at present, the posts for judges specified in the Judges Law of the People's Republic of China (PRC) also include the committee of the judicial committee.[264]

In accordance with Article 16 of the Judges Law of the PRC, there are four posts and twelve grades of judges.[265] In order to implement the grade system of judges provided for in the Judges Law of the PRC, the Organisational Department of the CPC Central Committee, the Ministry of Human Resources and the Supreme People's Court issued an Interim Provision on the Grades of Judges of the People's Republic of China (PRC) on 12th December 1997, which explicitly provides for the organisation, evaluation, promotion, demotion and cancellation of grades of judges. At present, the problem of establishing the grades of judges for the twelve grades is being temporarily addressed in accordance with this Provision. The grading of judges into twelve grades refers mainly to existing service categories and to the original grades of Chinese judges,[266] and corresponds to the established circumstances at various levels of the People's Courts of China. In accordance with the provisions of Paragraph 2 of Article 18 and of Article 5 of the Interim Provision on the Grades of Judges of the PRC, judges of twelve grades are grouped into four posts as follows:

- Chief Justice. Paragraph 2 of Article 18 explicitly provides that "the President of the Supreme People's Court is Chief Justice", i.e. there is only one Chief Justice, who is then the president of the Supreme People's Court. The president of the Supreme People's Court is elected by the National People's Congress and so becomes Chief Justice. In accordance with this provision, the position of Chief Justice is statutory, without any approval or grant procedure.
- Associate Justice. This includes Associate Justice, First Grade and Associate Justice, Second Grade.
- Senior Judge. This includes four grades (see the tables below).
- Judge. This includes five grades (see the tables below).

*Tab. 1.1: Summary table of the grades of judges*

264 Article 19 of the Judges Law of the PRC

265 See Article 5 of the Interim Provision on the Grades of Judges of the PRC

266 Article 4 of the Interim Provision on the Grades of Judges of the PRC stipulates that the grades of judges are established as judging posts.

| The four posts of judge | The twelve grades of judge | |
|---|---|---|
| Chief Justice | Chief Justice | A |
| Associate Justice | Associate Justice, First Grade | B |
| | Associate Justice, Second Grade | C |
| Senior Judge | Senior Judge, First Grade | D |
| | Senior Judge, Second Grade | E |
| | Senior Judge, Third Grade | F |
| | Senior Judge, Fourth Grade | G |
| Judge | Judge, First Grade | H |
| | Judge, Second Grade | I |
| | Judge, Third Grade | J |
| | Judge, Fourth Grade | K |
| | Judge, Fifth Grade | L |

*Tab. 1.2: Correlation between judges' posts and judges' grades*

| | Supreme People's Court | Higher People's Court | Intermediat People's Court | Basic People's Court |
|---|---|---|---|---|
| President | A | C | D–F | F–G |
| Vice-President | B–C | D–F | E–G | G–H |
| Member of a Judicial Committee | C–E | E–G | F–H | G–I |
| Chief Judge of a Division | D–E | E–G | F–H | G–I |
| Associate Chief Judge of a Division | D–F | E–H | F–I | G–J |
| Judge | D–G | E–I | F–J | G–K |

| | | | | |
|---|---|---|---|---|
| Assistant Judge | H–J | H–K | I–L | J–L |

The conditions for judges in China are generally stipulated for assistant judges. Chinese judges are selected and promoted uniformly to courts at various levels. Candidate judges can be recruited by the Higher Courts or the Supreme People's Court at the very start and, after two or three years' probation period, appointed as assistant judges, and can become Judge, Third Grade or even Judge, First Grade. However, if candidate judges are recruited by the Basic Courts, they will only be Judge, Fifth Grade after being appointed as assistant judges. Because this method of promotion cuts off the intercommunion between courts, many elite candidates only consider higher-instance courts when pursuing a career as a judge.

Moreover, in accordance with the Judges Law of the PRC as amended in 2001, the President and Vice-President are to be chosen and appointed from judges and those qualified as judges.[267] "Those qualified as judges" as mentioned here relates only to the general conditions provided for by Article 9 of the Judges Law of the PRC,[268] similar to the conditions for civil servants and not including the professional qualification of "passing the unified state examination for judicial qualification" as provided for by Paragraph 1 of Article 12. This professional qualification applies only to junior judges, and not to presidents or vice-presidents transferred to courts from other departments. Therefore, the President and Vice-President do not have to pass the unified state examination for judicial qualification in order to become eligible for judicial service. In short, the President – as the head and supervisor of judges – is in fact also the director of the judicial committee dealing with difficult cases, but only needs to be qualified as a general civil servant and does not need to be qualified for judicial service in courts. This is a major distinction between the conditions for judges in China and Germany.

## (2) Conditions for Judges in China

### *(a) History*

The conditions for judicial selection in China have grown organically and have developed away from laxity towards more rigidity. In the early founding years of the People's Republic of China, due to the political and social circumstances of the time, a large number of judges who were familiar with the law were

267 Paragraph 2 of Article 12 of the Judges Law of the PRC

268 See http://www.npc.gov.cn/npc/flsyywd/xianfa/2002-07/11/content_297407.htm

purged from courts and replaced by those who were not familiar with the law but were firm in their proletarian stance. In legislation, neither the Interim Organic Regulation of the People's Courts of 1951 nor the Organic Law of the People's Courts of 1954 required judges to be professionals. During the Cultural Revolution, courts alternated between being controlled by the army and being dissolved.[269] After the Cultural Revolution, the Organic Law of the People's Courts as agreed at the Second Session of the Fifth National People's Congress in 1979 stipulated that any citizen who had reached the age of 23 and had the right to vote and stand for election could be elected as President or appointed as Vice-President, Chief Judge of a Division, Associate Chief Judge of a Division, Judge or Assistant Judge, except for persons who had been deprived of their political rights.[270] In accordance with this provision, those who had reached the age of 23 and had not been deprived of their political rights were eligible to serve as judges. In 1983, the Organic Law of the People's Courts was amended. This amendment imposed some restrictions concerning the necessary competence for the post of judge. It stipulates that judges of the People's Courts shall possess professional knowledge of the law.[271] The Judges Law of the PRC passed by the Eighth Standing Committee of the National People's Congress in 1995 raised the conditions for judges by stipulating for the first time that a judge shall have received a junior college education and by introducing the unified state examination for judges to be appointed as such.[272] The Judges Law of the PRC was amended again in 2001, enhancing the necessary qualifications for judges to the effect that judges shall have acquired an undergraduate education at an institution of higher or further education. The first unified state examination for judicial qualification was arranged in 2002.[273] However, passing the unified state exam-

---

269 Huang Yan, Review and Structure of the System of Judicial Selection, http://www.lawbook.com.cn/lw/lw_view.asp?no=6367

270 Article 34 of the Organic Law of the People's Courts of 1979

271 Article 34 of the Organic Law of the People's Courts, amended in 1983 to include the second paragraph: "Judges of the People's Courts shall possess professional knowledge of the law".

272 Article 2 of the Interim Provisions Concerning the Examination for Judges and Assistant Judges of the Supreme People's Court to be Appointed as Such for the First Time stipulates that "judges and assistant judges to be appointed as such for the first time shall pass the unified state examination". Article 3 stipulates that "the committee for the examination and appraisal of judges of the Supreme People's Court is the competent body for drafting the unified state examination for judges and assistant judges to be appointed as such for the first time and for organising and holding the unified state examination".

273 Before the Judges Law of the PRC was amended in 2001, examinations for legal occupational qualification in China were separate. As mentioned above, the examination for

ination for judicial qualification is just a basic condition for judges to be appointed as such for the first time, and is the lowest qualification for such candidates. Those who pass this examination can apply to take civil service examinations organised by the People's Courts at various levels. Only applicants who come out top in the civil service examination and pass an interview, a political behaviour examination and a physical examination can be recruited to the courts. After a certain period of time, applicants may take the examination for judges to be appointed as such for the first time, organised by the courts. If they pass this examination, they become candidate judges and must then wait to be nominated as judges by the president of the court they work for. This aspect shall be elaborated on further below in my analysis of the selection procedure.

### *(b) Provisions of Laws Currently in Effect*

The conditions for judges in China are uniformly provided for by the Judges Law of the PRC, passed by the Ninth Standing Committee of the National People's Congress in 2001. However, the conditions concerning educational background can be mitigated in minor aspects, as detailed below.

The conditions for judges are included not only in Chapter IV "Conditions for Judges" but also in the provisions concerning the unified state examination for judicial qualification, in Article 12 of Chapter V "Appointment and Removal" and Article 51 of Chapter XVII "Supplementary Articles", which will each be discussed in detail further below.

#### (i) Necessary Competences for the Post of Judge

1. To be a national of the People's Republic of China (PRC), i.e. judges must be Chinese citizens and cannot be foreigners or stateless persons. Also, in accordance with the provisions of the Law of Nationality,[274] the PRC does not recognise dual nationality for any Chinese national. Hence, a judge must be a national of the PRC and cannot also be a national of one or more other counties.

---

judges to be appointed as such for the first time was organised by the Supreme People's Court, and the examination for procurators to be appointed as such for the first time was organised by the Supreme People's Procuratorate. These two examinations were generally organised within an internal system. The examination for the qualification as a lawyer, organised by the Department of Justice, was the only examination of legal occupational qualification open to the whole of society, and began to be organised in 1986, being held each year in the middle of October, a total of 15 times by 2000. After the Judges Law of the PRC was amended in 2001, the examination for the qualification as a lawyer to be held in October of that year was replaced by the first uniform state examination for the qualification of legal practitioners in March 2002.

274 Article 3 of the Law of Nationality of the People's Republic of China

2. To have reached the age of 23. Article 34 of the Organic Law of the People's Courts stipulates that judges shall be citizens who have reached the age of 23 and who have the right to vote and to stand for election. The provision of having reached the age of 23 means completed years of life, i.e. the minimum age which judges have to have already reached. More generally, the specifics of the occupation of judge require judges to have a rich legal knowledge, social experience, human experience and the capacity to deal with all kinds of complicated problems. If judges are too young, it is difficult for them to adjudicate. Therefore, when the Judges Law of the PRC was to be amended in 2001, many suggested that the minimum age for judges should be raised. Because the age of 23 is provided for in the Organic Law of the People's Courts, this can simply be amended when the Organic Law of the People's Courts is amended. Hence, when the Judges Law of the PRC was amended in 2001, the minimum age of judges was not amended for the time being.

3. To endorse the Constitution of the PRC.

4. To be of fine political and professional quality and to be of good conduct. To be of fine professional quality means that judges should be learned in their profession, familiar with the work of judges, and capable of dealing with problems in cases, using the correct legal methods. To be of good conduct means that judges should be of sound character, habits and conduct, should consciously respect social morality, and should adhere to the principles of professional ethics and polite behaviour. Only then can an image of judges who execute laws fairly and evenly be established. According to remarks concerning the Judges Law of the PRC made on the official website of the National People's Congress of China, to have fine political quality means that "judges are members of staff of government organisations, hence judges should adhere to the national political system and the basic principles provided for by the Constitution, should be highly politically conscious, should have perceptive insight and a strong sense of political responsibility. Only then can the task entrusted to judges by the Constitution and the legislature be properly completed." Thus, we may say that fine political quality is the political basis on which judges can work well.[275] Explained in this way, fine political quality and the German requirement that judges shall "ensure that the principles of freedom and democracy provided for in the Basic Law are maintained at all times" are equally satisfactory in their outcome, albeit different in their approaches.

5. To be in good health.

---

275 See http://www.npc.gov.cn/npc/flsyywd/xianfa/2002-07/11/content_297407.htm

6. To have been in law for at least two years, in the case of graduates from colleges or universities specialising in law or from colleges or universities not specialising in law but who have professional knowledge of the law, or to have been in law for at least three years in the case of those appointed as judges of a Higher People's Court or the Supreme People's Court, or to have been in law for at least one year in the case of Bachelors of Law, Doctors of Law or Bachelors or Doctors of other subjects who have professional knowledge of the law, or to have been in law for at least two years for those appointed as judges of a Higher People's Court or the Supreme People's Court, which was an important amendment to the Judges Law of the PRC in 2001.

In accordance with Paragraph 1 (6) of Article 9 of the Judges Law of the PRC, the required educational background and the set number of years for judges to have worked are such that they are "to have worked for at least two years, in the case of graduates from colleges or universities specialising in law or from colleges or universities not specialising in law but who have professional knowledge of the law, or to have worked for at least one year in the case of Bachelors of Law; Masters of Law and Doctors of Law may not be subject to the aforementioned requirements for the set number of years for judges to have worked".

The new Judges Law of the PRC amended the former Judges Law of the PRC in three aspects of the conditions concerning educational background and the set number of years for judges to have worked. The first raised the conditions of educational background, from the stipulation of graduates from institutions of higher education_specialising in law or from institutions of higher education not specialising in law but who have professional knowledge of the law, to the stipulation of graduates from colleges or universities specialising in law or from colleges or universities not specialising in law but who have professional knowledge of the law. The second raised the conditions of professional quality in the field of law, changing "to have worked" to "to have been in law". The third raised the number of years set for judges to have been in law, and raised the number of years set for judges of a Higher People's Court or the Supreme People's Court to have been in law.

The six requirements mentioned above are to be simultaneously satisfied by the judges, as provided for in Paragraph 1 of Article 9 in Chapter IV of the Judges Law of the PRC. With the exception of the sixth requirement that judges shall have professional knowledge of the law, which does embody the special character of the occupation of judges, all the other requirements are practically the same as the basic requirements for civil servants, in particular the requirement for good political character, though they neglect the basic requirement of neutrality and independence inherent to the occupation of judge.

7. To have passed the unified state examination for judicial qualification. Paragraph 1 of Article 12 of the Judges Law of the PRC stipulates that persons to be appointed as judges shall be selected, through strict appraisal, from among those who have passed the unified state examination for judicial qualification and are the best qualified for the post in accordance with the standards of having both professional ability and political integrity. In accordance with this provision, in addition to satisfying the basic requirement provided for by Article 9 of merely having passed the unified state examination for judicial qualification, candidates can also have a qualification as judges to be appointed. The system of the unified state examination for judicial qualification is provided for in Article 11 of the Judges Law of the PRC, which stipulates that "the State shall organise the unified state examination for the qualification as judges to be appointed, procurators to be appointed and lawyers". In 2002, the Supreme People's Court and the Supreme People's Procuratorate formulated the Implementation of the Unified State Examination for Judicial Qualification (for Trial Implementation). This was brought into effect in 2002, and in March of that year, the first unified state examination for judicial qualification was organised. It has now been held six times. In total, more than 190,000 people have passed the examination. The pass rate is 13.8%.[276]

In accordance with this Implementation, the unified state examination for judicial qualification is held once a year. The Ministry of Justice is responsible for this examination. Except for the provision of the age limit, the conditions for taking this examination are the same as the conditions for judges as provided for in Paragraph 1 of Article 9 of the Judges Law of the PRC.

The contents of the examination for judicial qualification are decided by the Ministry of Justice, and include theoretical jurisprudence, applied jurisprudence, applicable law, legal practice and legal ethics. The examination is held over two days. During the two days, examinees are required to answer four examination papers. The first paper tests examinees' general knowledge, including philosophical jurisprudence, legal history, the constitution, economic law, international law, international private law, international economic law, legal ethics and professional responsibility. The second paper covers the criminal and administrative legal system, including criminal law, criminal procedural law, administrative law and administrative procedural law. The third paper includes topics on the civil and business legal system, including civil law, business law and civil procedural law (including systems of arbitration). The fourth paper involves case analysis and writing judicial documents and essays, including the topic areas of the first, second and third papers. The first, second and third papers are

276 See http://www.legalinfo.gov.cn/sfks/node_101.htm

machine-readable multiple-choice questions and the allotted time is 180 minutes in each case. The maximum possible marks on each of the four papers is 150, hence the maximum possible overall mark is 600. Those who get 360 marks or more usually pass the examination.

The unified state examination for judicial qualification is marked uniformly throughout the country. The examinees' marks and pass marks for each year are promulgated by the State Office for the Unified State Examination for Judicial Qualification of the Ministry of Justice. An examinee's mark in the unified state examination for judicial qualification is immediately valid. If an examinee disagrees with the mark given, he can apply for the mark to be rechecked by due process. Those who pass the unified state examination for judicial qualification are granted the Judicial Qualification Credentials uniformly issued by the Ministry of Justice.

Interestingly, it may be noted that the provision of having to pass the unified state examination for judicial qualification appears in the chapter on judicial selection in the Judges Law of the PRC and not in the chapter on conditions for judges. A review of Article 12 reveals that only those to be appointed as judges are required to pass the unified state examination for judicial qualification, whereas Paragraph 2 of Article 12 stipulates that presidents and vice-presidents shall be selected from among judges and others best qualified for the post. As mentioned above, presidents and vice-presidents are required to be qualified for the post of judge, but do not have to have passed the unified state examination for judicial qualification. In practice, it seems strange that "those who are ignorant of law cannot be junior judges, but presidents leading judges".[277] Thus, for example, if someone working in a court cannot pass the unified state examination for judicial qualification because they are poor at taking examinations, they cannot gain the qualification of assistant judge, but by taking office as a Vice-President in a Basic People's Court in some remote area, perhaps through special connections, for a period of time, they can become a judge by default, thus gaining the qualification of judge which others can only obtain by taking the unified state examination of judicial qualification over and over again.[278]

(ii) Conditions for Taking and Passing the Examination

The third paragraph of Article 9 of the Judges Law of the PRC gives certain discretion to local legislation with regard to the education of judges, particularly in areas where it may be difficult to obtain an education as stipulated in subparagraph 6 of the first paragraph of Article 9, such that it is possible to reduce

277 Gao Yifei, The President Who Was Not a Judge, Illuminated Research, 7th November 2007

278 See Gao Yifei above

the educational conditions to that of graduating from a specialised institution of higher education within a certain time limit, subject to review and confirmation by the Supreme People's Court. This takes into account the fact that different areas within China are unequally developed, and it is very difficult in some places to apply the condition of graduating from a college or university. In accordance with this paragraph, such places can reduce the educational conditions to that of graduating from a specialised institution of higher education within a certain time limit, subject to review and confirmation by the Supreme People's Court. This provision for "areas where it may be difficult to apply the education conditions" is intended to apply for example to remote mountainous areas and minority areas, which have a less developed economy and find it difficult to elect judges subject to the educational conditions stipulated in Paragraph 1 (6) of Article 9 of the Judges Law of the PRC. Correspondingly, the Implementation of the Unified State Examination for Judicial Qualification (for Trial Implementation) reduces the conditions for taking the examination, in these areas, to that of graduating from institutions of higher education specialising in law.[279] Also in accordance with provisions of the Judges Law of the PRC, the areas which may reduce the conditions for taking the unified state examination for judicial qualification correspondingly also enjoy discretionary powers to reduce the pass marks on the examination for judicial qualification. For example, in 2007, the pass mark on the examination for judicial qualification was nominally 360, but was 320 in the areas with reduced conditions, and was reduced to 290 in Tibet.[280] However, because successful candidates in these areas pass the examination of judicial qualification with a lower score, their certificates are different from those who pass the examination according to the nominal score, and they

279 According to the list of areas which may reduce the conditions for taking the unified state examination of judicial qualification, as issued by the Ministry of Justice, and the supplement notice issued in 2008 by the Ministry of Justice concerning standardisation of the areas which may reduce the conditions for taking the unified state examination of judicial qualification, these areas include 31 provinces and cities nationwide, including the whole of the Tibet Autonomous Region and totalling more than 900 counties and cities, but exclude Beijing, Tianjin, Shanghai, Jiangsu, Fujian and Shandong, which may not reduce the conditions for taking the unified state examination of judicial qualification, see http://www.legalinfo.gov.cn/misc/2008-07/21/content_905777.htm, http://www.legalinfo.gov.cn/misc/2008-07/21/content_905762.htm

280 See the official website of the Ministry of Justice: http://www.legalinfo.gov.cn/moj/sfkss/node_226.htm

can only then take judicial posts in the area in which they passed the examination.[281]

(iii) Conditions for Exclusion

In accordance with Article 10 in Chapter IV of the Judges Law of the PRC, the following persons cannot be elected as judges: those who have received criminal punishment for perpetrating a crime[282]; or those who have been discharged from the civil service.[283]

(iv) Retrospective Effect

Paragraph 2 of Article 9 of the Judges Law of the PRC stipulates that those who do not possess the educational qualifications stipulated in Paragraph 1 shall receive commensurate training. The former Judges Law of the PRC only stipulated a minimum condition of educational qualification as that of graduating from specialist institutions of higher education, whereas the new Judges Law of the PRC raises this condition to that of graduating from colleges or universities, hence those who did not graduate from colleges or universities but are already judges shall receive appropriate training retrospectively. This paragraph also stipulates that the retraining measures shall be arranged by the Supreme People's Court.

---

281 This is to prevent candidates from trying to pass the examination of judicial qualification with a lower score by transferring to an area with reduced conditions. For example, someone in Beijing who has taken and failed the examination many times might transfer to some area in Yunnan and then pass with 330 marks. But he would only receive the reduced-standard certificate B, and not the nominal certificate A. The holder of Certificate B can only take a judicial post in the area in which he passed the examination, i.e. in this case, the area in Yunnan.

282 Such crimes are divided into intentional crimes and negligent crimes. In accordance with criminal law, criminal punishment is divided into principal punishment which includes public monitoring (compulsory restraint), criminal detention, fixed-term imprisonment, life imprisonment and capital punishment, and supplementary punishment which includes fines, deprivation of political rights and confiscation of property. Those who have received criminal punishment cannot be appointed as judges.

283 "Discharged from the civil service" means being discharged by one's work unit by legal procedures. "The civil service" means employment in organs of state, state-owned companies, state-owned enterprises, government-sponsored institutions and people's organisations. There can be various reasons for being discharged from the civil service, but whatever the reason, those who have been discharged from the civil service cannot be appointed as judges.

## Section II Conditions for Judges in Germany

### (1) Types of German Judge

#### *(a) Judges Appointed for Life (Richter auf Lebenszeit)*

Judges appointed for life are duly appointed judges and are independent in terms of their identity and adjudication. In accordance with the tradition of German law and the provisions of the German Judges Act (*Deutsches Richtergesetz = DRiG*), judges are in principle appointed for life and it is the exception for judges not to serve until retirement. Except where special provision is made by federal laws, only judges appointed for life can serve as court judges. If there are a number of judges at one court, the judge appointed for life shall be the president.[284] Most judges in Germany are appointed for life. All German citizens have the right to become judges appointed for life, as long as they satisfy the necessary qualifications for judges and have been engaged in the business of judges for more than three years.

Appointing for life ensures the independence of judges, since there are only very rare instances of judges appointed for life being dismissed or transferred. The German Judges Act specifies the instances in which judges can be dismissed. Generally, the grounds for dismissing a judge have to be confirmed by a judge, with legal effect.[285]

#### *(b) Judges Appointed for a Fixed Term (Richter auf Zeit)*

Judges appointed for a fixed term are judges who dispatch the office of judge for a fixed period of time only, but are still also judges appointed in due form. Judges appointed for a fixed term are very much the exception in Germany.[286] The conditions of their election and the responsibilities they bear are specified by federal law.[287] For example, judges in the Federal Constitutional Court sit for a fixed term of 12 years and cannot be re-elected to serve another term.[288]

---

284 Article 8 of the German Judges Act

285 Paragraph 2 of Article 30 of the German Judges Act

286 The terms of office for some judges in state constitutional courts are fixed, see for example Paragraph 3 of Article 68 of the Baden-Württemberg Constitution, and Paragraph 2 of Article 130 of the Hessian Constitution.

287 Article 11 of the German Judges Act

288 Paragraphs 1 and 2 of Article 4 of the German Federal Constitutional Court Act

### (c) *Probationary Judges (Richter auf Probe)*

Judges appointed for life first have to be probationary judges for a certain period, before fully becoming judges appointed for life. The German Judges Act stipulates that the term for probationary judges be no longer than five years.[289] The employment contracts of probationary judges are provisional, since the appointing agencies have the right within the legal framework to terminate such employment contracts. If probationary judges are not appointed as another type of judge within the maximum term specified by law, they are dismissed.[290] Although probationary judges have the right to adjudicate independently, the guarantee of their independence of identity is less than that of judges appointed for life. For example, it is possible for probationary judges to be dismissed within two years of being appointed, without any specific reason. The appointment and dismissal of probationary judges is decided by the supreme agency responsible, without the prior permission of the court.[291] Probationary judges who are dismissed can only apply to the disciplinary Service Court for examination after the event. Moreover, probationary judges do not have the guarantee (as judges appointed for life do) of not being transferred arbitrarily: during the probationary period of five years, they may be transferred without their consent to other courts, to judicial or administrative office or to a public prosecutor's office.

### (d) *Judges on Commission (Richter kraft Auftrags)*

Those who have been public officials for life or public officials for a fixed term can be made judges on commission, if they are to be made judges appointed for life in the future.[292] The establishment of posts for judges on commission is based on the fact that the adjudications in such courts, such as administrative courts, finance courts, social courts and the federal patent courts, may deal with non-legal particularities, so when electing judges, some of the work shall be assigned to administrative officers. However, since such administrative officers have never adjudicated, it is not suitable for them to be made judges appointed

289 Some states shorten this term: Bremen and Hesse, for example, stipulate only three and a half years (Paragraph 2 of Article 7 of the Bremen Judges Act; Article 21 of the Hessian Judges Act).

290 Paragraph 1 of Article 22 of the German Judges Act. Federal law makes a limiting provision. Paragraph 2 of Article 22 of the German Judges Act stipulates that probationary judges can be dismissed after three or four years.

291 Paragraph 1, sub-section 4 c) of Article 62 and Paragraph 4 c) of Article 78 of the German Judges Act

292 Article 14 of the German Judges Act

for life straight away. In order to enable them to become judges and adjudicate, the post of judge on commission has been established in order to resolve the aforementioned problem. However, if judges on commission are not made judges appointed for life within two years, their employment contract as judge is terminated and they return to their former post.[293] Aside from this, the employment contract of judges on commission is provisional, similar to that of probationary judges.

## (2) Conditions for German Judges

The conditions for judges in Germany are uniformly stipulated. Article 9 of the German Judges Act stipulates the conditions for becoming a judge, including: (i) to be a German citizen in accordance with Article 116 of the German Basic Law; (ii) to guarantee to advocate at all times the principles of freedom and democracy enshrined in the Basic Law; (iii) to be qualified to become a judge, as stipulated in Articles 5 to 7 of the German Judges Act; (iv) to have the necessary social capacities. Of these conditions, it is clear that Condition (iii) is the most significant for qualifying as a judge. I shall therefore discuss the provisions of this condition in detail below.

Article 5 of the German Judges Act (Competence for Judicial Office) comprises the key provisions regarding the capabilities of judges. The approach to obtaining the judicial qualification includes: studying law as a specialist subject at college or university; passing the first state examination; completing practical legal training and passing the second state examination. The first state examination includes examination in the candidate's major field of study (*Schwerpunktbereichsprüfung*) and the state examination on compulsory topics (*Pflichtfachprüfung*).

### *(a) University Education in Law*

The provisions concerning university studies in Article 5a of the German Judges Act specify the period of study, subject, periods of practical experience, etc. Article 5a was amended in 2003 by changing the period of study from three and a half to four years; however, advanced candidates in the *Schwerpunktbereichsprüfung* of the judicial examination may be excluded from this. The content of studies includes not only the core of civil law, criminal law and administrative law, but also such basic legal knowledge as procedural law, EU law, jurisprudence, legal philosophy, legal history and legal sociology. In addition, Article 5a, Paragraph 2, second sentence of the German Judges Act again underlines the

293 Paragraph 1 of Article 16 of the German Judges Act

necessity of legal foreign-language knowledge and experience in legal studies.[294] Each *Land* can independently opt to set legal foreign-language skills as a compulsory topic for students learning jurisprudence.[295] It is impossible to cover all existant German law in four years, hence studies have to focus on the major legal issues. Students have to have a good knowledge of the major codes of German law and must learn how to apply statute law and how to operate in judicial proceedings. Thus, key aspects to be included in the content of studies for students learning jurisprudence are "judicatory, legal administrative and legal consultation practice, including negotiation management, presentation skills, rhetoric, mediation, and interrogation and communication skills", as stipulated in Article 5a, Paragraph 3, first sentence of the German Judges Act. In addition, the second sentence in Article 5a, Paragraph 3 of the German Judges Act stipulates that students learning jurisprudence shall participate in at least three months of practical legal training.

#### *(b) The First State Examination*

As mentioned above, the first state examination includes the university examination in the candidate's major field of study and the state examination on compulsory topics. Article 5d of the German Judges Act includes provisions concerning the contents and topic areas of the state judicial examination and the university examination on legal subjects. In accordance with Article 5d, Paragraph 1, first sentence, the state and university judicial examinations shall cover judicatory, legal administrative and legal consultation practice for students majoring in jurisprudence, including the "key aspects" mentioned above (see again Article 5a, Paragraph 3, first sentence of the German Judges Act). The content of the examination should include legal foreign-language skills. Within this framework, Article 5d, Paragraph 2, first sentence prescribes the content of the first state judicial examination to the effect that the content of the university examination in the candidate's major field of study and of the state examination on compulsory topics may be completed by studying for four and a half years. Article 5d, Paragraph 2, second sentence additionally prescribes that during the university examination in the candidate's major field of study, examinees shall hand in at least one written piece of work. The state examination on compulsory

294 Joachim Münch (ed.), Die neue Juristenausbildung: Chancen, Perspektiven und Risiken, Boorberg, Stuttgart 2004, p. 94

295 Peter Gilles, Nikolaj Fischer, translated by Zhang Chenguo: Legal Education Reform in Germany (original title: "Juristenausbildung 2003: Anmerkungen zur neuesten Ausbildungsreform" = "Legal Education in 2003: Remarks on the Latest Education Reform"), in: NJW 2003, pp. 707-711

topics includes both written and oral examinations. The university examination in the candidate's major field of study is conducted at the university, and the state examination on compulsory topics is held by judicial examination authorities in each *Land.* Generally, invigilators are professors and legal practitioners (judges, public prosecutors, administrative officers, lawyers, etc.). The state examination on compulsory topics generally includes eight written examinations and one oral examination. The marks from the oral examination form one third of the final marks. The failure rate on the examination is different in each *Land* and ranged from 19.9% to 54.8% in 2006, the average failure rate being 29.3%.[296] In accordance with the provisions of Article 5d, Paragraph 5, first sentence of the German Judges Act, the state examination on compulsory judicial subjects can only be retaken once. Article 5d, Paragraph 5, second sentence states that if an examinee enters themselves early for the examination and gains the stipulated marks, the unsuccessful examination shall be struck from the record. In other words, the marks from this second attempt are treated as if they were a first attempt (the so-called *Freischußregelung* or "free-shot provision"). Once the examinations have been passed, certificates are issued by the respective *Land.* In accordance with the provisions of the first part of the fourth sentence in Paragraph 2 of Article 5d, the certificate records the two marks from the university examination in the candidate's major field of study and the state examination on compulsory topics, and a total mark for the first judicial examination, to which the first mark contributes 30% and the second mark 70%. Students who pass this examination become trainee judges (*Referendar*) and later, once they have completed their trainee service and taken the second state examination, qualified legal practitioners (*Volljurist*).

### *(c) Preparatory Service*

There are no special training authorities for judges in Germany. Those who are eligible by having passed the first state examination are assigned throughout the country by the Federal Department of Justice, in order to receive practical and vocational training. In accordance with the provisions of Article 5b of the German Judges Act, the period of traineeship or "preparatory service" is two years and shall be completely at both compulsory and optional training agencies. The compulsory training agencies include: ordinary civil courts; criminal courts or procuratorates; administrative agencies; and law firms. The duration of the traineeship at each compulsory agency shall be at least three months, or nine

296 Bundesamt für Justiz, Referat III 3, 2224 III - B7 221/2007 Ausbildungsstatistik, Stand: 6. Februar 2008 (*Federal Office of Justice, Department III 3, 2224 III - B7 221/2007 Statistics on Education, dated 6th February 2008*)

months in the case of a law firm. The duration of the period of preparatory service can be extended in exceptional circumstances, though not on the grounds of inadequate performance. During their preparatory service in courts and procuratorates, trainees shall participate in court trials, attend court meetings as a non-voting delegate, compile judgement documents and handle the prosecution of moderate cases as procurators. During their preparatory service in a law firm, they shall represent a party in court. During their preparatory service in an administrative agency, they shall draw up various kinds of legal and other documents. Moreover, trainees can during their preparatory service execute the office of a civil servant (*Beamtenverhältnis auf Widerruf*) and receive a living allowance from the Department of Justice.

#### *(d) The Second State Examination*

Once they have completed their legal preparatory service, trainee judges may take the second state examination. Building on the basis established by the first state examination, the second state examination further examines candidates on the compulsory topics and in particular specialist subjects selected by the examinees themselves. It includes 12 written examinations and one oral examination, wherein the oral examination represents one fifth of the total marks. The failure rate for the second state judicial examination is thought to range between 10% and 20%, with 17.4% as the average failure rate in 2006.[297]

Those who pass the second state judicial examination shall have qualified as judges. The education of judges as stipulated by federal legislation is further specified in each *Land* by means of laws and ordinances.[298] The *Volljurist* who passes these examinations may qualify as a lawyer, senior administrative officer or notary public.

Regarding the competence to execute the office of a judge, Article 7 of the German Judges Act stipulates that "any full Professor of Law at a university within the area of application of this law is qualified to exercise the functions of a judge", which is the only exception to a legal vocation. However, the first German state judicial examination is in fact the graduation examination for university law students. Those who wish to engage in research are generally recommended by advisers, and excellent students are selected at tutors' meetings. Such students can easily pass the second state judicial examination. Consequently, most Professors of Law obtain the qualification of judge in accordance

297 Bundesamt für Justiz, Referat III 3, 2224 III - B7 221/2007 Ausbildungsstatistik, Stand: 6. Februar 2008 (*Federal Office of Justice, Department III 3, 2224 III - B7 221/2007 Statistics on Education, dated 6th February 2008*)

298 Article 5c of the German Judges Act

with Article 5 of the Judges Act. Article 7 of the German Judges Act thus becomes something of a null provision which is rarely applied.[299]

## Section III Comparison

The provisions regarding the conditions for judges in China are clearly different to those in Germany; however, the principles of nationality and supporting the national constitution are similar.

### (1) Age Requirements

The Judges Law of the PRC requires that judges be at least 23 years of age; the German Judges Act does not make provisions in this respect, although the German Federal Constitutional Court Act does specify that judges of the Federal Constitutional Court have to be older than 40 years of age.[300] Graduate students from college or university are generally 21 to 23 years of age, and become judges after working for one or two years. Hence, in theory, it is usual for a judge to be about 25 years of age or older. However, although there is no provision on an age requirement in Germany, those wishing to become judges have to study at college or university for four or five years, complete their preparatory service and pass a probationary period of three to three and half years after been admitted to court. Hence, they are at least 29 years of age by the time they become judges.[301] In fact, only a very small number of judges in Germany are younger than 30 years of age, and all federal judges are older than 45 years of age.[302] By comparison, Chinese judges are very young, and too young to have acquired a wealth of social experience. It is not a fundamental intention of the judge's vocation to learn to deal with complex social disputes from books alone. In Germany, it is felt that legal practitioners (*Juristen*) should not be appointed as judges prematurely. The thinker Rothenberger thought that the minimum age for judges should be 30, and that only a minority of judges should be younger than

299 Weng Yuesheng, Safeguards Regarding the Qualifications and Methods of Appointment and the Ranks of West German Judges, in his work: Administrative Law and the Modern State under the Rule of Law, p. 515

300 Paragraph 1 of Article 3 of the Federal Constitutional Court Act (*Gesetz über das Bundesverfassungsgericht* = BVerfGG)

301 Albrecht Wagner, Der Richter: Geschichte, aktuelle Fragen, Reformprobleme, Karlsruhe 1959, p. 138

302 Albrecht Wagner, Der Richter: Geschichte, aktuelle Fragen, Reformprobleme, Karlsruhe 1959, p. 134

35 years of age.[303] Judges who are too young will not be able to identify with others because they are not mature enough, whereas trials require judges to have well-rounded sensibilities and certain inter-relational capacities.[304]

### (2) Educational Requirements

The Judges Law of the PRC requires that candidate judges shall have graduated from a college or university, but need not have specialised in law. Those who have graduated from colleges or universities without specialising in law, but who possess the necessary professional legal knowledge, may become candidate judges. The German provisions specify four years of study majoring in law at a college or university, preparatory service and the two state examinations. The German educational system for majoring in law is different from that in China in that it does not comprise bachelor's and master's degrees, but only the state examinations. Students specialising in law who pass the first state examination receive a diploma corresponding to the *Diplom* diploma of other specialist fields, and can apply to study for a doctorate. Preparatory service and the second state examination may be undertaken before, during or after study for a doctorate. The Judges Law of the PRC is comparatively less rigid in its requirements regarding candidate judges' qualifications in areas of specialist study; for example, the Judges Law of the PRC stipulates that students who have graduated from a college or university without specialising in law, but who possess the necessary professional legal knowledge, may become candidate judges. This raises the question of what constitutes "possessing the necessary professional legal knowledge". This provision is very vague and general in its wording and cannot be precisely defined in practice. It is, however, doubtful that those who have only engaged in legal work for a few years can have developed the necessary professional character and insight, akin to those who have graduated from college or university and majored in law.

### (3) Requirements for the Judicial Examination

Correspondingly, the Chinese judicial examination is not open solely to students majoring in law; students who have graduated from other college or university faculties may also take the judicial examination. In Germany, however, the judicial examination is the state examination for students specialising in law only. The Chinese judicial examination comprises just one examination, which is a written examination, and no oral examination, whereas the German state exam-

303 Wolfgang Steinlechner, Der Richter im dritten Reich, Mainz 1974, p. 111
304 Wolfgang Steinlechner, Der Richter im dritten Reich, Mainz 1974, p. 112

ination is held in two sittings, each comprising a written and oral examination. The written examination tests students' capacity to recall information and to apply the knowledge which they have acquired, but their response times can only be tested by oral examination. It may be said that the Chinese judicial examination has no requirement regarding judges' response times, which clearly does not therefore correspond to the demands of the judge's vocation: the various cases which judges are confronted with differ in a myriad of ways; a candidate judge who has the ability to make a reasoned and just verdict but who loses his head when confronted with a new situation will not be a competent judge.

### (4) Health Requirements

The Judges Law of the PRC stipulates that candidate judges must be in good health, whereas the German Judges Act makes no provisions in this respect. Ever since the General Standard of Medical Examination for Recruiting Civil Servants (for Trial Implementation)[305] was jointly issued by the Personnel Department and the Ministry of Public Health of the State Council of the People's Republic of China, candidate judges have also had to take a medical examination in accordance with this general standard and can only be recruited once they have passed it. The General Standard stipulates that those who show evidence of any of 26 illnesses including various forms of heart disease, high blood pressure, blood disorders and other conditions (including corrected binocular vision of less than 0.8) are disqualified. Before this General Standard was issued, the Standards of Medical Examination for Civil Servants across 31 provinces and cities in China disqualified all disease carriers, thus excluding some 120,000,000 hepatitis B carriers in China from becoming civil servants.[306] A lawsuit[307] clai-

305 See http://www.gov.cn/fwxx/gwz2008/content_784142.htm

306 Carrying hepatitis B merely means that the virus may mutate in the future or may not, or may mutate but become denatured. Documented research has shown that in many cases, the virus does not mutate during the carrier's lifetime and the person is only identified as a hepatitis B carrier after death. However, many hepatitis B carriers pay a high social cost, being deprived of the opportunity to study and/or work. Testing for hepatitis B is therefore a great burden to carriers. See "Petition to Request the Examination of Unconstitutional Limitations on the Employment of Hepatitis B Carriers as Civil Servants in the 31 National Provinces, Regions and Cities and an Increase in Legal Protection for Hepatitis B Carriers".

307 It should be noted that the plaintiff in the case, Zhang Xianzhu, was a graduate student of West Anhui University and came first in the civil service examinations in 2003, but was refused because the medical examination found him to be infected with hepatitis B. It is noteworthy that Zhang Xianzhu was not even hepatitis B positive for the "major three" (HBsAg = hepatitis B surface antigen, HBeAg = hepatitis B e antigen and

ming "discrimination against hepatitis" brought national attention to the issue of hepatitis B carriers in 2003. A corresponding website was set up, and members jointly signed a Petition for Review of Constitutionality, calling for discussion and modification of the relevant laws and regulations, and submitted it to the National People's Congress (NPC). Finally, the Personnel Department and the Ministry of Public Health jointly issued the General Standard of Medical Examination which was applied nationally and explicitly stipulated that "carriers of the hepatitis B pathogen who are tested and found to not be suffering from hepatitis, shall qualify".[308] By contrast, Article 71 of the German Social Code, Volume 9 (SGB IX) stipulates that public employers (*öffentliche Arbeitgeber*) have to employ a certain proportion of severely disabled workers; Article 128 stipulates that the appointment of civil servants and judges shall also abide by the provisions of Article 71.[309] To be sure, adjudication work requires judges to have good character and sense; a strong physique may certainly help judges to better deal with difficult cases, but this is clearly not a basic requirement – judges are ultimately civil servants and not athletes. The Judges Law of the PRC would seem to be trying to put the cart before the horse in this respect.

### (5) Practical Experience Requirements

The Judges Law of the PRC makes no provisions regarding candidate judges' practical experience, save that candidate judges can only be appointed as judges once they have worked for one or two years at court. These standards are much lower than the provisions of the German Judges Act, which stipulates three to five years' practising experience. In Germany, those who become candidate

---

HBcAb = antibodies to the hepatitis B core antigen) or the "minor three" (HBsAg = hepatitis B surface antigen, HBeAb = antibodies to the hepatitis B e antigen and HBcAb = antibodies to the hepatitis B core antigen), was only rated 1 on the 5-point hepatitis B determination scale (where 5 points is positive) and had the normal liver function of a normal, non-contagious carrier. At the end of October 2003, after lengthy but fruitless negotiations, he took the Wuhu City Bureau of Personnel to court on the grounds of "hostile discrimination and violation of working rights due to infection with hepatitis B".

308 See the General Standard of Medical Examination for Recruiting Civil Servants (for Trial Implementation), Article 7, second sentence

309 During the Third Reich, by contrast, good health and a lack of disability were prerequisites for judges, since in that regime, physical disability was regarded as a disfigurement which would affect the development of a person's spirit and character, hence judges had to have a strong physique, a good constitution, and the courage and strong will to overcome difficulties. Ailing judges were to be dismissed if they could not execute their duties. See Wolfgang Steinlechner, Der Richter im dritten Reich, pp. 113-114

judges have to complete two years of preparatory service, as mentioned above, during which time trainees (*Referendaren*) undergo compulsory practical and vocational training at all kinds of legal vocational training agencies for specified periods, and select legal agencies to practice at. It is well-known that law is an applied science, which does not deal with natural knowledge but rather with human social interaction. It may thus be said that where there is a lack of appreciation of society, there is lack of appreciation of law. Consequently, countries all around the world attach great importance to the acquisition of practical experience by candidate judges. In China, however, candidate judges have a serious lack of practical legal experience, which is regarded by some scholars[310] as "one of the reasons that present judges in China have such a poor capacity to handle cases, and handle them inefficiently".

## (6) Miscellaneous

### *(a) Different Levels of Court*

In China, the qualification as a judge is uniform; there is no substantial difference in the qualifications of judges at different courts and at various levels. In Germany, however, judges can initially only be appointed as probationary judges, working as assistant judges in district courts and regional or federal state (*Land*) courts before becoming judges appointed for life after three and a half to five years. By being promoted, judges can gradually attain higher levels and the opportunity to judge at higher-level courts. It is impossible for judges in Germany to directly enter the higher *Land* courts. Generally, judges who have worked in ordinary courts for over ten years may be promoted to positions as judges in higher courts such as the higher *Land* courts. All federal judges are promoted from the *Land* courts. The conditions stipulated in the German Judges Act are indeed initially intended for district probationary judges. In China, by contrast, graduates who satisfy the conditions provided for in the Judges Law of the PRC can directly apply for a position as judge in courts at various levels, although presidents and vice-presidents are likely to be appointed from among judges of other local courts or college professors, and judges at the Higher People's Courts and the Supreme People's Court, which are higher than the local courts, are usually recruited internally, wherein all graduates from Chinese colleges or universities can take the recruitment examination for the Higher People's Courts and the Supreme People's Court and become judges at these courts by passing the examination. Since the civil service examination was established in China,

310 Chen Weidong, Han Dongxing, Research on the Election of Judges, Legal Forum, 5th May 2002, p. 110

the Supreme People's Court has recruited three to five candidate judges by holding personnel examinations almost every year. Although the Judges Law of the PRC stipulates that judges at the Higher People's Courts and the Supreme People's Court should have more work experience of practising law than judges in other, lower courts, it is doubtful whether working for just one year can satisfy the requirements for professional knowledge and judicial experience necessary for the Higher People's Courts and the Supreme People's Court, as the second and final instance, respectively.

It is well known that courts at different levels have different jurisdictions. The judges at ordinary courts generally deal with the more straightforward cases, whereas the judges at the higher courts always deal with the more significant and/or difficult cases and adjudicate appeals arising from cases tried by judges of the lower courts. Thus, judges of courts at different levels shall have different qualifications and experiences. In this sense, the conditions in China do differ in accordance with the different levels of courts and are not dependent on the same standard and/or requirements.

*(b) Differences Between Areas*

The Judges Law of the PRC allows a certain discretion to local legislation in areas where it is difficult to apply the Judges Law of the PRC in terms of the educational conditions for judges which it stipulates. This is because different circumstances prevail across the various provinces and cities within China, and there is an imbalance in their respective level of development. Federal Law in Germany also cedes some legislative freedom to the federal states (*Länder*). For example, all the *Länder* have a certain latitude in the content and organisation of the state examinations. The level of difficulty of the judicial examination may vary slightly from *Land* to *Land*, though always within the essential framework provided for by the German Judges Act. Those who pass the examination in one *Land* can embark on a legal vocation in any other *Land*.[311] This is based on the intuition that there is not much difference between areas in the nature and quality of candidate judges. In China, however, the candidate judges in different areas vary greatly in terms of their educational background and capacity to analyse and resolve problems, as tested in the judicial examination. Although such candidate judges may be limited in their legal vocation to the area with reduced conditions in which they passed the judicial examination, the requirements for just adjudication of cases in said area with reduced conditions should be the same as for those in other areas. There are also differences in economic devel-

311 Paragraph 2 of Article 6 of the German Judges Act

opment between different areas of Germany, but this should not prevent all areas from having judges of the same calibre. Where standards for legal practitioners are reduced in some areas merely because these areas have a lower level of economic development, it is worth discussing whether this is reasonable.

Moreover, although the German Judges Act does not stipulate that those who commit a crime or have been discharged from the civil service cannot be judges, there is a Federal Central Register of Convictions (*Bundeszentralregister*) in Germany which registers crimes and irregularities at the federal level, and when recruiting civil servants, the records of those entering for the examination are generally checked. Those who have any records of irregularities cannot be civil servants, including judges. Article 19, Paragraph 1, Section 4 of the German Judges Act stipulates that if, after a judge has been appointed, it emerges that he or she has been or is to be convicted of a major or minor crime which would seem to indicate that they are not suitable for the office of judge, then the appointment shall be revoked. Consequently, committing a crime will exclude a candidate from becoming a judge in Germany, the same as in China.

## Section IV Process of Judicial Selection in China

### (1) Civil Service Examination and Recruitment of Candidate Judges

The Interim Regulations on State Civil Servants was implemented in China on 1st October 1993. These Regulations qualify the rights and obligations, classification of posts, recruitment, evaluation, rewards, promotion and demotion, salary, insurance, resignation, removal, administration, supervision, etc. of civil servants. The system of civil service examination and recruitment of civil servants has been formed in accordance with these Regulations, and local governments then stipulate corresponding measures for implementing and enforcing the Regulations in accordance with their circumstances, configuring the civil service examination system to include written examination, oral tests, physical examination, evaluation and supervision, such that civil servants recruited by examination enter the system via an institutionalised route. The Civil Service Law of the People's Republic of China, implemented on 1st January 2006, stipulates that civil servants for non-leading posts at or below the level of senior section member and at other levels of corresponding posts shall be recruited and employed through open examination, strict review, competition on an equal footing and selection on merit.[312]

312 Article 21 of the Civil Service Law of the People's Republic of China

Unlike in Germany, it is not the case in China that anyone who passes the unified state examination for judicial qualification and qualifies within the legal profession can automatically become a candidate judge; rather, those wishing to become candidate judges have to take the civil service examination, i.e. "probationary judges" in China are recruited using the recruitment system for civil servants.[313]

Article 22 of the Civil Service Law of the PRC stipulates that the recruitment of civil servants for central government and institutions directly under it shall be organised by the central civil service management departments and that the recruitment of civil servants at the local level shall be organised by the provincial civil service management departments and that where necessary, the provincial civil service management departments may delegate this organisational work to municipal civil service management departments of cities which are divided into administrative districts. In accordance with this provision, the courts at the different levels each year submit a list of candidates to be recruited to the respective personnel department, for examination and approval. The personnel departments devise final recruitment plans for all civil service departments, including the courts, and issue them. Those civil servants who wish to apply to become judges and who satisfy the conditions[314] shall take the unified examination organised by the personnel department. The examination is generally divided into administrative aptitude tests and essay tests, set and graded by the personnel departments at the difficult levels. The personnel department then forwards all the materials on each candidate to the respective departments, who confirm a certain proportion as interviewees based on their marks and in accordance with the planned numbers of new recruits. As of the interview stage, all recruitment procedures are to be controlled by the courts, for example the number of interviewees, the interviewers, the questions, the method of assessment, the proportion of interviewees who pass the interview and may take the physical examination, and the number of recruits. Once past the interview stage, candidates are instructed to take the physical examination in a hospital designated by

---

313 The relevant principle issued by the Supreme People's Court has stated that in future, the process of judicial selection will not require candidates to take part in the civil service examination. Details of the future method of judicial selection may well be based on this, but such provisions have not yet been issued.

314 Up until a few years ago, the conditions for recruiting judges in local courts included that the candidates should be Party members, however this requirement has since been abandoned. Courts now pay more attention to a judge's areas of expertise and education background. For example, one condition for recruiting judges to the Supreme People's Court in 2008 was that those taking the examinations should have a doctorate specialising in law.

the organising department, so as to ensure that those past the interview stage also satisfy the physical requirements for judges as mentioned above (the same as for other civil servants). Those who pass the physical examination are then examined as to their political behaviour, i.e. the organising department examines the candidate's files, visit their teachers, classmates and friends, and notes their living status and the evaluation of them by others. Candidates who are ultimately recruited are required to sign a service contract for a certain period of service. It should be noted that the recruitment of civil servants for central government and at the local level are not mutually exclusive, i.e. a candidate can for example simultaneously apply to both the Supreme People's Court and a local court such as in Guangzhou or Shanghai, as long as the examination dates in these cities do not conflict.

Once recruited by a court, candidates become candidate judges. Their legal status is basically the same as that of probationary judges in German law. However, Chinese law does not prescribe a fixed number of years before probationary judges can be appointed as judges for life (in China, they are promoted from among assistant judges). The number of years can be one or two years or also four or five years. The procedures for judicial selection outlined below are based on the assumption that candidates have applied to courts and become candidate judges.

## (2) Procedures for Judicial Selection

### *(a) Statutory Principal Organs and Procedures*

Paragraphs 2 to 6 of Article 11 of the Judges Law of the PRC stipulate the authorities and procedures for appointing judges, as follows:

- The President of the Supreme People's Court shall be elected by the National People's Congress. The vice-presidents, members of the judicial committee, chief judges and associate chief judges of divisions and judges shall be appointed by the Standing Committee of the National People's Congress upon the recommendation of the President of the Supreme People's Court.
- The presidents of the local People's Courts at various levels shall be elected by the local People's Congresses at various levels. The vice-presidents, members of the judicial committees, chief judges and associate chief judges of divisions and judges shall be appointed by the Standing Committees of the People's Congresses at the corresponding levels upon the recommendation of the presidents of those courts.
- The presidents of the Intermediate People's Courts set up in prefectures of the provinces or autonomous regions or set in the municipalities directly

under the Central Government shall be appointed by the Standing Committees of the People's Congresses of the provinces, autonomous regions or municipalities directly under the Central Government on the basis of the nominations made by the respective councils of chairmen. The vice-presidents, members of the judicial committee, chief judges and associate chief judges of divisions and judges shall be appointed by the Standing Committees of the People's Congresses of the provinces, autonomous regions or municipalities directly under the Central Government upon the recommendations of the presidents of the Higher People's Courts.

- The presidents of the local People's Courts at various levels set up in the national autonomous areas shall be elected by the People's Congresses at various levels of the national autonomous areas. The vice-presidents, members of the judicial committees, chief judges and associate chief judges of divisions and judges shall be appointed by the Standing Committees of the People's Congresses at the corresponding levels upon the recommendations of the presidents of those courts.
- Assistant judges of the People's Courts shall be appointed by the presidents of those courts.[315] Article 35 of the Organic Law of the People's Courts of the People's Republic of China makes similar provisions, except that the appointment of assistant judges is provided for separately, in Article 37, and in that this article stipulates that courts and not presidents shall appoint the assistant judges.[316]

Thus, according to the above provisions, there are three principal organs in charge of judicial selection: firstly, the People's Congresses at various levels take charge of electing court presidents at various levels; secondly, the Standing Committees of the People's Congresses at various levels take charge of appointing the vice-presidents, members of the judicial committees, chief judges and associate chief judges of divisions and judges of courts at various levels upon the recommendation of the presidents of those courts; thirdly, the court presidents at various levels or the courts at various levels take charge of appointing assistant judges to those courts. The procedures for judicial selection can be di-

315 Why does the Judges Law of the PRC make this provision? The official website of the National People's Congress explains that: "In the People's Courts, there is a transition period as an assistant judge before becoming an appointed judge, in order for judges to acquire practical experience, which is conducive to judges better fulfilling their responsibilities when holding their own trials and to improving their professional capabilities and overall character. In terms of practical working requirements, assistant judges of People's Courts are appointed or removed by the court presidents". See http://www.npc.gov.cn/npc/flsyywd/xianfa/2002-07/11/content_297406.htm

316 Paragraph 1 of Article 37 of the Organic Law of the People's Courts

vided into two forms, namely direct election and judicial appointment. The assistant judges of courts at various levels are directly appointed by the presidents of those courts, hence this is a form of judicial appointment. The vice-presidents, members of the judicial committees, chief judges and associate chief judges of divisions and judges of courts at various levels are nominated by the court presidents at various levels and appointed by the Standing Committee of the People's Congress at those levels, wherein "appointing" means voting for or against the nomination made by the court president. Hence, this is in fact the same as electing the presidents of the courts at various levels and is a form of direct election.

### (b) *Principal Organs and Procedures in Practice*

In practice, there are no explicit provisions regarding the procedures for direct election or judicial appointment. Court presidents are generally nominated by the corresponding Party Committee, and the nomination is sent to the People's Congress of the same level. The election by the People's Congress is based on a one-member-one-vote system, and those who receive a majority of votes can be elected.[317] The term of office for court presidents is five years, the same as that of the People's Congress. Both can be re-elected to serve another term. The nomination of other court judges is worked out by the Party Committee or political department of the courts (the cadre department in some courts) and sent to the People's Congress by the court presidents; other judges are appointed providing half of the Standing Committee of the People's Congress approve the nomination by the court president.

It is known that, since both election by the People's Congress and appointment by the Standing Committee of the People's Congress are procedural examinations in which election or appointment is decided only by a personal introduction of the candidate judges and since they usually never exercise their right to veto candidate judges, they are in fact merely executing the procedure of election or appointment provided for by law.[318] The appointment of judges is in fact decided by the respective courts, especially by the heads of the respective courts. The appointment of a judge first has to be recommended by the head of the respective division or court, then examined by the personnel department of said court, and finally decided by the Party Committee (usually composed of presidents and/or vice-presidents).[319] Thus, we can see that the presidents of the courts at various levels are principal organs in appointing in a factual sense, and

317 Article 20 of the Organic Law of the Local People's Congresses

318 Ma Jianhua, Research on the Professionalisation of Judges, pp. 44-45

319 Su Li, Bringing the Law to the Countryside, p. 77

the People's Congresses at various levels and their respective Standing Committees have little influence on the appointment of judges, with the exception of the court presidents. Thus, court presidents have both direct and indirect powers of appointment – indirect in that court presidents nominate vice-presidents, members of the judicial committees, chief judges and associate chief judges of divisions and judges to the Standing Committee of the respective People's Congress, who then appoint them, and directly in that court presidents have the power to appoint assistant judges to the courts over which they preside.

In China, the departments involved in judicial selection include not only administrative departments, judicial departments and legislative departments, but also Party and governmental organs. If these authorities can restrain each other and reach a balance, they do not impair the independence of judges. In reality, however, these authorities respectively control each link of judicial selection and endanger the independence of judges in various respects. But the most serious threat is the court itself. Initially, the recruitment of candidate judges is controlled entirely by the personnel department of local government, since examinations and marks are handled solely by the personnel department and the personnel department is likely to use this power to benefit examinees; the process of interview and examining political behaviour, however, is controlled within the purview of the judiciary. It is well-known that in China, the interview process has no criteria and is the easier to manipulate, and this process is organised and executed by the courts themselves. We can put aside the question of whether interviewers have a capacity for professional review or whether professional criteria have been stipulated, since there is no comparison in this respect between China and Germany. In Chinese courts, there is no neutral organ similar to the Committee of Judicial Selection. The interviewer is usually the head of the court, i.e. heads of court such as court presidents decide whether someone can be recruited to a court and become a candidate judge at said court.

After entering court, candidate judges are increasingly dependent on the president of the court. As is clear from the procedures for judicial selection mentioned above, court presidents have the power to appoint assistant judges. Assistant judge is already a formal post as judge. Although, in accordance with the provisions of law,[320] their duty is to help judges in their work, their duties are in practice the same as those of judges. They can also adjudicate cases by themselves and are sometimes the most senior judge. The differences between assistant judges and judges may thus be said to merely be those of administrative post and grade, and there is little difference in terms of their executive power of adjudication. In practice, the method by which the courts at various levels recruit

320 Paragraph 2 of Article 37 of the Organic Law of the People's Courts

assistant judges is that the personnel departments of the courts first submit candidate judges to the Party Committees of the courts in accordance with the needs of the courts, then the Party Committees of the courts vote on the candidate judges by way of democratic centralism (the opinions of the court presidents are decisive), and finally the presidents appoint the candidates selected. Similarly, the removal of an assistant judge is also undertaken by the president, once the Party Committee of the court has investigated and made a decision. Clearly, therefore, gaining or forfeiting the status of assistant judge is heavily dependent on the assessment by a head of court such as a president or vice-president. Thus, once candidate judges become assistant judges, it is difficult for them to shake off pressure and interference from more senior judges, let alone for them to be able to adjudicate cases according to their own ideas.

Judges other than assistant judges are nominated by the court presidents and appointed by the Standing Committees of the People's Congresses, in accordance with the law. There can be no doubt that the independence of judges is seriously endangered: because of the variety of posts of Chinese judges, different judges appointed for life in the same court can have different posts (from Assistant Judge to President) and correspondingly different grades and salaries, hence the process of judicial selection is in fact also the process of promotion. Those who work hard and show obvious achievement following their appointment as assistant judges will be appointed judges within a few years, and among judges, those who show superior capacity and whose work is to a high quality will be appointed as associate chief judges and chief judges of divisions. The heads of the respective courts have the last say in these matters. Whether heads of court use these powers to decide many important matters justly and not just to interfere with the adjudication of judges and the independence of judges depends on the self-discipline of the individuals in question, since there is no force either in legal theory or in practice to curtail the exercise of these powers.

So do the heads of court who have these powers exercise them justly? We have seen from the conditions for judicial selection mentioned above that court presidents do not have to pass the judicial examination. Court presidents are also different from other judges in that they are usually transferred to courts from other departments and not promoted from among lower-grade judges. Reviewing the résumé of the current President of the Supreme People's Court, Wang Shengjun, reveals that his degree major was in history and that his employment history includes some Party posts and judicial posts but that he had had no experience of working in courts before assuming the office of President of the

Supreme People's Court.[321] However, the majority of previous presidents share this trait. Since the end of 2007, presidents of the provincial Higher People's Courts and provincial Chief Procurators have been regulated at the national level in China.[322] Thus, it can be seen that court presidents are not different to other cadres of state organs in China, or at least differ only in the areas in which they lead, and their appointment and removal essentially depend on the policy decisions regarding appointment and removal of cadres of government at various levels, as recommended by the Party Committee of government at various levels and nominated through examination by the secretary's meeting of the Party Committee of the People's Congress.[323] This shows that it is in fact the Party Committee of government at various levels or the organisational department of the Party Committee who controls the appointment of court presidents, who in turn decide on the promotion, demotion, recruitment and removal of other judges. Judges cannot retain their independence under these circumstances. Indeed, the secretary of the local Party Committee, the Standing Committee or the heads and even staff members of organisational departments of the Party Committee can all interfere with the adjudication by courts and judges by the means of reporting, directing, writing notes and calling.[324] If this situation is to change, the present system of judicial selection has to be changed, to ensure the independence of judges, wherein the German system may be used as a reference.

## Section V Process of Judicial Selection in Germany

In Germany, from the federal level to the federal state or regional (*Land*) level, there are rigid legal provisions on the process of judicial selection. Within the framework provided by Article 92 of the Basic Law, each *Land* establishes a Committee of Judicial Selection, as does the Federation, which plays an important role in judicial selection.

---

321 Résumé of President Wang Shengjun of the Supreme People's Court of the PRC, from the website of the National People's Congress, see http://www.npc.gov.cn/huiyi/dbdh/11/2008-03/16/content_1418888.htm

322 Regulation of the Presidents of the Higher People's Courts and Provincial Chief Procurators, Xinhua website, 25th December 2007, see http://news.xinhuanet.com/legal/2007-12/25/content_7310406.htm

323 See Paragraph 1 of Article 4 and Articles 16, 20 and 44 of the "Party and Government Administration Leadership Cadre's Working Regulations on Selection and Appointment" as printed and distributed by the Chinese Communist Party Central Committee on 9th July 2002, http://news.xinhuanet.com/ziliao/2003-01/18/content_695422_1.htm

324 Tan Shigui, Research on Issues of Judicial Independence, p. 106

## (1) Judges of the Constitutional Courts

### *(a) Judges of the Federal Constitutional Court*

The Federal Constitutional Court is composed of two panels or senates (*Senate*), each of which has eight judges.[325] In accordance with the second sentence of Paragraph 1 of Article 94 of the Basic Law (*Grundgesetz = GG*) and Paragraph 1 of Article 5 of the Federal Constitutional Court Act (*Bundesverfassungsgerichtsgesetz = BVerfGG*), the *Bundestag* (the lower house of the German Federal Parliament) and the *Bundesrat* (the upper house of the German Federal Parliament) each select half the judges of each senate. The selection process is defined in Articles 6 to 9 of BVerfGG.[326] There are differences between the *Bundestag* and the *Bundesrat*. In accordance with Article 7 of BVerfGG, the *Bundesrat* selects judges directly, whereas in accordance with Article 6 of BVerfGG, the *Bundestag* selects judges indirectly.

#### (i) Selection Process in the *Bundestag*

In accordance with Paragraphs 1 and 2 of Article 6 of BVerfGG, the *Bundestag* sets up a selection committee composed of 12 members of the *Bundestag*. Each parliamentary group may propose candidates for the selection committee. The number of candidates elected on each list is calculated from the total number of votes cast for each list in accordance with the d'Hondt method. The members are elected in the sequence in which their names appear on the list.[327]

The selection committee is a comparatively independent body, and once elected, cannot be elected anew. It does not form part of any parliamentary group or the *Bundestag*. Its members are not constrained by any instructions or orders from without. Neither the parliament nor any parliamentary group has the right to require the selection committee to re-select, since the committee does not receive instructions or orders from without. If a member of the selection committee dies, retires, loses their status as a member or is forced to leave the committee, they are replaced by the next member on the same list calculated in accordance with the d'Hondt method.[328] The eldest member of the selection committee calls and chairs a meeting of the committee to select the judges.[329]

---

325 Paragraphs 1 and 2 of Article 2 of the Federal Constitutional Court Act (*Bundesverfassungsgerichtsgesetz = BVerfGG*)

326 See Thorsten Erwin Dietrich, Richterwahlausschüsse und demokratische Legitimation, pp. 22 ff; Werner Billing, Das Problem der Richterwahl zum Bundesverfassungsgericht, in: Ordo Politicus, Volume 11 (1969), pp. 121 ff

327 Paragraph 2 of Article 6 of BVerfGG

328 Werner Billing, Das Problem der Richterwahl zum Bundesverfassungsgericht, in: Ordo Politicus, Volume 11 (1969), p. 124

329 Paragraph 3 of Article 6 of BVerfGG

There are no explicit legal provisions as to how the selection committee is to select the judges. In practice, the members of the selection committee vote on lists of candidates nominated anonymously by each parliamentary group.[330] Each member has one vote on the list submitted by each parliamentary group. The candidates on the lists are selected in accordance with the number of votes they have received. An elected judge must receive at least eight votes.[331] The outcome of selection by the selection committee is final and does not require the approval of the *Bundestag*.

(ii) Selection Process in the *Bundesrat*

The Federal Constitutional Court Act does not stipulate how judges are to be selected in the *Bundesrat*; however, the second half of Paragraph 3 of Article 52 of GG and Article 29 of the Rules of Procedure of the Federal Council (*Geschäftsordnung des Bundesrates = GOBR*) stipulate that voting is undertaken at a public (or optionally non-public) session. In accordance with Article 7 of BVerfGG, candidates need to receive a two-thirds majority of the votes of the *Bundesrat* in order to be elected.[332] The term of office for judges of the Federal Constitutional Court is 12 years, and they cannot be re-elected once they have reached retirement at the age of 68.[333]

### *(b) Judges of Land Constitutional Courts*

The judges of *Land* constitutional courts are usually selected by the parliament of the respective *Land*. Nearly all *Land* constitutions and *Land* Constitutional Court Acts stipulate that the judges of the *Land* constitutional courts are selected by parliament. There are some differences in the provisions for the selection process in each *Land*. For example, the laws of Baden-Württemberg, Bavaria and Hamburg stipulate that candidates must receive a two-thirds majority of votes, whereas the laws of Saxony-Anhalt and Lower Saxony merely stipulate that candidates must receive an absolute majority of the votes cast by the members of parliament present.

---

330 The list submitted by each parliamentary group is proposed by the chairmen of the parliamentary group and approved at a parliamentary group meeting.

331 Paragraph 5 of Article 6 of BVerfGG

332 See Thorsten Erwin Dietrich, Richterwahlausschüsse und demokratische Legitimation, p. 22 ff; Werner Billing, Das Problem der Richterwahl zum Bundesverfassungsgericht, in: Ordo Politicus, Volume 11 (1969), pp. 121 ff

333 Article 4 of BVerfGG

## (2) Federal Judges

### *(a) The Federal Court of Justice*

At the end of December 2008, there were 458 federal judges in Germany,[334] comprised of 427 judges at the Federal Court of Justice and 31 judges at other federal courts. In accordance with the provisions of Paragraph 1 of Article 95 of the Basic Law, the Federation shall establish the Federal Court of Justice, the Federal Administrative Court, the Federal Finance Court, the Federal Labour Court and the Federal Social Court as supreme courts of ordinary, administrative, financial, labour and social jurisdiction. The judges of these courts are selected in accordance with the provisions of Paragraph 2 of Article 95 of the Basic Law, which stipulate that the judges of each of these courts shall be chosen jointly by the competent Federal Minister and a committee for the selection of judges consisting of the competent *Land* ministers and an equal number of members elected by the *Bundestag*. Articles 1 and 2 of the Judicial Selection Act (*Richterwahlgesetz* = *RiWG*) contain the same provisions as the above-mentioned sections of the Basic Law. The method of selection employed by the *Bundestag* is the same as that employed by the Committee of Judicial Selection in the case of the Federal Constitutional Court.[335] The only difference is that members of the selection committee need not necessarily be members of the *Bundestag* but must have the right to be elected (as specified in Paragraph 2 of Article 38 of GG)[336] and must have experience of judicial life (*Rechtsleben*); however, in practice, the members of the Committee of Judicial Selection are usually also members of the *Bundestag*.[337] After the election of a new *Bundestag*, the members of the Committee of Judicial Selection are also re-elected. Membership of the Committee of Judicial Selection is also automatically forfeited as a result of death, losing the right to be elected, dropping out voluntarily or being required to be re-elected.[338]

The members of the Committee of Judicial Selection and the competent Federal Ministers have the right to propose candidates to be appointed as federal judges, but the federal ministers have no right to vote and are only involved in

---

334 See Statistisches Bundesamt, Ausgewählte Zahlen für die Rechtspflege - Fachserie 10, Reihe 1–2009, Stand: 22.12.2009 (*Federal Office of Statistics, Selected Figures for the Judicature - specialist series 10, set 1–2009, dated 22nd December 2009*)

335 Paragraph 2 of Article 5 of RiWG

336 Paragraph 1 of Article 4 of RiWG

337 Thorsten Erwin Dietrich, Richterwahlausschüsse und demokratische Legitimation, p. 139

338 Thorsten Erwin Dietrich, Richterwahlausschüsse und demokratische Legitimation, p. 138

selection.[339] The Committee examines whether a candidate meets the personal and formal requirements for a federal judge, in the absence of the candidate, from the candidate's personnel files provided by the competent Federal Minister and a report delivered by two members of the committee appointed for this purpose.[340] The committee then decides by an anonymous vote. Candidates receiving a majority of the votes are elected, and the vote is valid as long as both a majority of the committee members who are Federal Ministers (*Mitglieder kraft Amts*) and a majority of the members who have been selected to the committee (*Mitglieder kraft Wahl*) are present.[341] If the competent Federal Minister agrees with the outcome of selection, he shall submit a request to the Federal President for the chosen candidates to be appointed as federal judges.[342] In principle, the Federal President has the right to oppose some or all of the requested appointments, but in practice, this situation rarely arises.[343]

Moreover, in accordance with the provisions of Article 54 of the German Judges Act (*Deutsches Richtergesetz* = *DRiG*), a presiding council (*Präsidialrat*) is established for each supreme federal court, which is composed of the President, Vice-President and five judges (in the case of the Federal Court of Justice; three in the case of the other supreme federal courts). In accordance with Article 55 of the German Judges Act, the *Präsidialrat* is to be consulted before a judge is selected or appointed. Its main function is to be invited by the Committee of Judicial Selection to submit a written opinion on the personal and formal suitability of candidates, but in accordance with the provisions of Article 57 of the German Judges Act, it is merely a prerequisite that the opinion of the *Präsidialrat* be sought, and the *Präsidialrat* has no actual say in the final nomination and/or appointment.[344]

#### *(b) Other Federal Courts*

##### (i) Disciplinary Court

In accordance with the authority provided by Paragraphs 1 and 4 of Article 96 of GG, the Federation may establish a federal court for disciplinary proceedings

---

339 Paragraph 1 of Article 10 and Paragraph 1 of Article 9 of RiWG

340 Paragraphs 2 and 3 of Article 10 and Article 11 of RiWG

341 Article 12 of RiWG

342 Article 13 of RiWG, Paragraph 1 of Article 60 of GG

343 Van-Hoa To, Judicial Independence: Legal Research on its Theoretical Aspects, Practices from Germany, the United States of America, France and Vietnam, and Recommendations for Vietnam, Lund 2006, p. 179

344 Diethard Oppermann, Richterberufung und richterliche Unabhängigkeit, Marburg 1966, pp. 147-148

against, and for proceedings on complaints by, persons in the federal public service (i.e. federal disciplinary courts). In accordance with the Federal Disciplinary Ordinance (*Bundesdisziplinarordnung* = *BDO*), which has since been superseded by the Federal Disciplinary Act (*Bundesdisziplinargesetz* = *BDG*), the federal disciplinary court was established at Frankfurt on the Main and its divisions defined by areas of jurisdiction. Adjudication is undertaken by one presiding judge and two civil servants acting as lay judges. Presiding judges are nominated by the Federal Minister of Justice and appointed by the Federal President in accordance with Paragraph 1 of Article 60 of GG. The adjudication of the court is to be approved by the Federal Chancellor or competent Federal Minister.

(ii) Service Court

The Federal Service Court is established as a special panel of the Federal Court of Justice in accordance with Article 61 of DRiG and is charged with making final adjudications in disciplinary cases involving federal judges and in appeals (*Revision*) against adjudications made by *Land* service courts. The panel is composed of one presiding judge, two permanent assistant judges and two non-permanent assistant judges. The presiding judge and the permanent assistant judges must be judges of the federal ordinary court, whereas the non-permanent assistant judges are appointed by the presiding board (*Präsidium*) of the federal ordinary court, within the limits of the court's autonomy.

(iii) Military Court

Military courts are established by the Federal Ministry of Defence and are charged with adjudicating cases concerning military affairs and soldiers. There are currently two military courts in Germany: a southern military court in Munich and a northern military court in Münster. Their jurisdiction is established by the Ordinance on the Establishment of Military Courts.[345] Adjudicating panels are always composed of one presiding judge and two soldiers as honorary assistant judges. Presiding judges are nominated by the Minister of Defence and appointed by the Federal President. The courts of appeals for military courts are military divisions within the federal administrative court, each of which is composed of three professional judges and two honorary judges, who are appointed in the same way as other judges of federal administrative courts.

345 Verordnung über die Errichtung von Truppendienstgerichten vom 16. Mai 2006 (BGBl. I S. 1262)

### (iv) Patent Court

The judges of the patent court established in 1961 are nominated by the Minister of Justice and appointed by the Federal President. The selection and appointment process for the judges of this court do not exhibit any particularities.

## (3) *Land* Judges

At the end of December 2008, there were 19,643 state judges in Germany.[346] In accordance with the provisions of Paragraph 4 of Article 98 of GG, each *Land* has the right to legislate that *Land* judges are appointed jointly by the minister of the *Land* Department of Justice and a Committee of Judicial Selection. This is different from the provision in Paragraph 2 of Article 95 of GG that a Committee of Judicial Selection is established in order to select federal court judges; the provisions of Paragraph 4 of Article 98 of GG concern authorisation. Each *Land* has the right to decide whether to establish a Committee of Judicial Selection, but cannot exclude the *Land* Minister of Justice when performing judicial selection according to Land regulations. Nine federal states (*Länder*) including Berlin, Brandenburg, Bremen, Baden-Württemberg, Hesse, Hamburg, the Rhineland Palatinate, Schleswig-Holstein and Thuringia have so far established Committees of Judicial Selection; the other *Länder* select judges by an administrative method. The administrative method of appointment usually means that judges are appointed by the *Land* Department of Justice or by the *Land* government. There are different regulations in each *Land*. The administrative method of appointment is regarded as a method which inhibits the independence of judges,[347] though this will not be discussed in detail here. Rather, I shall discuss here the selection process for the Committee of Judicial Selection. Because Paragraph 4 of Article 98 of GG and the corresponding annotations do not place restrictions on the selection method or the number of members of the Committee of Judicial Selection, there are differences between the *Länder* in these respects. I shall take Berlin as an example and use it to introduce the process of judicial selection by way of a Committee of Judicial Selection.

---

346 See Statistisches Bundesamt, Ausgewählte Zahlen für die Rechtspflege - Fachserie 10, Reihe 1–2009, Stand: 22.12.2009 (*Federal Office of Statistics, Selected Figures for the Judicature - specialist series 10, set 1–2009, dated 22nd December 2009*)

347 For further details, please see: Oppermann, Richterberufung und richterliche Unabhängigkeit, Marburg 1966, pp. 44 ff; Ernst Teubner, Die Bestellung zum Berufsrichter in Bund und Ländern: Entwicklung, Modelle, Analysen, Cologne 1984, p. 91; Hilke Thiedemann, Judicial Independence – Eine rechtsvergleichende Untersuchung der Sicherung unabhängiger Rechtsprechung in Südafrika und Deutschland, Baden-Baden 2007, pp. 212-213; Saltanat Khorrami, Das Einstellungs- und Beförderungsverfahren englischer und deutscher Richter, Hamburg 2005, p. 24

Berlin was the first *Land* to legislate on the status and selection of judges by way of *Land* laws. At present, Articles 2 and 9 to 18 of the Berlin Judges Act make provisions for judicial selection. Except for the president of the higher *Land* court, all court judges are selected by the Committee of Judicial Selection.

The Committee of Judicial Selection in Berlin consists of 15 members, including seven selected by the *Land* parliament, five who are judges (two from ordinary courts, and one judge from each of the administrative court, the labour court and the social court) and one lawyer and one procurator. If a judge from a finance court is selected, they replace one of the two judges from ordinary courts, so there is still a total of five judges. Additionally, in accordance with provisions of the Basic Law, the *Land* Senator for Justice (*Senator für Justiz*) shall in principle decide on the appointment and promotion of judges together with the Committee of Judicial Selection, though he or she has no voting rights.

The seven members selected by the *Land* parliament need not be members of the *Land* parliament, but rather may be elected to the committee as long as they receive a two-thirds majority of the votes cast by the members of the *Land* parliament present.

The committee members who are judges are selected from a list of nominated judges, the committee members who are procurators are selected from a list of nominated procurators, and the committee members who are lawyers are selected from a list of nominations provided by the bar association (*Rechtsanwaltskammer*).

The outcome of selection is valid as long as more than half of the members of the Committee of Judicial Selection are present. All decisions which receive more than half the votes cast are carried.

The Committee of Judicial Selection decides not only on the selection but also on the promotion of judges. Three years at the latest after being appointed as probationary judges, or two years at the latest after being appointed as Judges on Commission, the Committee of Judicial Selection decides whether said judge can be appointed as a judge appointed for life. When deciding on the appointment of judges, the Committee of Judicial Selection mainly examines the character of the candidates and whether their professional activities hitherto satisfy the requirements for judges and how well they are likely to abide by the principles of liberal democracy as set out in the Basic Law and the Constitution of the State of Berlin.

In deciding on appointments and promotions, the Committee of Judicial Selection shall select the best qualified in terms of their capabilities, qualities and professional qualifications, without taking into account their sex, parentage, race, beliefs, religion and or political views, industrial affiliation, origin or other relationships.[348] The *Land* Department of Justice appoints and promotes judges in accordance with the decision of the Committee of Judicial Selection.

It is thus clear that, both at the federal level and *Land* level, the Committee of Judicial Selection and administrative bodies play an important role in the appointment of judges in Germany. The method of administrative appointment is usually criticised for making the judiciary an instrument of government, which impairs the independence of judges. However, some research finds that this method of appointment does not affect the independence of judges in Germany,[349] since the first selection of (probationary) judges is made according to professional capacity, and is not a political selection. Indeed, only 2% of probationary judges are dismissed and not appointed as judges appointed for life after the three-year probationary period.[350] Thus, the process of judicial selection has little influence on the independence of judges. Rather, the factors which are likely to influence the independence of judges arise during the application process by legal practitioners to be probationary judges, and in the promotion of judges.[351]

In Germany, those who want to be judges have to start out as the judges of ordinary courts or the assistant judges of *Land* courts, as probationary judges. The first step in a judge's career is to become a judge appointed for life in the ordinary courts or *Land* courts. Those aspiring to attain posts as higher-level judges have to begin with a post as a lower-level judge. It is impossible to directly occupy a post as a higher-level judge, for example a presiding judge at a *Land* court or a judge at a higher *Land* court. In Germany, there are ten different ranks (R1-10) of judges' salaries.[352] The most frequent promotion is from Rank R1 (including the judges of ordinary courts and *Land* courts) to Rank R2 (that of presiding judges at *Land* courts and judges of higher *Land* courts). Few judges have a chance at the subsequent promotions, such as the promotion to presiding judge of a higher *Land* court (R3), Court President or Vice-President higher

348 Thorsten Erwin Dietrich, Richterwahlausschüsse und demokratische Legitimation, p. 106

349 Van-Hoa To, Judicial Independence: Legal Research on its Theoretical Aspects, Practices from Germany, the United States of America, France and Vietnam, and Recommendations for Vietnam, Lund 2006, p. 179

350 Saltanat Khorrami, Das Einstellungs- und Beförderungsverfahren englischer und deutscher Richter, Hamburg 2005, p. 23

351 See the opinion advanced in Saltanat Khorrami, Das Einstellungs- und Beförderungsverfahren englischer und deutscher Richter, Hamburg 2005, p. 23

352 See R1-10 in the Appendices to the Federal Remuneration Act (*Bundesbesoldungsgesetz = BBesG*)

*Land* court (R3 and above) or of a federal court (R6).[353] It may be concluded that since the chance of these promotions is remote, it is not the specific attraction for judges, and judges also cannot ingratiate themselves with their superiors or leaders in order to expedite their promotion, which would impair the independence of judges.

In Germany, those who wish to become ordinary judges first have to apply to the *Land* Department of Justice. When posts as judge become vacant, this is announced by the Department of Justice in a bulletin. Those who satisfy the preliminary requirements may submit their application to the Department of Justice. Unlike in China, the applicants need not have taken the civil service examination and can enter their application as long as they have taken the second state examination and attained the marks required by the *Land* Department of Justice. The Bavarian Department of Justice, for example, specifies when publicly recruiting judges that only those who have attained more than eight marks in the second state examination may submit their application; eight is an above-average mark and applicants can thus at least in part deduce from this the severity of the competition.[354] The personnel department of the Department of Justice will formally examine applicants' capabilities, qualifications and professional experience, pick out the most outstanding, invite them to a personal interview and then confirm the contract of employment. In fact, the precondition for ordinary judges is that the marks from the state examinations be higher than the average marks, meaning over nine marks (*vollbefriedigend* or "above-average") in both of the two state examinations. At present, only 15% of graduates attain this standard. Recently, some *Länder* have introduced an Assessment Centre method of recruitment, whereby the materials submitted by applicants are filtered, and applicants are then invited to take a test at the Assessment Centre. The test is divided into three parts, namely group discussions, individual interviews and practical challenges. After the tests have all been completed, the Assessment Centre makes proposals as to which applicants should be recruited and informs the applicants accordingly.[355] Because the Assessment Centre is composed of

353 Saltanat Khorrami, Das Einstellungs- und Beförderungsverfahren englischer und deutscher Richter, Hamburg 2005, p. 119

354 See the official website of the Bavarian State Ministry of Justice: http://www.justiz.bayern.de/ministerium/berufe/rista/00042/

355 Gero Debusmann, Zum Berufsbild des Richters: Vortrag anlässlich der Informations- und Bewerbungsmesse „JurStart“ am 19. Mai 2005 in Münster (*paper delivered at the "JurStart" information and advertising trade fair on 19th May 2005 in Münster*)

judges from many courts, they are likely to have little influence on the ordinary judges in the future.[356]

Another significant difference as compared to China is that in Germany, ordinary judges are assigned to work in many different ordinary courts or *Land* courts in different areas in the course of their first three years. They are therefore not directed by the same court president for the whole of their probationary period, but rather by many different department heads of different courts, and therefore establish only a limited relationship with each court because of their frequent changes of area, hence it is essentially impossible for such relationships to influence their work.[357]

## Section VI Comparison

As compared to Germany, the process of judicial selection in China has numerous ambiguities and limitations which seriously endanger the independence of judges. For example, the law does not deliver explicit provisions regarding the process of judicial selection and appointment. There is no unified standard for selection and appointment. Most ordinary judges are recruited and appointed as judges appointed for life by the heads of their courts. Moreover, the head of their court can influence their future promotions. All these factors lead most Chinese judges to not resist interference and influence from within their courts. How independently they adjudicate rests entirely on their self-discipline and decisions made by the head of their court.

In China, ordinary judges are selected according to the same standards and procedures as other civil servants, whereas in Germany, there are special bodies and procedures for this. The fact that candidate judges take a unified civil service examination is irrelevant, since the process is easy to corrupt if any of the procedures or bodies involved in this process are not infallibly designed. As discussed above, examinations and grades are controlled entirely by the government personnel department, and the procedures from the interview stage onwards are controlled by the courts themselves. These two bodies each concern themselves only with their own business and do not co-ordinate with or supervise each other, which can easily lead to inequities. It is well-know that many examinees who come first in the civil service examination ultimately fail to be recruited, usually because their interviews go very badly. Attention needs to be

356 Saltanat Khorrami, Das Einstellungs- und Beförderungsverfahren englischer und deutscher Richter, Hamburg 2005, pp. 113-114

357 Saltanat Khorrami, Das Einstellungs- und Beförderungsverfahren englischer und deutscher Richter, Hamburg 2005, p. 115

paid to the key role which the heads of courts play in this process, since there are no unified provisions regarding the content of interviews and the assessment criteria, all of which is not revealed to candidates afterwards.

Moreover, while promotion in China is achieved step-by-step as in Germany, there is parallel selection at the higher and lower courts, and promotion usually means transfer by an administrative method without a renewed selection process. The capacities of judges thus depend on the level of the courts at which their primarily work, jokingly referred to as "determinism at birth". Even excellent judges at lower-level courts find it difficult to apply to become judges at higher-level courts. One result of this is that the judges at higher-level courts are unfamiliar with the mode of operation of judges at lower-level courts and have no experience of the Basic People's Courts.

Finally, court presidents in China obtain their posts via the promoting cadre and not judicial selection, and the candidates are decided by the local Party Committee (while the local Party Committee usually invites suggestions for the higher courts in advance, there can be no doubt that it is the local Party Committee who plays the leading role). Due to the interaction of the election of new heads of the local Party and the government, the local Party Committee does not usually pay much attention to the professional qualities and judicial experience of such candidates, but rather to their political qualities and the level of their previous administrative posts, with the result that the professional qualities of court presidents have been neglected for a long time in China, and there is the abnormal phenomenon whereby "non-professionals" lead "professionals".[358]

From the foregoing, it is evident that in order to tangibly improve the system of judicial selection in China and ensure the independence of judges, it is first necessary to strengthen legislation and unify the methods and standards of judicial selection across the country, in a similar way to that in which the Basic Law in Germany creates the Committee of Judicial Selection. It has been reported in the media that a Method of Judicial Selection (for Trial Implementation) will address opinions on all these aspects and will be issued in the near future.[359] Hopefully, this Method shall deliver a more refined set of provisions regarding the system of judicial selection. Secondly, the civil service examination needs to be removed as a requirement for candidate judges, as it is not relevant to judicial selection. Thirdly, a special body for judicial selection such as a Committee of Judicial Selection needs to be established in China, replacing the monopoly sta-

358 Guo Zegao, On the System of Judicial Selection, http://hngf.gov.cn/theory/artilce_list.asp?id=1704&l_class=3

359 See article of 26th April 2007 from the Xinhua news agency website: http://news.xinhuanet.com/legal/2007-04/26/content_6032011.htm

tus which court presidents currently enjoy in the process of judicial selection. Such special bodies would most appropriately be composed of judges, procurators, lawyers and professors of law, would be established at the provincial level and would be responsible for judicial selection within a provincial area. Finally, judges of higher courts, lower courts and court presidents should be promoted stage by stage and not transferred by an administrative method. They should be examined and interviewed by the special body for judicial selection. Judges at the higher courts should not be selected directly from among ordinary judges, but rather promoted from the lower courts to the higher courts in stages, which will prevent judges' careers being decided right at the beginning, and will prevent interference in the adjudication of judges due to their fear of disobeying the head of their court.

# Chapter II Service Supervision (*Dienstaufsicht*) of Judges

The service supervision of judges means the power and action which authorised state organs employ in order to monitor whether judges satisfy the obligations of duty[360] and conduct themselves in the requisite manner.[361]

The service supervision of judges involves monitoring whether judges operate within their jurisdiction; it is in fact the supervision of state jurisdiction. It will be generally recognised that this power has two sides to it: one is organised, positive and creative; and the other is destructive, aggressive and corrosive. Without restrictions, this power would run wild and infringe civil and national interests. As a state power, this jurisdiction can destroy a society if not restricted effectively. Abuse of jurisdiction will cause the people to lose confidence in the law, thus endangering the authority of the law. All such powers, including that of jurisdiction, therefore have to be restricted and supervised.

Supervision of jurisdiction is the supervision of the service of judges who exercise jurisdiction. It is well-known that no-one who exercises power is utterly infallible or incorruptible. Many ideologists point out that human nature is both good and bad. James Madison, an architect of the American Constitution, said: "If men were angels, no government would be necessary. If angels were to govern men, neither external nor internal controls on government would be neces-

360 See Henning Stanicki, Die Dienstnachschau – Ein Eingriff in die richterliche Unabhängigkeit?, DRiZ (1986), pp. 329, 330

361 See the German Federal Court of Justice (*Bundesgerichtshof* = *BGH*) judgement of 21st December 1976, in: DRiZ (1977), p. 151

sary."[362] The French political thinker Charles de Secondat, Baron de Montesquieu, also pointed out that: "Constant experience shows us that every man invested with power is apt to abuse it, and to carry his authority as far as it will go."[363] As such everymen, judges are also only flesh and blood and have relatives and friends. Without effective restriction and supervision, judges could also exercise the power which they wield to satisfy their own selfish desires.[364] The service supervision aims to ensure that judges execute their posts appropriately and to avoid any delay or decline in justice.[365] Therefore, countries around the world establish systems for the supervision of judges' posts as a whole.

On the other hand, however, the supervision of posts must not interfere with the independence of judges. The German Judges Act expressly stipulates that judges shall receive supervision in their posts only where this does not interfere with their judicial independence.[366] Because both the independence of judges and the supervision of posts are principles established in the Basic Law, they are in a constantly strained relationship of pros and cons. The more strained the relationship becomes, the more departments tend to supervise the adjudication by judges.[367] It is difficult to delineate their ambits; nonetheless, Germany has not abolished the system of supervising judges' posts. But to prevent the independence of judges from being damaged, Germany sets strict limits on the supervisory organs responsible for judges' posts and on the supervisory methods permitted, and provides relief measures for judges.

In Germany's experience, the supervision of judges' posts generally involves a system of impeachment and discipline and a system of assessment and evaluation. In China, because the judiciary is highly corrupt,[368] the relationship between the independence of judges and the supervision of judges' posts is very strained, and there are many forms of supervision and many kinds of state organs and social forces which can supervise judges' posts. Each of these shall be discussed in the following.

---

362 Collected Works of Federal Partisans, p. 264

363 The Spirit of the Laws, p. 154

364 Ma Jianhua, Research on the Professionalisation of Judges, pp. 95 ff

365 Cheng Chunyi, The Independence of Judges and the Service Supervision, master's thesis at Taiwan National University Politics Department, June 1988, p. 127

366 Paragraph 1 of Article 26 of DRiG

367 Günter Schmidt-Räntsch, Deutsches Richtergesetz, 3rd edition, Munich, pp. 228-229

368 Liang Huixing, Judicial Corruption at an Unacceptable Level, in: Southern Metropolis Daily, 13th March 2009

## Section I The Service Supervision of Judges in China

The service supervision of judges as it currently stands may be broadly divided into two parts, namely internal supervision and external supervision. Internal supervision is the supervision of judges by the internal offices of the courts. External supervision is the supervision of judges by other organs.

### (1) External Supervision

External service supervision of judges may be further divided into two types, namely legally binding supervision and non-legally binding supervision. Legally binding supervision is legally effective supervision implemented by the state organs according to their legal authority and procedures in the name of the state and includes supervision by the legislature and supervision by prosecutorial organs. Non-legally binding supervision is an umbrella term for social supervision and includes various forms of supervision such as Party Commissions, news media and the masses.

#### *(a) Legally Binding Supervision*

##### (i) Supervision by the Legislature

Paragraph 3 of Article 3 of the Chinese Constitution stipulates that all administrative, judicial and procuratorial organs of the State are created by the People's Congresses to which they are responsible and by which they are supervised. Article 67 of the Constitution stipulates that one of the authorities of the Standing Committee of the National People's Congress is "to supervise the work of the State Council, the Central Military Commission, the Supreme People's Court and the Supreme People's Procuratorate" (Section 6). Article 104 stipulates that: "The Standing Committee of a local People's Congress at or above the county level discusses and decides on major issues in all fields of work in its administrative area and supervises the work of the People's Government, the People's Court and the People's Procuratorate at the corresponding level." In addition, Article 5 of the Supervisory Law stipulates that: "the Standing Committee of the People's Congress at various levels supervises the work of the People's Government, the People's Court and the People's Procuratorate at the corresponding level and promotes the legality of administrative acts and the justice of adjudication". It is thus clear that in China, the People's Congress and its Standing Committee are the legal organs supervising judges' service. The supervision of the courts by the People's Congress has been discussed in Section I of Chapter I on the relationship between the courts and the legislature, and can be divided into supervision in a general sense and supervision of individual cases. This supervision concerns the courts as a whole and stresses a supervision of the courts by the People's Congress which is legislative and the highest organ of state power. This chapter focuses on the supervision of individual judges rather than the supervision of the courts as a whole. Service supervision of judges by the People's Congress and its Standing Committee is implemented by deposing judges from their posts.

1. Removal

Removal applies to the presidents of courts at various levels (except a minority of the presidents of Special Intermediate People's Courts).[369] But there are no provisions as to the institutions in which removal can be applied. In practice, removal is usually applied where presidents of courts breach the law, fail in their duty or commit serious mistakes. In 2006, when answering a personnel delegate of the Standing Committee of a People's Congress at the provincial level as to whether the president of the Higher People's Court in that province could be removed, the Legislative Affairs Work Committee under the Standing Committee of the National People's Congress pointed out that removal could also be applied where leaders could neither perform their duties nor resign, such as where leaders are ill and cannot perform their duties for this reason. Removal could then be applied. But this answer was misleading, since it did not distinguish between reasons for removal and deposition. In accordance with the provi-

369 In accordance with the provisions of Article 30 of the Constitution, the administrative division of the People's Republic of China takes four forms: firstly, the nation; secondly, provinces (including municipalities directly under the jurisdiction of the Central Government and autonomous regions); thirdly, cities (including counties and autonomous prefectures); and fourthly, townships (including towns and nationality townships, i.e. autonomous townships of ethnic minorities). The People's Congresses are correspondingly divided into these four divisions. According to the system of organisation of Chinese courts as mentioned above, the Supreme People's Court, the Higher People's Courts, the Intermediate People's Courts and the Basic People's Courts are also divided according to these four administrative regional divisions, such that the presidents of Intermediate People's Courts are elected by the People's Congress of cities or counties in accordance with the third of the above divisions. But there are also exceptions in this general principle - for example, some provinces establish districts rather than cities or counties. These districts have no corresponding People's Congress. Also, the four municipalities directly under the jurisdiction of the Central Government only establish districts as townships dominated by local People's Courts. The Intermediate People's Courts above Basic People's Courts have no corresponding administrative regional division or corresponding People's Congress. The Special Intermediate People's Courts mentioned in this dissertation are those Intermediate People's Courts having no corresponding People's Congress.

sions on removal in the Judges Law of the People's Republic of China (PRC),[370] the president of the Higher People's Court of that province should be deposed, not removed, if he is ill and cannot perform his duties.

In accordance with the provisions of Paragraph 2 of Article 36 of the Organic Law of the People's Courts and Paragraphs 2 and 3 of Article 13 of the Judges Law of the PRC, the president of the Supreme People's Court is removed by the National People's Congress, and the presidents of local People's Courts at various levels are removed by the People's Congress at the corresponding level. The presidents and other judges of the minority of Special Intermediate People's Courts mentioned above who are the presidents of Intermediate People's Courts set up in prefectures, provinces and municipalities directly under the Central Government are removed by the Standing Committee of the People's Congress of the corresponding provinces or municipalities directly under the Central Government.[371] The presidents of these courts are not elected by the People's Congress at the corresponding level, hence they are also not removed by it but rather by the Standing Committee of the People's Congress at the corresponding level.

The procedure of removal is stipulated in the provisions of Article 15 of the Organic Law of the National People's Congress which state that: "proposals for the removal of the President of the Supreme People's Court or the Procurator-General of the Supreme People's Procuratorate may be submitted by three or more delegates or at least one tenth of the total number of deputies to the National People's Congress; the presidium shall refer such proposals to the Congress for deliberation." Paragraph 1 of Article 26 of the Organic Law of the Local People's Congresses and People's Governments at Various Levels stipulates that: "when a local People's Congress at or above the county level is in session, its presidium, its standing committee, or a group of at least one tenth of its deputies may submit a proposal to remove from office members of its standing committee or members of the People's Government, the president of the People's Court or the chief procurator of the People's Procuratorate at the corresponding level; the presidium shall refer such proposals to the Congress for deliberation." Paragraphs 3 of this Article stipulates that: "in a proposal for removal from office, reasons for the removal shall clearly be stated"; Paragraphs 4 stipulates that: "persons having been proposed for removal from office shall have the right to defend themselves at a meeting of the presidium or at the plenary meeting of a session, or to submit their defence in writing. The defence

370 Paragraph 5 of Article 13 of the Judges Law of the PRC

371 Paragraph 2 of Article 34 of the Organic Law of the People's Courts; Paragraph 4 of Article 11 of the Judges Law of the PRC

made at the meeting of the presidium or the written defence shall be printed and distributed to participants of the session by the presidium"; Paragraph 5 stipulates that: "the proposal for removal from office submitted to a local People's Congress at or above the county level shall, after being distributed by the presidium to the participants for deliberation, be submitted to the plenary meeting of the session for voting; or the presidium shall, subject to the decision of the plenary meeting of the session, propose to organise an investigation committee, and the proposal for removal from office shall be deliberated and decided at the next session of the People's Congress at the corresponding level on the basis of the report prepared by the investigation committee."

In accordance with these provisions, the organs which can propose a removal include three or more delegates or at least one tenth of the total number of deputies of the National People's Congress and the presidium, the standing committee, or a group of at least one tenth of the deputies of the local People's Congress at various levels. The procedure of removal is that the proponent submits the proposal for removal to the presidium for deliberation, and the presidium, having deliberated, submits it to the plenary meeting of the session for voting or proposes to organise an investigation committee, depending on the decision made at the plenary meeting of the session. The People's Congress at the corresponding level then decides at its next session on the basis of the report prepared by the investigation committee. Before the decision in the plenary meeting, persons who have been proposed for removal from office have the right to defend themselves at the meeting or to submit their defence in writing, which shall be printed and distributed to participants of the session by the presidium.

Additionally, Article 20 of the Local Organic Law stipulates that the adoption of a decision requires a majority vote of more than half of all the deputies of the People's Congress at various levels. Thus, the adoption of a proposal for removal of the presidents of courts also requires a majority vote of more than half of all the deputies.

2. Dismissal

Like removal, dismissal is usually applicable when judges breach laws or commit serious mistakes. Dismissal is applicable to all vice-presidents, chief judges of divisions, assistant chief judges of divisions, members of judicial committee, judges at various levels and presidents of some Special Intermediate People's Courts. In accordance with the provisions of Article 44 of the Supervisory Law, the local standing committee of the People's Congress at or above the county level – when the corresponding People's Congress is not in session – dismisses vice-presidents of courts, chief judges of divisions, assistant judges of divisions, members of judicial committee, judges, presidents of Intermediate People's Courts (this only applies here to presidents of Intermediate People's Courts established in prefectures, provinces and municipalities directly under the Central Government).

Dismissal is similar to removal in its nature and function. The power to dismiss of the Standing Committee of the People's Congress, as the permanent organ of the corresponding People's Congress, is indeed merely an extension of the power to dismiss of the People's Congress. Similarly, the Supervisory Law stipulates the procedures for advancing, dealing with and deliberating on proposals for dismissal and consulting the provisions on dismissal in the local Organic Law. The general principle of removal and dismissal is "those who elect or appoint can also remove or dismiss". Election is complemented by removal and appointment by dismissal. The presidents of courts are elected by the People's Congress, hence they are also to be dismissed by the People's Congress by a vote, which is the process of dismissal. Other personnel of the courts are nominated by the presidents of those courts and appointed by the Standing Committee of the People's Congress, hence the standing committee has the power to dismiss for example the relevant judges.

In accordance with the provisions of Article 45 of the Supervisory Law, the courts at various levels, the council of chairmen of the standing committee at various levels or a group of at least one fifth of the component members of the standing committee at various levels may propose the dismissal of judges, i.e. the proposal is not accepted directly by the Standing Committee of the People's Congress but is rather submitted to the council of chairmen of the Standing Committee of the People's Congress to be deliberated, who then decide whether or not to submit the proposal to the Standing Committee of the People's Congress to be decided. The council of chairmen of the Standing Committee of the People's Congress can also decide to establish an investigation committee. A subsequent council of the standing committee may then pass a resolution on the basis of the report produced by the investigation committee. In accordance with Article 46 of the Supervisory Law, the proposal for dismissal shall state the object and reasons of the proposal for dismissal, and relevant materials shall be provided with it. Before the decision, persons who have been proposed for dismissal have the right to defend themselves at the council of the standing committee, or to submit their defence in writing, which shall be printed and distributed to the council of the standing committee by the council of chairmen. The proposal for dismissal shall then be decided by secret ballot and shall be passed by a majority of all the members of the standing committee.

Dismissal as decided by the Standing Committee of the People's Congress is different from "dismissal from one's post" as a disciplinary punishment for civil servants. Civil servants are the agents who execute public duties, are incorporated into the national administrative system and are paid by the state treasury, including those elected and appointed by the People's Congress and its Standing Committee. In accordance with the provisions of the Civil Servant Law of the PRC, civil servants who violate the law or rules of discipline and are to be held accountable shall be punished in accordance with the Civil Servant Law of the PRC. Sanctions include a disciplinary warning, a demerit recorded, a grave demerit recorded, demotion, dismissal from one's post and discharge from public employment,[372] wherein dismissal from one's post is a disciplinary sanction in which civil servants are dismissed from their duties and which is generally approved by the organs responsible for approving and dismissing civil servants. The result of both dismissal as decided by the Standing Committee of the People's Congress and dismissal from one's post as a disciplinary punishment is that civil servants are relieved of their duties. The difference is that the sanction of dismissal is a form of disciplinary supervision and thus essentially of administrative management. Those who violate the rules of discipline and are punished according to the conditions and standards of disciplinary punishment have the right to appeal or apply for a review. Dismissal as decided by the Standing Committee of the People's Congress is a form of political supervision. In essence, it is the supervision and checking of one organ of state power by another organ of state power. There is no relief measure whereby those who are dismissed may appeal or apply for a review.

3. Deposition

Deposition is where the Standing Committee of the People's Congress deposes members of state organs who were elected and appointed by it. In accordance with the provisions of Article 13 of the Judges Law of the PRC, a proposal to depose a judge may be advanced if the judge fulfils any of the following criteria:

(1) having forfeited nationality of the PRC;
(2) having been transferred from the court;
(3) having no need to maintain an original post after changing to a new post;
(4) having been determined to be incompetent in the post through appraisal;
(5) being unable to perform the functions and duties of a judge for a long period of time due to poor health;
(6) having retired;
(7) having resigned or been dismissed;
(8) being disqualified from continuing to hold the post because of violation of discipline, law or commission of a crime.

372 Articles 55 and 56 of the Civil Servant Law

Deposition is a power of the Standing Committee of the People's Congress, but there are differences in nature between deposition and removal and dismissal. Both removal and dismissal are penal, indicating that those removed or dismissed have committed mistakes such as breach discipline or serious misconduct or even violating the law. Deposition, however, is not penal in nature. Individuals can be deposed due to a transfer, an exchange of personnel, the expiry of term of office and/or retirement (Sections 1 to 7 in Article 13 of the Judges Law of the PRC). It was thus not correct for the Legislative Affairs Work Committee under the Standing Committee of the National People's Congress to respond that the president could be deposed by the procedure of dismissal. In this case, the president to be removed has committed no mistake, hence deposition and not dismissal should be applied. Although in some cases of deposition, the judge is at fault (see Section 8 of Article 13 of the Judges Law of the PRC), the extent of fault is less than in the case of dismissal and removal and/or a further determination of the nature of their behaviour must be awaited and they are currently unfit to continue in their present office for this reason.

Deposition differs from dismissal both in its nature and in its procedures. The procedure whereby the Standing Committee of the People's Congress decides to depose an individual is generally as follows: (1) the president of the court who proposed the individual's appointment proposes that they be deposed; (2) it is generally required that the reasons of deposition be simply stated in the proposal for deposition; (3) the standing committee votes on the proposal for deposition after having deliberated on it. The procedures of deliberating and deciding on the proposal for deposition are simpler here than in the case of removal.

### 4. The Relationship between the Procedure of Removal or Dismissal and the Procedure of Criminal Sanction

In accordance with the provisions of the Criminal Procedure Law,[373] cases in which judges commit crimes are investigated and prosecuted by the People's

373 Paragraph 2 of Article 18 of the Criminal Procedure Law stipulates that the People's Procuratorate shall file a case for investigation of a crime of embezzlement and bribery, crime of dereliction of duty by a State functionary, crime infringing upon the citizen's rights of a person committed by a State functionary by abusing his power, such as illegal detention, extorting confessions by torture, reprisal and calumniation or illegal search, or crime infringing upon citizen's democratic rights. If cases involving other grave crimes committed by State functionaries by taking advantage of their functions and powers need to be handled directly by the People's Procuratorates, they may be placed on file for investigation by the People's Procuratorates upon a decision by the People's Procuratorates at or above the provincial level.

Procuratorate and adjudicated by the People's Court. In accordance with Article 12 of the Methods of Punishment in Adjudicative Discipline of the People's Courts, as issued by the Supreme People's Court in 1998, judges who receive a criminal sentence shall be discharged, and those who do not require sentencing as punishment for a minor crime shall be dismissed or discharged. In accordance with this provision, judges who commit a crime are in practice generally removed or dismissed from their posts as judges by the People's Congress or the Standing Committee of the People's Congress which elected or appointed them.

(ii) Supervision by Prosecutorial Organisations

In accordance with the Constitution, the People's Procuratorate is the state legal supervisory organisation. Service supervision of judges by the People's Procuratorate includes the following two aspects:

1. Supervision of Litigation

This form of supervision means that if a superior People's Procuratorate finds that evidence in a case handled by a lower People's Court was insufficient, the law was wrongly applied, legal procedures were violated and/or a judge violated the law, it can present a protest against the legally effective judgement or ruling rendered by the lower People's Court in accordance with the procedure of judicial supervision (i.e. the procedure discussed in Section I on the System of Trial Supervision).

2. Supervision of Crimes by Judges

The People's Procuratorate may, in accordance with its functions and powers, investigate and prosecute judges who have taken bribes, committed malpractice for personal gain and/or abused the law in the verdict rendered after adjudicating a case.

*(b) Non-Legally Binding Supervision*

Non-legally binding (social) supervision is where political or social organisations, other than state organs, and citizens perform supervision which is not directly legally binding. This supervision may take the following three forms:

(i) Supervision by the Party Committee

As the party in power, the Chinese Communist Party has the power to legally supervise party organisations and party members in the state organs. Based on this political principle, the Party Committee has the power to supervise the behaviour of Party judges; in particular, the disciplinary examination department of the Party has the power to supervise and punish any violations of Party discipline by Party judges. Indeed, because the Organisational Department of the

Party Committee has a certain influence and decision-making power in the appointment and dismissal of cadres in courts, it plays a role in supervising and restricting judges. Although this form of supervision is not legally binding, it does in practice influence the independence of judges. In recent years, many notable cases where judges have violated the law have been handled by the commission for disciplinary inspection of the supervisory organs of the Party.[374] In 2006, as a first example, many judges of the Intermediate People's Courts in Shenzhen were investigated according to the so-called two-fold directive[375] by the Central Commission for Disciplinary Inspection, and during this period, the daily work of the courts was managed by the Shenzhen Commission for Discipline.[376]

(ii) Supervision by the News Media

News media such as the press, magazines, television and radio broadcasts and the internet can publish, evaluate and supervise the adjudication by judges

---

374 The commission for disciplinary inspection is the supervisory organ of the Chinese Communist Party, having the function of enforcing party conduct and party discipline and fighting corruption and implementing the system of secretarial responsibility. As an organ of the Chinese Communist Party, the commission for disciplinary inspection generally works together with the supervisory department of the anti-corruption department of governments at various local levels. It should be noted that the commission for disciplinary inspection of the Chinese Communist Party is not a state organ and has no power imbued by the Constitution, and its exact nature has never even been determined. But within the special scenario in China, the commission for disciplinary inspection replaces procuratorates in inspecting state civil servants and even replaces the security department in investigating and handling criminal cases.

375 The two-fold directive means investigation at an appointed place within an appointed period and is a measure of disciplinary inspection and investigation by the Chinese Communist Party. It generally involves senior Party and political members being investigated and restricted in their freedom before an investigation by prosecutorial organisations, which is a separate examination. In general, a leader who is being investigated according to the two-fold directive is likely to be dismissed and put on trial. This scenario of being "investigated according to the two-fold directive" comes from Paragraph 3 of Article 28 of the Regulations of the Chinese Communist Party on Disciplinary Examination which "requires the relevant persons to explain the problem involved at the appointed place and within the appointed period". Generally, investigation according to the two-fold directive is applied to corrupt elements; leaders who are being investigated according to the two-fold directive are always removed from their homes or offices or restricted in their freedom when taking part in meetings. Although the investigation is for an appointed period, there are no explicit provisions on the duration of this period.

376 See the article "Many Judges at Shenzhen Intermediate People's Court being Investigated according to the 'Two-fold Directive'" of 7th November 2006, http://www.gmw.cn/content/2006-11/07/content_504081.htm

through live broadcasts of trials, news reports and journalist criticism. Because there is no supervisory law for news media, supervision of judges' behaviour in their posts by the news media usually oversteps the mark, preventing proper adjudication by judges and interfering with the independence of judges. Judges are only required to obey the law and adjudicate according to the law, but reports by news media, including instigative criticism, always bring a great pressure of public opinion to bear on judges, hence judges are ultimately likely to make a verdict in accordance with public opinion and not the law, such as in the case of Liu Yong which caused a great stir a few years ago[377] and the more recent case of Xu Ting.[378]

---

377 On 17th April 2002, in a trial of the first instance at Tieling Intermediate People's Court in Liaoning Province, Liu Yong was sentenced to death as a summary punishment for the crime of wilful and malicious injury together with several other offences. On 11th August 2003, Liaoning Higher People's Court passed sentence in a trial of the second instance, withdrawing the punishment for the crime of wilful and malicious injury and the civil compensation to the plaintiff, Hu Yan, from a separate civil action and passing a suspended death sentence with a two-year suspension of execution for the crime of wilful and malicious injury. It was said that an "opinion paper" published by some legal experts played a major role in this case. When Liu Yong's sentence was changed to a suspended death sentence with a two-year suspension of execution, nearly all the news media and the press voiced their opinion and a fierce discussion began among citizens on the internet. Suspicion, criticism, condemnation, satire and cursing were heard without end. Disappointment and anger were overflowing. The majority of voices were calling: "Liu Yong should be sentenced to death. The judiciary is not just." The counsel for Liu Yong's defence and the legal experts who had issued the opinion paper were criticised as "shameless hacks accepting illegal earnings". The Liaoning Higher People's Court was criticised for "bending the law in its administration of justice" and humiliated. The Supreme People's Court therefore brought the case to trial and restored the death sentence for Liu Yong. Some approved of a proper final trial and considered that public opinion had overcome the opinion of the experts. See Zou Ju, The Role of the News Media in the Balance and Guiding of Social and Public Opinion in the Case of Liu Yong, from: the Death of Socrates speeches, News Knowledge, 2004, No. 4.

378 On 21st April 2006, Xu Ting withdrew 175,000 Yuan and Xu's friend Guo Anshan withdrew 180,000 Yuan from an ATM by exploiting a malfunction. Guo later returned the money and gave himself up and was sentenced to a year's imprisonment. Xu Ting was arrested after a year on the run and sentenced to life imprisonment at a trial of the first instance. On 22nd February 2008, Xu Ting's case was reheard and he was sentenced to five year's imprisonment and a 20,000 Yuan fine. After Xu Ting was sentenced to life imprisonment in December 2007 for withdrawing money from an ATM, all the news media paid close attention to the case and it was widely discussed. The counsel for the defence, Yang Zhenping, expressed the opinion that supervision by the news media had played an important role. The decision for a retrial illustrates the power

(iii) Supervision by the Masses

According to Article 7 of the Judges Law of the People's Republic of China, one of the obligations of judges is to accept legal supervision and supervision by the masses.[379] Citizens and social organisations can supervise the adjudication by judges by implementing the Constitution and exercising their right of expression (including freedom of speech, freedom of the press, freedom of assembly, freedom of association, freedom of procession and freedom of demonstration), right of appeal, right of accusation, right of impeachment by law. In practice, the masses supervise judges most usually by reporting violations to procuratorial organisations or disciplinary committees. With the development of the internet, Chinese people are currently very enthusiastic about evaluating the adjudication by judges. In the case of Xu Ting as mentioned above, for example, a large number of "netizens" (i.e. citizens online) on the Tianya forum, one of the most popular networks, severely criticised the sentence of life imprisonment passed at the trial of the first instance, which in turn attracted the even closer attention of the news media and their continuous reporting, which ultimately moved the judges to change the original sentence.

Through the system of external supervision for judges in China, aimed at avoiding judicial corruption and preventing judges from abusing their powers, China has established many supervisory systems for the adjudication by judges. Whether legally binding supervision or non-legally binding supervision, both have such influence and the supervisory systems are so strict that they in fact interfere with the independence of judges. Continuous reporting by the news media for example causes an original sentence to be changed by the courts, and the influence of the Party Committee, including its disciplinary committee, means that judges do not try to eliminate the interference in trials by these departments, and the right of the People's Congress and its standing committee to

---

of the news media and public opinion. See Sina News Net http://news.sina.com.cn/s/l/2008-03-31/163515262649.shtml The Xinjing Newspaper also reported on 1st April 2008 that after sitting in on the trial, Chen Shu – delegate of the National People's Congress and secretary-general of the Guangzhou bar association – had approved of the sentence passed at the trial of the first instance. She pointed out that Xu Ting had the news media to thank for his eventual sentence. The lawyer Shen Wuchao commented that without continuous reporting by the news media, there would have been little chance of changing the sentence or securing a retrial. Shen Wuchao found that "the retrial in this case shows that the law in China is both serious and principled but also humane and provides limitless options for procedural review to parties such as Xu Ting. His final sentence was changed, showing how the law can reflect the will of the people." http://news.sina.com.cn/s/l/2008-04-01/014115263668.shtml

379 Section 7 of Article 7 of the Judges Law of the PRC

remove, dismiss and depose also mean that judges will not adjudicate cases independently in the face of interference from delegates of the People's Congress. On the other hand, however, the incidence of judges breaching the law or rules of discipline has also not diminished but has in fact increased. In recent years, instances of judges having to be punished have become almost too numerous to count,[380] hence the Supreme People's Court has repeatedly stressed that supervision needs to be further strengthened. The result has been phenomenal. So is there a serious flaw in the system of internal supervision of the courts?

## (2) Internal Supervision

In accordance with the Organic Law of the People's Courts and the Judges Law of the PRC, internal service supervision of judges is exercised by means of examination, appraisal and discipline. These shall be examined individually in the following.

### *(a) The System of Examination and Appraisal of Judges*

#### (i) The Organs for Examination and Appraisal

Chapter 8 of the Judges Law of the PRC stipulates the system of examination and appraisal of judges. In accordance with Article 19 of the Judges Law of the PRC, People's Courts examine and appraise judges, and in accordance with Article 46 of the Judges Law of the PRC, the People's Court establishes a commission for the examination and assessment of judges, and the functions and duties of the commission are to guide the training, examination, appraisal and assessment of judges. Article 47 additionally stipulates that the chairmanship of a commission for the examination and assessment of judges shall be assumed by the president of the court it belongs to, and that the commission for the examination and assessment of judges shall be composed of five to nine persons. In view of the broad terms and general nature of these provisions, it is in practice the case that courts usually devise additional internal provisions based on the above stipulations. These additional internal provisions vary depending on a court's situation. Taking the Second Intermediate People's Court of Beijing as an example, its provisions regarding the commission for examination and appraisal – as established in its Interim Procedures on Examining the Aims of Posts (For Trial Implementation) – are that: "the court shall establish a leading team for examination which is composed of the Party of the court and the chairmanship of which is assumed by the president of the court (Article 30). The

380 In 2007 alone, there were 218 cases of breaking the law and violating the rules of discipline, see the Work Report of the Supreme People's Court in 2008.

commission for examination and appraisal is established under the leading team for examination and is composed of the presidents in charge and the main leaders of various departments, and its chairmanship is assumed concurrently by the president of the court and its vice-chairmanship is assumed by the main leaders of the political department and the supervisory department. There are two administrative offices under the commission for examination and appraisal, one is the team for commenting on and examining cases and is established within the supervisory office; the other is the team for the examination and appraisal of non-judicial work and is established within the political department (Article 31). The teams for examination and appraisal are established in various departments, are led by the leader of those departments, are composed by key members of those departments and take charge of the examination and appraisal of the departments to which they belong (Article 32)." According to these Interim Procedures, there is a leading examination team composed of the members of the Party of the court above the commission for the examination and appraisal of the Second Intermediate Court in Beijing. It centrally guides the examination and appraisal of the court as a whole and resolves the major issues of examination by discussion (Article 30). Many teams for examination and appraisal are established under it and they also examine and appraise. Examination and appraisal are classified into two parts: judicial work is presented for comment and examination of the cases to the team established in the supervisory office; and the non-judicial work is presented for examination and appraisal to the team established in the political department.

(ii) The Content of Examination and Appraisal

In accordance with the provisions of Article 21 of the Judges Law of the PRC, the content of the examination and appraisal of judges includes achievements in their judicial work, their ideology and moral character, their competence in judicial work and their mastery of the theories of law, as well as their attitude towards and style of work. However, emphasis is to be laid on their achievements in judicial work.

1. "Achievements in judicial work" means the judges' achievements in their judicial works, including the quality, quantity, efficiency of their judicial work and the social benefits and awards.
2. "Ideology and moral character" means the judges' politics and ideology, their style of work, their professional ethics and their sound moral character, including whether they exemplarily abide by the Constitution and the laws, regulations and other regulatory documents, whether they serve the people wholeheartedly, maintain close links with the masses and accept supervision

by the masses, whether they continue to conscientiously learn the theoretical works of the Party and advance their political character and knowledge of political theory, whether they are devoted to their duties, keep state secrets, keep judicial work confidential, enforce the law impartially, are not swayed by personal considerations and are fair and just in their handling of affairs.
3. "Competence in judicial work" means their competence in theoretical and applied judicial work, and their competence in establishing facts and applying the law.
4. "Mastery of the theories of law" means their degree of learning, mastery and application of legal theory, wherein legal theory includes both basic legal theory and more specialised departmental legal theory such as criminal law, civil law, economic law, administrative law and procedure law. In practice, it means in particular the legal theory which needs to be mastered by judges dealing with specific judicial work.
5. "Attitude towards work" means how they deal with actual cases, whether they treat every case seriously and how they deal with the relationship between their work and personal life.
6. "Style of work" means, in the course of trying cases, whether judges are open and just, whether they discriminate against certain parties, whether or not they treat legal representatives equally, and whether they hear cases in good time and correctly.[381]

In practice, and again taking the Second Intermediate People's Court of Beijing as an example, the content of the examination of judges as established by this court – in accordance with its Interim Procedures on Examining the Aims of Posts (For Trial Implementation) – includes five parts, namely the aim of developing a qualified contingent (including three parts, namely political education, development of a Party and Youth League and establishment of a clean and honest administration), the basic aim of judicial work, the aim of disseminating information, the aim of administrative management and the aim of reform and innovation.

The content of the aim of developing a qualified contingent is centred on the provisions of Article 21 of the Judges Law of the PRC, as enumerated above in Section 2 (the ideology and moral character), Section 5 (attitude to work) and Section 6 (style of work). For example, the details regarding Section 2 specifically stipulate that not less than 12 hours every quarter should be spent in learning political theory and political activities (political study and activities are usu-

381 The explanations in 1. to 6. are quoted from the official internet site of the National People's Congress, see http://210.82.31.30/zgrdw/common/zw.jsp?label=WXZLK&id=297403&pdmc=1137

ally held between 4 p.m. and 6 p.m. every Tuesday and Thursday), and each person should spend not less than 10 days a year learning political theory. There are unscheduled tests on political learning, in which the average mark of various departments is required to be more than 80. The aspects covered in Section 5 are that judges shall appear in court on time, receive parties on time and are not permitted to treat parties "coldly, harshly or impatiently". Section 6 includes that every department shall make an honest analysis of their situation every quarter, develop education aimed at the problems which exist and take minutes of the analysis meeting. Reports and criticisms regarding issues of honest politics and style of adjudication (including letters, visits and telephone calls) should be less than one for every ten people in a department (rounded up to the nearest ten).

The basic aim of judicial work is included in Sections 1 and 3. In Sections 1, the rate of cases concluded is the most important standard of examination. The aim established in the Interim Procedures of this court is that the rate of cases concluded shall be not less than 40% in the first quarter, 65% in the second quarter, 80% in the third quarter and 85% percent in the fourth quarter. The quality of case handling is another requirement, including that in each quarter, the rate of revised judgements shall be less than 15%, the rate of lawsuits remanded for a retrial shall be less than 2% and the rate of mistakes in general folders shall be less than 5%. The last requirement is the time limit for concluding a trial. The rate of cases which exceed the time limit for concluding a trial for no reason shall be less than 2%. The rate of cases at the executive division which exceed the time limit for executing a judgement shall be less than 10%. In order to realise the aims in Section 3, this court expressly stipulates that each department shall organise practical learning or special lectures lasting more than four hours each month.

The aim of disseminating information is covered in Section 4. This court stipulates that in every quarter, there shall be more than two pieces of written material of investigation, including essays which investigate and research all kinds of important and difficult questions, investigation reports on judicial work and reviews of legal academic conferences.

The aim of administrative management and the aim of reform and innovation are established by this court essentially in accordance with the Civil Servant Law, which includes an attendance checking system, requirement for correct apparel and repast for judges, and even that playing cards, chess and ball games during working hours and drinking at noon are forbidden.

### (iii) The Procedure of Examination and Appraisal

In accordance with the provisions of Article 22 of the Judges Law of the PRC, judges are examined routinely and annually. There is no specific procedure or method of examination and appraisal stipulated in the Judges Law of the PRC. The Second Intermediate People's Court of Beijing will again be taken as an example in order to explain the practice which courts adopt.

In accordance with the provision in the Judges Law of the PRC for a routine and annual method of examination, the method of examination at the Second Intermediate People's Court of Beijing stipulates that routine examination is carried out once every quarter. The basic procedure is that at the end of each quarter, every department submits a written summary to the commission for examination and appraisal of this court regarding its performance towards each aim, and the commission for examination and appraisal of this court then examines and appraises the performance of each department. The commission principally examines and appraises the cases concluded. The commission for examination and appraisal of this court examines and appraises on the basis of collective investigation and discussion. All examinations and appraisals are completed before the $10^{th}$ day of the first month of the next quarter. An annual examination is carried out on the basis of summaries submitted at the end of the year, the procedure of which is similar to that of the routine examination.

(iv) The Results of Examination and Appraisal

In accordance with the provisions of Article 22 of the Judges Law of the PRC, the results of the annual examination and appraisal shall fall into three grades: excellent, competent and incompetent. These results of the examination and appraisal form the basis for regulating the award, punishment, training, removal, dismissal, grade and salary of judges. Furthermore, in accordance with the provisions of Paragraph 1 of Article 38 of the Judges Law of the PRC, judges who are confirmed by annual appraisal as being incompetent for two successive years shall be dismissed. In the method of examination used at the Second Intermediate People's Court of Beijing, the results of examination and appraisal influence the salary and awards of judges mainly on the basis of the results of routine examinations and appraisals. The results of the annual examinations and appraisals are not mentioned in the method of this court and have no influence. The rate of cases concluded by each division may be considered as an example. In divisions which achieve their aim, the court shall distribute 2,000 Yuan to each person in the first quarter, 2,200 Yuan in the second quarter, 2,300 Yuan in the third quarter, 2,400 Yuan in the fourth quarter, and no more than 2,700 Yuan each time. In divisions which do not achieve the required rate of cases concluded, and in which the rate of revised judgements and lawsuits remanded for a retrial exceeds 1% and the rate of mistakes in general folders exceeds 2%, the court shall deduct 15 to 30 Yuan from each person in any one quarter.

### (b) *The System of Disciplining Judges*

The legal provisions in China on a system of disciplining judges are disordered and unmethodical. Content on disciplinary organs, causes, methods and procedures appear sporadically in relevant laws such as the Judges Law of the PRC, the Methods of the People's Courts on Adjudicative Discipline and Punishment, the Methods of the People's Courts on the Accountability of Judges for Illegal Adjudication, the Interim Provisions of the People's Courts on Supervision, the Interim Measures of the People's Courts on Investigating and Punishing Activities which Violate the Law and the Rules of Discipline of the Supervision Department, the Criminal Law of the People's Republic of China and the Code of Judicial Ethics for Judges.

#### (i) The Organs of Discipline

There are no specific provisions in the Judges Law of the PRC on the organs of discipline. In accordance with the Interim Provisions of the People's Courts on Supervision, the supervisory organs of the People's Courts at various levels in China are the special organs which exercise the function of supervising and manage supervision and preside over the supervision of court staff.[382]

##### 1. Functions

The functions of supervisory organs include supervising and examining that courts and their staff administer laws, regulations, policies and rules of discipline, accepting and hearing charges filed and exposing violations of the law and rules of discipline by courts and their staff, imposing disciplinary sanctions against court staff who violate the law and rules of discipline, and hearing pleas from court staff who have suffered a disciplinary sanction.[383]

##### 2. The Organs and their Personnel[384]

The supervisory departments of the Supreme People's Court, the Higher People's Courts and the Intermediate People's Courts establish supervisory offices which lead and manage the supervision of the courts in their areas of jurisdiction and supervise all the departments of their courts and staff, and the lower courts and their presidents and vice-presidents. Basic People's Courts establish supervisory offices or supervisors which supervise all the departments of their courts and staff.

The supervisory office of the Supreme People's Court establishes one director and two deputy directors. The supervisory offices of the Higher People's

382 Article 2 of the Interim Provisions of the People's Courts on Supervision

383 Article 16 of the Interim Provisions of the People's Courts on Supervision

384 Articles 8 to 12 of the Interim Provisions of the People's Courts on Supervision

Courts and the Intermediate People's Courts establish one director, one or two deputy directors and a number of supervisors and assistant supervisors who are on a par with judges or assistant judges. The appointment of supervisors of the supervisory offices of local courts at various levels is to be reported to and approved by the supervisory office of a higher court.

(ii) Categories of Discipline

In accordance with Paragraph 1 of Article 32 of the Judges Law of the PRC and the Methods of the People's Courts on Adjudicative Discipline and Punishment, there are six types of disciplinary sanction which may be imposed on judges, including: a disciplinary warning; a demerit recorded; a grave demerit recorded; demotion; dismissal from one's post; and discharge from public employment. These are the same as the categories of disciplinary sanction for public servants in general.

These six administrative disciplinary measures range from the mild to the severe, depending on the extent to which adjudicative discipline is violated, wherein a disciplinary warning, a demerit recorded and a grave demerit recorded represent the milder administrative punishments. If the offence is a minor offence or a first offence and/or has had no major negative consequences, then a disciplinary warning, a demerit recorded or a grave demerit recorded are imposed, depending on the situation, in order to re-educate the offender and as a warning to others. By contrast, demotion, dismissal from one's post and discharge from public employment represent the more severe administrative punishments and are applied to more serious offences which do have major negative consequences.

In accordance with the provisions of Articles 14 to 17 of the Methods of the People's Courts on Adjudicative Discipline and Punishment, "Demotion means a reduction of one grade. If the offender is already on the lowest grade, a grave demerit recorded may be imposed". "Dismissal from one's post means dismissal from the original post and a simultaneous reduction in grade and salary. A new post shall be notified following a reduction of one or more grades and the corresponding grade and salary shall be determined by the new post." "The post and grade of a judge who has been discharged from public employment shall be simultaneously revoked. However, a judge elected and appointed by legal procedure shall be discharged from public employment by legal procedure."

In addition, Paragraph 2 of Article 34 of the Judges Law of the PRC stipulates that: "The salary of a judge who has been dismissed from their post shall at the same time be reduced and his or her grade demoted." Being "dismissed from their post" means that a judge who commits one of the 13 acts listed in Article 30 of the Judges Law of the PRC is dismissed from their original post in accordance with the Methods of the People's Courts on Adjudicative Discipline and Punishment issued by the Supreme People's Court. "The salary shall at the same time be reduced and his or her grade demoted" means that when a judge is dismissed from their post, their salary and grade shall correspondingly be demoted. By how much the salary and grade are to be demoted is determined in accordance with the severity of the offence and the provisions of the Supreme People's Court and other relevant departments.

(iii) Grounds for Disciplinary Measures

1. The Provisions of the Judges Law of the PRC

The system of discipline in China is different from that of Germany. The disciplinary measures for judges are not restricted to violations of their post or the like. The Judges Law of the PRC merely specifies in general terms a number of situations which merit discipline, in which judges use their posts for criminal ends, including general offences and violating the rules of discipline and judicial ethics for judges. The grounds for disciplinary measures specified in Article 30 of the Judges Law of the PRC include the following acts:

- to spread statements damaging the prestige of the State; to join illegal organisations; to take part in such activities as assembly, procession and demonstration against the State; and to participate in strikes;
- to embezzle money or accept bribes;
- to bend the law for personal gain;
- to extort confessions by torture;
- to conceal or falsify evidence;
- to divulge State secrets or secrets of one's judicial work;
- to abuse functions and powers; and to infringe upon the legitimate rights and interests of citizens, legal persons or other organisations;
- to neglect one's duty so as to wrongly judge a case or to cause heavy losses to a party concerned;
- to intentionally delay the handling of a case so as to adversely affect the work;
- to take advantage of one's functions and powers so as to seek gain for oneself or others;
- to engage in profit-making activities;
- to meet parties concerned or their agents without authorisation and to attend dinners or accept presents given by parties concerned or their agents; or
- to commit other acts in violation of the law or the rules of discipline.

2. The Provisions of the Methods of the People's Courts on Adjudicative Discipline and Punishment

In the Judges Law of the PRC, the provisions regarding the acts for which judges should be punished are only specified in principle and not elaborated, and there are no provisions as to which punishments should be applied to which acts. The Methods of the People's Courts on Adjudicative Discipline and Punishment supplement this and make provisions for the different punishment situations:

- Judges who violate the provisions of the law, do not accept and hear cases which should be accepted and heard, or illegally accept and hear cases which should not be accepted nor heard, shall suffer a disciplinary measure ranging from a disciplinary warning to a grave demerit recorded. Judges who accept and hear cases in secret shall suffer a disciplinary measure ranging from a grave demerit recorded to dismissal from their post. Judges who do not accept and hear cases which should be accepted and heard as a result of negligence, or illegally accept and hear cases which should not be accepted or heard, in a way incurring serious consequences shall suffer a disciplinary measure ranging from a disciplinary warning to a grave demerit recorded.
- Except for situations such as provided for in law, judges who recommend and introduce lawyers or attorneys to the parties in accepted cases, or who introduce cases to lawyers or others, in a way incurring serious consequences shall suffer a disciplinary measure ranging from a disciplinary warning to a grave demerit recorded. Judges who furthermore profit from this shall suffer a disciplinary measure ranging from a demerit recorded to discharge from public employment.
- Judges who know the legal conditions for withdrawal and do not withdraw of their own accord, or deliberately do not apply the legal conditions for withdrawal, and interfere with the just adjudication of a case, shall suffer a disciplinary measure ranging from a disciplinary warning to a grave demerit recorded.
- Judges who meet privately with parties and/or their attorneys in accepted cases in a way incurring serious consequences shall suffer a disciplinary measure ranging from a disciplinary warning to a grave demerit recorded.
- Judges who interfere presumptuously in the adjudication of lower People's Courts shall suffer a disciplinary measure ranging from a disciplinary warning to a grave demerit recorded.
- Judges who accept gifts from parties and/or their attorneys, or require parties and/or their attorneys to pay fees which should be paid by the judge, shall suffer a disciplinary measure ranging from a disciplinary warning to a grave demerit recorded.

- Judges who accept dinner invitations from parties and/or their attorneys, or take part in entertainment paid for by parties and/or their attorneys, in a way incurring serious consequences shall suffer a disciplinary measure ranging from a disciplinary warning to a grave demerit recorded.
- Judges who borrow money, vehicles, telecommunication facilities or other items from parties and/or their attorneys for their own use, or accept preferential treatment proved by parties and/or their attorneys in purchasing merchandise, furnishings and the like, shall suffer a disciplinary measure ranging from a disciplinary warning to a grave demerit recorded. If the circumstances are serious, judges shall suffer a disciplinary measure ranging from demotion to discharge from public employment.
- Judges who violate the provisions of the charging method for legal fees at the People's Courts, increase the legal fees, extend the range of charges or elevate the charges, or presumptuously reduce, exempt or suspend legal fees or require parties to sponsor the court in a way incurring serious consequences shall suffer a disciplinary measure ranging from a disciplinary warning to a grave demerit recorded.
- Judges who share out without permission, misappropriate or embezzle legal fees, fines, case-related temporary deposits and other gains shall suffer a disciplinary measure ranging from a disciplinary warning to a grave demerit recorded. If the circumstances are serious, judges shall suffer a disciplinary measure ranging from demotion to discharge from public employment.
- Judges who fail to collect evidence concerning major facts requested by parties and/or their attorneys for objective reasons, leading to an incorrect decision, shall suffer a disciplinary measure ranging from a disciplinary warning to dismissal from their post.
- Judges who fail to identify, inspect, enquire into or check evidence concerning major facts, or deliberately fail to retain evidence which should be retained, leading to an incorrect decision shall suffer a disciplinary measure ranging from a disciplinary warning to a grave demerit recorded.
- Judges who alter, hide, forge, steal or damage evidence on purpose shall suffer a disciplinary measure ranging from a grave demerit recorded to discharge from public employment.
- Judges who instigate, support or authorise others to give false testimony shall suffer a disciplinary measure ranging from demotion to discharge from public employment.
- Judges who collect evidence using threats or the lure or promise of gain shall suffer a disciplinary measure ranging from a disciplinary warning to a grave demerit recorded. If the circumstances are serious, they shall suffer a disci-

plinary measure ranging from demotion to discharge from public employment.

- Judges who intimidate or entice parties to withdraw an action shall suffer a disciplinary measure ranging from a disciplinary warning to a grave demerit recorded.
- Judges who tamper with, forge or damage trial records on purpose shall suffer a disciplinary measure ranging from a disciplinary warning to a grave demerit recorded. If the circumstances are serious, they shall suffer a disciplinary measure ranging from demotion to discharge from public employment.
- Judges who keep major evidence or particular material from a collegial panel or judicial committee, or provide forged material shall suffer a disciplinary measure ranging from a discipline warning to a grave demerit recorded. If the circumstances are serious, they shall suffer a disciplinary measure ranging from demotion to discharge from public employment. Those who omit major evidence or particular material, leading to an incorrect decision, shall suffer a disciplinary measure ranging from a disciplinary warning to a grave demerit recorded.
- Judges who deliberately violate the facts or the law, leading to an incorrect decision, shall suffer a disciplinary measure ranging from a disciplinary warning to a grave demerit recorded. If the circumstances are serious, they shall suffer a disciplinary measure ranging from demotion to discharge from public employment. If they make an incorrect decision as a result of negligence, in a way incurring serious consequences, they shall suffer a disciplinary measure ranging from a disciplinary warning to a grave demerit recorded.
- Judges who tamper with, forge or damage the discussion records of the collegial panel or judicial committee on purpose shall suffer a disciplinary measure ranging from a grave demerit recorded to discharge form public employment.
- Judges who refuse to report to judicial committee, or fail to execute a decision made by a higher People's Court, shall suffer a disciplinary measure ranging from a disciplinary warning to a grave demerit recorded.
- Judges who leak the contents of a discussion by the collegial panel or judicial committee, or leak other trial secrets, shall suffer a disciplinary measure ranging from a disciplinary warning to a grave demerit recorded. If the circumstances are serious, they shall suffer a disciplinary measure ranging from demotion to discharge from public employment.
- Judges who deliberately violate the provisions of the law or enforce illegal measures or remove measures of preservation regarding property, causing parties to lose their property, shall suffer a disciplinary measure ranging from

a disciplinary warning to a grave demerit recorded. If the circumstances are serious, they shall suffer a disciplinary measure ranging from a demotion to discharge from public employment. If they remove measures of preservation regarding property as a result of negligence, in a way incurring serious consequences, they shall suffer a disciplinary measure ranging from a disciplinary warning to a grave demerit recorded.

- Judges who commit errors prior to executing judgement, causing parties or others to lose property, shall suffer a disciplinary measure ranging from a disciplinary warning to a grave demerit recorded.
- Judges who illegally administer the property of parties or others on purpose, causing them to lose property, shall suffer a disciplinary measure ranging from a disciplinary warning to a grave demerit recorded. If the circumstances are serious, they shall suffer a disciplinary measure ranging from demotion to discharge from public employment.
- Judges who deliberately make excessive use of seizure of property, detention in custody, wage freezes or the disposal of property, causing parties to lose property, shall suffer a disciplinary measure ranging from a disciplinary warning to a grave demerit recorded. If the circumstances are serious, they shall suffer a disciplinary measure ranging from demotion to dismissal from their post.
- Judges who incite relevant departments to raise or drop prices when evaluating administered property, causing parties to lose property, shall suffer a disciplinary measure ranging from a disciplinary warning to a grave demerit recorded.
- Judges who deliberately make repeated use of seizure of property, detention in custody, wage freezes or the disposal of property, causing parties to lose property, shall suffer a disciplinary measure ranging from a disciplinary warning to a grave demerit recorded.
- Judges who deliberately violate laws concerning temporary respite, suspension of execution or termination of execution, causing parties to lose property, shall suffer a disciplinary measure ranging from a disciplinary warning to a grave demerit recorded. If the circumstances are serious, they shall suffer a disciplinary measure ranging from demotion to dismissal from their post.
- Judges who embezzle, withhold, personally apportion or misappropriate administered property shall suffer a disciplinary measure ranging from a disciplinary warning to a grave demerit recorded. If the circumstances are serious, they shall suffer a disciplinary measure ranging from demotion to discharge from public employment.
- Judges who provide secret information to those being prosecuted, enabling them to transfer, hide or sell off administered property and avoid prosecution,

shall suffer a disciplinary measure ranging from a disciplinary warning to a grave demerit recorded.

- Judges who draft charge documents in secret or deliberately violate decisions by the collegial panel or judicial committee when drafting charge documents shall suffer a disciplinary measure ranging from a disciplinary warning to a grave demerit recorded. If the circumstances are serious, they shall suffer a disciplinary measure ranging from demotion to discharge from public employment. If there are mistakes in the charge documents as a result of negligence, in a way incurring serious consequences, they shall suffer a disciplinary measure ranging from a disciplinary warning to a grave demerit recorded.
- Judges who deliver charge documents illegally, in a way incurring serious consequences, shall suffer a disciplinary measure ranging from a disciplinary warning to a grave demerit recorded.
- Judges who without good cause, do not duly assist the People's Courts of other jurisdictions in accordance with the law, in a way incurring serious consequences, shall suffer a disciplinary measure ranging from a disciplinary warning to a grave demerit recorded.
- Judges who hamper or interfere with the judges of the People's Courts of other jurisdictions in their investigations or collection of evidence, or adopt illegal enforcement measures or remove measures of preservation regarding property, in a way incurring serious consequences, shall suffer a discipline from a disciplinary warning to a grave demerit recorded.
- Judges who deliberately adopt illegal enforcement measures shall suffer a disciplinary measure ranging from a disciplinary warning to a grave demerit recorded. If the circumstances are serious, they shall suffer a disciplinary measure ranging from demotion to discharge from public employment. Judges who adopt illegal enforcement measures as a result of negligence, causing a party serious injury or death, shall suffer a disciplinary measure ranging from demotion to discharge from public employment.
- Judges who violate the law by reducing sentences or granting parole on crimes which do not meet the requirements for such a reduction or parole shall suffer a disciplinary measure ranging from a disciplinary warning to a grave demerit recorded. If the circumstances are serious, they shall suffer a disciplinary measure ranging from demotion to discharge from public employment.
- Judges who intentionally delay the handling of a case for personal reasons shall suffer a disciplinary measure ranging from a disciplinary warning to a grave demerit recorded. If the circumstances are serious, they shall suffer a disciplinary measure ranging from demotion to discharge from public employment. If judges delay the handing of a case as a result of negligence, in a

way incurring serious consequences, they shall suffer a disciplinary measure ranging from a disciplinary warning to a grave demerit recorded.

- Judges who handle cases, demand payment or bring suspects up for trial in secret shall suffer a disciplinary measure ranging from a disciplinary warning to a grave demerit recorded. If the circumstances are serious, they shall suffer a disciplinary measure ranging from demotion to discharge from public employment.
- Judges who keep suspects under lax guard as they are brought up for trial or transported under escort, causing the suspects to escape, shall suffer a disciplinary measure ranging from a grave demerit recorded to discharge from public employment.
- Judges who deliberately damage rolls or other charge documents, affecting the normal process of judicial work, shall suffer a disciplinary measure ranging from a disciplinary warning to a grave demerit recorded. If the circumstances are serious, they shall suffer a disciplinary measure ranging from demotion to discharge from public employment. If they lose rolls or secretly lend rolls or other charge documents to others, in a way incurring serious consequences, they shall suffer a disciplinary measure ranging from a disciplinary warning to a grave demerit recorded.
- Judicial experts who deliberately draw incorrect expert conclusions shall suffer a disciplinary measure ranging from a disciplinary warning to a grave demerit recorded. If the circumstances are serious, they shall suffer a disciplinary measure ranging from demotion to discharge from public employment. If they draw incorrect expert conclusions as a result of negligence, in a way incurring serious consequences, they shall suffer a disciplinary measure ranging from a disciplinary warning to a grave demerit recorded.
- Judges who use guns or ammunition outside the regulations, causing them to be missing or in a way incurring other serious consequences, shall suffer a disciplinary measure ranging from a disciplinary warning to a grave demerit recorded. If they cause human casualties, they shall suffer a disciplinary measure ranging from dismissal from their post to discharge from public employment.
- Judges who use or store police equipment outside the regulations, causing it to be missing or in a way incurring other serious consequences, shall suffer a disciplinary measure ranging from a disciplinary warning to a grave demerit recorded. If they cause human casualties, they shall suffer a disciplinary measure ranging from dismissal from their post to discharge from public employment.
- Judges who drink while on duty, generating a bad influence, shall suffer a disciplinary measure ranging from a disciplinary warning to a grave demerit

recorded. If the circumstances are serious, they shall suffer a disciplinary measure ranging from demotion to discharge from public employment.

- Judges who beat, scold, insult or humiliate litigants or their relatives shall suffer a disciplinary measure ranging from a disciplinary warning to a grave demerit recorded. If the circumstances are serious, they shall suffer a disciplinary measure ranging from dismissal from their post to discharge from public employment.
- Judges who sleep with litigants or their relatives in their cases shall suffer a disciplinary measure ranging from a disciplinary warning to a grave demerit recorded.
- Judges in charge of supervision and management who fail to correct or report any act violating the law or rules of discipline shall suffer a disciplinary measure ranging from a disciplinary warning to a grave demerit recorded. If the circumstances are serious, they shall suffer a disciplinary measure ranging from demotion to discharge from public employment.

It can be seen from the above provisions that the rules of discipline concerning judges' acts which violate the law are very broad and exceed the equivalent provisions in Germany. Some scholars consider that such strict rules of disciplines for judges address the situation that the characters of judges have a very low standing generally in China at present.[385]

(iv) The Procedure of Disciplinary Measures

Article 33 of the Judges Law of the PRC merely stipulates very generally that: "A sanction shall be authorised and procedures gone through in accordance with the relevant regulations", wherein "the relevant regulations" means the implementing method promulgated by the Supreme People's Court, consisting mainly of the Interim Measures of the People's Courts on Investigating and Punishing Activities which Violate the Law and the Rules of Discipline of the Supervision Department, and the Criminal Law of the People's Republic of China. In accordance with these Interim Measures, the basic procedures by which the supervision departments of the People's Courts investigate and punish activities which violate the law and the rules of discipline are as follows:

---

385 Framework of the Judges Law of the PRC, p. 208; Wang Pan / Cheng Zhengju, Judicial Independence and Judicial Fairness, China People's Public Security University Press, Beijing 2002, p. 541; Xie Youping, Establishing Judicial Fairness, China Procuratorate Press, Beijing 2005, pp. 280-281

1. Accepting and Hearing[386]

Court staff may be accused orally or in writing of acts which violate the law and/or rules of disciplines. An oral accusation shall be recorded by supervisors and signed or sealed by the accusers once they have confirmed that the records are correct. Written accusations may be required to be accompanied by evidence provided by the accusers at the behest of supervisors. If accusers wish their names to remain secret, this can be granted by supervisors.

If an initial investigation finds that acts by a judge have violated the law and/or rules of discipline and merit a disciplinary measure, the case shall be placed on file and investigated. If the acts do not violate the law and/or rules of discipline or the accusations are incorrect, the case shall not be placed on file and the reasons why the case has not been placed on file may be communicated to the accusers, depending on the specific circumstances of the case.

2. Placing a Case on File[387]

If a case is to be placed on file, a person in charge shall write a report about placing the case on file, attach the materials of the accusation and initial investigation and submit the file to the senior authorities for examination and approval. Once said senior authorities have approved this, they shall report it to the relevant authorities for placing the case on file.

3. Investigation[388]

Investigation refers to the activities whereby the supervisory departments verify the facts and circumstances and collect and interpret evidence. Investigations shall be concluded within three months. During the investigation, the accused shall be interviewed and confessions or statements of defence shall be heard. After completion of the investigation, investigation reports shall be drawn up, the content of which shall include the origin of the case, a basic introduction of the accused, the grounds for placing the case on file, aspects of the accusation, a confirmation or rejection of the accusation, whether the nature of confirmed

386 Articles 14 to 16 of the Interim Measures of the People's Courts on Investigating and Punishing Activities which Violate the Law and the Rules of Discipline of the Supervision Department

387 Articles 17 to 21 of the Interim Measures of the People's Courts on Investigating and Punishing Activities which Violate the Law and the Rules of Discipline of the Supervision Department

388 Articles 22 to 29 of the Interim Measures of the People's Courts on Investigating and Punishing Activities which Violate the Law and the Rules of Discipline of the Supervision Department

acts violates the law or rules of discipline, the liability of those involved, the attitude of the accused and the opinion of the investigation team.

4. Adjudication[389]

The supervisory office of the Intermediate People's Courts establish an adjudication team and Higher People's Courts and the Supreme People's Court establish an adjudication committee to adjudicate such cases. If an adjudicative or disciplinary decision is to be made in a case following the investigation, it shall be submitted to the adjudication team or adjudication committee to be adjudicated. Adjudication includes reviewing all the material of the case, verifying the facts and evidence and discussing all aspects of the case.

5. Disciplinary Measures[390]

Once a case has been adjudicated and discussed, if a disciplinary measure below a grave demerit recorded is to be imposed on the accused, this disciplinary measure is imposed directly by the supervisory department. If a disciplinary measure above demotion is to be imposed, the supervisory department recommends the disciplinary measure and submits this recommendation to the president for approval.

If a disciplinary measure of discharge from public employment is to be imposed on a judge of a Basic People's Court, the supervisory office of the Intermediate People's Court shall submit the disciplinary opinion to its Board of Court Affairs for approval. If a disciplinary measure of discharge from public employment is to be imposed on a judge of an Intermediate People's Courts or a Higher People's Court, the supervisory office of this court shall submit the disciplinary opinion to its Board of Court Affairs for approval and report to the supervisory office of the higher court to have this put on file.

The disciplinary decision shall be signed by the disciplined judges, although whether they agree with the discipline or not does not affect whether the disciplinary decision is executed or not.

389 Articles 30 to 35 of the Interim Measures of the People's Courts on Investigating and Punishing Activities which Violate the Law and the Rules of Discipline of the Supervision Department

390 Articles 36 to 43 of the Interim Measures of the People's Courts on Investigating and Punishing Activities which Violate the Law and the Rules of Discipline of the Supervision Department

## 6. Appeal and Re-examination[391]

Disciplined judges who do not agree with a disciplinary decision may appeal to the supervisory department of the People's Court which made the disciplinary decision or to the supervisory department of the next higher People's Court. After receiving an appeal request, the supervisory department shall establish another investigation team to review all the facts considered in the original disciplinary decision and punishment applied. The review of cases involving violation of the rules of discipline shall be concluded within three months. If the original disciplinary measure is considered to have been correct, the appeal shall be dismissed and the original decision shall be confirmed. If the original disciplinary measure is considered to have been incorrect, it shall be revoked and may be replaced by a new disciplinary measure.

### *(c) The Influence of Internal Supervision on the Independence of Judges*

Interior service supervision of judges through the aforementioned examination and disciplinary system is implemented by many different persons and organs, hence the independence of judges is threatened in a variety of ways.

#### (i) Presidents

The Judges Law of the PRC stipulates that the president of a court is the chairman of a commission for the examination and assessment of judges, and all courts implement this provision of the Judges Law of the PRC. Although in the Second Intermediate People's Court of Beijing, there is no commission for examination and assessment under the leading team for examination and assessment, wherein the chairman is the president and examination and assessment are divided into two parts, namely judicial work and non-judicial work, which are examined and assessed separately by the supervisory office and the political department, the final result of examination and assessment still has to be passed by the leading team for examination and assessment which is chaired by the president. The members of this team cannot assume this post without the approval of the president. Their future promotions also depend on the president. Thus, it may be assumed that anything which the president objects to cannot then be approved by other members of the team, and anything which the president approves also then has to be approved by the other members of the team. In fact, both the supervisory office and the political department under the commission for examination and assessment are the departments for carrying out admin-

391 Articles 44 to 49 of the Interim Measures of the People's Courts on Investigating and Punishing Activities which Violate the Law and the Rules of Discipline of the Supervision Department

istrative management and supervision in lieu of the president. The results of examination and assessment affect not only the salary and bonuses of judges, but also their future promotions. At the same time, the president has the final decision within the supervisory office, since the supervisory office can only impose disciplinary measures below a grave demerit recorded, and any disciplinary measures above this have to be approved by the president. Thus, the president can almost be said to wield absolute power over judges. If judges wish to be promoted, to get an increase in salary and/or to not be punished for mistakes, they must follow the president's lead, hence their decisions are not made independently of interference from the president. In the service supervision, the independence of judges is not fulfilled with respect to the president, but is rather completely suppressed by the power of the president.

(ii) Chief Judges of a Division

The chief judges of a division are an extension of the power of the presidents. They monitor judges by examining, assessing and supervising their daily work.

(iii) Supervisory Departments

The supervisory departments are established in courts and supervise the discipline of judges. Because they are established in the courts and their disciplinary recommendations are decided by the president, they in fact become the administrative supervisory commission of the president. But there are no restrictions on the presidents who hold power. Although the law stipulates that the supervisory departments of higher courts supervise the presidents of lower courts, this is not possible in practice, and it should not be the case that higher courts have a complete grasp on the work situation of lower courts, hence they cannot supervise the presidents of lower courts.

It may be concluded that whether the internal supervisory system of courts in China is successful is completely dependent on the presidents of courts, because the core of all powers reside with the court presidents and there are no restrictions on these powers. This aspect is very different to Germany. In Germany, the supervisory departments do include officials including presidents, but the methods of supervising judges are very limited. Above these officials and supervisory departments, there are independent post divisions with whom judges can initiate appeal procedures if they feel their rights have been infringed. In China, laws do not restrict the methods of discipline to judgements made by supervisory departments, but endow courts with broad disciplinary powers to restrict judges. These disciplinary measures are not made by an independent department but by interior organs of the courts. Also, there is not then a procedure of court trial as there is in Germany. The discipline of judges is both imprudent and severe. As long as the presidents of courts have the power to supervise the daily actions of judges, decide the results of the examination of judges, decide the disciplinary measures imposed on judges and are not restricted in these powers, judges will without doubt always be hugely under the influence of the courts and unable to be truly independent. In practice, judges who commit a crime are usually found out and punished by external supervision (generally by the commission for disciplinary inspection) and many cases deal with the court as a whole, since in a court in which the president almost monopolises the power, judges who violate the rules of discipline with the president's consent should not be punished, and if the president violates the law and/or rules of discipline, none of the judges in the court as a whole will dare to object. Cases in recent years have for example included Tian Fengqi, the former president of the Higher People's Court of Liaoning province, Mai Chongkai, the former president of the Higher People's Court of Guangdong province, Jia Yongxiang, the former president of the Intermediate People's Court of Shenyang city, Zhou Wenxuan, the former president of the Intermediate People's Court of Wuhan city, Tang Jikai, the former vice-president of the Intermediate People's Court of Changsha city, and Shang Jun, Liu Jiayi, and Zhang Zimin, all former presidents of the Intermediate People's Court of Fuyang city, were sentenced for bribery, corruption and embezzlement. Many of these cases deal with a large number of judges – the bribery case involving Wu Zhenhan for example featured more than ten court officials and judges, and more than thirty defendants in total.[392] Because their powers are concentrated and restrictions are lacking, court presidents are indeed a "high-risk group" for corruption. Absolute power corrupts absolutely. Under the pressure of the president's powers, judges either go along with their schemes or object and achieve nothing. Although judges should, through the strict procedures of appointment, be of good character and upright and not ones to stoop to fawning or favouritism, under the authority of their presidents, few judges are able to go their own way for fear of being discharged from public employment or dismissed from their post. Clearly, until this situation in which presidents cling on to power is changed, it is hard to know where to begin with the independence of judges.

By all accounts, there are many systems and methods for supervising and restricting judges, including the external and internal, the legally binding and non-legally binding. It is almost inconceivable how judges can be independent under

392 See the article of 11th November 2006 on Xinhua Net: Why Presidents are a "High-Risk Group" for Corruption, http://news.xinhuanet.com/comments/200611/11/content_5315970.htm, last retrieved on 24th March 2010.

such a rigid supervisory system. Conversely, these systems do not prevent judicial corruption as might be supposed. The independence of judges has disappeared under the system of service supervision, and the supervisory system does not achieve the effect of restricting powers. It may be said that the ill-conceived design of this system has made the supervisory system of judges' service in China essentially ineffective. By comparison, the German supervisory system is clearly more highly developed.

## Section II The Service Supervision of Judges in Germany[393]

Paragraph 1 of Article 26 of the German Judges Act prescribes that judges shall be subject only to such supervision of their service as does not damage their independence. The service supervision is thus a legal system acknowledged in law. However, the independence of judges is a system guaranteed by the Constitution, bearing constitutional benefits, hence the service supervision may under no circumstances violate the independence of judges. In another words, the independence of judges has priority.[394] It is very difficult to draw a line between the necessary service supervision and the independence of judges, but the latter can neither negate the necessity for nor abolish the service supervision of judges in Germany.[395] Except for the judges of the constitutional court, more than 17,000 judges are subject to the service supervision. Unlike China, Germany has neither a strict, unified policy on the service supervision of judges nor the various supervisory methods and organs which exist in China. In accordance with the German Judges Act, the service supervision of judges in Germany may be divided into three aspects, namely examination and appraisal, punishment and impeachment.

### (1) The Scope and Limitation of the Service Supervision

Paragraph 2 of Article 26 of the German Judges Act stipulates that judges who improperly execute their official functions may be cautioned and exhorted to

393 Günter Schmidt-Räntsch, Jürgen Schmidt-Räntsch, Deutsches Richtergesetz (DRiG), Kommentar, 6th edition, Munich 2008, p. 423 ff

394 Wolfgang Meyer, Dienstaufsicht, richterliche Unabhängigkeit und Zusatzgutachten ohne richterliche Ernennung, in: German Judges Journal (*Deutsche Richterzeitung = DRiZ*) 1981, pp. 22, 24; Karl Krützmann, Zur richterlichen Unabhängigkeit im verfaßten Gemeinwesen des Grundgesetzes, DRiZ (1985), pp. 201, 206

395 Günter Schmidt-Räntsch, Jürgen Schmidt-Räntsch, Deutsches Richtergesetz (DRiG), Kommentar, 6th edition, Munich 2008, p. 359

properly complete their duties without delay. It may be seen from this provision that the service supervision of judges under the German legal system may include supervising judges and urging them to comport themselves legally, providing this does not harm their independence. However, there are no unified laws or regulations on the service supervision for the courts of all the different federal departments. There are only a few sources of corresponding provisions, as enumerated below:

#### *(a) The Federal Constitutional Court*

The Federal Constitutional Court is the supreme federal organ, having the same status as the *Bundestag*, the *Bundesrat*, the president and the federal government and free from any service supervision conducted by other departments. Furthermore, since the Federal Constitutional Court is a constitutional institution and in view of the special status of constitutional judges with regard to punishment, only the Federal Constitutional Court[396] and no other institution, including the president of the Federal Constitutional Court, can supervise the service of federal constitutional judges.[397]

#### *(b) Law Courts*

The federal law courts include the Federal Court of Justice and the Federal Patent Court. In the Federal Court of Justice, supervisory power over posts is exercised by the Federal Minister of Justice and the president of the Federal Court of Justice. The Federal Patent Court applies the regulations of the Federal Court of Justice. The service supervision in the law courts and superior courts in the various *Länder* is executed by the Minister of Justice, and the service supervision of judges in district courts is executed by the president of each court.[398]

#### *(c) Administrative Courts*

The president of an administrative court supervises the service of all the judges within it. The superior supervisory institution of the administrative courts is the president of the superior administrative court.[399]

---

396 Article 105 of BVerfGG

397 Günter Schmidt-Räntsch, Jürgen Schmidt-Räntsch, Deutsches Richtergesetz (DRiG), Kommentar, 6th edition, Munich 2008, p. 231

398 Günter Schmidt-Räntsch, Jürgen Schmidt-Räntsch, Deutsches Richtergesetz (DRiG), Kommentar, 6th edition, Munich 2008, p. 231

399 Paragraphs 1 and 2 of Article 38 of the Administrative Court Code (*Verwaltungsgerichtsordnung = VwGO*)

### (d) *Labour Courts*

In accordance with the provisions of Paragraph 1 of Article 15 of ArbGG, the supreme labour courts in the various *Länder*, together with the administrative organisations in the respective *Länder*, supervise the service of the labour court judges in the first instance. In addition, the Federal Minister of Labour, together with the Federal Minister of Justice, supervises the service of judges of the Federal Labour Court.[400] There are three instances in labour court trials. The institutions which have the power to supervise service are permitted to authorise the presidents or presiding judges (*Vorsitzende*) of the various labour courts to exercise the power to supervise service.[401]

### (e) *Social Courts*

The governments of the various *Länder* supervise the service of the social court judges of the respective *Länder*,[402] and the Federal Minister of Labour has the power to supervise the service of the Federal Social Court. The governments of the various *Länder* and the Federal Minister of Labour are permitted to authorise the presidents or presiding judges of the various courts to exercise the power to supervise service.[403]

### (f) *Finance Courts*

The power to supervise service in each finance court is exercised by its president.[404]

The ministers, presidents and other senior officials mentioned above cannot direct judges on how to adjudicate, but they can direct judges in the area of judicial or court administration and make decisions on personnel matters involving judges.[405]

The service supervision of judges in Germany is limited to that which does not violate the independence of judges, so any external disciplinary behaviour outside the core scope of adjudication is subject to the service supervision. Mat-

---

400 The first sentence of Paragraph 1 of Article 34 of ArbGG

401 Paragraph 2 of Article 15, Paragraph 2 of Article 34 and the second sentence of Paragraph 2 of Article 40 of ArbGG

402 Paragraph 2 of Article 9 and Paragraph 2 of Article 30 of SGG

403 Paragraph 2 of Article 9, Paragraph 2 of Article 30 and the second sentence of Paragraph 3 of Article 38 of SGG.

404 Article 31 of FGO

405 Günter Schmidt-Räntsch, Jürgen Schmidt-Räntsch, Deutsches Richtergesetz (DRiG), Kommentar, 6th edition, Munich 2008, Article 26, margin number 19

ters which are considered to be within the core scope of adjudication, aside from the content of Paragraph 2 of Article 26 of the German Judges Act, include sorting evidence and determining the value of evidence, the manner of compiling records and the content of these records, the relationship between the chief judge and assistant judges, reaching a consensus and the judges' opinion in procedures of disqualification.[406] Because the choice of words in a judgement belongs to the external scope, it can also be the subject of supervision. Moreover, external forms and rules of discipline concerning judges' behaviour in their posts,[407] such as the brief end-of-year report on the reasons for cases not yet completed, the wearing and cost of judges' robes and the training of apprentices who have passed the first state examination, which have nothing to do with the core scope of the independence of judges, can also be the subject of supervision.[408]

## (2) The Manner of Service Supervision

The relationships of judges form the basis of their rights and obligations, and the concept of supervising judges on the basis of their working relationships and loyalty derives from the idea of supervising the behaviour of judges and courts so as to ensure that judges execute their obligations completely and that the legal function of courts is fully realised. The service supervision is therefore divided into court supervision (i.e. supervision by authorities or *Behördenaufsicht*) and the supervision of judges. The manner of the service supervision of judges may include the following:

### *(a) Observation (Beobachtung)*

The supervisory institutions or senior officials shall regularly observe whether judges execute their duties in accordance with their obligations, often by examining their professional work, requesting files and materials and requesting reports. Observation may be initiated either by the supervisory institution or upon appeal by other parties.[409]

---

406 Günter Schmidt-Räntsch, Jürgen Schmidt-Räntsch, Deutsches Richtergesetz (DRiG), Kommentar, 6th edition, Munich 2008, p. 238

407 Judgement of 17th October 1977 by the German Federal Court of Justice (the service court of the federation), NJW 1978, p. 825

408 Günter Schmidt-Räntsch, Jürgen Schmidt-Räntsch, Deutsches Richtergesetz (DRiG), Kommentar, 6th edition, Munich 2008, p. 237

409 Karl-Heinz Dinslage, Richterliche Unabhängigkeit und Dienstaufsicht, DRiZ (1960), p. 201; Herbert Arndt, Die Dienstaufsicht über Richter in der Rechtsprechung des Bundesgerichtshofes, DRiZ (1978), p. 299

*(b) Correction (Berichtung)*

Correction is a response to observation. It has various specific connotations depending on the specific circumstances, and may be either a response in the mind of the supervisors, such as a mental impressions while examining a judge, or in an external form as views and expectations towards judges, such as noting the opinions of other courts, pushing them to pay attention, or making recommendations to judges on how to proceed in a case, even criticising judges, and so on.[410]

In accordance with Paragraph 2 of Article 26 of the German Judges Act, if judges improperly execute their official functions, the supervisory institutions or senior officials may decide to take the measures of cautioning (*vorbehalten*) them and exhorting (*ermahnen*) them to properly complete their duties without delay. When a caution is to be issued is judged objectively on the facts, hence this is a material measure and not a personal one, so the supervisors cannot make a subjective evaluation which goes against the judge's personal judgement and then criticise or blame the judge.[411] Exhorting is aimed at evoking a sense of responsibility[412] in the future behaviour of judges,[413] hence it cannot be directed to a specific case.[414]

However, where the supervisors consider that cautioning and exhorting are not sufficient in view of the extent of illegality or breach of duty in a judge's behaviour, they may also take the following more extreme measures, depending on the severity of the case:

(i) Disciplinary Action[415]

The supervisory institution or senior officials shall issue a reprimand (*Verweis*) against judges who commit dereliction of duty, in accordance with Paragraph 1 of Article 64 of the German Judges Act.

(ii) The Formal Procedure of Disciplinary Action[416]

Where a judge has acted illegally or in breach of duty and the circumstances are found to be serious following investigation, then the responsible organ at which

---

410 Karl-Heinz Dinslage, Richterliche Unabhängigkeit und Dienstaufsicht, DRiZ (1960), p. 201; Herbert Arndt, Die Dienstaufsicht über Richter in der Rechtsprechung des Bundesgerichtshofes, DRiZ (1978), p. 299

411 Decisions by the Federal Court of Justice in Civil Cases (*Entscheidungen des Bundesgerichtshofs in Zivilsachen = BGHZ*), Volume 46 (1966), 147, 150; BGHZ, Volume 67 (1976), 184, 188

412 BGHZ 51 (1969), 280, 286

413 BGH, DRiZ (1973), p. 280

414 BGHZ 51 (1969), 280, 286

415 See the content of (c) Disciplinary Measures below

416 See the content of (d) Disciplinary Procedure below

the accused judge works shall be required to apply to the service court to begin formal disciplinary proceedings. In formal disciplinary proceedings, there are seven types of disciplinary measures which may upon request be imposed on normal civil servants. In accordance with Paragraph 2 of Article 64 of the German Judges Act, however, the only measures which may be imposed on judges of the Federal Court of Justice are those of a caution, a fine or dismissal from office.

### (3) Service Courts

The German Judges Act stipulates that disciplinary measures against judges are to be handled by the service courts. Issues relating to the independence of judges, such as the nullity or revocation of appointments, dismissal from office, filling in for other judges, secondment or the assignment to part-time positions, are subject to the jurisdiction of the service courts. Generally speaking, service courts have jurisdiction of final judgement on the following cases:

(a) disciplinary cases, including disciplinary cases involving retired judges;
(b) cases of transfer due to judicial interests;
(c) cases involving judges appointed for life and judges appointed for a fixed term and concerning (i) nullity of an appointment; (ii) revocation of an appointment; (iii) dismissal from office; (iv) order to retire due to incompetence; (v) restricted assignment due to limits on working capability;
(d) appeal cases against the following measures: (i) punishment for altering the organisation of the court; (ii) secondment in accordance with Paragraph 3 of Article 37 of the German Judges Act; (iii) nullity of an appointment, revocation of an appointment, deposition or dismissal against a probationary judge or a judge on commission, or an order to retire due to incompetence; (iv) assignment to a part-time position; (v) supervisory measures taken in accordance with Paragraph 3 of Article 26 of the German Judges Act; (vi) restricting a judge's workload or stopping or suspending payment of their salary while they retain their office, in accordance with Articles 48a to 48c;
(e) appeal cases against judgements by *Land* service courts.[417]

The most particular of these is that the service courts shall decide on permission for supervisory measures (*Zulässigkeit von Maßnahmen der Dienstaufsicht*). The service courts are established separately at the federal level and in the *Länder*, wherein the Federal Service Court is established in the (ordinary) Federal Court of Justice and composed of one chief judge (who cannot be the president or vice-president of the court), two permanent associate judges and two

417 Article 79 of DRiG

non-permanent associate judges. The chief judge and the permanent associate judges are judges of the (ordinary) Federal Court of Justice. The non-permanent associate judges are the judges appointed for life at courts of the same branch of courts as the accused works at.[418]

The Federal Service Court has the jurisdiction of the first instance and the final instance for all judges at the federal level, and is the appeal court of the service courts in the various *Länder*. In order to maintain the independence of the service courts, their judges are not appointed by administrative organisations but rather by the presidium of the court at which the service court is established.[419]

In accordance with the jurisdiction of the service courts, the trial procedure can take one of three forms: disciplinary procedures, transfer procedures and examination procedures (including the jurisdiction of items (c) and (d) mentioned above). All cases in the various *Länder* which apply these three types of procedure can be appealed at the Federal Service Court, in order to maintain a consistency in judgements. However, disciplinary procedures can only be appealed in this way if the *Land* has passed provisions for its disciplinary procedures to be appealed at the federal court and if the appeal has been permitted by the state service court because it satisfies the requirements stipulated in Paragraph 1[420] and Paragraphs 3[421] of Article 81 of the German Judges Act.

## (4) The System of Appraisal of Judges

### *(a) The Character and Purpose of Appraisal*

In Germany, it is generally agreed that *dienstliche Beurteilung* is one of the supervisory measures for judges' service.[422] The German Judges Act does not make explicit provisions, but Article 46 stipulates that: "where this Act does not make any provisions to the contrary, the legal position for judges serving at the federal level corresponds to the provisions applied to federal civil servants, ex-

418 Paragraphs 1 and 2 of Article 61 of DRiG

419 Paragraph 3 of Article 77 of DRiG

420 These requirements are that (i) the case concerns a matter of principle, or (ii) the judgement deviates from a decision by the Federal Service Court and this discrepancy is the basis of the appeal.

421 These requirements are that (i) the court judging the case was not properly composed, or (ii) a judge was involved in the decision who was excluded from acting as a judge by law or was successfully dismissed due to concerns of prejudice, or (iii) grounds for the judgement were not provided.

422 Gerhard Bluhm, Die Beurteilung des Richters und seine Unabhängigkeit, DRiZ (1971), p. 330; BGH, DRiZ (1984), p. 365

cept for special regulations." It is known that in practice, the appraisal of federal judges are regulated by the provisions on appraisal in the Federal Civil Servants Act (*Bundesbeamtengesetz = BBG*). The provisions on the appraisal of judges in the judges laws of the *Länder* are generally the same as those of Article 46 of the German Judges Act. The aim of the appraisal of judges is to investigate their average capability, professional capability, specialities and personal tendencies so that when assigning routine work, materials are available showing what specialities judges have and what posts they may be particular suitable for and serving as a reference in regulating their posts over time.[423] The results of appraisal are also the facts which decide judges' promotions.[424]

### *(b) The Organs of Appraisal*

Appraisal, as one form of the service supervision, is usually carried out by the supervisors of judges' service (usually the president of the court and/or a chief judge authorised by the president). However, some scholars consider that if appraisal is carried out by the supervisors of service, this places control over the appointment and promotion of judges in their hands, which will lead to the assimilation of judges as they give up their own opinions in order to curry favour with those who hold sway over appraisal and yield, thus damaging the independence of judges. If those who hold sway over appraisal take part in the joint conferences on cases, then they also deliberate on the case and cannot objectively examine the behaviour of other judges. Moreover, those who hold sway over appraisal usually authorise the chief judge to examine members of the court and usually accept the conclusions of the appraisal by the chief judge as they are, hence the appraisal recorded by those who hold sway over appraisal is essentially based on hearsay. It has thus been suggested that appraisal should be carried out by an independent commission (*Gremium*), and some advocate adopting the Austrian system of examining judges, in which judges are examined by a personnel committee of the court composed of the president and vice-president, together with elected delegate judges. In practice at the moment, however, it is the view of the Federal Constitutional Court that appraisal as carried out by the supervisors of service is permitted by the various laws and that it is therefore not necessary for this to be changed.

423 Günter Schmidt-Räntsch, Jürgen Schmidt-Räntsch, Deutsches Richtergesetz (DRiG), Kommentar, 6th edition, Munich 2008, p. 242

424 Fritz Baur, Die Beurteilung des Richters und seine Unabhängigkeit, DRiZ (1973), p. 6

### (c) *The Content of Appraisal*

Appraisal of judges should be independent of individual cases and should consider aspects such as the average capabilities of judges, in particular their knowledge of law, grasp of the facts and their ability to control the proceedings. The content of appraisal shall include the behaviour of judges in the past but should not affect the behaviour of judges in the future, hence the content of appraisal must not affect judges either directly or indirectly through mental influence in terms of how they may adjudicate or make decisions in cases in the future. Within this framework, each *Land* can decide the details of the content of appraisal for itself. Taking the appraisal measures in Saxony as an example, this *Land* divides the content of appraisal into nine parts: professional knowledge, perceptivity, verbal skills of expression, written skills of expression, handling capacity, interpersonal skills, communications skills, implementation skills and mental strength. Each aspect is graded as 1 (very far above average), 2 (far above average), 3 (above average), 4 (average or better), 5 (average only), 6 (below average). The overall marks are then graded as: extremely eligible, very eligible, quite eligible, eligible, not overly eligible, ineligible.

### (d) *The Result of Appraisal*

Because the purpose of examining judges is to appraise their capabilities and work achievements in order to decide their future promotions, the appraisal of judges in Germany does not have legal implications or appraisal bonuses and does not affect examinee's rank or wealth. In this respect, although the appraisal procedure and the disciplinary procedure run parallel, they are entirely different.

## (5) The System of Discipline

Discipline is a punitive measure imposed on judges who violate their obligations, in order to preserve state discipline, and involves cautioning and exhorting judges to properly complete their duties before the fact, and punishing them after the fact and removing them from office if they are not capable of continuing to act as judges.[425] In accordance with Articles 46, 63 and 64 of the German Judges Act, discipline of judges of the German federation is subject to the provisions of the Federal Disciplinary Act (*Bundesdisziplinargesetz*) unless otherwise specified in the German Judges Act.

---

425 Günter Schmidt-Räntsch, Jürgen Schmidt-Räntsch, Deutsches Richtergesetz (DRiG), Kommentar, 6th edition, Munich 2008, p. 242

### *(a) Disciplinary Organs*

In Germany, before the German Judges Act was issued, disciplinary cases involving judges were generally handled by the disciplinary organ for civil servants, i.e. the Disciplinary Court, using the cautious and rigorous provisions in the Federal Disciplinary Act on the procedures for disciplining judges. However, the German Judges Act then entirely supplanted these special provisions for judges in the Federal Disciplinary Act on Civil Servants and established a Judges Service Court in charge of disciplinary matters involving judges. The Federal Judges Service Court, established especially for federal judges, is established in the ordinary Federal Court of Justice and composed of one chief judge, two permanent associate judges and two non-permanent associate judges. The chief judge and associate judges are all judges of the ordinary Federal Court of Justice, and the non-permanent associate judges are judges appointed for life at courts of the same branch of courts as the accused works at. But the president and vice-president who enjoy a measure of administrative power do not serve as judges at the Service Court, in order to avoid the possibility of them being both the plaintiff and judge in a disciplinary case. Only judges of the Federal Constitutional Court, because of their elevated position, are not subject to the provisions on discipline in the German Judges Act. The jurisdiction of the Service Court is very broad and is not limited to adjudicating disciplinary cases. It also adjudicates other disputes such as the transfer, appointment, removal, order to retire, secondment and assignment to part-time positions of judges and orders from superior organs which violate adjudicative independence. In addition, the German Judges Act also stipulates in detail the trial procedure of the Service Court. In accordance with the provisions of Paragraph 4 of Article 61 and Paragraph 1 of Article 63 of the German Judges Act, the Service Court shall be regarded as a civil court when trying disciplinary cases and subject to the provisions of the Federal Disciplinary Act.

### *(b) Grounds for Disciplinary Measures*

The German Judges Act does not make specific provisions on the grounds for disciplinary measures against judges. In accordance with Paragraph 1 of Article 63 of the German Judges Act, this aspect shall be subject to the provisions of the Federal Disciplinary Act. Article 2 of the Federal Disciplinary Act stipulates that the grounds for disciplinary measures against German federal civil servants are divided into two areas: breach of duty committed by civil servants during the period of their employment as civil servants; and behaviour regarded as breach of duty committed by retired civil servants after retirement.

It is thus clear that the starting point for disciplinary measures against judges and the object of disciplinary proceedings is breach of duty. Breach of duty means a deliberate or negligent breach of one's duty as a judge,[426] which encompasses both the objective aspect of dereliction of duty (*Pflichtwidrigkeit*) and the subjective aspect of responsibility (*Verantwortlichkeit*). The law does not attempt to enumerate which behaviours count as a breach duty, and it is only possible to make general provisions for the duties of judges, as also for other civil servants, and not specific provisions on each and every form of behaviour. A decision as to whether particular behaviour is a breach of duty must be made in accordance with the specific circumstances of a case.

(i) The Objective Aspect of Breach of Duty – Breach of Obligations

Judges who breach the duties detailed in the following shall be subject to disciplinary proceedings.

1. The Special Duties Stipulated in the German Judges Act

Articles 38 to Article 43 of the German Judges Act specify the special duties of judges which apply to all federal and *Land* judges.

- In accordance with Article 38, judges have a duty of oath, the content of which is different to that of ordinary civil servants and reads as follows: I hereby swear to execute the office of judge in accordance with the Basic Law of the Federal Republic of Germany and in accordance with the law, to pass judgements to the best of my knowledge and conscience, to treat all persons equally in the eyes of the law, and to serve only the causes of truth and justice, so help me God". However, judges who breach this duty are not subject to disciplinary procedures but are rather relieved of office in accordance with Section 1 of Paragraph 2 of Article 21 of the German Judges Act.
- In accordance with Article 39 of the German Judges Act, judges have an obligation to maintain their independence. They must comport themselves, both within and outside of their office and in political activities in such a way as to never threaten the confidence of the people in their independence.
- Article 40 of the German Judges Act stipulates that judges should not as a rule act as arbitrators, arbitral expert witnesses or mediators. In accordance with Article 41 of the German Judges Act, judges cannot act as legal expert witnesses or provide remunerated legal advice.
- In accordance with Article 42 of the German Judges Act, judges can only take on such concurrent positions in judicial administration or court adminis-

426 Günter Schmidt-Räntsch, Jürgen Schmidt-Räntsch, Deutsches Richtergesetz (DRiG), Kommentar, 6th edition, Munich 2008, p. 242

tration as do not breach the provisions of Article 4. Judges who apply to participate in such activities shall accept the responsibilities arising from them.

- Article 43 of the German Judges Act stipulates that judges have a duty of confidence with regard to the course of events during deliberations and voting, even after they have left office.

2. Duties Stipulated in the Federal Civil Servants Act

In accordance with Article 46 of the German Judges Act, the common judicial and extra-judicial duties stipulated in the Federal Civil Servants Act (Articles 60 to 75) shall also apply to federal judges, unless specified otherwise in the German Judges Act.

The common judicial and extra-judicial duties stipulated in Articles 60 to 75 of the Federal Civil Servants Act are as follows:

- A duty to serve the people as a whole: civil servants must serve the people as a whole and not a particular group.
- A duty to safeguard the Basic Law: civil servants must in their conduct safeguard the free democratic basic order enshrined in the Basic Law.
- A duty to moderate political activities: civil servants shall exercise self-restraint in their political activities, maintaining a level of moderation and restraint appropriate to their position in public life and the requirements of their official obligations.
- A duty of devotion to their duties: civil servants must be completely committed to their profession and execute their office selflessly and to the best of their ability.
- A duty to maintain the dignity of their office: civil servants must maintain the dignity of their office in their behaviour both within and outside of their office.
- A duty to superiors: civil servants must advise and support their superiors, enforce the orders of their superiors and follow the general guidelines of their superiors, except where particular legal provisions stipulate that they are not subject to directives but only to the law.
- A duty to defend the legality of their official actions: civil servants who have concerns about the legality of an official directive must immediately raise these concerns with their direct superior. If the directive is maintained and their concerns have not been allayed, civil servants must address their concerns to their superior or superiors at the next highest level. If these superiors confirm the directive, the civil servant must enforce the directive but is then exempt of any personal responsibility.

- A duty to take an oath of office: civil servants shall take an oath as they assume their office which reads as follows: “I hereby swear to safeguard the Basic Law and all laws which are valid in the Federal Republic of Germany and to fulfil my obligations of office faithfully, so help me God.”
- A duty of exemption from certain official acts: civil servants must be exempted from performing official acts which would relate to themselves or their relatives. The supreme supervisory authority or an authority appointed by it can ban civil servants from performing their official business if there are pressing official reasons for this.
- A duty of confidentiality: civil servants must maintain confidentiality on official matters which come into their knowledge in the course of their official work, even beyond the field of their employer and after they have left office, must not disclose such matters within or outside the court without permission. Heads of departments decide who shall provide information to the media.
- A duty not to accept a concurrent position.
- A duty not to accept rewards or gifts: civil servants must not demand or accept rewards or gifts relating to their office, during their tenure or after they have left office, unless permitted by the supreme supervisory authority or a subordinate supervisory authority appointed by it. Civil servants may only accept a title, an honorary decoration or a certificate of merit from a foreign sovereign or government with the permission of the Federal President.
- A duty to observe working hours: civil servants shall observe the general working hours of their position, although the average working time per week should not exceed 44 hours. Civil services may work beyond this limit within the framework of judicial emergencies, special circumstances or on-call duty, although even the extended working time per week should not exceed 54 hours.
- A duty not to neglect their work: civil servants cannot refuse to execute their duties personally without the permission of their superiors. If incapacitated by illness, they should submit a doctor’s certificate. Civil servants who refuse to perform their duties without permission cannot receive their salary for this period.
- A duty to accept limitation on choice of domicile: if required by official matters, the supervisory superiors of civil servants have the power to order them to locate their domicile within a certain distance of the location of their post or to move into accommodation provided by the employer. In case of emergency situations, superiors also have the power to order civil servants to remain in the vicinity of the location of their post outside working hours.

- A duty of appropriate uniform: the Federal President issues provisions on the working attire which civil servants should wear while performing their duties, and those who perform specific duties should wear specific working attire.
- A duty to avoid business conflicts: within five years of retiring and receiving a retirement pension or within three years of retiring at the age of 65, civil servants who acquired a part-time position during their last five years of service which relates to their post and affects the benefits of their post can apply to the second supreme supervisory authority for permission to continue executing the part-time position. If the second supreme supervisory authority considers the position to hamper the interests of the original post, it can refuse the application.

3. Actions by Retired or Former Judges which Constitute a Breach of Duty

In accordance with Article 46 of the Judges Act and Paragraph 2 of Article 77 of the Federal Civil Servants Act, retired judges or former judges receiving living allowance shall also be regarded as in breach of duty and subject to disciplinary measures for the following actions:

- actions contrary to the free democratic basic order enshrined in the Basic Law;
- participation in actions aimed at undermining the continued existence or security of the Federal Republic of Germany;
- breaches of the duty of confidentiality in accordance with Article 67 of the Federal Civil Servants Act or breaches of the duty of disclosure specified in Article 67 of the Federal Civil Servants Act or breaches of the duty not to accept rewards or gifts specified in Article 71 of the Federal Civil Servants Act;
- violations of the provisions of Paragraphs 1 or 2 of Article 46 or of Article 57 of the Federal Civil Servants Act for not accepting re-appointment to public institutions as civil servants for valid reasons, which refers to when retired civil servants who can accept a new post, and civil servants who have been retired due to incapacity and are now capable again, do not accept re-appointment by the federal government to serve in public institutions.

(ii) The Subjective Aspect of breach of duty – Responsibility

The subjective aspect of breach of duty is that judges are responsible for their behaviour, i.e. they have the mental capacity to be accountable (*Zurechnungsfähigkeit*) and thus a responsibility for deliberate or negligent breaches of duty.

1. Mental Incapacity (*Unzurechnungsfähigkeit*)

If judges are affected by a mental illness or become retarded or demented such that they cannot govern their own behaviour or make their own decisions or dealings, then they shall be considered to be mentally incapable.[427]

2. Intent

Intent includes direct intent and indirect intent, which means that judges do not wish to breach their obligations but through inaction allow their obligations to be breached. A negligent breach of obligations is also a breach of duty, whatever the degree of negligence; even slight negligence is a breach of duty.

Viewed from the subjective aspect, only judges who are not aware at the time that their behaviour is a breach of duty cannot be disciplined.

*(c) Disciplinary Measures*

Paragraph 2 of Article 64 of German Judges Act contains provisions specifically for judges of supreme federal courts, though the disciplinary measures in the Federal Disciplinary Act are not otherwise changed. In accordance with Paragraph 1 of Article 63 of the German Judges Act and Article 5 of the Federal Disciplinary Act, the types of disciplinary measure are as follows:

(i) Disciplinary Measures for Serving Judges

1. Reprimand (*Verweis*)[428]

A reprimand is an admonishment issued in particular by a senior official to a civil servant in writing. Critical comments, such as a correction, warning, denouncement or similar comment, which is not identified as a reprimand does not constitute a disciplinary measure.

2. Fine (*Geldbuße*)[429]

The amount of a fine should not exceed the civil servant's monthly salary. If the disciplined party does not receive a salary or trainee's grant, the fine should not exceed € 500.

3. Reduction in Salary (*Kürzung der Dienstbezüge*)[430]

The amount of the reduction in salary should not exceed one fifth of the original salary, and the duration of the reduced salary should not exceed three years. The

427 Article 20 of the German Penal Code (*Strafgesetzbuch = StGB*); Articles 104 and 105 of the German Civil Code (*Bürgerliches Gesetzbuch = BGB*)

428 Article 6 of the Federal Disciplinary Act (*Bundesdisziplinargesetz = BDG*)

429 Article 7 of BDG

430 Article 8 of BDG

total amount of the reduction in pension for retired judges is applied to the average monthly pension for the six months prior to the disciplinary procedure. Judges cannot be promoted for the duration of the reduced salary from the date on which the disciplinary judgement can no longer be appealed.

4. Demotion to a Post with a Lower Final Basic Salary (*Zurückstufung*)[431]

From the time the judgement of demotion can no longer be appealed, the disciplined party loses all their rights derived from the previous position and draws the salary derived from the new position following demotion. Additionally, the disciplined party cannot be promoted for at least five years from the time the judgement of demotion can no longer be appealed.

5. Dismissal from the Civil Service (*Entfernung aus dem Beamtenverhältnis*)[432]

Once dismissed from office, the disciplined party can no longer claim their salary or maintenance grant and lose the right to use their official title or any titles or privileges conferred by their office or to wear their official attire. Judges who are dismissed from office simultaneously forfeit their pension rights.

(ii) Disciplinary Measures for Retired Judges

1. Reduction in Pension[433]

The reduction in pension should not exceed one fifth of the original pension, and the duration of the reduced pension should not exceed three years.

2. Forfeit of Pension[434]

Judges who forfeit their pension through a disciplinary measure are not only deprived of their pension but also lose their right to claim maintenance, including provision for dependants, and the right to use their official title or any titles or privileges conferred by their office or to wear their official attire. Retired judges (including those who are retired because of dismissal from office) can only be disciplined with a reduction in pension or forfeit of pension.

The seven disciplinary measures mentioned above can only be employed when Federal Disciplinary Prosecutors prosecute federal judges through the Service Court of the Federal Court of Justice by way of formal disciplinary proceedings. In accordance with the Federal Disciplinary Act, the supervisory authorities or senior officials of civil servants can impose the disciplinary measures of reprimand, fine, reduction in salary and reduction in pension. The supreme

431 Article 9 of BDG

432 Article 10 of BDG

433 Article 11 of BDG

434 Article 12 of BDG

supervisory authority can reduce salaries up to the highest limit; the senior officials directly under the supreme supervisory authority can only reduce salaries by up to one fifth of the original salary and only for a period of up to two years.[435] In the case of retired civil servants, the supreme supervisory authority can decide to reduce their pension,[436] but in accordance with Paragraph 1 of Article 64 of the German Judges Act, the supervisory departments of judges' service and senior officials can only reprimand judges, and other disciplinary measures have be imposed through formal disciplinary proceedings.

(iii) Disciplinary Measures for Judges of the Supreme Federal Courts

Paragraph 2 of Article 64 of the German Judges Act limits the disciplinary measures which can be imposed on judges of the supreme courts in the various *Länder*, to the effect that the disciplinary measures which can be imposed on judges of the supreme courts in the various *Länder* are limited to only three of the aforementioned forms, namely reprimand, fine and dismissal from office, and must be imposed by the service courts of the Federal Court of Justice by way of formal disciplinary proceedings.

(iv) Disciplinary Measures for Judges of Constitutional Courts

If the judges of Constitutional Courts breach their obligations or behave improperly (including behaviour which would destroy their reputation) and are sentenced to more than six months imprisonment by a court, or are no longer suitable to function as a judge because of a serious breach of obligation, then all the judges of the Federal Constitutional Court may form a collegial panel of their own volition and decide by a two-thirds majority to request that the president remove the disciplined party from office (Article 105 of the Federal Constitutional Court Act (*Bundesverfassungsgerichtsgesetz = BVerfGG*)).

(v) Disciplinary Measures for Probationary Judges and Judges on Commission

In accordance with Paragraph 3 of Article 5 of the Federal Disciplinary Act, probationary judges only can be disciplined with a reprimand or fine. Additionally, in accordance with Paragraph 3 of Article 22 and Article 23, if breaches of duty by probationary judges or judges on commission are to be disciplined, they shall be removed from office, without formal disciplinary proceedings.

435 Paragraph 3 of Article 33 of BDG

436 Paragraph 4 of Article 33 and Article 84 of BDG

### (d) *Disciplinary Procedure*[437]

The disciplinary procedure for federal judges shall apply the provisions of the Federal Disciplinary Act as well as the special provisions of the German Judges Act (such as Paragraphs 2 and 3 of Article 63 of the German Judges Act). The procedure can be divided into two stages, namely the investigation before the procedure and then the formal disciplinary procedure. This shall be discussed separately below.

#### (i) The Investigation before the Procedure

The disciplinary procedure begins with an investigation. When senior officials are informed that judges are suspected of committing a breach of duty, they shall investigate in order to clarify the facts. The investigation is the obligation of the senior official. Senior officials shall investigate all the circumstances which are favourable or unfavourable to the judge to be disciplined[438] and give the judge in question the chance to voice their opinions on the situation, so far as this does not harm the aim of the investigation.[439] However, the judge to be disciplined must be notified of the result of the investigation and has the right to request further investigation.[440]

If the investigation reveals that there was no breach of duty, or if the senior officials consider it inappropriate to discipline the judge, the senior officials shall terminate the procedure at once and notify the judge to be disciplined and the federal disciplinary prosecutors accordingly. If there has been a breach of duty but the circumstances are very mild, the senior officials may take careful stock of the overall conduct of the judge and decide to take disciplinary action in writing within the limits of their functions and powers, with reasons attached, and deliver this to the judge to be disciplined and notify the federal disciplinary prosecutors accordingly. If there has been a breach of duty and the circumstances are serious, then the senior officials have no power to take action, and the supreme supervisory authority of the judge to be disciplined shall apply to the Federal Service Court to initiate a formal disciplinary procedure.[441]

#### (ii) The Formal Disciplinary Procedure

As mentioned above, the supreme supervisory authority of the judge to be disciplined applies to the Service Court having jurisdiction to initiate the formal dis-

437 On the Supervision of Judges and Adjudicative Independence, pp. 28 ff

438 Paragraph 1 of Article 21 of BDG

439 Paragraph 1 of Article 20 of BDG

440 Article 30 of BDG

441 Article 31 of BDG; Günter Schmidt-Räntsch, Jürgen Schmidt-Räntsch, Deutsches Richtergesetz (DRiG), Kommentar, 6th edition, Munich 2008, p. 677

ciplinary procedure for federal judges. However, judges can also voluntarily request that a formal disciplinary procedure be initiated, in order to exonerate themselves of the suspicion of a breach of duty.[442]

The formal disciplinary procedure can be divided into the procedure of investigation and the trial procedure at the Service Court. However, if the facts have been clarified, the procedure of investigation can be omitted with the permission of the federal public prosecutor. Conversely, the departments which can initiate the formal disciplinary procedure appoint one individual, either at the beginning of the formal disciplinary procedure or during the formal disciplinary procedure, who has the official capacity of a judge or satisfies the requirements of the first sentence of Article 110 of the German Judges Act, to carry out the investigation. This investigator shall investigate independently, exempt of orders, with the same status as the investigating judges in criminal litigation procedures. Once the facts have been investigated and clarified, and the aims of the investigation have been reached, the investigator shall submit a concluding report and all relevant documents to the department which initiated the formal disciplinary procedure. The federal public prosecutor shall also be notified of this report, and the department which initiated the formal disciplinary procedure shall decide whether to terminate the procedure or continue and have it tried at the Service Court.

Decisions by the service courts can take one of the following three forms:

- a decision to impose disciplinary measures;
- a decision not to impose disciplinary measures because a breach of duty cannot be proven;
- a decision to terminate the disciplinary procedure if the requirements of Paragraphs 1 and 3 of Article 22 of the Federal Disciplinary Act are fulfilled.

Decisions by the service courts are final decisions, but it is possible to apply for a retrial if the legal conditions for this are met.

Additionally, in the formal disciplinary procedure, the supreme department in charge of the judge to be disciplined may apply to the Federal Service Court for a decision to suspend the judge from duty and temporarily stop their pay; or if the grounds for imposing disciplinary measures are removed, the supreme department in charge of the judge to be disciplined may apply to the Federal Service Court for a decision to revoke the aforementioned disciplinary measures. Once the Service Court has made a decision, it delivers the decision in question to the judge to be disciplined and to the supreme department in charge of the judge.

442 Paragraph 1 of Article 18 of BDG; Paragraph 3 of Article 26 of DRiG

## (6) The System of Impeachment

The constitutional basis for the system of impeachment for German judges is Article 98 of the Basic Law, in which Paragraph 2 stipulates that if a federal judge infringes the principles of the Basic Law or the constitutional order of a *Land* in his or her official capacity or unofficially, the Federal Constitutional Court, upon application by the *Bundestag*, may by a two-thirds majority order that the judge be transferred or retired. In the case of an intentional infringement, it may order the judge to be dismissed. Paragraph 5 of this article also stipulates that the *Länder* may enact provisions regarding *Land* judges which correspond to those of Paragraph (2) of Article 98 of the Basic Law, wherein existing *Land* constitutional law shall not be affected and the decision in cases of judicial impeachment shall rest with the Federal Constitutional Court. Therefore, all powers to try judges for impeachment are held by the Federal Constitutional Court. Paragraph 9 of Article 13 of the Federal Constitutional Court Act of 1951 clearly stipulates that the Federal Constitutional Court has jurisdiction over the procedure for impeaching federal and *Land* judges, and Articles 58 to 62 of the Federal Constitutional Court Act stipulate detailed provisions for the trial procedure.[443] However, since the Basic Law was promulgated, this system of impeachment for judges has never actually been employed.[444]

### *(a) The Organs of Impeachment*

#### (i) The Organs of Proposal

In accordance with the provisions of Paragraph 2 of Article 98 of the Basic Law, the organ of proposal for the impeachment of federal judges is the *Bundestag*.

The organ of proposal for the impeachment of judges in the various *Länder* depends on what is stipulated in the respective *Land* constitution, which may or may not be similar to the Basic Law. For example, the *Land* constitutions of both Saxony-Anhalt and North Rhine-Westphalia stipulate that the organ of proposal for the impeachment of their *Land* judges is the *Land* parliament,[445] but the constitution of Berlin does not make any provisions on this matter.

Thus, the organs of proposal for the impeachment of judges may be different depending on the status of judges. The organ of proposal for the impeachment of

443 Konrad Hesse, Grundzüge des Verfassungsrechts der Bundesrepublik Deutschland, 15th edition, Heidelberg 1985, margin number 689, pp. 256 ff

444 Karl-Heinz Seifert, Dieter Hömig (ed.), Grundgesetz für die Bundesrepublik Deutschland, Kommentar, 8th edition, Nomos, Baden-Baden 2007, Article 98, margin number 2, p. 464

445 Article 3 of the Constitution of North Rhine-Westphalia; Article 84 of the Constitution of Saxony-Anhalt

federal judges is the *Bundestag*, but the organ of proposal for the impeachment of *Land* judges is (often) the respective *Land* parliament.

(ii) The Organs of Impeachment Trials

In accordance with the provisions of Paragraph 5 of Article 98 of the Basic Law, the organ of impeachment trials, whether of federal judges or *Land* judges, is the Federal Constitutional Court.

*(b) The Grounds for Impeachment*

Paragraph 2 of Article 98 of the Basic Law specifies the grounds for impeaching judges, which include the following two acts as committed by a judge either in his or her official capacity or unofficially, and either deliberately or negligently as stipulated in the German Judges Act:

- infringing the principles of the Basic Law;
- infringing the constitutional order of a *Land*.

There is no substantive difference here between infringing the principles of the Basic Law and infringing the constitutional order of a *Land*, both of which mean breaching either the Basic Law or basic provisions of the various *Land* constitutions. Because the system of impeachment places particular emphasis on political responsibility, judges who breach the constitutional order do not necessarily have to meet the conditions for a breach of the official rules of conduct, hence an act which infringes the constitutional order but unofficially is still grounds for impeachment.

*(c) The Punishment of Impeachment*

In accordance with the provisions of Paragraph 2 of Article 98 of the Basic Law, the Federal Constitutional Court shall distinguish between deliberate and negligent breaches when trying impeachment cases involving judges, and may choose from sentences including dismissal from office (*Entlassung*), transfer to another post (*in ein anderes Amt versetzen*) and an order to retire (*in den Ruhestand versetzen*), depending on the circumstances of the case. If neither of the two aforementioned acts obtains, a decision that the constitutional order has not been infringed should be passed.

If judges are found to have infringed the principles of the Basic Law or constitutional order of a *Land* "deliberately", they can – in addition to the possibility of being transferred to another post or retired – also be sentenced to be removed from office. If judges are found to have infringed the principles of the Basic Law or constitutional order of a *Land*, not deliberately but rather only negligently, then they can only be transferred to another post or retired and not removed from office.

### *(d) The Procedure of the Impeachment Trial*

#### (i) The Procedure of Proposal

In accordance with Article 98 of the Basic Law, a motion for impeachment proposed by the *Bundestag* must be agreed by more than two thirds of its members. Paragraph 1 of Article 58 of the Federal Constitutional Court Act stipulates that the procedure for impeaching judges also applies the provisions in Articles 49 to 55 relating to impeaching the Federal President, except for the provisions in Article 50 on the time limit for proposing such a motion, hence it is not necessary to propose a motion for impeachment of a judge to the Federal Constitutional Court within three months of the judge in question infringing the principles of the Basic Law or the constitutional order of a *Land.* However, in accordance with Paragraph 3 of Article 58 of the Federal Constitutional Court Act, impeachment shall no longer be permissible if two years have expired since the irreversible completion of the judicial proceedings in which the Federal judge is claimed to have committed the infringement, except that – in accordance with Paragraph 2 of Article 58 of the Federal Constitutional Court Act – if a federal judge is accused of an infringement in his official capacity, the *Bundestag* shall not decide until the irreversible completion of the judicial proceedings or, if formal disciplinary proceedings have previously been instituted for the same infringement, until such proceedings have been commenced, and impeachment shall no longer be permissible if six months have expired since the irreversible completion of the judicial proceedings in which the federal judge is claimed to have committed the infringement.

In accordance with the provisions of Article 49 of the Federal Constitutional Court Act, the proposal shall be in the form of a bill and shall be submitted to the Federal Constitutional Court. The bill must specify the act or omission (*Unterlassung*) for which impeachment is being proposed, the evidence and the relevant provisions of the Constitution or law which are claimed to have been infringed.

#### (ii) The Trial Procedure

Once the *Bundestag* has proposed a motion for the impeachment of a judge, it shall commission a delegate to appear before the Federal Constitutional Court once formal trial proceedings have been opened.[446] The Federal Constitutional Court shall pass sentence in the form of one of the three disciplinary measures

446 Paragraph 4 of Article 58 of BVerfGG

stipulated in Article 98 of the Basic Law or shall declare the judge in question to not have infringed the Constitution or other laws. If the Federal Constitutional Court passes a sentence of removal from office, the impeached judge shall lose his or her post immediately after the sentence has been announced. If the Federal Constitutional Court passes a sentence of retirement, the authority which exercises jurisdiction over the removal of federal judges shall take charge of executing this sentence. The sentence shall be delivered to the Federal President, the *Bundestag* and the Federal Government, with the grounds for the decision attached. The trial procedure for *Land* judges is the same as that for federal judges in accordance with the provisions of Article 62 of the Federal Constitutional Court Act.

*(e) Relief Measures*

Strictly speaking, the German system of impeachment is different from the disciplinary system for civil servants; it is a responsibility of great political significance which is granted to special public servants such as the President and judges, and is essentially a special system designed within the Constitution. Therefore, if it is confirmed by the sentence of the Federal Constitutional Court in an impeachment trial that the Federal President has infringed the Basic Law or other federal laws deliberately, the Federal President will immediately lose his or her position as president so as to take the entire political responsibility and shall not have access to any relief measures. The impeachment of judges, by contrast, bears some aspects of a criminal judgement, such that for example in accordance with the provisions of Article 61 of the Federal Constitutional Court Act, if some new evidence comes to light after sentence has been passed and this evidence is sufficient to justify a change in the original sentence, then in order to ensure that it benefits the impeached judge, the original sentence can be subjected to a retrial as a relief measure.

*(f) The Relationship Between Crime and Impeachment and Between Discipline and Impeachment*

The impeachment of judges and criminal prosecution have a close relationship with the discipline of judges. Paragraph 2 of Article 58 and Article 60 of the Federal Constitutional Court Act specify the relationship between the two:

- If a judge is being prosecuted under criminal law, for an act which also infringed the Basic Law or the constitutional order of a *Land*, the impeachment procedure cannot be proposed until the criminal proceedings have been concluded. This is known as the "principle of crime before impeachment".

- If a judge is being tried for impeachment by the Federal Constitutional Court, a disciplinary procedure based on the same facts must be suspended. If the Federal Constitutional Court sentences the judge to removal from office, transfer to another post or orders him or her into retirement, other procedures should not be pending, although the disciplinary procedure can be continued if the Federal Constitutional Court finds the judge innocent. This is known as the "principle of impeachment before discipline".

### (7) Summary

Article 92 of the Basic Law stipulates that judicial power is vested in the judges. In addition, Article 97 of the Basic Law provides for the independence of judges and stipulates that judges shall be subject only to the law. This does not however deny that judges must also be supervised, the same as any other public servants. Hence, Article 26 of the German Judges Act clearly affirms that judges are to be officially supervised. The service supervision is aimed at exhorting judges to execute their duties legally and without delay and at preventing judges from executing their duties illegally and is limited to maintaining the independence of judges. The supervision of judges by supervisors includes observation and correction. Observation is mainly appraisal of the behaviour of judges in office. The promotion and removal or retention of judges may be influenced by the result of appraisal. Correction is mainly an investigation by supervisors of breaches of duty by judges within and outside of their office, and different there are different ways of handling these depending on the circumstances. If, after investigation, the circumstances are considered to be mild, supervisors may decide to impose measures such as cautioning and/or exhorting, or also disciplinary measures such that a reprimand and/or fine. If the circumstances are considered to be serious, supervisors may apply to the Service Court to initiate a formal disciplinary procedure aimed at a sentence of punishment. However, if a judge has seriously infringed the principles of the Basic Law or the constitutional order of a *Land*, which cannot suitably be punished according to the principles governing ordinary acts of office, then supervisors may also propose a motion for impeachment to the Federal Constitutional Court in order to remove the judge from office. If judges feel that a particular supervisory measure is damaging to their independence, they may apply to the Service Court for a decision on the legality of the measure. If the measure is not an administrative punishment in the sense of the Administrative Court Act, then the court may be able to stop this supervisory measure which is damaging to the independence of judges.

German measures for judicial supervision have meaning in principle, since the final say in conflicts between judges and supervisors of service lies with the courts. In this way, the independence of judges can be safeguarded to the highest degree.

## Section III Comparison

Because there are no clear provisions on safeguarding the independence of judges in the Chinese Constitution, judicial supervision in China does not have the specific limits which obtain in Germany and ensure that the independence of judges cannot be infringed. German laws prescribe strict limits on supervisors and their supervisory measures and establish an independent authority, the Service Court, which examines whether particular supervisory measures are proper, in order to safeguard the independence of judges. In China, by contrast, there are no such considerations at all, hence there is no independence of judges at all because of the various confused and unsystematic provisions, especially those which mean that the power to examine and discipline judges is entirely vested in the court presidents. The right to recall court presidents held by the People's Congress and its Standing Committee still wallows at the base of the system because the grounds for investigation are unclear and the procedures vague, as a result of which the service supervision by the president has practically no function. Some supervisory measures which are not stipulated in law and have no legal effect are applied to the supervision of judges in practice, such as the supervision by the disciplinary department of the Party and the supervision by the news media. It is nearly impossible for judges in China to be independent in view of these numerous and unrestricted forms of supervision. There is therefore an urgent need to change the current situation of numerous and unrestricted forms of judicial supervision, learn from the German laws which strictly limit supervisors and supervisory authorities and establish special (and likewise restricted) disciplinary authorities, so as to safeguard the independence of judges.

### (1) The System of Appraisal

Compared to their systems of discipline and impeachment, China and Germany have the most similarities in their system of appraisal; for example, the appraisal of judges in both countries is carried out in courts, and the powers of appraisal are held by court presidents and presiding judges authorised by said presidents. The results of appraisal influence individual promotion, although in Germany, the results of appraisal do not directly influence judges' salaries or rewards, and in China, judges get different rewards or even fines depending on the results.

Because German laws clearly limit the service supervision such that it cannot damage the independence of judges, it is the case that although appraisal in both countries includes evaluating the official character of trials and individual capabilities, German law emphasises that appraisal can only evaluate the past behaviour of judges and does not affect the future behaviour of judges. Supervisors cannot directly or indirectly control judges by psychological means, nor can they govern how judges will adjudicate or make decisions in the future. In China, by contrast, appraisal more or less includes such enforcement, such as for example the requirement for a certain rate of cases to be concluded by judges at the Second Intermediate People's Court of Beijing.

## (2) The Disciplinary System

### *(a) Legal Provisions*

The German Judges Act and the Federal Disciplinary Act in Germany provide very comprehensive stipulations on the grounds for disciplinary measures, the organs of discipline, the measures and procedures of discipline and the relief measures for judges, whereas in China, there is no dedicated disciplinary law and the provisions for disciplining judges appear sporadically in various related laws and measures by the Supreme People's Court, including the Judges Law of the PRC, the Methods of the People's Courts on Adjudicative Discipline and Punishment, the Methods of the People's Courts on the Accountability of Judges for Illegal Adjudication, the Interim Provisions of the People's Courts on Supervision, the Interim Measures of the People's Courts on Investigating and Punishing Activities which Violate the Law and the Rules of Discipline of the Supervision Department, the Criminal Law of the People's Republic of China and the Code of Judicial Ethics for Judges. This is very disordered and unsystematic.

### *(b) Organs of Discipline*

The Chinese organs of discipline are the supervisory departments established in courts. The supervisors and judges work in the same court, so they unavoidably have a very close relationship. Such relationships and acquaintances are likely to prevent supervisors from imposing disciplinary measures fairly and justly on judges as their close colleagues. Hence in practice, the provisions on the professional discipline of judges and disciplinary measures are not enforced effectively, and behaviour which breaches the rules of discipline for judges (such as meeting interested parties without permission) is not properly punished, because the disciplinary authorities are largely established in the same courts and in accordance with the Interim Measures of the People's Courts on Investigating and Punishing Activities which Violate the Law and the Rules of Discipline of the Supervision Department, punishments above demotion have to be approved by the court president, hence the presidents in fact have complete control over the power to discipline judges in the court as a whole, which obviously makes judges administratively more dependent on the presidents and damages the independence of judges. The fact that court presidents have sole control of such powers, even in major issues, also causes discipline to be improperly enforced. In this respect, the German disciplinary system whereby the special Service Courts try disciplinary cases is more independent and just.

### (c) Subjects of Disciplinary Measures

The range of those subject to disciplinary measures in Germany is limited to serving judges and retired judges. The organs of discipline have no powers to investigate or discipline other persons employed by the courts, such as judges' assistants, clerks of the court, court registrars, executors, bailiffs and so on. By contrast, the range of those subject to the jurisdiction of the disciplinary departments of Chinese courts includes not only judges but also clerks of courts, executors, bailiffs, administrative management staff, the staff of subordinate public works and so on.

### (d) The Grounds for Discipline

The grounds for disciplining judges in Germany are breaches of duty, either within of outside their office and either deliberate or negligent, whereas in China, there are no general provisions on the grounds for disciplinary measures, but rather specific provisions including criminal behaviour by judges involving the function of their office and behaviour by judges which breaches professional ethics.

### (e) The Disciplinary Measures

In accordance with the provisions of the German Judges Act, the disciplinary measures imposed by supervisors can only include a reprimand, a fine or a reduction in salary; other, more severe measures can only be imposed by the Service Court. In China, by contrast, all disciplinary measures are imposed by the supervisory departments of the courts where the judges work; even the most severe disciplinary measures only require the approval of the president of the court. This system does not in any way consider the wellbeing of judges and means that judges have no independence under the supervision of the supervisory departments.

### (3) The System of Impeachment

In Germany, the system of discipline is stipulated by administrative law and the system of impeachment is stipulated by the constitution. Article 98 of the Basic Law explicitly establishes a system of constitutional obligations required of judges, whereas in China, there is still no system of constitutional obligations for judges to be subject to. The existing supervisory system whereby the People's Congress and its Standing Committee recall, dismiss or remove judges from office is the same as the disciplinary system, both of which investigate ordinary illegal acts by judges and not the violation of obligations under the Constitution. They are merely tried by different authorities and apply different measures.

Generally speaking, impeachment is established in order for the institutions of public authority to investigate violations of legal obligations by administrative senior officers, advanced administrative staff or individuals who try to independently exert the authority of their office. In China, the People's Congress and its Standing Committee are the institutions of public opinion; they are supposed to supervise judges by means of impeachment and investigate violations of judges' constitutional obligations, but through the disciplinary system. However, the two systems are confused in China, leading to judges being investigated by multiple authorities for breaches of duty but not being investigated by anyone for unconstitutional acts.

### (4) Other aspects

Except for the system of impeachment and the system of appraisal and discipline, German judges are not officially supervised by any other authorities, whereas in China, the institutions of the Party also have the power to investigate judges directly; even the news media can in practice influence the sentences imposed on judges through comment and public agitation. This flood of unrestricted supervision means that judges cannot be independent. Such supervision is also impossible to implement in a just and impartial manner.

From the above comparison, it may be seen that the system of judicial supervision in China has many aspects which are still inappropriate. The true independence of judges can only be expected once these aspects have been improved one by one.

Firstly, it is necessary to unify the various relevant provisions in law. It would be best to incorporate and so unify the various provisions on the system of judicial supervision into the Judges Law of the PRC, to avoid confusion due to the current sporadic nature of the various laws and regulations.

Secondly, it is necessary to include provisions in the Judges Law of the PRC on the organs of judicial supervision, the measures of supervision and corresponding limits on supervision, such that no bodies other than the organs of judicial supervision have direct or indirect power to investigate violations of judges' obligations.

Thirdly, it is necessary to distinguish between disciplinary measures and impeachment, to limit the supervisory measures of the People's Congress and its Standing Committee to investigating violations of judges' constitutional obligations, and ensuring that other breaches of duty are investigated by the disciplinary authorities.

Fourthly, it is necessary to establish special disciplinary authorities in the same vein as the Service Courts in Germany and ensure that all official disputes involving judges are tried by the disciplinary authority, in order to attain the ideal scenario whereby judges are in particular protected by the Constitution.

Lastly, it is necessary to establish a disciplinary law as soon as possible which explicitly identifies the various grounds for disciplinary measures and the measures themselves and establishes a specific disciplinary procedure.

# (B) Independence from the Legislature

## Chapter III The Independence of Judges from the Legislature

It has been seen from the discussion in the first chapter of this dissertation relating to the substantive independence of judges that the tense relationship between the substantive independence of judges and the legislative powers stems from the binding character of the law, which is to say judges shall be controlled by the law. Upon careful observation, it can be seen that nowadays, legislators with comprehensive functions have limited all aspects of life in society by positive legislation. Thus, the standards adopted by the legislature are no longer entirely orientated according to judicial principles but rather serve for social planning.[447] This means that judges who apply these standards become policy judges in the sense of product-active social structuring. Because the framework for such social structuring is provided by the law, judges will be biased in their adjudication.[448] Legislators cannot only change the legal framework of the business of

447 See also Allgemeine Staatslehre, p. 326. Accordingly, the content of judicial independence has to include the functions of examination and balance, because they play a role in the social integration of complex crowds. See Arndt, DRiZ 1972, 41 (42)

448 See Friedrich Heydte, Richterfunktion und "Richtergesetz", in: Forschungen und Berichte aus dem öffentlichen Recht, Gedächtnisschrift für Walter Jellinek, edited by Otto Bachof, Martin Drath, Otto Gönnenwein and Ernst Walz, Munich 1955, p. 493

the courts by amending laws at any time, but can also revise the laws and regulations on the organisation of the courts and the status of judges in a way which would influence justice, such as altering jurisdictions and/or amending the laws and regulations on how judges are appointed, their salary and the grounds and procedures for their dismissal.[449] In Germany, the bias caused by the application of the law by judges is regarded as indirectly damaging the principles of "prohibiting influence" enshrined in Paragraph 1 of Article 97 of the Basic Law. The influence of the legislature on the judiciary may be regarded as a legal means by which state powers check and balance each other,[450] and not all changes to the judicial system damage the independence of judges. The judicial system also has to constantly adjust to social change in order to conform to the requirements of social development. On this occasion, the principle of the independence of judges has to give way to the benefits of democratic supervision.[451] Because judges do not work outside the bounds of social development under the basic principle of loyalty to the state and the constitution, they cannot obstruct the essential development of the state and society by positively applying effective laws.[452]

If political forces try to use their powers under the system of judicial supervision to get the judiciary to follow their lead, then the independence of judges will be threatened. Countries around the world therefore generally limit judicial supervision to the constitution.[453] As an important means of balancing state

---

449 In view of its significance for judicial independence, these measures belong to the legislature in Germany, although the legislature may delegate these powers to administrative organisations for execution. See BVerfGE Volume 2, 307 (316, 326); Detterbeck, in: Sachs, Michael, Grundgesetz, Kommentar, 5th edition, Munich 2009, Article 97, margin number 38

450 Because parliament can only amend laws with the approval of a majority, all of these decisions are legalised by democratic means.

451 See Hilke Thiedemann, Judicial Independence – Eine rechtsvergleichende Untersuchung der Sicherung unabhängiger Rechtsprechung in Südafrika und Deutschland, Baden-Baden 2007, p. 238

452 See Lars Immisch, Der sozialistische Richter in der DDR und seine Unabhängigkeit, Frankfurt on the Main 1997, p. 20

453 However, Article 126 of the Chinese Constitution merely stipulates that the People's Courts exercise judicial power independently, in accordance with the provisions of the law, and are not subject to interference by any administrative organ, public organisation or individual, but does not refer to interference from the legislature. People's Congress, as a legislative body, is also responsible for the organisation court supervision; courts must report on their work to the People's Congress and may be interrogated by it, see Articles 62, 67 and 71 of the Chinese Constitution.

powers, the judiciary can review constitutionality and under certain circumstances declare laws and regulations to be null and void.

## Section I Formal and Informal Influence of the Legislature

Legislators provide the conditions under which courts decide legal disputes; thus, judges have to judge independently within this framework. On the one hand, out of a need to ensure the independence of judges, such legislative methods of the legislature cannot act directly on certain proceedings, such as an individual law or a specific law. On the other hand, legislators can guide some specific types of cases to be decided by other means, by amending legislation in a general and abstract way. In this regard, the principle of judicial independence also represents the separation of the law and politics. Although judges are generally bound by the law in accordance with the constitution, and enjoy the independence to interpret the law in specific cases, general abstract laws will equally be able to approximately specify the judgement in an individual case.[454] There are many deciding factors in the judgement of a case, such as the degree of specification in laws and regulations, new and old legal norms and varying degrees of amendment or revision to laws and regulations. The laws approved by legislators exist once they come into effect, i.e. political organs change the existing conditions of laws only by revoking or amending them, but as soon as laws have come into effect, they are applied and interpreted by judges, and political organs are no longer able to influence them.[455]

If the application of laws and regulations develops contrary to the wishes of the policy makers, the political organs will have to amend them for the future, but cannot affect the past.[456] In this respect, external political forces cannot influence the application of the law in individual cases. Legislators are only permitted to supervise the judiciary democratically by way of altering the legal framework for the future.[457] Amending laws whenever judicial practice is disas-

454 Dieter Grimm, Die Verfassung und die Politik: Einsprüche in Störfällen, Munich 2001, p. 26

455 Dieter Grimm, Die Verfassung und die Politik: Einsprüche in Störfällen, Munich 2001, p. 23. The interpretation of laws may additionally be influenced by academic circles and the zeitgeist.

456 This is the principle that laws do not have retroactive force, see Dieter Grimm, Die Verfassung und die Politik: Einsprüche in Störfällen, Munich 2001, p. 26

457 See Gertrude Lübbe-Wolf, Unabhängige Richter im Interesse der Demokratie – Mut zu unbequemen Entscheidungen, in: Neue Zürcher Zeitung of 16th February 2005, p. 11. Because such amendments by the legislature conform to the principle of approval by a

sociated from legislative aims or social reality is otherwise forbidden. The constitution, as the safeguard of basic western constitutional values, must have constancy[458] and be amendable only in accordance with rigid procedures.[459]

In Germany, it is forbidden to interefere with the independence of judges in any informal way or to try to influence individual cases or exert pressure on judges. The parliament shall assess courts decisions cautiously, but cannot interfere in the actual work of courts. But in China, in accordance with the system of Special Investigation Committees established by the Constitution, the National People's Congress, as the legislature, can decide to supervise the Special Investigation Committees established for individual cases, so it is possible for supervision after the event to change the court's decision.[460] The "Law of the People's Republic of China on Supervision by the Standing Committees of the People's Congresses at Various Levels", approved by the Standing Committee of the National People's Congress on 27th August 2006 and enforced on 1st January 2007, does not provide for the direct supervision of individual cases but does stipulate rigid provisions on the procedures by which supervisory committees are started and operated, thus restraining the application of supervision to individual cases at least to a certain extent. It is hoped that once the Law on Super-

---

parliamentary majority, they are democratic and legal and do not fundamentally damage the judiciary.

458 Paragraph 3 of Article 79 of the Basic Law stipulates that amendments to the Basic Law affecting the division of the Federation into *Länder*, their participation on principle in the legislative process, or the principles laid down in Articles 1 and 20 shall be inadmissible. These are the basic principles of human dignity, republicanism, democracy, the rule of law and the social state. An amendment of Paragraph 3 of Article 79 is under debate; opposing views include Ingo von Münch, Staatsrecht 1, 6th edition, Stuttgart 2000, margin number 89; see also Bryde, in: von Münch/Kunig, Grundgesetz-Kommentar, Volume 3, Article 79, margin number 27. In China, there is no perpetual safeguard provision in the Constitution. The basic value of the Constitution that are dignity, equality, personal rights and freedom, uppermost authority of the Constitution, and the principle of ruling by law are provided separately in preface, the first chapter and the second chapter. They are safeguarded by rigid amending procedure, see the next note.

459 Article 64 of the Chinese Constitution stipulates that amendments to the Constitution are to be proposed by the Standing Committee of the National People's Congress or by more than one fifth of the deputies to the National People's Congress and adopted by a vote of more than two thirds of all the deputies to the Congress. But in Germany, Paragraph 2 of Article 79 of the Basic Law stipulates that laws which alter the provisions of the Constitution shall be carried by two thirds of the members of the *Bundestag* and two thirds of the votes of the *Bundesrat*.

460 See also Chapter 3 of Part 1 of this dissertation on the relationship between courts and legislative authorities

vision formally takes effect, supervision of the judiciary by the National People's Congress will be constitutionalised over time, and the supervision of individual cases will be gradually consigned to history.[461]

In addition, the judiciary will be financially influenced to a certain extent by the legislature. The legislature can govern the operational capacity of courts through their annual financial budget, providing for example more financial support to some courts than others.[462] Although this has not directly influenced some judges or the content of judges' decisions, it could be changed if the judiciary budgeted independently. This way, however, judges' representatives have to negotiate directly at parliament on their conditions, which is also likely to lead to a certain formal dependency.[463]

## Section II Means of Balancing the Legislature – Judges' Power of Judicial Review

The independence of judges from the legislature is reflected in the courts' power to review constitutionality. In a legal system in which the Constitution is paramount, judges are in principle subject only to constitutional laws and regulations. If the judiciary is to be effective, judges have to be independent of the legislature; courts must be able to review laws and regulations established by legislators; and the judiciary must have the power to review their constitutionality and declare them null and void if the circumstances are deemed to warrant this. In countries which operate a system of constitutional government which pursues the ideal of the rule of law, supervision of the powers of the legislature is essential. Judges are not then forced to apply laws which are unconstitutional.

The Chinese Constitution differs from that of Germany in that it does not grant the courts these powers to review laws.[464] The political system of the Peo-

461 See Zhou Anping, Liu Huigui, Criticisms of the System of Supervision of Individual Cases by the National People's Congress, Chinese Justice, 2006, No. 11, pp. 31-32

462 Budgetary restraints on judges can be seen in Wolfgang Hoffmann-Riem, Gewaltenteilung – mehr Eigenverantwortung für die Justiz?, in: DRiZ 2000, p.18 (19)

463 See Hilke Thiedemann, Judicial Independence – Eine rechtsvergleichende Untersuchung der Sicherung unabhängiger Rechtsprechung in Südafrika und Deutschland, Baden-Baden 2007, pp. 241

464 Some scholars believe that although the Constitution does not establish a system of judicial review, it does establish the principle that a citizen has the right to accuse state organs and state functionaries of violating the law or neglecting their duties, and the principle that all state organs have to abide by the law and the Constitution or they will be deemed to be guilty of malpractice, and the principle that courts exercise their powers of examination and approval independently in accordance with the law, which pro-

ple's Congress operated in China means that the National People's Congress establishes and amends the Constitution, the National People's Congress and its Standing Committee interpret the Constitution and supervise its application, and the National People's Congress and its Standing Committee establish and amend laws. In this type of political system, the National People's Congress is the highest organ of state power and the Standing Committee of the National People's Congress is a component of said highest organ of state power. All other state organs are subordinate to the National People's Congress and its Standing Committee, and the National People's Congress and its Standing Committee supervise and pass decisions on other state organs. Based on this supervisor-supervisee relationship, other state organs are neither qualified nor entitled to review whether or not laws established by the National People's Congress and its Standing Committee violate the Constitution. Therefore, courts cannot review the constitutionality of laws established by the National People's Congress and its Standing Committee. Only the National People's Congress and its Standing Committee themselves can determine the constitutionality of laws established by them.[465] But in accordance with the provisions of the Legislation Law, courts do have the power of judicial review over administrative regulations, local decrees, autonomous decrees, special decrees and rules and other normative documents.[466] In accordance with Article 90 of the Legislation Law, if any courts be-

vides the essential constitutional basis for the system of judicial review. The most immediate legal basis for the system of judicial review is Article 5 of the Administrative Procedure Law, which stipulates that the People's Courts have the power to review the legality of specific administrative acts. In the opinion of these scholars, the People's Courts only exercise their power of judicial review in the course of adjudicating administrative cases. See Mo Jihong, New Theories on Constitutional Government IV: On the System of Judicial Review in China, http://article.chinalawinfo.com/article/user/article_display.asp?ArticleID=24838 (retrieved on 16th October 2008) Scholars who oppose this believe that if the Constitution merely specifies the paramount status of the Constitution (see the preface and Article 5) but does not explicitly authorise judicial review, it cannot be said that a system of judicial review has been established. If a system of judicial review is deemed to have been established, then the Constitution should stipulate provisions for a system of judicial intervention in its chapter on exercising rights, see Zhang Qianfan, From a Constitution to Constitutional Government, in: Research on Comparative Law, 2008, Volume 1, p. 75

465 See Hu Jinguang, On the Review of the Constitutionality of Laws, in: Northern Law, 2007, Volume 2, p. 65

466 It is necessary here to strictly delineate what is meant by laws and other kinds of legal norms. Laws are where the National People's Congress and its Standing Committee establish legal norms (Article 7 of the Legislation Law). Administrative regulations are

lieve that particular administrative regulations, local decrees, autonomous decrees or special decrees violate the Constitution and/or the law, they have the power to propose a review to the National People's Congress. In Germany, all courts have the power to review constitutionality and legality, though judges do not have the power to refuse to apply a law (*Verwerfungskompetenz*) or to declare a formal law null and void; only the Federal Constitutional Court has this power.[467] Once the Federal Constitutional Court finds a law to be constitutional, all courts are bound by this decision.[468] This arrangement maintains unity between the Constitution and the legal system and respects the authority of Parliament in the sense of the separation of powers.[469]

Since the Administrative Procedure Law was approved in 1989 and established an administrative procedure in China, the status of judges has fundamentally changed. The Administrative Procedure Law provides the courts with the power to apply legal reference, which means that when trying administrative cases, courts can "refer to"[470] the ministerial rules of the State Council and to local government rules and regulations.[471] This has been interpreted as courts having the

---

regulations established by the State Council; local regulations are norms established by the local People's Congress and its Standing Committee; autonomous decrees and special decrees are norms established by the People's Congress of an autonomous area and its Standing Committee; regulations include local regulations and ministerial rules, wherein local regulations are established by local government and ministerial rules are established by ministries of the State Council under their respective authorities (Articles 56, 63, 66 and 71 of the Legislation Law). Their order of precedence is as follows: the Constitution > laws > administrative regulations > local regulations > rules (local rules, ministerial rules). The flexible provisions on autonomous decrees and special decrees with respect to the Constitution and laws are only implemented in autonomous areas, see Articles 79 to 81 of the Legislation Law.

467 See Article 100 of the Basic Law. However, in the case of informal laws and regulations (laws, rules and regulations), all courts have the power to refuse to apply them.

468 On the basis of the essential principle that regulations which violate laws are null and void, such regulations would be null and void from the beginning, in Germany and in China.

469 In the case of Germany, this aspect can be seen in BVerfGE Volume 1, 184 (195, 197) and Volume 42, 42 (49).

470 "Refer to" means here that People's courts do not automatically have to apply such rules and regulations, but should first review whether such rules and regulations are in line with superior laws and so decide whether to apply them or not as the case may be. See Deng Chukai's positive-law analysis "Referring to Rules and Regulations", in: People's Court Gazette, 25th December 2009

471 See Article 53 of the Administrative Procedure Law

power to review the legality of these rules and regulations.[472] In practice, the power of courts to review laws and regulations is not limited to such rules and regulations but has for some time extended to local government rules and regulations.[473] After the Legislation Law came into force in 2000, the Supreme People's Court continued to reaffirm that courts have the power to review local government rules and regulations.[474] The "Bulletin of the Supreme People's Court" also published many cases in which local courts refused to apply local government rules and regulations, and these cases no doubt guide courts across the country.[475]

The courts have the power of judicial review not only in administrative procedures but also in civil procedures. The fourth "Bulletin of the Supreme People's Court" in 2004 published the dispute case in which Taifeng Hotels Ltd.

---

472 See Mo Jihong, New Theories on Constitutional Government IV: On the System of Judicial Review in China, http://article.chinalawinfo.com/article/user/article_display.asp?ArticleID=24838 (retrieved on 16th October 2008)

473 The Supreme People's Court has repeatedly clarified in its past legal interpretations that courts have the power to decide whether local government regulations are in line with superior laws and to apply superior laws directly. In 1993, for example, the Supreme People's Court refused to apply a local government regulation in Fujian Province in its "Law Letter No. 16 (1993)". The local government regulation in question stipulated that anyone caught fishing without a license "may have his fishing vessel confiscated", whereas the Fisheries Law merely stipulates "may have his fishing equipment confiscated" in the same instance. The Supreme People's Court affirmed in its letter of reply that this provision was not in line with the provisions of the Fisheries Law and directed the lower courts "to execute the provisions of laws and administrative regulations if the provisions of local government regulations are not in line with those of the laws and administrative regulations."

474 For example, in its "Reply on Issues of How the Law is to be Applied When People's Courts Try Road Traffic Administrative Cases" ([1999] Xing Ta Zi No. 29) made on 1st February 2001, the Supreme People's Court clarified again that when the provisions of local government regulations are inconsistent with those of the Road Law, the relative provisions of the Road Law shall be applied.

475 For example, the first Bulletin in 1998 published a case in which the Water and Electricity Survey Design and Research Institute of Fujian province refused to accept an administrative punishment imposed by the Provincial Department of Geology and Mineral Resources. In this case, the Intermediate People's Court of Fuzhou found that the administrative department in charge of "geothermal energy" had decided on the basis of a local government regulation of Fujian Province which was "not in line with the provisions of laws and administrative regulations" and that it was inappropriate for said administrative organ to "consider itself to have administrative management power over matters of geothermal energy in accordance with this local government regulation."

Co. sued Datong city Land Administration Bureau over the assignment of land-use rights. In this case, a government regulation of Shanxi province has been applied which stipulated that if the assignee of land-use rights fails to carry out their contract, the assignment fees paid shall not be reimbursed. The Intermediate People's Court of Datong, in accordance with the "General Provisions of Civil Law" and the "Interim Regulations on the Assignment and Transfer of Land-Use Rights for State-Owned Land in Urban Areas", found that the transgressing party in this case was only liable for the deposit and had the right to have the assignment fees reimbursed. Thus, the court refused to apply the provincial government regulation. The Higher People's Court of Shanxi province not only upheld the judgement of the first instance but also stated in more detail that the provisions of this regulation were "null and void because they are neither authorised by nor in line with administrative laws and regulations."[476]

The above analysis of the provisions in Chinese law and trial practice make clear that courts have in cases had overall power to review regulations and in particular local government rules and regulations. This power of review has included not only a *de facto* "refusal to apply" a rule or regulation but also a nominal "affirmation" that it is "null and void", although this merely means that it is null in that individual case and does not have any general force of constraint beyond the individual case. Completely nullifying a regulation still involves going through the legislative procedure, which means that the organs which established the regulation "amend" or "abolish" it, or that other organs with the requisite powers "revise" or "revoke" it. However, it must be conceded that due to the limited extent of the constitutional framework, courts in China still cannot review laws as such, and judges still lack independent status with respect to the supreme legislative organs. Because of the dominating status of the National People's Congress and its Standing Committee, it is unlikely that courts will review or abolish laws, but the National People's Congress and its Standing Committee can approve any laws. Although the Legislation Law provides a way of declaring a law null and void,[477] the lack of provisions on procedure make this difficult to implement.

---

476 However, what the courts refused to apply in this civil case was not a local government regulation which had been approved by the provincial People's Congress but rather a subordinate, first-level provincial government rule; however, the significance of this case was that it was the first time a court had publicly "affirmed the subordinate law to be null and void". In the aforementioned cases, courts had merely determined that superior laws and subordinate laws were at odds and had applied the superior law directly but had not publicly affirmed that the subordinate law was null and void.

477 Paragraph 1 of Article 88 of the Legislation Law

The provisions on judges' power of review clarifies the constitutional interpretation of the function of judges with respect to the law:[478] judges must be subject to the law, but laws and regulations established by the legislature must firstly be constitutional before judges and courts are subject to them. The judges' power of review develops their independence within this framework and prevents interference or violation of the Constitution in individual cases. Although in this sense, the power to review laws allows the judiciary to interfere in political affairs, this does not result either in a politicisation of the judiciary or in a judicialisation of political affairs.[479] Judges' power of review strengthens their position with respect to the political authorities, but the reasons of their emergence and existence are essentially based on changes in legal interpretation.[480]

If every court had the power of judicial review, there would be a basic problem in that judges could declare laws and regulations – established by legislators by democratic and legal procedure – null and void, without themselves submitting to a democratic and legal procedure.[481] This problem is conclusively resolved by the separation of powers and constitutional government, meaning that the Constitution is not only the foundation stone of the state but also the standard for legislative power.[482] Judges' power of review is not a challenge to the principle of democracy, but rules out the distorting interference of other people's

478 The power of judges to examine laws and regulations is not the only requirement of the principle of the rule of law, but also that of supervising legislative power based on the principle of the separation of powers. See Maunz/Dürig, Grundgesetz: Kommentar, Munich 2009, Volume 6, Article 100, margin number 2

479 Maunz/Dürig, Grundgesetz: Kommentar, Munich 2009, Volume 6, Article 100, margin number 2. With respect to the influence of political aims on the procedure of examining laws and regulations, see Martin Shapiro, The European Court of Justice, in: Peter H. Russel, David M. O'Brien (eds.), Judicial Independence in the Age of Democracy: Critical Perspectives from Around the World, London 2001, pp. 273, 279

480 Judicial review in America was first permitted in the case of Marbury v. Madison, 5 US 137 (1803). With respect to the establishment of legal and regulatory review by constitutional courts in the USA and Europe see Wolfgang Hoffmann-Riem, Das Ringen um die verfassungsgerichtliche Normkontrolle in den USA und Europa, in: Law Practitioner's Gazette (*JuristenZeitung = JZ*) 2003, pp. 269-275. See also Winfried Brugger, Kampf um die Verfassungsgerichtsbarkeit: 200 Jahre Marbury v. Madison, in: Legal Instruction (*Juristische Schulung = JuS*) 2003, p. 320-325

481 In Germany, a simple majority of judges at constitutional courts who hear a case can decide to refuse to apply a law, see the second sentence of Paragraph 4 of Article 15 of BVerfGG.

482 In controversial political matters in particular, it is possible for decisions by judges to become a form of oligarchic governance, see Wolfgang Meyer, in: von Münch/Kunig, Grundgesetz-Kommentar, Volume 3, Article 100, margin number 2

volitions in the course of applying and interpreting the law, ensuring the people's volition as contained in laws is realised.[483]

In practice, courts have to exercise self-restraint in order to avoid becoming too radical and violating legislation.[484] The other way of preventing courts from supervising too much is an ideal set of procedural provisions whereby the procedures of judicial review and regulation are not all controlled by the courts, but rather organs which are identified by the Constitution and permitted to apply file an application (abstract review),[485] or a constitutional review of a particular law is carried out in an individual case (concrete review).[486]

In Germany, abstract judicial review is exercised only by constitutional courts,[487] and concrete judicial review is shared by constitutional courts and general courts. If a general court believes a law to be constitutional, it can presume the constitutionality of the law and decide to apply said law. If a court believes a law to be unconstitutional, it shall suspend the action in accordance with the first sentence of Paragraph 1 of Article 100 of the Basic Law; if a law violates the Basic Law, it shall be submitted to the Federal Constitutional Court. Only the Federal Constitutional Court can declare a law to be null and void because it violates the Basic Law (monopoly veto);[488] courts cannot decide by themselves to refuse a law, since this would not only cause laws to become unstable (for example, court A believes a law to be constitutional and applies it, but court B

---

483 Gertrude Lübbe-Wolf, Unabhängige Richter im Interesse der Demokratie – Mut zu unbequemen Entscheidungen, in: Neue Zürcher Zeitung of 16th February 2005, p. 11

484 The means for this is that before courts can declare a law to be in violation of the Constitution, they must first explain how the law does conform to the Constitution. See Hilke Thiedemann, Judicial Independence – Eine rechtsvergleichende Untersuchung der Sicherung unabhängiger Rechtsprechung in Südafrika und Deutschland, Baden-Baden 2007, p. 245

485 In China, as stated above, the provisions of Article 88 of the Legislation Law mean that only the National People's Congress has the power to revise or revoke inappropriate laws established by its Standing Committee. But in the case of other regulations below the level of laws, any organ or individual can file an application for review to the Standing Committee of the National People's Congress (Article 90 of the Legislation Law). In Germany, by contrast, the second sentence of Paragraph 1 of Article 93 of the Basic Law stipulates that only the Federal Government, *Land* governments or a third of the members of the *Bundestag* can apply for abstract review.

486 The Basic Law stipulates an abstract review procedure and a concrete review procedure, but in practice, the abstract procedure is only rarely implemented. See Christiane Chlosta, Nur dem Gesetz unterworfen?, Frankfurt on the Main 2005, p. 205

487 This relates only to laws which have been formally approved by parliament.

488 Günter Schmidt-Räntsch, Jürgen Schmidt-Räntsch, Deutsches Richtergesetz (DRiG), Kommentar, 6th edition, Munich 2008, Article 25, margin number 18, p. 353

believes the same law to be unconstitutional and refuses to apply it) but would also allow individual courts to violate democratic and legal decisions by legislators, thus damaging the authority of the legislators.[489] Therefore, the limits on the authority to refuse to apply laws are exercised by the Federal Constitutional Court alone. Judges can ascertain that a law is constitutional and so apply it, but if they believe it to be unconstitutional, they must submit it to the Federal Constitutional Court.

In China, the judiciary rarely infringes on the legislature through the practice of judicial review. Courts tend to assume that measures taken by legislative organs are constitutional. One case where the judiciary is considered to have infringed on the legislature is the "Luoyang Seed Case" which caused a furore in legal circles soon after it transpired. As a result, judges' power of judicial review began to be examined more closely and thoughtfully.

## Section III The Luoyang Seed Case and Judges' Power of Judicial Review in China

Motivated by the idea of combining the legislature and the executive, the existing Chinese Constitution establishes the system of the National People's Congress as the underlying political system.[490] The National People's Congress enjoys a higher status than any other state organ within the system of state power. In response to the National People's Congress having exerted little effect for a long time after the founding of the People's Republic of China, the current Constitution (of 1982) further strengthened the status of the National People's Congress as the organ of supreme power.[491] The National People's Congress is not only the supreme organ of the legislature, but also supervises other central organs.[492] All state organs shall observe and execute the laws established by the National People's Congress and the resolutions approved by it. Correspondingly, local People's Congresses at various levels and other organs of power at the same level shall also observe them.[493] Many scholars therefore believe that

489 Christoph Degenhart, Staatsrecht 1, Staatsorganisationsrecht, 19th revised edition, Heidelberg 2003, margin number 620, p. 249

490 Article 57 of the Chinese Constitution

491 Wang Shuwen, Zhou Yanrui: New Developments in the System of the People's Congress, in: Zhang Youyu, Essays on the Constitution (Forum on Law and Order in China), Social Sciences Literature 2003, p. 164

492 See the provisions of Article 62 of the Constitution on the powers of the People's Congress

493 See Article 104 of the Constitution

organs other than the People's Congress (such as courts) reviewing the normative declarations made by the National People's Congress would conflict with the system of the National People's Congress of China.[494] The Luoyang Seed Case occurred in China's Henan province in 2003 and nicely exemplifies the tense relationship between the idea of the supreme National People's Congress and the system of judicial review.

## (1) Main Points of the Case

On 27th May 2003, while adjudicating a dispute over compensation for seed, the Intermediate People's Court of Luoyang in Henan province became embroiled in a legal conflict. In the court hearing, the plaintiff (the Ruyang County Seed Company) and the defendant (the Yichuan County Seed Company) debated intensely over how to calculate the amount of compensation. The plaintiff wanted to apply the Seed Law passed by the Standing Committee of the National People's Congress in 2001 and calculate the amount of compensation according to the "market price", whereas the defendant wanted to apply the Regulation of Henan Province on Crops and Seed and calculate the amount of compensation according to the "government-set price range". Upon conclusion of the trial, the Intermediate People's Court of Luoyang issued the 26th Civil Judgement of the Court of Luoyang (2003), which stated that: "Since the enactment of the Seed Law, the price of sweet corn seed has been governed by the market. The Regulation of Henan Province on Crops and Seed, as a local regulation of lower legal precedence, is null and void since it is not in line with the provisions of the Seed Law." Both the plaintiff and the defendant refused to accept the judgement and appealed to the Higher People's Court of Henan Province.

The statement in the judgement by the Intermediate People's Court of Luoyang strongly aroused the ire of the People's Congress of Henan Province, who considered that "the action in the 26th Civil Judgement of the Court of Luoyang (2003) of declaring the local regulation null and void constituted a substantive review of the legality of a local regulation approved by the Standing Committee of the provincial People's Congress and so violated the system of the National People's Congress of China and infringed on the powers of the proper state organs and was thus a serious transgression of law."[495] On 18th October 2003, the

494 See Zhang Qianfan, From a Constitution to Constitutional Government, in: Developments in the Law in Mainland China, Taiwan, Hong Kong and Macau in 2006 (Book One), edited by Tang Dezong, Wang Pengxiang, Taiwan Xin Xuelin Publishing House 2007, p. 59

495 The 18th document of the legal system office of the Standing Committee of the People's Congress of Henan province (2003), 13th October 2003

General Office of the Standing Committee of the People's Congress of Henan province issued a "Declaration on the Illegal Action in the Civil Judgement by the Intermediate People's Court of Luoyang in Declaring the Content of a Relevant Local Regulation, Approved by the Standing Committee of the People's Congress of Henan Province, to be Null and Void" and ordered the Higher People's Court of Henan province "to deal severely with this serious illegal action by the Intermediate People's Court of Luoyang and to punish the individual directly responsible and the associated leadership." Following this order, the leading Party group of the Intermediate People's Court of Luoyang decided to remove the deputy presiding judge Zhao Guangyun who had issued the Civil Judgement and the presiding judge Li Huijuan who was the commissioner in this case from their posts, and to dismiss the assistant judge to Li Huijuan, although this decision was ultimately not carried out.

After the Higher People's Court had accepted this case, it asked for instructions from the Supreme People's Court. On 30th March 2004, the Supreme People's Court issued its "Response to the Request for Instructions in the Case of the Disputed Sweet Corn Seed Replenishment Contract Between the Ruyang County Seed Company, Henan Province and the Yichuan County Seed Company, Henan Province" and highlighted that Article 79 of the Legislation Law stipulates that: "the efficacy of laws is greater than that of administrative regulations, local rules and regulations. The efficacy of administrative regulations is greater than that of local rules and regulations." Article 4 of the Contract Law of the PRC explains that: "once the Contract Law has been enacted, the People's Courts shall confirm a contract to be valid or null and void in accordance with the laws made by the National People's Congress and its Standing Committee and administrative regulations made by the State Council and not in accordance with the local regulations or administrative rules." In accordance with the above provisions, when People's Courts are trying cases and believe the provisions of local regulations to be out of line with those of laws and/or administrative regulations, they shall apply the relevant provisions of the laws and/or administrative regulations. The final judgement by the Higher People's Court of Henan Province upheld the original judgement by the Intermediate People's Court of Luoyang.[496]

## (2) Issues

The Luoyang Seed Case unleashed a heated discussion in legal science circles in China. The issues involved in this case are extensive, and the discussion on

496 For more details on the Luoyang Seed Case, see Zeng Jinsheng, Reinvestigating the Case of Li Huijuan, in: Trends of the Times, People's Daily 2004, Volume 9

judges' power of judicial review came to comprise two related aspects: one is whether courts have the power to review legislation made by the local People's Congress; the other is the relationship between the courts and the People's Congress and how courts can and/or should exercise their jurisdiction independently.

The first aspect is a technical issue. When normative documents from different levels exist but contradict each other, judges have to choose one to apply. In this case, if the Intermediate People's Court wished to apply the relevant provisions of the Seed Law in its judgement, it could have opted for one of the following approaches:

- Applying the provisions of the Seed Law directly, but not commenting on the efficacy of the provincial Regulation on Crops and Seed, which is the approach most scholars favoured, since in accordance with Article 100 of the Constitution, the People's Congress of Henan province has the power to make local regulations, although the premise for this is that the local regulations cannot conflict with the Constitution, laws or administrative regulations. Furthermore, the "Response on How to Interpret and Execute Laws" emphasises that if, when trying a case, courts find that local regulations conflict with laws made by the state organ of supreme power, they should execute the laws made by the state organ of supreme power,[497] and in view of the instructions of the Supreme People's Court to the Higher People's Court of Fujian province regarding the Fisheries Law, it may be concluded that courts have the power to directly apply the laws of greater precedence without declaring the regulations which conflict with the superior law null and void.[498]
- Exercising the power of judicial review to a limited extent by reviewing the efficacy of the subordinate laws and applying the superior laws, i.e. reviewing the subordinate laws in the judgement and highlighting the provisions in the subordinate laws which conflict with those of the superior laws, and possibly declaring the provisions which conflict with the superior laws to be null and void, depending on the sprit of the Constitution and the Legislation Law. This was the approach taken by Li Huijuan at the Intermediate People's Court of Luoyang in the first instance.
- Suspending the trial on the basis of the system established by the Legislation Law and writing a dispatch to one's superiors asking for instructions, step by

497 See the Response to Several Issues on How to Interpret and Execute Laws by the Legal Work Committee of the Standing Committee of the National People's Congress (I) 18. How to Execute When Local Regulations Conflict with State Laws (17th November 1989)

498 Wang Zhenmin, The System of Constitutional Review in China, China University of Political Science and Law Press, Beijing 2004, p. 267

step up to the Supreme People's Court, whereupon the Supreme People's Court shall direct the Standing Committee of the National People's Congress to review the law or regulation in question in accordance with Article 90 of the Legislation Law.

The first approach turns the action whereby courts review normative documents into an action whereby courts merely select which law to apply and thus not only avoids direct conflict between the courts and the People's Congress but also achieves the desired aim of applying the law which has greater precedence. This approaches deliberately avoids the issue of the efficacy levels of different laws and regulations, and regards the regulations having greater precedence not as having to be applied but merely as being selectable as the regulation of choice. As for the second approach, the fact that many scholars supported Judge Li Huijuan does not alter the fact that courts in China are not authorised to review the constitutionality of laws and regulations, hence there was no firm legal foundation for the Intermediate People's Court of Luoyang to directly declare, in the first instance, that the provincial local regulations were null and void.

The third approach is simply the scheme of judicial review established by the existing Chinese Constitution and the framework of the Legislation Law. In accordance with the provisions of the Constitution and the Legislation Law, when judges find during a trial that local regulations or administrative regulations are not in line with state laws, they should suspend the trial and report the matter to their court. The court then reports the matter to the Supreme People's Court, and then in accordance with the Legislation Law, the Supreme People's Court directs the Standing Committee of the National People's Congress to review the matter. After completing its review, the Standing Committee of the National People's Congress makes a decision and the court may then pass a judgement on the basis of this decision. In the Luoyang Seed Case, for example, the court had the power to apply to the Standing Committee of the National People's Congress for a review of the local regulations by Henan Province, by way of the procedure stipulated in the Legislation Law. In practice, however, the Standing Committee of the National People's Congress only meets every two months and has a heavy legislative workload, so courts who report such issues up through the various hierarchical levels would have to delay the adjudication of cases indefinitely. In point of fact, the Standing Committee of the National

People's Congress has so far not started any procedure of reviewing normative documents.[499]

## (3) Reflection and Comparison with Judicial Review by Judges in Germany

### *(a) Courts' Limited Powers of Judicial Review*

The above discussion of the Luoyang Seed Case and the practice of judicial review by the courts in China reveal that although judicial review by the courts in China is not affirmed by the Constitution, the Legislation Law has made some positive provisions. Most Chinese scholars currently resolve the power of judicial review into the power of constitutional review and the power of legal review.[500]

#### (i) The Power of Constitutional Review

Since the Chinese Constitution stipulates that the power to interpret the Constitution and supervise its implementation is held by the National People's Congress and its Standing Committee,[501] Article 90 of the Legislation Law correspondingly stipulates that if courts believe regulations of a lower precedence than laws conflict with the Constitution and laws, they should apply to the Standing Committee of the National People's Congress for review, but courts have no power of constitutional review.[502]

#### (ii) The Power of Legal Review

In accordance with the provisions of the first paragraph of Article 90 of the Legislation Law and the Administrative Procedure Law, when courts try specific contested administrative actions, they must rely on administrative regulations, local regulations, autonomous regulations and specific regulations, and if they

499 Zhang Qianfan, Dealing with the Constitution Conscientiously: On the Necessity and Feasibility of Constitutional Government Review, in: Chinese and Foreign Jurisprudence, 2003, Volume 5, p. 560

500 See the distinction of the courts' powers of judicial review in Hu Jinguang, On the Void of Judicial Review in China (in: Henan Social Sciences, September 2006, Volume 5), pp. 72-73

501 The second paragraph of Article 62 of the Constitution stipulates that the National People's Congress supervises the implementation of the Constitution. The first paragraph of Article 67 stipulates that the Standing Committee of the National People's Congress supervises the implementation of the Constitution.

502 Hu Jinguang, On the Void of Judicial Review in China, p. 73; Research on the Judicial Review of Abstract Behaviour in China, in: Xiamen University Legal Review, Volume 13, Xiamen University Press, June 2007 edition, pp. 37-39

encounter a conflict between regulations, departmental rules and local regulations, they should submit a request to the State Council for an interpretation and decision. Courts should refer to rules and regulations when adjudicating on the legality of particular administrative actions. Thus, courts have no power of legal review with respect to regulations above the level of rules, but do have powers of legal review for regulations below the level of rules.[503]

This author does not find this idea appropriate. Although the Constitution does not expressly imbue courts with the power to interpret it,[504] courts inevitably encounter issues of whether laws and regulations conform to the Constitution in the course of adjudicating specific cases and have to decide on the constitutionality of the laws and regulations. Courts interpret the Constitution in the course of applying a particular regulation. This is analogous to the legal review by courts. In Germany's system, there is no division of constitutionality and legality in the power of judicial review by the courts, but merely a division between the power to ascertain regulations and the power to refuse to apply them. In the view of this author, China could draw entirely on the experience of this system of judicial review and improve the character of its own system.

### *(b) Comparison with Germany*

The objects of German judicial review can be divided into formal laws (*formelle Gesetze*) and rules below laws (*untergesetzliches Recht*). The criteria for this distinction are whether they were passed by parliament and whether they have come into effect. Only those which were passed by parliament (including the *Bundestag* and the *Land* legislatures) and have come into effect on the basis of this may be called formal laws. With regard to formal laws, all courts only have the power to ascertain, i.e. to ascertain their constitutionality and legality in order to decide whether to apply them. If a court suspects that they are unconsti-

503 Hu Jinguang, Research on the Judicial Review of Abstract Behaviour in China, in: Xiamen University Legal Review, Volume 13, Xiamen University Press, June 2007 edition, pp. 37-39

504 Article 67 of the current Chinese Constitution stipulates that the Standing Committee of the National People's Congress has the power to interpret the Constitution, but the Constitution's concept of interpretation is based merely on theory and ideas and fails to translate into a workable system in practice, hence the Standing Committee of the National People's Congress fails to exercise this power effectively and indeed has never actually interpreted the Constitution once. See Nie Yongqing, Liu Yanming, Thoughts on Constitutional Amendment – An Interview with the Constitutional Expert Professor Xu Qing, in: Law and Society, 1999, Volume 3, quoted from Xie Weiyan, On the Autonomous Development of Constitutional Law, http://www.gongfa.com/xiewyxianfazizhuxing.htm (retrieved on 15th October 2008)

tutional or illegal, it cannot itself decide to refuse them but can only submit them to the relevant constitutional court and continue the proceedings once the constitutional court has made a decision.

With regard to the rules below laws, all courts have the power to refuse to apply them, but their validity can also be contested before the relevant administrative court in order for a decision to be passed. If the administrative court affirms that the rule is null and void, the nullity decision is then generally binding.[505]

With regard to levels of efficacy in China, regulations made by the legislature have greater precedence than those made by administrative organs, and to confirm the absolute power of central authorities over local authorities, the level of efficacy of regulations made by central administrative organs is higher than that of regulations made by the local legislature, which is very different to Germany.

Correspondingly, judges in China have the power to ascertain facts and apply regulations of all levels of efficacy in their cases, but the Constitution and laws do not clarify this power of judicial review. In view of the aforementioned written response by the Supreme People's Court and the Standing Committee of the National People's Congress, judges also have the power to refuse to apply any regulations. In this respect, judges in China have more power of judicial review than judges in Germany do in practice (except that the power of judicial review exercised by the constitutional courts in Germany is not exercised by the courts in China but by the legislature). What judges in China cannot do is explicitly declare particular regulations to be null and void, although even in Germany, regulations which have been found and declared to be null and void by an administrative court by administrative procedure can only be submitted to the authority which has the jurisdiction to decide on their validity if their efficacy is in doubt.

### *(c) The Abuse of Judicial Review in China*

As can be seen from the differences between China and Germany as mentioned above, the current arrangement of judges' power of judicial review in China is completely inappropriate, and the ways in which it is open to abuse are obvious:

- The power of judges to exercise judicial review has not been confirmed by the Constitution or laws, although their power to ascertain laws is already widely exercised in practice.

505 Paragraph 5 of Article 47 of VwGO

- Judges cannot declare regulations to be null and void, but can refuse to apply any regulation at will, which would cause the same case to lead to different judgements under different judges and thus goes against the unity of the legal system.
- When judges doubt the validity of a regulation, they must submit it for the legislature to decide whether the regulation is valid or not, which is clearly not the same effect as supervision. The restriction and balance of judges, whether with respect to the legislature or the executive, cannot be realised and the independence of judges from two authorities cannot be safeguarded.

### *(d) Proposals for Improvement*

In view of the limitation and practice of the courts' power of judicial review in China, it is the opinion of this author that things will be clearer if the power of judicial review is divided into a power to ascertain and a power to refuse to apply, as in the German approach, and that it is time for the Constitution and laws to confirm judges' power of judicial power.

The Legislation Law should then define the limits within which judges can refuse to apply regulations. Judges should not be able to refuse to apply all laws, such as the Constitution and other laws. This could not only lead to loss of authority for the Constitution, but would also fail to prevent judges from choosing to apply local regulations because of local advantages, leading to central laws becoming null and void and judgements becoming localised.

The scope of administrative proceedings should be expanded on again. The validity of rules below laws should be affirmed by administrative proceedings and should have a unified level of efficacy. Individual judges should be prevented from choosing from different regulations when coming to apply them, such that judgements are unified and unity in the national legal system is established.

Finally, an independent authority should be established under the National People's Congress to review the validity of laws. As is well known, judges cannot judge this by themselves. Judges submit the laws which they suspect of being null and void to the National People's Congress or Standing Committee which made the law, and they then review the law which they themselves passed, which hardly seems above reproach; and as if to prove that the system is unworkable, the National People's Congress and its Standing Committee have in fact never actually declared a law to be null and void. Many scholars in China propose establishing a committee which is independent of the National People's Congress to exercise the power of judicial review, like constitutional courts in

Germany.[506] Although the political function of this committee would be very different to that of constitutional courts, it would have the power to review regulations nationwide and in a frequent and highly efficient way, which would at least temporarily make up for the defects in the existing system.

# (C) Independence within the Judicial branch

## Chapter IV The Administration and Organisation of Courts

In the administrative sphere of the courts, administrative organisations can indirectly interfere with the judiciary. Whether in China or Germany, there is a global trend whereby the judiciary is trying to be free of the administrative responsibility in the administrative sphere of courts, which mainly means the independence of courts on the strength of their own budget and independence in personnel matters.

Theoretically, the organisation and administration of courts does not belong directly to the core mission of courts which is to decide cases, but courts are incapable of accomplishing this mission without certain material labour resources.[507] It can be said that the organisation and administration of courts has the purpose of ensuring that judges decide cases objectively and impartially, without any external interference or influence.[508] The responsibility for managing the administrative affairs of courts is generally shared by judicial departments and courts, but some matters are managed by judges themselves in order to guarantee their independence.[509] Where the budgets of courts are involved, the legislature also participates in management.

In China, the internal function of the administrative management of courts is exercised by the Supreme People's Court and the Presidents of courts. In prac-

---

506 Zhang Qianfan, Dealing with the Constitution Conscientiously: On the Necessity and Feasibility of Constitutional Government Review, in: Chinese and Foreign Jurisprudence, 2003, Volume 5, p. 560; Wang Shuwen, On Safeguarding Constitutional Implementation, in: China Legal Science, 1992, Volume 6; Wu Jialin, On the Necessity and Feasibility of Establishing a Constitutional Inspectorate, in: Law Review, 1991, Volume 2

507 See Kissel/Mayer, Gerichtsverfassungsgesetz (GVG): Kommentar, 4th edition, Munich 2005, p. 142, margin number 34

508 See also Degenhart, Staatsrecht 1, Staatsorganisationsrecht, 19th revised edition, Heidelberg 2003, Article 11, margin number 700, p. 288

509 The IBA (International Bar Association) Minimum Standards of Judicial Independence require the judiciary to have special jurisdiction over its legal affairs.

tice, courts also have the function of regulating their own internal management procedures, although the Constitution does not authorise this power. The issues of providing goods, materials and labour and the budgets of courts also largely come under the purview of the Supreme People's Court and various courts. The Ministry of Justice is mainly responsible for managing the affairs of lawyers and prisons.[510]

In Germany, the functions of the administrative management of courts are shared by the various Ministries of Justice[511] and the presidents of courts (they are in charge of the court institutions which fulfil administrative functions) and *Präsidialrichter*.[512] Judges have to be restricted by all kinds of directives in the sphere of administrative affairs, but matters which fall within the autonomous domain of judges may not be interfered with in any way from without.[513]

In the matter of the administrative management of courts, the balance in the system of democratic accountability and the independence of judges should receive particular attention. In purely external matters of court management such as personnel matters, judges cannot have substantive independence but rather have to be directed by administrative organs. But matters relating to the sphere of judgements have to be governed by the courts themselves and not influenced by parties in lawsuits or by the State. Otherwise, it is possible that the judge-

510 See the Regulation of the Ministry of Justice on Functional Allocation, Internal Institutions and Workforce promulgated by the State Council on 24th June 1998. In 2002, the qualification examination for lawyers was abolished in China; the qualification examinations for judges, procurators and lawyers were unified in the Judicial Examination. The mandate of the Ministry of Justice was changed from the qualification examination for lawyers only to the unified Judicial Examination, i.e. including judges, thus broadening its role.

511 Ministers of the Ministry of Justice also negotiate the judiciary's annual budget when the Parliament sets the budget each year.

512 Activities relating to administrative functions for the benefit of judges are excluded from the core activities of judges. Hoffmann-Riem emphasises a mixed mode of management but does not specify how to divide the powers, see DRiZ 2000, p.18. In addition to providing the necessary location and working conditions, the administrative management of courts also includes personnel allocation and personnel management (nomination, appointment, dismissal, promotion and punishment) and service supervision, see Kissel/Mayer, Gerichtsverfassungsgesetz (GVG): Kommentar, 4th edition, Munich 2005, Article 12, margin number 85

513 These matters include distributing work, scheduling cases and maintaining court registers.

ments of judges will be affected.[514] The autonomy of courts is an important factor in guaranteeing the independence of judges.

## Section I The Provision of Goods and Materials to the Courts

Appropriate working conditions are one of the prerequisites for judges to administer justice independently.[515] If the State is to provide effective legal protection to citizens, then it must also provide sufficient equipment and materials to courts.[516] Like their German counterparts, Chinese judges have mild criticism for their working conditions. The judicial functions which they are to fulfil are becoming more and more complex, but the financial resources provided are becoming insufficient for their workload.[517] A deficiency of funds[518] will firstly influence the quality of justice, and it would be possible for the administrative

514 It is possible for the judiciary to be interfered with through court administration, for example by changing judges' positions and/or transferring, punishing or rewarding judges.

515 These measures include appropriate office facilities so that judges can work efficiently, have access to technological assistance and can research cases in depth and reasonably substantiate judgements in cases.

516 This is derived from the right of citizens to just judgement and rapid execution under the principle of the rule of law, cf. Paragraph 1 of Article 6 of the European Convention on Human Rights (*Europäische Menschenrechtskonvention = EMRK*). See also Article 10 of the IBA Minimum Standards of Judicial Independence.

517 Most Chinese judges do not have their own office, secretary or other assistants. Taking as an example what this author witnessed at the Second Intermediate People's Court of Beijing, more than ten judges may share one office, and in less-developed areas of the country, judges' working conditions are even more severe. In Germany, the problem of badly needed funds for the judiciary was the topic of the 61st Meeting of German Legal Practitioners in 1996. See Manfred Zuleeg, Der Wandel der deutschen Judikative in Zeiten knapper Mittel, in: the Legal Policy Journal (*Zeitschrift für Rechtspolitik = ZRP*), Volume 33 (2000), Issue 11, p. 483-489

518 The immediate consequence of a deficiency of funds is a reduction in the number of posts for judges and non-judges and a poor provision of technical literature and technological assistance. In China, some courts cannot even pay back the cost of erecting court buildings. For example, the Yangpu district Court in the city of Shenzhen fell into arrears on the repayment of construction capital by 2.6 million Yuan even while the court building was under construction. See the Preliminary Investigation on Reform of the System of Guaranteeing Funds for the Court of Yangpu, in: Legal Forum of the Special Economic Zones, 2003, Volume 77. In Germany, more and more courts are being merged; in order to reduce costs, different procedures are being merged into a single procedure.

and legislative organisations to indirectly influence the judiciary,[519] especially when individuals in the judiciary are dependent on the related expenses,[520] because they control how the judges of courts are provided with labour and administrative resources and how collegial panels are established.

Citizens require their right to just judicial procedure to be realised and require courts to have an appropriate provision of resources, such as court offices and qualified judges who receive adequate salaries. Therefore, the Federal Service Court of Germany stipulates in particular that the provision of judicial resources should not be made so efficient as to interfere with the independences of judges.[521]

Mindful of the possibility of the legislature or administrative organisations controlling and influencing courts, Germany has tried to place the budgeting of courts within the autonomous sphere of the courts such that the courts themselves are in charge of their budgets. By contrast, China is thinking of incorporating the funding of Basic People's Courts into the unified central budget.

In fact, the badly needed funds of courts are a rather prominent and common problem in China,[522] and particularly serious in poverty-stricken areas.[523] Fund-

---

519 The legislature restricts the activities of courts by deciding on the establishment of courts, and the administrative organisations have the power over court personnel matters and decide on the arrangement of personnel in courts; on the other hand, these actions by the legislature and administrative organisations are supervised by the judiciary, see Kissel/Mayer, Gerichtsverfassungsgesetz (GVG): Kommentar, Introduction, margin number 170; Wolfgang Heyde, Rechtsprechung, in: Ernst Benda, Werner Maihofer, Hans-Jochen Vogel (eds.), Handbuch des Verfassungsrechts, 2nd edition, Berlin 1994, Article 33, margin number 76

520 The ministers of the Ministry of Justice cannot set budgets based on the types of disputes, otherwise judges would not want to handle the expensive cases and would consider the costs whenever handling a case, which would lead them to handle only cheaper cases, cf. Stephan Haberland, Problemfelder für die richterliche Unabhängigkeit, in: DRiZ 2002, p. 301

521 With respect to Paragraph 3 of Article 26 of DRiG, the specific action by a judicial department of providing unreasonable working conditions is not directed at a specific judge, hence it does not fall within the measures of service supervision, see BGH (the service court of the Federation), judgement of 3rd November 2004, in: DRiZ 2005, pp. 83 f.

522 For example, when the vice-president of the Higher People's Court of Hubei Province tried to compile a survey and study of the Basic People's Courts, he found that many courts did not even have a telephone number, and even when they did, he often could not get through because the court had failed to pay the telephone bill and the line had therefore been cut off. In one court, only one telephone in the President's office was in normal working order. Due to a shortage of funds, courts often failed to pay their staff for months at a time and/or could only maintain basic operations by borrowing, and the

ing for local Basic People's Courts currently comes from local finance, hence the amount of local allocation directly influences the normal operations of courts, hence the shortcomings in the system allow local administrative authorities to interfere with the judiciary. Many poverty-stricken areas have insufficient funds, so they have to leave courts to support themselves by their own efforts. If the courts have no extra income, they are difficult to continue,[524] so "income" becomes the most difficult problem for the presidents of courts at various levels.[525]

It is often seen that courts specify a target amount in cases,[526] which can only be a source of concern, since judges will treat cases unequally and are likely to compete to handle the cases which carry large target amounts and refuse to handle smaller cases. What is worse is that it is more difficult for judges to refuse economic temptations if there is no guarantee on their salary, rendering them incapable of pronouncing an independent judgement.

Since the new method of the State Council for the payment of court costs was promulgated,[527] the problem of funding for courts has become even more serious. The original purpose of this new method for the payment of court costs was to reduce court costs in order to solve the problem that it was difficult for citizens to bring cases to court because they had to pay so much. For example, the court costs for a divorce case are now just 50 Yuan. The fees for a division of property were also reduced from 1% of the value of the property to 0.5%.[528] However, the new method inadvertently enhances the difficult funding position

---

water and electricity supply were frequently cut off. See the report in the First Finance and Economics Daily, 14th November 2005: Judicial Reform Shoulders Heavy Responsibilities, Funding for Courts Looking Up

523 See also the report in the People's Court Paper, 7th May 1993: Serious Deficiencies in Funding for Basic People's Courts in Poverty-Stricken Areas

524 See the related discussion in Shen Deyong, A System of Courts Adapted to the Market Economy Should be Established, in: People's Court Paper, 6th June 1994

525 He Weifang, Two Problems of the System of Judicial Management in China, in: Social Sciences of China, 1997, Volume 6, p. 123

526 A lawyer at the Huiye Law Firm in Shanghai, Wu Dong, once handled a case in Shandong; because the target amount in the case was nearly one million Yuan, the judge in this case called him to give him a warm welcome, because after hearing this case, he would have reached his target. See the report in the First Finance Daily, 14th November 2005: Judicial Reform Shoulders Heavy Responsibilities, Funding for Courts Looking Up

527 The new Method for the Payment of Court Costs was approved by the State Council on 8th December 2006 and has been in force since 1st April 2007.

528 See Section 1 of Paragraph 2 of Article 13 of the Method for the Payment of Court Costs

of courts. On the one hand, the income from court costs has been reduced, while on the another hand, the number of cases and the cost of handling cases has increased. For example, the Huqiu Court in Suzhou in Jiangsu province compiled the statistics and found that in the month following the implementation of the new method for the payment of court costs, the number of cases accepted by this court almost doubled, but the income from court costs was just 300,000 Yuan, a quarter of what it had been before the reform.[529] In addition, the cost of operating such district courts is about ten million Yuan each year.[530] This is a considerable discrepancy.

In 2007, in order to solve the problem that the Basic People's Courts at the district level in central and western China have insufficient funds, China's central financing committee assigned three billion Yuan as a special fund aimed at resolving the funding difficulties at local courts created by the reform of court costs and to help local courts establish a mechanism for safeguarding funding for local courts.[531] Strengthening the guarantees on judicial funding was included in the Government Work Report by the National People's Congress in 2008. The central financing committee subsequently allocated four billion Yuan (including one billion Yuan committed in 2007) to subsidise the funding of case handling in the Basic People's Courts in its Report on the Executive Situation of the Central and Local Budget in 2007 and the Protocol on the Central and Local Budget in 2008.[532]

At present, reform of the financial capabilities of the Basic People's Courts in China is being led by the central financing committee and formulated by the Judicial Provisions Administration of the Supreme People's Court in concert with other departments. According to projections and calculations, all local court funding will be incorporated into the guarantee system of the central financing

---

529 See the report in the Legal Daily of 8th May 2007: One Month after the Implementation of the New Method of Court Costs and Some Courts are Faced with Strains on their Funding

530 He Weifang, Judicial Reform Begins Again: the Funding for Basic People's Courts is to be Incorporated into the Central Budget, in: 21st Century Economic Report of 5th December 2008

531 See the report in the People's Daily, 19th September 2007, Central Financing Committee Establishes a System of Special Funds to Subsidise Courts in their Handling of Cases

532 See the report in the Procuratorial Daily, 10th March 2008, Government Work Report Orders a Strengthening of the Guarantees on Judicial Funding

committee, and the central financing committee will increase expenditure by about forty billion Yuan each year.[533]

## Section II The Autonomy of Courts

Effective administrative management of courts can prevent the court judiciary from being improperly influenced. There are many ways of exerting political influence in the personnel policies and financial resources of courts. In many countries, it is therefore required that the judiciary enjoys greater freedom to manage its own affairs.[534] This requirement for autonomy of courts has extended to independence in the judicial budget and in appointing and promoting judges. Although, as powers of court autonomy, this is less pressing than the principle of the independence of judges itself, allowing the judiciary to be responsible for its own affairs will further strengthen the standing of judicial power in proportion to other state powers.[535]

It is noteworthy that the international trend is currently towards strengthening judicial independence by establishing autonomous committees of judges.[536] At present, nearly all countries in continental Europe have established the Supreme Judges' Committees (*Richterräte*) or Judicial Committees (*Justizräte*) in their legal system.[537] They merely differ slightly in their emphasis: some mainly protect the independence of judges and the autonomy of courts with respect to

533 He Weifang, Judicial Reform Begins Again: the Funding for Basic People's Courts is to be Incorporated into the Central Budget, in: 21st Century Economic Report of 5th December 2008

534 For an international comparison of the autonomy of courts, see Hanspeter Teetzmann, Selbstverwaltung der Justiz in Europa: Nachholbedarf für Deutschland?, in: DRiZ 2002, p. 394

535 In Germany, the budget of the Supreme Court comes under the purview of the Federal Ministry of Justice, except for the Federal Labour Court and the Federal Social Court (which are respectively budgeted by the Federal Ministry of Labour and the Federal Ministry of Social Affairs). The budget of *Land* courts are set by the respective *Land* Ministry of Justice. After reviewing the annual budget for the courts, the ministers of the various ministries submit it to the Cabinet, the Cabinet discusses and votes on it and then submits it to Parliament. Parliament approves it as one component of the overall budget. The financial resources are governed by the various ministries, but are also to be supervised by the Federal Audit Office. The Federal Constitutional Court is an exception; it makes its own budget and submits it only to the Ministry of Finance.

536 See Carlo Guarnieri, Appointment and Career of Judges in Continental Europe: the Rise of Judicial Self-Government, in: Legal Studies 2004, Volume 24, Issue 1-2, p. 169

537 Such Judicial Committees are generally comprised of delegate judges and non-judicial members.

personnel matters (such as appointment, promotion, training and discipline),[538] while others emphasise the active functions with respect to financial and administrative management, and judicial organisation and leadership of courts.[539] But establishing these institutions clearly weakens the potency of administrative organisations which always otherwise influence these areas, and thus strengthens the independence of the judiciary in its affairs.[540]

Germany is one of the few European countries which have not established such institutions.[541] Some scholars suggest encouraging judges to participate in judicial management in order to strengthen the independence of judges.[542] The mode of Judicial Committees in other European countries is an appropriate one which can be taken as a reference.[543] But there are still some opposing voices which reject the administrative autonomy of the courts.[544]

---

538 The Judicial Committees of Southern Europe essentially belong to this group, see Giacomo Oberto, Richterliche Unabhängigkeit – rechtsvergleichende Betrachtung ihrer institutionellen Ausgestaltung in den Ländern Europas, in: ZRP 2004, pp. 207 ff

539 This cannot strictly be said to be an autonomous organisation of courts, see Giacomo Oberto, Richterliche Unabhängigkeit – rechtsvergleichende Betrachtung ihrer institutionellen Ausgestaltung in den Ländern Europas, in: ZRP 2004, pp. 207 ff

540 The degree of judicial independence is clearly improved if judges occupy the majority of seats on such autonomous committees and are elected directly by their fellow judges, cf. Carlo Guarnieri, Judicial Independence in Latin Countries of Western Europe, in: Peter H. Russel, David M. O'Brien (eds.), Judicial Independence in the Age of Democracy, Critical Perspectives from Around the World, University Press of Virginia, Charlottesville 2001, p. 111

541 See Hanspeter Teetzmann, Selbstverwaltung der Justiz: Rechtsvergleichender Überblick, in: DRiZ 2003, pp. 44 f. One investigation by the International Association of Judges (*Internationale Richtervereinigung*) shows that only Germany and the Czech Republic have no higher autonomous organisations; Austria establishes the Personnel Office in the individual states of the federation, which has a power of proposal on the distribution of judges' posts. See Hanspeter Teetzmann, Selbstverwaltung der Justiz in Europa: Nachholbedarf für Deutschland?, in: DRiZ 2002, p. 394

542 See Lutz Frauendorf, Zur richterlichen Selbstverwaltung im demokratischen Rechtsstaat, in: Public Administration (*die öffentliche Verwaltung = DÖV*) 1980, pp. 553 ff; Hoffmann-Riem, in: DRiZ 2000, pp. 18 ff

543 See Carlo Guarnieri, Appointment and Career of Judges in Continental Europe: the Rise of Judicial Self-Government, in Legal Studies 2004, pp. 169 ff

544 Some think that the administrative autonomy of judges does not benefit judges because judges will be more heavily burdened if they manage their own administration than if a third party is in charge of it. If a third party is in charge of administration, judges can concentrate solely on their judicial work. See die Stellungnahme Hamburger Verwaltungsrichter in dem Abschlussbericht der Arbeitsgruppe II, p. 114

In China, there are also currently many discussions on removing administrative management from the purview of administrative organisations. At present, the funds of the local courts at various levels are budgeted by the people's government of statistics and allocated by government financial departments after discussion and approval by the People's Congress at the same level. In this system, courts and judges have to be at the head of the government and its financial departments at the same level. In practice, the cases involving governments and financial departments are always won completely by the government or financial department.[545] If administrative organisations control the administrative affairs of courts, there is a danger that they have administrative control over the judiciary and threaten the independence of judges. Therefore, courts should be isolated from administrative organisations and acquire more autonomy, in particular in their budget and in appointing judges.[546]

## Section III Prohibiting Extraordinary Courts (*Ausnahmegerichte*), Ad-Hoc Courts (*Ad-Hoc-Gerichte*) and Special Courts (*Sondergerichte*)

The Chinese Constitution does not contain provisions prohibiting the establishment of extraordinary courts, but in accordance with the provisions of the Legislation Law,[547] the establishment, organisation and powers of the People's Courts belong to the legislative power of the National People's Congress and its Standing Committee and only are provided by law. Therefore, if additional courts were established, the National People's Congress would legislate. In Germany, Paragraph 1 of Article 101 of the Basic Law not only stipulates that it is forbid-

545 Tan Shigui, Research on Issues of Judicial Independence, p. 17

546 It is known by comparison that if courts hold more power over their budget and over appointing, promoting and punishing judges, the "collective independence" of courts will be greatly strengthened. But the independence of courts in these respects does not mean that courts will be in a position to oppose the administrative organisations, and if courts were in charge of their own budget, they would subject to new political interests when judicial delegates have to appear every year before Parliament and explain the reasons for their financial requirements. Ministers will then communicate and negotiate with each other, so that the courts fulfil their functions as independently from political influence as possible. See Shimon Shetreet, Judicial Independence: New Conceptual Dimensions and Contemporary Challenges, in: Shimon Shetreet, Jules Deschênes, Judicial Independence: The Contemporary Debate, Dordrecht 1985, Chapter 52, pp. 646 f

547 Paragraph 2 of Article 8 of the Legislation Law

den to establish extraordinary courts,[548] but also stipulates the legal rights of judges (which are the general abstract promises which judges shall enjoy in order to exercise their powers) in order to prevent the establishment of courts from being arbitrarily controlled. Paragraph 2 of Article 101 of the Basic Law establishes that there are legal restrictions on the establishment of special courts.

Only when the State has a sense of responsibility for the basic principle of the rule of law can the legal restrictions on establishing new courts effectively guard against the establishment of extraordinary courts. In China, the danger of extraordinary courts being established currently derives essentially from the Supreme People's Court, since the Supreme People's Court can not only approve the abolition and establishment of different courts, but also can give an official response to requests from areas to establish development zone courts.[549] In 1992, for example, the Supreme People's Court approved the abolition of 47 Basic People's Courts and the establishment of four Intermediate People's Courts and 47 Basic People's Courts;[550] between January and March of 1993, the Supreme People's Court approved the abolition of two Intermediate People's Courts and 15 Basic People's Court and the establishment of three Intermediate People's Courts and 17 Basic People's Courts.[551] So far as there is a legal basis for establishing Intermediate People's Courts and Basic People's Courts, it is merely that they are approved by the Supreme People's Court exceeding its powers. There is no legal basis for establishing the development zone courts, which represent an arbitrary change in the system of establishing courts.[552]

---

548 In accordance with the explanations of the Federal Constitutional Court, extraordinary courts are "courts established for some specific case outside the bounds of legal jurisdiction", see BVerfGE 14, 56 (72), with further references.

549 "Development area" is the short name for the National Economic and Technological Development Zones. They are independent economic areas whose establishment is decided by the State Council and the People's government at the provincial level and in which preferential policies and flexible measures similar to those of the Special Economic Zones are applied to foreign investors. (The People's Pictorial, September 1987)

550 The Bulletin of the Supreme People's Court, 1993, Volume 1, p. 34

551 The Bulletin of the Supreme People's Court, 1993, Volume 2, p. 71

552 In 1984, the State Council approved the establishment of 14 National Economic and Technological Development Zones. After this, all areas successively established economic and technological development zones or new high-tech industrial development zones of various names. But these development zones are just special areas for implementing the open-door policy to the outside world, introducing foreign technology and developing economic and specialist areas, but not a level of administrative divisions. In accordance with Article 30 of the Constitution, development zones are not Chinese administrative divisions. In accordance with the Constitution and the Organic Law of the People's Courts, Chinese courts are established at four levels including the Supreme

In approving the abolition and establishment of courts, the Supreme People's Court is not only adopting the legislative role of the National People's Congress and its Standing Committee but thereby also in fact makes itself the leading organisation of all courts. The law is now no longer the only basis on which courts exercise their jurisdiction; rather, courts can exercise their powers at any time in accordance with the opinions and rules and regulations of the Supreme People's Court.[553]

## Section IV Hierarchical Dependence (*hierarchische Abhängigkeit*)

Another poorly perceived influence which threatens the independence of judges comes from the judiciary itself. The basic principle of the independence of judges is also applied internally. Specifically, other judges – especially senior judges or the presidents of courts – are forbidden to influence the adjudication by judges by exploiting the hierarchical relationships at court. In particular in difficult cases or cases without precedent, the independence of judges cannot resist the influence of senior judges, such that the independence of the individual judge is lacking.

### (1) Control by the Judicial Instances (instanzgerichtliche Urteilskontrolle)

In order to prevent judges from monopolising power arbitrarily and to guarantee that laws are applied correctly, general procedure laws provide a system of control by judicial instances. In 1971, the Federal Constitutional Court of Germany confirmed in a judgement that Paragraph 1 of Article 97 of the Basic Law merely authorises judges to exercise their jurisdiction and does not deal with the powers of judges.[554] Therefore, it is permissible for judges to control other judges and to issue directives in individual cases with respect to "the decisions

---

People's Court, the Higher People's Courts, the Intermediate People's Courts and the Basic People's Courts (see the Part 1, Chapter III, Section II of this dissertation on the establishment of Chinese courts). Basic People's Courts should accordingly be established in counties, municipalities, autonomous prefectures, towns, townships and nationality townships, but not development zones.

553 See also Liu Songshan, Development Zone Courts Represent the Unconstitutional and Illegal Establishment of Judicial Authorities, in: Jurisprudence, 2005, Volume 5, p. 29

554 See BVerfGE 31, 137 (140) and 12, 67 (71) before it. In this case, the Federal Constitutional Court decided that it was permissible for judges to be restricted by the judgements of higher-level courts.

of judges",[555] while many in Germany currently take the view that the independence of judges includes the independence of jurisdiction, so judges should not be restrained by the legal opinions of other courts.[556]

In practice, if a court of a higher instance has issued a certain legal opinion in a particular case, this opinion will also leave judges with a slight sense of pressure when judging specific cases. Generally, judges will not want their judgements to be revoked, which would dent their sense of professional pride. In particular in countries, such as Germany, where the occupation of judge is similar to that of civil servants, the more one's judgements are reversed, the more harm this may do to one's professional advancement.[557] In this respect, there is a certain degree of invisible pressure from the higher instances in Germany.[558] But courts of higher instances can also accept and adopt new arguments advanced by courts of lower instances. In China, it has always been a formal constraint that courts of lower instances apply the judgements of courts of higher instances.

Article 127 of the Chinese Constitution stipulates that the Supreme People's Court supervises the administration of justice by the local People's Courts and special People's Courts at various levels. The People's Courts at higher levels supervise the administration of justice by the People's courts at lower levels. It is difficult to decide what is meant here by "supervise". In China, the prominent problem is that courts at lower levels request instructions from courts at higher levels in certain specific cases. This system of requiring the courts at higher levels to issue instructional opinions is regarded as a form of "non-procedural judicial supervision" by the mainstream. But aside from the system of instructional opinions, the courts at higher levels can even by their own initiative direct cases being heard by the courts at lower levels because of their "major influence". Senior Chinese judicial officials explain the rationality of this supervision and instruction as follows:

---

555 Bettermann, Die Unabhängigkeit der Gerichte und der gesetzliche Richter, in: Bettermann, Nipperdey, Scheuner, Die Grundrechte, Volume 3, 2nd semi-volume – Rechtspflege und Grundrechtsschutz, Berlin 1959, p. 523

556 They may then make judgements according to their own opinion, even if this opinion differs from that of higher-level courts; they may even correct or abandon judgements which they themselves made.

557 Regarding the possibility of promotion, see Max Rheinstein, Wer wacht über die Wächter?, in: JuS 1974, p. 409

558 However, judges in Germany can under any circumstances judge cases according to their own opinion, even if different from that of others, and even if judges express such an opinion in order to object to an existing judicial opinion, even one of a higher-level court.

"In the majority of instances, the courts at lower levels request instructions from the courts at higher levels in cases which they feel are difficult. If the courts at higher levels consider the cases being heard by the courts at lower levels to have a major influence, they will issue directives by their own initiative which are conducive to applying and executing laws correctly and can correct misjudged cases even in the initial stage."[559]

These intentions may be rational and benign, but the arbitrary factors are sufficient to skew the whole litigation system and make an independent judgement by the courts at lower levels impossible. There are no articles of law or judicial interpretations to decide what defines cases which the courts at lower levels feel are difficult or what defines cases which the courts at higher levels consider to have major influence. In practice, these may become a pretext for arbitrary interference. Not only would the provisions of the Organic Law of the People's Courts regarding the different instances have no function, but the right of parties to question judgements of the first instance by way of appeal would be violated.[560]

## (2) The Internal Dependence of Courts

It is possible for the independence of judges to be threatened by dependency between colleagues within the same court or dependency on higher officials. Although courts ensure through the framework and personnel that judges in various social relationships are the judges of law,[561] contact between colleagues may still influence the content of judges' adjudications. These influences, not easy to discover, usually lie hidden in the unofficial sphere. There are many probable factors in the pressure on judges, such as the opinions of presiding judges, the opinions of the presidents of courts, the allocation of professional work, the restrictions of the opinions of other judges in collegial panels, the concurrent posts required in the profession, the allocation of resources, the service supervision, evaluation within posts and the anticipation of promotion.[562]

It is possible that the system of collegial panels, like the judicial court of the higher courts in Germany, has a special influence in damaging the independence of judges' jurisdiction. It is impossible to realise the independence of individual

---

559 Liu Jiachen, Litigation and its Axiology, Beijing Normal University Press, 1993, p. 46. The writer is a member of the Judicial Committee of the Supreme People's Court.

560 See He Weifang, Two Problems of the System of Judicial Management in China, in: Social Sciences of China, 1997, Volume 6, p. 128

561 See Hoffmann-Riem, in: DRiZ 2000, p. 18

562 See Schulze-Fielitz, in: Horst Dreier, Grundgesetz. Kommentar, Volume 3, Tübingen 2000, Article 97, margin number 37

judges if one judge (usually the presiding judge) of a collegial panel actually enjoys leadership status.[563] Under these circumstances, the individual judge on a collegial panel may simply repeat the legal opinion of others because of a perceived pressure to do so.[564]

In order to prevent such dependency, a legal system ought to be established in such a way that judges can maintain their own opinions even if they are different from the majority of other opinions. In principle, all the judges have the same voting rights in collegial panels (*Kollegialgremien*).[565] In order to prevent any special influence by the presiding judge of collegial panels in voting, a particular voting sequence should be separately established.[566] In Germany, the different opinions which the judges express in the joint conference can only be made public when the Federal Constitutional Court make judgements.[567] All the voting results of other courts fall within the boundaries of joint conference[568] and cannot be made public, to protect the authority of judges and their judgements.[569] Because judges are certain to discuss and consult on such matters in their deliberations before voting, this may potentially influence the fairness of judges.

---

563 According to the decision of 29th February 1996 by the Federal Constitutional Court, the presiding judge of a collegial panel is not allowed to amend the judgement of an individual judge, NJW 1996, pp. 2149 ff

564 The judges of higher courts often describe the experience that the joint conference of the collegial panel is just a balance of all the suggestions and legal opinions, and in practice, the opinion of chief judge is usually applied.

565 To prevent the ballot to be the same, the numbers of the members of collegial panel are usually confirmed to be odd. Only under the circumstances of Paragraph 4 of Article 196 of GVG can the chief judge have the decisive vote. It is impossible to waive their vote, see Article 195 of GVG

566 In Germany, the sequence of voting is decided by the judges' seniority. Those who have the shortest length of service vote before those who have the longest length of service, lay judges vote before judges, if a clerk (*Berichterstatter*) has been appointed, they vote first, and the presiding judge votes last, see Article 197 of GVG

567 Paragraph 2 of Article 30 of BVerfGG. Since 1971, judges who veto may write their differing opinion into the minutes of the collegial panel.

568 In 1958, Article 43 of DRiG stipulates with regard to the secrecy of joint conference that judges are required to maintain confidentiality on joint conferences and the course of voting in collegial panels even after their tenure has ended. But in the event of a veto, the names of judges who vetoed are never allowed to be made public, cf. Kopp/Schenke, Verwaltungsgerichtsordnung, 11th edition, Munich, Article 55, margin number 14. The obligation that judges maintain confidentiality is merely a matter of professional ethics (nobility of office).

569 If the parties know the judgement is not decided by judges coincidently, their degree to accept may be reduced.

However, the motive behind the secrecy of joint conference is to promote the independence of adjudication.[570]

The collegial system is also a fundamental judicial system provided by the Organic Law of the People's Courts of the People's Republic of China.[571] But in practice, it is merely a formality. Nominally, cases are judged by collegial panels, but in reality they are judged only by the judge handling the case. Some presiding judges even simply notify the other members of the collegial panel once they have made their judgement.[572] Although the Set of Regulations of the Supreme People's Court on the Work of Collegial Panels of the People's Courts specifies that when the collegial panel discusses a case, the judge handling the case shall give their opinion first on the facts of the case, whether the evidence is reliable and complete, and on the applicable law. If the presiding judge is the judge handling a case, he or she gives his or her opinion last. When deliberating on the judgement, the presiding judge gives his or her opinion last.[573] The presiding judge shall summarise the conclusive opinions of the collegial panel which have emerged from the discussions. But in reality, when discussing cases, the members of collegial panels usually simply declare their position on the basis of the opinion of the judge handling the case, by listening to the report by the judge handling the case and reviewing the file. The so-called democratic resolution exists in name only, because in China, the collegial panel does not in fact have any independent jurisdiction. Its power is always infringed on by presidents and presiding judges. Adjudication without judgement or judgement without adjudication have become the norm in the Chinese judiciary.[574] Given that presidents and presiding judges interfere with the judicial power of judges through their powers of administrative management, it is difficult for individual judges to be independent. The so-called independence of judges in joint conference has lost its meaning.

---

570 See Günter Schmidt-Räntsch, Jürgen Schmidt-Räntsch, Deutsches Richtergesetz (DRiG), Kommentar, 6th edition, Munich 2008, Article 43, margin number 3; see also Rolf Lamprecht, Richter contra Richter, Baden-Baden 1992, p.28

571 See the first sentence in Article 10 of the Organic Law of the People's Courts of the People's Republic of China

572 Hou Yilin, Perfecting the System of Collegial Panels with Respect to the System of Selecting and Appointing Presiding Judges, in: Legal Systems and Society, 2008, Volume 11 (No. 2 of 2), p. 148

573 Article 10 of the Set of Regulations of the Supreme People's Court on the Work of Collegial Panels of the People's Courts (approved by the Judicial Committee of the Supreme People's Court at its 1234th meeting, 30th July 2002)

574 Lin Jingsong, Reflections on the System of Deliberation in Chinese Collegial Panels, in: Jurisprudence, 2005, Volume 10, p. 17

Immediately after the reunification of Germany, there was a special form of law whereby judges relied on the officials at higher levels in the short-term period after the laws of the Federal Republic of Germany began to come into effect in the areas of the former East German.[575] This is somewhat similar to the dependent relationship between newly appointed, inexperienced judges and older, experienced judges.[576] Although such dependence is unavoidable in practice, presiding judges do not in fact have the power to arbitrarily change the judgement of any judge.[577] Except for examining judgements by other judges according to the provisions on the different instances of trial in accordance with procedural law, it is forbidden to examine the judgements of other judges. It is not permitted for presiding judges of collegial panels to amend the judgements of other judges, because it infringes on the independence of judges.

## Section V Manipulation in the Distribution of Work

If courts try to influence specific cases by distributing work in such a way as to engineer a desirable result or by trying to identify and exploit previous trends in judgements, then the independence of judges is threatened. But as long as the Organic Law of the People's Courts and the procedure law stipulate in advance how cases are to be distributed among individual judges and judicial organisations, this danger can be precluded.

In Germany, the Basic Law provides the protection of "statutory judges"[578] for setting abstract regulations for the standard distribution of work in advance.

---

575 Judges in the areas of the former East Germany previously regarded the purpose of training as being to implement socialist reform. After reunification, the Basic Law was effective in all areas of the reintegrated Federal Republic of Germany. In order to help judges in the former East Germany apply the new laws based on the Basic Law, it was in practice necessary for "visiting judges" from the former West Germany to direct them. In order to ensure that the aforementioned directives were carried out, the posts at higher levels, such as that of presiding judge or court president, were usually held by judges from the former West Germany. See the press report, Mit Ost-Erfahrung an ein Bundesgericht, in the *Frankfurter Allgemeine Zeitung (FAZ)* of 9th September 2004, p. 10

576 The relevant discussion can be seen in He Weifang, Two Problems of the System of Judicial Management in China, in: Social Sciences of China, 1997, Volume 6, p. 127

577 See BVerfG, in: NJW 1996, p. 2149. In this case, the president of an administrative court abridged and amended the judgement in a case in order to bring the judge under pressure. The Service Court considered such an action to be a breach of duty (breaching the independence of judges) and temporarily removed the president from his post.

578 The second sentence in Paragraph 1 of Article 101 of GG decrees that no-one may be removed from the jurisdiction of his lawful judge.

This function is usually realised by a work distribution plan in courts and is approved by courts by means of autonomous proposals from judges at the beginning of each financial year. In China, there is currently still no abstract regulation on the distribution of work. The presidents of courts can assign any case depending on the purpose and feasibility of the individual case. This flexibility in the distribution of cases is likely to be abused, especially when the procedure is not transparent. For example, in order to fulfil the expectations of government in particular cases, courts will assign these cases to judges known to be loyal to the government policies in question. Precisely because of this form of control, the image of judicial authorities has been seriously damaged in people's minds.

Some international principles require that it be decided in advance which judges shall handle which categories of cases. The basic principles of the United Nations on the independence of the judiciary merely stipulate that it is an autonomous problem of the courts to decide how to distribute cases among judges.[579] The minimum standards of the International Bar Association on the independence of the judiciary also require that work is distributed to judges by a system which is decided in advance and can only be changed under clearly defined conditions.[580] If cases are only distributed according to such a plan, then the independence of judges cannot be damaged by the distribution of cases by court presidents.[581] Plans for determining the distribution of cases in advance also exist in countries which employ a common law system, but the power of distribution then belongs to the presiding judges.[582] Therefore, the International Bar Association has accepted the concept of "statutory judges" (i.e. lawful or natural judges) in order to define the power of judges in advance, as is exactly the present practice in Germany,[583] while in international courts such as the

579 Article 14 of the basic principles stipulates that: "The assignment of cases to judges within the court to which they belong is an internal matter of judicial administration."

580 Article 11 a) of the IBA minimum standards stipulates that: "Division of work among judges should ordinarily be done under a predetermined plan, which can be changed in certain clearly defined circumstances."

581 Article 11 c) of the IBA minimum standards stipulates that: "Subject to (a), the exclusive responsibility for case assignment should be vested in a responsible judge, preferably the President of the Court."

582 Article 11 b) of the IBA minimum standards stipulates that: "In countries where the power of division of judicial work is vested in the Chief Justice, it is not considered inconsistent with judicial independence to accord to the Chief Justice the power to change the predetermined plan for sound reasons, preferably in consultation with the senior judges when practicable."

583 See Shimon Shetreet, Judicial Independence: New Conceptual Dimensions and Contemporary Challenges, in: Shimon Shetreet, Jules Deschênes, Judicial Independence: The Contemporary Debate, Dordrecht 1985, Chapter 52, pp. 393 f

European Court, most cases are distributed to sub-courts directly by the court presidents.[584]

## (1) German Protection of the Principle of Statutory Judges

In Germany, no one can be deprived of the constitutional protection of statutory judges, as contained in the Constitution.[585] As a protection of legal procedure, it requires that the decision as to who is appointed as judge of a case is made according to general objective rules, and as far as possible in advance.[586] It is forbidden to withdraw the purpose of the second sentence of Paragraph 1 of Article 101 of the Basic Law. According to judgements by the Federal Constitutional Court, this is to prevent the judiciary from being operated in such a way that judges are appointed by being handpicked to hear cases, and to eliminate so-called "cabinet justice" (*Kabinettsjustiz*).[587] Why is this a question of the inde-

584 Article 9 of the Rules of Procedure of the European Court of Justice stipulates that the court president assigns cases to all the law courts and appoints the Rapporteur in each case. All cases received are uniformly written into a detailed list at the beginning. All cases are decided by the whole court in principle, which means that after the written procedure, the court decides on a law court to continue judging the case. The rules of procedure also provide an exception clause whereby if the case concerns personnel of the court, the case is assigned directly to an individual law court according to a rota principle.

585 The provision that no one can be deprived of the constitutional protection of statutory judges has appeared in the German Constitution since 1849, see for example Article 175 of the Paulskirschen Constitution (*Paulskirschenverfassung*) of 1849, Article 7 of the Prussian Constitution of 1850, Article 105 of the Weimar Constitution of 1919, and the second sentence of Paragraph 1 of Article 101 of the Basic Law of 1949. The protective function of this article is mainly aimed at stopping administrative organisations from interfering in the judiciary, see Ulrike Seif, Recht und Justizhoheit, Historische Grundlagen des gesetzlichen Richters in Deutschland, England und Frankreich, Berlin 2003; Seif, Recht und Gerechtigkeit: die Garantie des gesetzlichen Richters und die Gewaltenteilungskonzeptionen des 17.-19. Jahrhunderts, in: Der Staat 2003, pp. 110 ff

586 BVerfGE 19, 52 (59 f); 22, 254 (258); 322 (327 f). Such protection has the function of existing performance and defence. See also Thomas Roth, Das Grundrecht auf den gesetzlichen Richter, Berlin 2000; Ernst Träger, Der gesetzliche Richter – aktuelle Fragen aus Verfassung und internationalem Recht, in Walther Fürst, Festschrift für Wolfgang Zeidler, Volume 1, Berlin 1987, pp. 123 ff. Although there is neither the need nor the ability for formal laws to decide which judges handle cases, legislators should establish a basic governing rule. The Constitution establishes specific rules according to the different forms of jurisdiction, different organisational forms and scales of courts, the number of judges at courts, the number of cases received and specific changes in the number of cases received, see BVerfGE 95, 322 (328).

587 See BVerfGE 4, 412 (416); 17, 294 (299)

pendence of judges and not just of the neutrality and objectivity of courts? One reason may be that the judge chosen would be expected to judge in a specific way and not be impartial. Confirming how cases are to be abstractly distributed in advance can reduce the possibility of the judiciary interfering with individual cases, because if cases are distributed in this way, judgements no longer depend on who is handling the case, but only on objective fixed standards. This not only protects the independence of judges, but also promotes the trust of parties involved and of the public in the fairness and objectivity of courts.[588]

In Germany, the provisions of the Constitution on the organisation of courts are realised by the specific provisions of basic laws[589] and are carried out in practice by courts as the means of establishing plans for distributing work within the framework of self-governance by judges in each year.[590] When assigning cases, the abstract standards are mainly the professional fields of judges and collegial panels.[591] In the collegial panels, the basic principle of distributing cases is that judges decide by resolution.[592] When confirming these rules on the limits of authority, the circumstance that judges are absent or unable to attend should be taken into the consideration in advance.[593]

---

588 BVerfGE 95, 322 (327): "If such trust is destroyed, the parties to a case would have to worry that judge handling the case is not the judge one would expect"; BVerfGE 17, 252: the first sentence of Paragraph 2 of Article 97 of GG strictly forbids the presiding board (*Präsidium*) of the court from excluding full-time judges from the judiciary when distributing work.

589 See Articles 21e and 21g of GVG

590 Article 21e of GVG stipulates that the presidium of the court decides the members of the collegial panel, appoints investigating judges, regulates delegate judges and distributes work. The deadline for the aforementioned arrangement shall be decided at the beginning of the judicial year. The president decides what adjudicative activities they are in charge of. Each judge can belong to various collegial panels at the same time.

591 One pattern of distribution is the alternative pattern, whereby cases are assigned by the court in the order in which they are received and judges are assigned them alternately. Alternatively, work is distributed according to specific fields or in the order of the name of the plaintiff or the name of the defendant. Sometimes, courts apply several of these patterns simultaneously.

592 In accordance with the judgement of 8th April 1997 by the Federal Constitutional Court (1 PBvU 1/95, BVerfGE 95), if there are too many members in the collegial panel, the court can decide the presiding judge in individual cases and not in advance in accordance with the abstract rules, which is clearly inconsistent with the principle of statutory judges protected by the Constitution. In these situations, however, the general abstract rules of deciding in advance have to give way to the specific situation. Before this, different tribunals of the Federal Constitutional Court had different opinions on this issue.

593 The first sentence of Paragraph 1 of Article 21g of GVG stipulates that the work of the collegial panel shall be distributed among all the members by a decision of all the pro-

If the rules on deciding the distribution of cases in advance are breached so as to arrange which judge handles a case, the parties in the case may appeal to the constitutional court.[594] But the judges themselves are not damaged in their individual rights.[595] If judges who have been assigned to handle a case in accordance with the abstract rules are personally or materially related to the parties in the case, then the partiality of the judge shall be prevented by additional rules.[596]

## (2) The Chinese Practice of Distributing Work

Aside from the fact that there are many special courts in China in addition to ordinary courts as in Germany, there are also different law courts for trying different types of cases, rather than a given type of case being assigned to different courts. For example, the Supreme People's Court establishes seven law courts, two criminal courts and four civil courts in addition to the administrative courts,[597] and all cases which enter the court are registered at the case-filing court. According to the website of the Supreme People's Court, the main function of its case-filing court is to "register all the kinds of cases handled by the Supreme People's Court", and having registered them within the jurisdiction of

---

fessional judges on the collegial panel. The principles according to which members are involved in proceedings shall be decided before the beginning of the judicial year and for the period of that year, and can only be amended when necessary because of too great a workload, too light a workload, or when individual members are changed or permanently incapacitated. In 1964, the Organic Law of the People's Courts incorporated the aforementioned provisions. Before that, the work at courts was distributed among members directly by the president and presiding judges.

594 See Section 4a of Paragraph 1 of Article 93 of GG and Paragraph 1 of Article 90 of BVerfGG. Breaches of the provisions in the second sentence in Paragraph 1 of Article 101 of GG are the grounds for the Federal Constitutional Court examining absolutely, cf. BVerfGE 20, 39 (40); see Kunig, in: Münch/Kunig, Grundgesetz-Kommentar, Volume 3, Article 101, margin number 22

595 Individual judges are protected by other forms of rights, such as the procedure of instituting the supervision of posts, see also Kunig, in: von Münch/Kunig, Grundgesetz-Kommentar, Volume 3, Article 101, margin number 18. Judges filing constitutional suits is just a measure directed against certain public powers, violating their statutory status as endowed by the State, see BVerfGE 15, 298 (301 f)

596 In accordance with the Federal Constitutional Court and the overwhelming majority of doctrines in Germany, the protection of statutory judges shall ensure judges satisfy all other conditions of the Constitution besides the rules mentioned above, see Kunig, in: Münch/Kunig, Grundgesetz-Kommentar, Volume 3, Article 101, margin number 17

597 The breakdown of the Supreme People's Court can be seen on the homepage of the Supreme People's Court: http://www.court.gov.cn/about/

the Supreme People's Court, to "transfer them to the relevant courts to be handled" and to "manage the time limits and procedures of all the kinds of cases tried by the Supreme People's Court".[598]

However, there are in reality no reliable rules in China as to how cases are to be distributed to the law courts once they have been accepted by the case-filing court. In the process of distributing cases, the independence of judges may be threatened or not taken into account.[599] In general, most factors concerning attempts to interfere with independent adjudication are centred on the course of events after cases have been distributed, i.e. after it has been decided which judge handles which case.

---

598 See the website of the Supreme People's Court: http://www.court.gov.cn/about/200302130028.htm

599 In China, all judges handling cases cannot refuse the interference of the president of the court, presiding judges or other powers supported by the president of the court and the presiding judges (this refers to all the factors mentioned in this dissertation, such as the absolute power of the court president over personnel appointments and removal, assessment, supervision and so on). Since the court president and presiding judges can interfere in the adjudication of any case if they wish, they do not need to interfere in the distribution of cases.

## Section VI Conclusions

### (1) Comparison

In Chinese courts, the degree of dependency between administrative levels is much higher than in Germany. German judges are only restrained by the law, but Chinese judges ask presiding judges and court presidents for instructions, and courts at lower levels ask courts at higher levels for instructions. German judges are permitted to have different opinions to others in the court; the pressure and influence on them from colleagues is much less than for Chinese judges, because Chinese judges are not only restrained by their court president and presiding judges in the procedures of election and appointment, supervision and assessment, but are also guided by them in other aspects of administrative management. The pressure on German judges from within the court and from courts at higher levels is slight, but in China, this pressure is obvious and universally acknowledged. This not only causes the authority of Chinese judges to suffer, but also makes court presidents and presiding judges into a high-risk group with regard to corruption, because if parties in a case wish to influence the judge's decision, they need only use the direct method of convincing a higher-level official above the judge to exert pressure on the judge.

In China, there is a lot of discussion at the moment about the lack of independence in the finance and budgeting of courts, such that courts are not able to be independent of the local government, which is another important reason why Chinese judges fail to try cases independently. When power over the financing and resources of courts lies with the administrative government, this is enough for the judiciary to not want to offend the administrative departments.[600] For example, if a case concerns the local government, then as long as the local government coerces the court through its powers over finance, such as the daily expenses of courts and the salaries of judges, the court president will have to direct the judge to be partial in favour of the government. Although the finance of courts is to be unified and incorporated into the central budget, this is merely a reform plan. The independence of judges be only be possible once courts truly no longer need worry about their finances and judges about their livelihood.

The organisation and administration of courts in China is not the same as in Germany. In Germany, all matters are governed by law, and all factors which might interfere with independent adjudication by judges are considered and averted. Although the measures are not perfect, there are in general no serious

600 Cai Dingjian, History and Reform, the Course of Establishing a Legal System in New China, China University of Political Science and Law Press, March 1999, Volume 1, p. 390

problems. But in China, there are still too many self-contradictory areas in this respect. On the one hand, courts are controlled by the administrative organisations with respect to finance and personnel, while on the other, the power of courts occasionally crosses the line. For example, the Supreme People's Court is approving the abolition and establishment of various kinds of courts. Powers which should not be exercised by courts are being exercised by courts, while areas where courts should enjoy self-governance are being restricted. Such an illogical system needs to be reformed as soon as possible.

Many Chinese scholars consider that in China today, the serious dependence of courts on local government is rooted in the illogical mode of establishing courts, whereby all local courts are established according to local administrative divisions and the finances of the courts at the different levels are determined by the local government at the corresponding level.[601] So far, the most attractive reform plan has been to reform the way courts are established, implementing vertical management[602] or a two-track system[603]. Although there is not the same

601 Jiao Hongchang, From the Localisation of Courts to the Two-Track System of Establishing Courts, in: Journal of the National School of Administration, 2000, Volume 1

602 The basic premise of vertical management is that the leadership system of Chinese courts implements a system of double leadership: on the one hand, receiving professional instruction and supervision from the judicial organs at higher levels, while on the other hand being restricted by the government at the same level with respect to personnel and finance. In order to break this status of multiple leadership, the plan of vertical leadership would be that: (1) the Central Committee establishes judicial work committees, the courts at various levels establish Party committees, the Party committee of the local courts at lower levels obey the Party committee of the local courts at higher levels and the Party committees at all subordinate levels obey the Supreme People's Court, and the Supreme People's Court obeys the Central Party Committee; (2) the funding of courts is uniform – the central financing committee sets a unified budget, and after the National People's Congress has approved the budget, the Supreme People's Court allocates, manages and distributes the funding to the courts at various levels in succession; (3) the personnel, finance and resources of the courts at higher levels and the courts at lower levels belong to the relationship of vertical leadership, and the judicial work serves as a balanced relationship of supervision. Courts implement the vertical leadership system from top to bottom, the courts at lower levels are led by the courts at higher levels in their organisation, administration and work, the courts throughout the country are led only by the Supreme People's Court, thus eliminating the interference of the Party in the specific affairs of the judiciary within the system and excluding the unreasonable interference of the administrative organisations (especially local government) in the judiciary and realising judicial independence. The specific discussion can be seen in Zhao Junru, The Current Situation of the Judicial Court System and Prospects for its Reform, in: Modern Law, October 1999, Volume 21, Issue 5; He Derong, Song Jian, Establishing a Judicial Court System with Chinese Characteristics, in: Application of

severe localisation of courts in Germany, the aspects that judicial areas and administrative areas coincide and that the finance of courts is incorporated into the local finance budget are similar to China. The reason is that the system of financially managing courts is not institutionalised and is inappropriate. Therefore, the most urgent task at hand is a reform of the financial management system of courts.

## (2) Opinions on Reform

### *(a) Funding*

Some scholars propose that the reform of court funding should come in two stages: the first stage is that the Supreme People's Court shall draw up the budget for itself and the special courts and submit this to the National People's Congress for approval, and finally the state financing committee shall allot funds in accordance with the budget. At the same time, the system of collecting litigation fees should be reformed. Parties engaging in litigation before the Supreme People's Court and the special courts shall pay their litigation fees to the central treasury. The Ministry of Finance appropriates these funds for the finance budget of the Supreme People's Court and special courts as approved by the National People's Congress, combining them with funds from the central budget. For the funds of Higher People's Courts, Intermediate People's Courts and Basic People's Courts, the provincial People's Congress decides the budget, the provincial financing committee enforces the budget and uniformly allocates it, and the provincial Higher People's Courts formulate the overall plan and distribution. In addition, a plan is implemented whereby the litigation fees are uniformly controlled by the provincial Higher People's Courts. The parties in dispute pay all their litigation fees to the state treasury at the same level, which is

---

Law, 2000, Volume 1; Wang Guochun, Wu Yugong, Existing Problems and Countermeasures in the Chinese Judicial System, in: Journal of Changde Normal College (Social Sciences Edition), September 2000, Volume 25, Issue 5

603 The so-called two-track system means establishing a system of central courts and a system of local courts. The central court system establishes a National Supreme Court, a National Appeal Court and a National District Court. The Supreme Court will still be established in Beijing. The Appeal Courts are established wherever there are governments of provinces and autonomous regions and cities and municipalities directly under the Central Government. The District Courts are established in central cities. A province or autonomous region can establish multiple District Courts. Their funds are uniformly allocated by the provincial financing committee, and judges are still appointed and removed by the local People's Congress and its Standing Committee. See Jiao Hongchang, From the Localisation of Courts to the Two-Track System of Establishing Courts, in: Journal of the National School of Administration, 2000 Volume 1

centred in the provincial state treasury. Provincial Ministries of Finance appropriate the sum through the finance budget for the provincial courts as a whole, as approved by the provincial People's Congress, combining it with the funds in the budget, and the provincial Higher People's Court formulates the overall plan and distribution in accordance with the planned financial cash flow balance of the courts at various levels in the province, in order to subsidise the handling fees of the courts at various levels in the province.

The second stage is that the funding of the courts throughout the country is reported by the Supreme People's Court to the National People's Congress, in order for it to decide the budget. The national financing committee executes the budget and uniformly allocates it, and the Supreme People's Court formulates the overall plan and distribution in accordance with the specific budgets of the courts at various levels in the country as a whole (including ordinary courts and special courts). In addition, a plan is implemented whereby the litigation fees are uniformly controlled by the Supreme People's Court. The parties in dispute pay all their litigation fees to the state treasury at the same level, which is centred in the central state treasury. The Ministry of Finance appropriates the sum through the finance budget for the courts in the country as a whole, as approved by the National People's Congress. The Supreme People's Court formulates the overall plan and distribution in accordance with the planned financial cash flow balance of the courts at various levels, in order to subsidise the handling fees of the courts at various levels.[604]

*(b) Reform of the Internal Organisation of Courts*

In accordance with the aforementioned reform plan of scholars, courts would be independent in their funding, and the possibility of the administrative organisations interfering with the judiciary would be reduced, although courts would only gain external independence. In order to guarantee the independence of judges, the internal organisation of courts would also have to be reformed, as explained above.

- Firstly, the powers of the president need to be regulated and restricted. The president of the court is not only the supreme head of the court's administrative affairs but also the supreme judge in the court. The president has the power to instruct, approve and decide in all areas, and has the power to or-

604 The relevant discussion can be found in Han Bo, Research on Reform of the Court System, People's Court Press, Beijing, May 2003, Volume 1, pp. 276-277

ganise and supervise the workings of court as a whole.[605] This causes the internal management of courts to be administrative in nature, and judges currently have no independence under any kind of administrative order. Therefore, in order to grant judges internal independence, the powers of the presidents firstly need to be limited. The administrative affairs of court may draw on the experience of the German method and establish committees of judges. The committees of judges decide by discussion.

- The second requirement is to strengthen the function of collegial panels. In order to actually exercise the jurisdiction of collegial panels as provided in law, the system of examining and approving cases firstly needs to be abolished. Although Chinese law does not stipulate that cases heard by collegial panels shall be examined and approved by the presiding judges or the president, in reality Chinese courts usually mix the president's and the presiding judges' administrative management function with their adjudicative function, leading judges to ask officials at higher levels for instruction either in administrative affairs or even in practical adjudicative affairs. In order to change this situation, it needs to be clarified that the president and presiding judges only have the function of judges when they are hearing cases and have the same status as other judges.
- The third requirement is to abolish as soon as possible the system whereby courts at lower levels request instructions from courts at higher levels. The purpose of having the different instances of court is to guarantee that the procedure of litigation is fair, and if this superior-subordinate relationship between the courts at higher levels and the courts at lower levels does not exist, both will be able to make judgements independently. If instructions are requested or directives issued in advance between the two instances, the so-called legal system in which the second instance is the final instance exists in name only, and the right of parties to appeal is meaningless.

605 Zhang Chunhe, On the Presidents of Courts, in: Jurisprudence Magazine, 1997, Volume 3, pp. 37-38

# B Independence of status

## Chapter V Guaranteeing the Status of Judges

Paragraph 1 of Article 97 of the Basic Law nearly perfectly guarantees the independence of judicial adjudication, and Paragraph 2 is directed to guaranteeing the independence of the status of judges and lays particular stress on specific problems of judicial independence by stipulating that: "judges appointed permanently to full-time positions may be involuntarily dismissed, permanently or temporarily suspended, transferred or retired before the expiration of their term of office only by virtue of judicial decision and only for the reasons and in the manner specified by the laws. The legislature may set age limits for the retirement of judges appointed for life. In the event of changes in the structure of courts or in their districts, judges may be transferred to another court or removed from office, provided they retain their full salary."

The independence of the status of judges principally means that judges cannot be arbitrarily dismissed or transferred,[606] in order to ensure the independence of judges' posts and to prevent judges from having misgivings about possible harm to their status if they do not obey the orders of superiors to pass a particular judgement. The independence of the status of judges is in direct and obvious principle relationship to the independence of adjudication. In other words, the independence of the status of judges is in some respects a precondition for adjudicative independence,[607] in order to adequately implement the independence of judicial adjudication. Independence of adjudication prohibits judges from being directed, but the guarantee of the independence of judges is not entirely the same thing, since judges who cannot be directed or instructed can still be suspended from their duties, dismissed or transferred in order to remove their status as judge, which can also damage the independence of judges. Not all judges are necessarily appointed for life, and judges who must fear for their position at any time cannot judge independently in accordance only with their conscience and the law. The status of judges must be secure enough that they can resist these influences and so pass their judgements with confidence, which depends on the level of guarantee of the independence of their status. The independence of the status of judges prohibits judges from being transferred in accordance with the affinities or animosities of judicial and administrative officers. It is therefore prohibited for judges to be involuntarily dismissed, permanently or temporarily

606 Konrad Hesse, Grundzüge des Verfassungsrechts der Bundesrepublik Deutschland, 15th edition, Heidelberg 1985, p. 212

607 Maunz/Dürig/Herzog, Grundgesetz: Kommentar, Munich 1980, Article 97, margin number 56

suspended, transferred or retired before the expiration of their term of office, unless by virtue of judicial decision and only for the reasons and in the manner specified by the law. But in Germany, only the status of judges who are formally employed (i.e. judges appointed for life and judges appointed for a fixed term) can be guaranteed in this way.[608] It may be said that the independence of the status of judges supplements the adjudicative independence, wherein the two complement each other in order to resist various kinds of damage to the independence of judicial adjudication.[609]

Because Germany has acknowledged the difference between judges and civil servants in general, it has established the German Judges Act in order to provide a personnel system specifically for judges. In order to guarantee the independence and status of judges, the German Judges Act stipulates that judges shall be appointed in writing[610] and defines the grounds for nullifying and withdrawing appointments,[611] the scope of supervision,[612] the main conditions and procedures by which judges may be dismissed, held in reserve, suspended from duty, retired and transferred, the establishment of Judicial Council (*Richterrat*) and Presiding Council (*Präsidialrat*) and the establishment of Service Courts, all of which are aimed at guaranteeing the independence of judges. In the following, the guarantee of the status of judges shall be discussed along these lines, and a comparison drawn with the Chinese system.

## Section I The German System of Guaranteeing the Status of Judges

### (1) A Summary of Guaranteeing the Status of Judges

#### *(a) Preconditions*

The guarantee of the independence of the status of judges appointed for life and judges appointed for a fixed term must firstly be dependent upon the judge having a post at a particular court.[613] Judges must have independence in their status and independence in their office not solely because they are judges but because they hold a particular post and execute the associated functions. Therefore, they

608 Article 30 of DRiG

609 Manfred Wolf, Eduard Kern, Gerichtsverfassungsrecht, Beck, 5th edition, Munich 1975, p. 134

610 Article 17 of DRiG

611 Articles 18 and 19 of DRiG

612 Article 26 of DRiG

613 Article 27 of DRiG

have to have been granted a judge's post in order for it to be possible or indeed meaningful to protect their independence in relation to said post. There is a difference here between the abstract office of judge (*abstraktes Richteramt*) and the concrete office of judge (*konkretes Richteramt*). The abstract office of judge yields the basic characteristics of the office of judge and the grades of salary, such as for example that of a junior judge appointed for life at a *Land* court. Although the abstract office of judge protects judges from being dismissed, judges are still susceptible to being transferred between courts. Article 27 of the German Judges Act prohibits fluid (*fliegende*) judicial posts by stipulating that judges shall be granted "a judgeship at a particular court," such as for example a judgeship at a *Land* court in a particular city. Only once a judge has been granted a definite post is the independence of his or her status absolutely guaranteed, because only judges who hold a concrete judgeship can subsequently be deemed to have been suspended from duty or transferred to another court. If a judge is not granted a concrete judgeship, he or she cannot act in court or be regarded as a statutory judge by a court.[614]

#### *(b) The Ban in Principle on Dismissal, Suspension, Transfer and Retirement*

Judges who have been formally appointed are in principle prohibited from being dismissed (*Entlassung*), permanently or temporarily suspended (*Amtsenthebung*), relocated (*Versetzung*) or ordered to retire (*Ruhestand*) before the expiry of their term of office. As long as their term of office has not expired, they enjoy full immobility (*volle Immobilität*) in principle. Therefore, when formally executing the measures mentioned above, the aim of guaranteeing the independence of status will be influenced, and other informal measures (*informelle Maßnahmen*) such as leave (*Beurlaubung*), secondment (*Abordnung*) or allocation of duties (*Geschäftsverteilung*) will also exert the same or nearly the same influence (which shows the close relationship between the independence of status and the independence of posts). Accordingly, the German Federal Constitutional Court has indicated in an individual case that effectively sidelining (*kaltstellen*) a judge by way of the allocation of duties, although almost a removal from adjudication, falls short of the provisions in the first sentence of Paragraph 2 of Article 97 of the Basic Law.[615] Under this interpretation, this article also includes the rights of judges engaged in professional activities.[616] Only in this way can the

---

614 Manfred Wolf, Eduard Kern, Gerichtsverfassungsrecht, Beck, 5th edition, Munich 1975, p. 136

615 BVerfGE 17, pp. 252 ff

616 Maunz/Dürig/Herzog, Grundgesetz: Kommentar, Munich 1980, Article 97, margin number 57

independence of judges be extensively safeguarded, enabling the judiciary to perform its tasks within the state under the rule of law.

In conclusion, the second paragraph of Article 97 of the Basic Law on the independence of the status of judges stipulates that, in addition to the measures enumerated, all actions which exert *de facto* the same influence as dismissal, suspension, temporary retirement and transfer to other courts are not permitted.[617]

#### *(c) Exceptions*

The independence of status permits some exceptions to the ban on transfer or suspension, namely that judges who are to be punished may be removed in this way by written approval, or courts may issue judgements on transfers and suspensions in accordance with legal grounds and legal procedures. From this point of view, this may be said to be an actual retention of the judge (*Richterbehalt*).[618] The German Judges Act stipulates detailed provisions in this regard.[619]

In addition, Article 31 of the German Judges Act stipulates the specific circumstances and grounds for transfer because of judicial interests,[620] under which a judge may be transferred if circumstances beyond the judge's judicial activities necessitate this in order to avoid an impairment of the course of justice. The section of this Act concerning the Service Courts of Judges further stipulates[621] that instances of transfer because of judicial interests shall be judged by the service courts.[622]

### (2) Dismissal

Article 21 of the German Judges Act stipulates the provisions for dismissing judges, which are applied to all judges holding posts at the Federal level and in the various *Länder*.[623] The special provisions for dismissing probationary judges and judges on commission are stipulated separately in Articles 22 and 23.

---

617 Manfred Wolf, Eduard Kern, Gerichtsverfassungsrecht, Beck, 5th edition, Munich 1975, p. 135

618 Paragraph 1 of Article 97 of GG

619 Articles 30 and 31 of DRiG

620 Article 31 of DRiG

621 See Maunz/Dürig/Herzog, Grundgesetz: Kommentar, Munich 1980, Article 97, margin number 57

622 Section 2 of Paragraph 1 of Article 62 of DRiG

623 Günter Schmidt-Räntsch, Jürgen Schmidt-Räntsch, Deutsches Richtergesetz (DRiG), Kommentar, 6th edition, Munich 2008, Article 21, margin number 2

The dismissal of judges can be divided into *ipso iure* dismissal or dismissal by law (*Entlassung kraft Gesetzes*) and appropriate dismissal or disciplinary dismissal by the competent authority (*Entlassung durch Verfügung der Dienstbehörde*). Similar to the provisions of the Federal Civil Servants Act (Articles 28 and 29 of BBG, Article 22 and Paragraph 1 of Article 23 of the Civil Servants Legal Framework Act (*Beamtenrechtsrahmengesetz = BRRG*), as of 1st April 2009: Articles 22 and 23 of the Civil Servants Status Act (*Beamtenstatusgesetz = BeamtStG*), the distinction between the two is essentially only the time of dismissal, since if judges do not agree with the dismissal imposed by the authorities, both forms of dismissal require that service courts then adjudicate and pass judgement.[624] It is not permitted by law to punish judges appointed for life or judges appointed for a fixed term by dismissing them. *Ipso iure* dismissal is of course decided by service courts passing a judgement, and the time of dismissal is the time when the cause of the dismissal occurred; appropriate dismissal is permitted by service courts by a declaration, and when the supreme authority concerned sanctions the dismissal, the dismissal is devised and promulgated. The grounds for dismissal are enumerated in the German Judges Act; the legislation of the various *Länder* cannot stipulate other grounds for dismissal beyond these.[625]

*(a) Ipso Iure Dismissal*

If there is cause for an *ipso iure* dismissal, it is not necessary to issue a dismissal having formal legal effect (*Entlassungsverfügung mit rechtsgestaltender Wirkung*), but rather merely to affirm it through the service courts, which merely involves a declaration.[626] In accordance with Article 21 of the German Judges Act, the grounds for an *ipso iure* dismissal include the following:

(i) Loss of German Identity as Defined in Article 116 of the Basic Law[627]

In accordance with Article 9 of the German Judges Act, being a German national is a precondition of appointment as a judge. If this condition is not imposed when a judge is appointed, then the appointment is invalid (Paragraph 2 of Article 18 of the German Judges Act). Judges who lose their German nationality

624 Günter Schmidt-Räntsch, Jürgen Schmidt-Räntsch, Deutsches Richtergesetz (DRiG), Kommentar, 6th edition, Munich 2008, Article 21, margin number 2

625 Günter Schmidt-Räntsch, Jürgen Schmidt-Räntsch, Deutsches Richtergesetz (DRiG), Kommentar, 6th edition, Munich 2008, Article 21, margin number 2

626 Günter Schmidt-Räntsch, Jürgen Schmidt-Räntsch, Deutsches Richtergesetz (DRiG), Kommentar, 6th edition, Munich 2008, Article 21, margin number 3

627 Günter Schmidt-Räntsch, Jürgen Schmidt-Räntsch, Deutsches Richtergesetz (DRiG), Kommentar, 6th edition, Munich 2008, Article 21, margin number 4

after their appointment shall be dismissed in accordance with the provisions of this article.

(ii) Entrance into Public Employment or a Public Office (*öffentlich-rechtliches Dienst- oder Amtsverhältnis*) for another employer (*Dienstherr*)

Judges are to devote all their energies to this office, hence it is forbidden in principle for judges to accept the responsibility for other posts or offices, except as otherwise specified by law or agreed upon with the supreme authority in charge of the judge and the new employer, wherein it is also possible with the agreement of the judge for the judge to continue his or her tenure as judge after adopting the new post (final sentence in Paragraph 1 of Article 21 of the German Judges Act).[628]

(iii) Appointment as a Professional Soldier (*Berufssoldat*) or Soldier on a Fixed-Term Contract (*Soldat auf Zeit*)

If judges are appointed as professional soldiers or soldiers on a fixed-term contract, even if their employer remains the same, they shall be dismissed.

The German Judges Act does not stipulate specifically for the situation in which the employer remains the same and for example judges are appointed as civil servants or conversely civil servants are appointed as judges.[629] If a civil servant appointed for life or a civil servant appointed for a fixed term is transferred so as to be appointed as a judge, then the provisions for judges on commission shall apply (Articles 14 to 16 of the German Judges Act). The individual's status as a civil servant is maintained, but their corresponding rights and obligations are suspended. If, however, a judge is simultaneously appointed as a civil servant, the provisions of Section 2 of Paragraph 1 of Article 21 of the German Judges Act cannot be applied, because the grounds on which judges are dismissed must in principle be rigidly explained. In addition, Paragraph 1 of Article 4 of the German Judges Act stipulates that judges are not allowed to be simultaneously engaged in the judiciary, the legislative and/or the executive, and except for the instances specified in Paragraph 2 of Article 4 of the German Judges Act,[630] judges shall not hold the office of civil servant and judge simultaneously.[631]

---

628 Günter Schmidt-Räntsch, Jürgen Schmidt-Räntsch, Deutsches Richtergesetz (DRiG), Kommentar, 6th edition, Munich 2008, Article 21, margin number 6

629 Günter Schmidt-Räntsch, Jürgen Schmidt-Räntsch, Deutsches Richtergesetz (DRiG), Kommentar, 6th edition, Munich 2008, Article 21, margin number 9

630 Paragraph 2 of Article 4 of the German Judges Act stipulates that in addition to their judicial duties, judges are allowed to engage in: (1) court administration duties; (2) other duties which are assigned to courts or judges by law; (3) research and teaching du-

*(b) Appropriate Dismissal (Entlassung durch Verfügung)*

Paragraph 2 of Article 21 of the German Judges Act enumerates six circumstances in which appropriate dismissal is applied, which is dismissal by disciplinary action. The supreme authority concerned has no powers of discretion and enforces the dismissal disciplinary action as soon as it is informed of the grounds for the appropriate dismissal.[632] In accordance with Paragraph 2 of Article 21 of the German Judges Act, the six grounds for appropriate dismissal are as follows:

(i) Refusal of Oath (Verweigerung der Eidesleistung)

In accordance with the provisions of Article 38 of the German Judges Act, judges are obliged to swear an oath. Whatever the reasons may be for refusing to take the oath, those who refuse to swear shall be dismissed.[633]

(ii) Membership of the *Bundestag* or of a *Landtag*

Judges who are members of the *Bundestag* or of a *Landtag* (one of the federal German state parliaments) when they are appointed as judges and fail to give up their mandate within an appropriate period set by the supreme competent authority shall be dismissed. This provision is derived from the theory of the Separation of Powers (the second sentence in Paragraph 2 of Article 20 of the Basic Law), and corresponds to Article 4 of the German Judges Act. This provision makes the legal consequences of being appointed judge far stricter than being appointed as a member of the *Bundestag* or of a *Landtag*. In the latter case, the Parliamentary Members Act of 18th February 1977 does not require dismissal but merely temporary suspension of the rights and obligations derived from the office of judge (Articles 5 and 8 of this Act), because judges are regarded in this Act as ordinary nationals to be appointed as members of parliament. By contrast, the German Judges Act emphasises the incompatibility (*Inkompatibilität*) of the status as judge with other duties and considers members of parliament unable to

---

ties at university-level institutions, public education institutions or official education institutions; (4) matters of examination; (5) the chairmanship of arbitration committees and corresponding independent committees as defined in the second sentence of Article 104 of the Federal Employees Representation Act (*Bundespersonalvertretungsgesetz = BPersVG*).

631 Günter Schmidt-Räntsch, Jürgen Schmidt-Räntsch, Deutsches Richtergesetz (DRiG), Kommentar, 6th edition, Munich 2008, Article 21, margin number 9a

632 Weng Yuesheng, Appointment Qualifications, Appointment Methods and Status Guarantees for German Judges, in his work: Administrative Law and the Modern State under the Rule of Law, p. 513

633 Günter Schmidt-Räntsch, Jürgen Schmidt-Räntsch, Deutsches Richtergesetz (DRiG), Kommentar, 6th edition, Munich 2008, Article 21, margin number 11

execute the office of judge, hence the situation whereby members of parliament are appointed as judges is not dealt with explicitly. If parliamentary members are appointed as judges and fail to give up their mandate within a certain period, they shall be dismissed. The competent authority also does not permit them to retain their position without pay (*ohne Dienstbezüge beurlauben*).[634]

(iii) Age Limit for Serving Judges

The age limit for serving judges is 67 years for federal judges (Paragraph 1 of Article 48 of the German Judges Act) or less depending on their year of birth (Paragraph 3 of Article 48 of the German Judges Act); the age limit in the various *Länder* depends on their respective provisions (Paragraph 2 of Article 76 of the German Judges Act). Judges who are over the age limit when they are appointed shall be dismissed, because it is feared they may be incompetent for the office of judge. Judges who are near the age limit when they are appointed and are or become incompetent for the office of judge shall be dismissed in accordance with the fifth criterion.

(iv) Written Request for Dismissal

The right of judges to be able to request that they resign cannot be given up in advance. Others are not allowed to violate judges' wishes by appointing or retaining them. Judges can apply to resign at any time, which is a declaration of will which has to be acknowledged by their counterpart (*empfangsbedürftige Willenserklärung*) and becomes effective once they have declared this wish. But an application for resignation can also be invalidated due to misunderstanding (*Irrtum*), fraud (*arglistige Täuschung*) or threat (*Drohung*). A valid application shall be confirmed as having been made clearly, positively and of the judge's own free will, and shall be presented in writing and specify the date on which resignation is to be declared to have occurred.[635]

(v) Age Limit or Incompetence for Office

If a judge reaches the age limit or is incompetent to perform the duties of his or her office, and the judge's employment is not terminated by the judge entering retirement, then the judge shall be dismissed.

634 Günter Schmidt-Räntsch, Jürgen Schmidt-Räntsch, Deutsches Richtergesetz (DRiG), Kommentar, 6th edition, Munich 2008, Article 21, margin number 12

635 Günter Schmidt-Räntsch, Jürgen Schmidt-Räntsch, Deutsches Richtergesetz (DRiG), Kommentar, 6th edition, Munich 2008, Article 21, margin number 16

#### (vi) Residence Abroad Without Permission[636]

Residing abroad without the permission of the supreme competent authority was once a criterion for *ipso iure* dismissal, but is now a criterion for appropriate dismissal and must be decided by the service court. It was found to be impracticable for residence abroad without the permission of the supreme competent authority to be a criterion for *ipso iure* dismissal. The residential locations of civil servants and judges are not now relevant in most cases. Judges are no longer required to reside at or near the court at which they are employed. In a modern viewpoint, changes in one's personal situation (such as a spouse's job or children's schools) which may necessitate a move, even abroad, are no longer considered that consequential by many civil servants. Therefore, most civil servants (including judges) have no idea that their residence abroad without permission, even within the EU, may lead to an *ipso iure* dismissal or are not even aware of the necessity to seek permission. The newly amended rules thus avoid the drawbacks of the old one.

The aim of the new rule is still to ensure the function of public administration. Employers must to able to reach their judges at any time. But generally speaking, they are merely obliged to reside at a location which is convenient with respect to their job, and that is all.

### *(c) Procedure for Dismissal*

#### (i) Dismissal by a Court Decision (Entlassung durch gerichtliche Entscheidung)

In the case of an *ipso iure* dismissal, a procedure is to be carried out whereby a court passes a decision. If the supreme competent authority feels that conditions for an *ipso iure* dismissal are met, it shall apply to the service court to initiate this procedure (Paragraph 3 of Article 66 and Article 83 of the German Judges Act). The court passes a valid decision and verifies the termination of judgeship and the time of termination. In accordance with the provisions of Article 35 of the German Judges Act, the supreme competent authority has the power to request that the court suspend judges from carrying out their official functions while the trial by the service court is pending. This procedure has to be implemented even if the judges themselves agree with the dismissal, as also applies in the case of invalid appointments.[637]

636 Günter Schmidt-Räntsch, Jürgen Schmidt-Räntsch, Deutsches Richtergesetz (DRiG), Kommentar, 6th edition, Munich 2008, Article 21, margin number 20

637 Günter Schmidt-Räntsch, Jürgen Schmidt-Räntsch, Deutsches Richtergesetz (DRiG), Kommentar, 6th edition, Munich 2008, Article 21, margin number 23

(ii) Dismissal Permitted by a Court Declaration

In the case of appropriate dismissal, courts do not confirm the dismissal but rather confirm that the supreme competent authority shall dismiss judges appointed for life or judges appointed for a fixed term (Paragraph 2 of Article 66 and Article 83 of the German Judges Act). If the judge being dismissed agrees with the dismissal, there is no need for a decision by the court. If judges agree with a dismissal, they are agreeing not only with the dismissal itself but also with the time of dismissal. If judges present a complete and valid declaration of agreement in writing, then the supreme competent authority can declare the dismissal.[638]

(iii) Dismissal upon Request (*Entlassung auf Antrag*)

There are no specific provisions in the German Judges Act regarding the procedure whereby judges request that they be able to resign. In accordance with Article 46 of the German Judges Act, the provisions of Article 33 of the Federal Civil Servants Act can be applied, which stipulates that the request for resignation must be made in writing and be presented to the competent authority. Providing the order for dismissal has not yet been issued, the request can been withdrawn within two weeks of being received by the competent authority, or longer with the permission of the competent authority.

*(d) Effect of Dismissal*

The rights and obligations of judges as derived from their office are eliminated by dismissal, but the more general rights and obligations of public law and loyalty in public service (*öffentlich-rechtlicher Dienst und Treueverhältnis*) which also pertain to judgeships continue to be valid, such as the obligation of confidentiality with respect to public affairs (*Amtsgeheimnis*) and joint conference (*Beratungsgeheimnis*), the obligation not to accept rewards and gifts, and the right to inspect their personnel file and to request the issue of a certificate of service, etc.

Termination of employment by dismissal also ends a judge's liability to disciplinary proceedings, and any pending formal disciplinary procedure for dismissal is also discontinued. If the dismissed judges was receiving pension benefits before their dismissal, then in accordance with the provisions of Article 77 (2) of the Federal Civil Servants Act, it is regarded as misconduct (*Dienstvergehen*) if a formerly serving judge violates the free democratic basic order enshrined in the Basic Law, participates in actions aimed at undermining the con-

638 Günter Schmidt-Räntsch, Jürgen Schmidt-Räntsch, Deutsches Richtergesetz (DRiG), Kommentar, 6th edition, Munich 2008, Article 21 margin number 24

tinued existence or security of the Federal Republic of Germany, breaches their duty of confidentiality or duty of disclosure or breaches their duty not to accept rewards or gifts, damage judicial interests and violate their obligations as stipulated in the second sentence of Paragraph 4 of Article 48 of the German Judges Act,[639] and the Federal Civil Servants Act is applied. If they are again appointed as judges or civil servants in the future, they can again be disciplined if they violate the provisions mentioned above.[640]

Unless otherwise stipulated in law, judges lose their right to request emoluments and pension benefits (*Dienst- und Versorgungsbezüge*) once they have been dismissed. If judges are dismissed because they are over the age limit or incompetent to perform the duties of their office, then pension benefits are still guaranteed. If they did not apply to resign, they may also request an interim allowance (*Übergangsgeld*) in accordance with the provisions of Article 46 of the German Judges Act which apply Article 47 of the Civil Service Pensions Act (*Beamtenversorgungsgesetz = BeamtVG*). Those dismissed in accordance with Paragraph 1 of Article 21 (*ipso iure* dismissal) or Sections 1 to 4 in Paragraph 2 of Article 21 of the German Judges Act cannot request an interim allowance (Paragraph 2 of Article 1 and Paragraph 3 of Article 47 of the Civil Service Pensions Act).

When judges are dismissed, the status, rank and titles conferred by their office are in principle forfeited upon dismissal, although there are exceptions since federal judges are permitted to apply the second sentence of Article 39 and the first sentence of Paragraph 3 of Article 86 of the Federal Civil Servants Act, but the position or title must be followed by the word "(retired)".[641]

639 The original provision of this sentence was that disabled judges who satisfy Article 1 of the Disability Act, are over 60 years old and request retirement shall guarantee that once retired, they shall not engage in duties or occupations paying over 425 Marks per month. However, the content of this provision has now been revised to the effect that judges who are severely disabled in the sense of Paragraph 2 of Article 2 of Book IX of the Social Code may request retirement when they are over 60 years old. Hence, the obligation of the original provision no longer obtains.

640 Günter Schmidt-Räntsch, Jürgen Schmidt-Räntsch, Deutsches Richtergesetz (DRiG), Kommentar, 6th edition, Munich 2008, Article 21, margin number 29

641 Günter Schmidt-Räntsch, Jürgen Schmidt-Räntsch, Deutsches Richtergesetz (DRiG), Kommentar, 6th edition, Munich 2008, Article 21, margin number 31

## (3) *Ipso Iure* Termination of Employment as Judge

### *(a) Termination by Court Decision*

Article 24 of the German Judges Act stipulates the circumstances under which judges lose their rights due to decisions of the criminal courts or the Federal Constitutional Court. This article applies both to federal judges and judges in the various *Länder*. Employment as Judge is terminated once the court's decision has been passed.

A court decision is the prerequisite for judges to lose their rights. Once employment has been terminated, Article 24 of the German Judges Act is no longer applied. The court decisions which in accordance with this provision result in judges losing their rights are to be made by German courts within the boundaries of applying the German Judges Act. What is meant here by "German courts" is the same as in Paragraph 1 of Article 41 of the Federal Civil Servants Act and excludes the courts of occupying powers (*Gerichte der Besatzungsmacht*) or judgement courts (*Spruchgerichte*). The decisions made by such courts may lead to a disciplinary procedure but not terminate judgeship. German courts shall make decisions within the effective scope of the German Judges Act, i.e. within the entirety of the current territory of the Federal Republic of Germany. Criminal courts or the Federal Constitutional Court shall declare the four specific punishments, additional punishments or legal responsibilities as stipulated by Article 24:[642]

- a custodial sentence of at most one year for a premeditated crime;
- a custodial sentence for a premeditated crime liable to prosecution according to the provisions regarding breach of the peace, high treason, endangering the democratic state under the rule of law or treason and endangering national security;
- deprivation of the right to hold public office;
- forfeiture of basic rights in accordance with Article 18 of the Basic Law.[643]

---

642 Günter Schmidt-Räntsch, Jürgen Schmidt-Räntsch, Deutsches Richtergesetz (DRiG), Kommentar, 6th edition, Munich 2008, Article 24, margin number 3

643 Article 18 of the Basic Law stipulates that whoever abuses the freedom of expression, in particular the freedom of the press (paragraph (1) of Article 5), the freedom of teaching (paragraph (3) of Article 5), the freedom of assembly (Article 8), the freedom of association (Article 9), the privacy of correspondence, posts and telecommunications (Article 10), the rights of property (Article 14), or the right of asylum (Article 16 a) in order to combat the free democratic basic order shall forfeit these basic rights. This forfeiture and its extent shall be declared by the Federal Constitutional Court.

With regards to the termination of employment by the decision made by a criminal court or the Federal Constitutional Court, the court or competent authority is not required to make any other declaration. But in accordance with the provisions of other detailed rules and regulations of application, federal judges will also receive a written notification.[644] If judges themselves do not believe that there has been a decision as stipulated in Article 24 of the German Judges Act, they may bring a case to court to confirm that judgeship continues to exist or to sue for payment of salary. Both these actions are governed by general administrative courts, not by the service courts.[645]

If judges have their employment terminated in accordance with the provisions of Article 24 of the German Judges Act, they lose the right to request their salary and allowances and may no longer use the titles conferred on the basis of their original of former professional positions. A judge's loss of rights may be excluded by presidential pardon. Judges who are dismissed but subsequently pardoned or reinstated following an appeal procedure are regarded as not having been dismissed and may continue to serve as a judge under the conditions of their former position and receive the same salary as before, although income derived from other work during this period shall be deducted. Judges are thus obliged to report such income. However, if federal judges are dismissed by disciplinary proceedings on the basis of facts established in the retrial or on the basis of a criminal judgement, they lose their rights as stipulated in Paragraph 1 of Article 41 of the Federal Civil Servants Act (i.e. the right to resume their post and draw a salary). In this case, the dismissal of the judges shall be put back to when they lost their rights in accordance with Article 24 of the German Judges Act, for which period the rights in Paragraph 1 of Article 41 of the Federal Civil Servants Act mentioned above are certainly lost. The judges of the various *Länder* are subject to the provisions of the respective *Land* laws.[646]

#### *(b) Termination due to Election to the Bundestag or a Land Legislative Body*

Article 36 (2) of the German Judges Act stipulates that if judges are elected to the German *Bundestag* or to the legislative body of a *Land* or are appointed with their permission as members of the federal government or members of a *Land*

644 Paragraph 3 of Article 1 of the *Durchführungsbestimmungen zur Anordnung des Bundespräsidenten über die Ernennung und Entlassung der Bundesbeamten und Richter im Bundesdienst* of 25th September 1969

645 Günter Schmidt-Räntsch, Jürgen Schmidt-Räntsch, Deutsches Richtergesetz (DRiG), Kommentar, 6th edition, Munich 2008, Article 24, margin number 8

646 Günter Schmidt-Räntsch, Jürgen Schmidt-Räntsch, Deutsches Richtergesetz (DRiG), Kommentar, 6th edition, Munich 2008, Article 24, margin number 9

government, they lose their rights and obligations as judges without the need for a court decision in accordance with the more detailed provisions of the law.

This provision is again based on the theory of the separation of constitutional powers and the consequential incompatibility of a position as judge.[647] If parliamentary members are appointed as judges, this is for the reasons mentioned above.

## (4) Relocation (*Versetzung*) and Suspension (*Amtsenthebung*) of Judges

### *(a) The Concept of Relocation and Suspension*

Neither the German Judges Act nor the Federal Civil Servants Act gives a legal definition of relocation. This concept derives from the first sentence in Paragraph 2 of Article 97 of the Basic Law. Relocation means that judges leave the court of their original position and go to serve as judge at another court. If a judge has more than one post, it is also considered relocation if he or she is only dismissed from one of them (Paragraph 3 of Article 30 of the German Judges Act). This does not change their employment status. A change in the place where they serve counts as relocation because judges who have been formally appointed must be granted a position as judge at a particular court, as stipulated in Paragraph 1 of Article 27 of the German Judges Act. A "particular court" means a concrete judgeship at a specific court and not an abstract position. Changing to another adjudicative post at the same court does not count as relocation.[648] Relocation is different from secondment. In the latter case, judges still retain their post at the original court when they are transferred to another court to work, whereas in the former case, their post at the original court is lost when they are transferred.[649]

---

647 Günter Schmidt-Räntsch, Jürgen Schmidt-Räntsch, Deutsches Richtergesetz (DRiG), Kommentar, 6th edition, Munich 2008, Article 36, margin number 2, p. 513

648 Because it does not count as relocation, it is not safeguarded by the legal elements and procedures of relocation. It is then likely that court presidia, taking the opportunity to distribution work, would send judges to other judicial courts without their permission. But because most of the members of the presidia are elected, they cannot in principle be easily changed once the work has been distributed. Only in the event of an emergency can judges be sent to other judicial courts; otherwise, they must be given the opportunity to express their opinions (see Paragraph 1 of Article 21 of the Court Constitution Act. This arrangement of the system reduces to a minimum the possibility of interfering in independent adjudication through the distribution of work.

649 Günter Schmidt-Räntsch, Jürgen Schmidt-Räntsch, Deutsches Richtergesetz (DRiG), Kommentar, 6th edition, Munich 2008, Article 30, margin number 7

Suspension means that judges lose their original post as judge and are not granted another post as judge. The status of being employed is maintained in the event of suspension, as also with relocation, and judges' rights and obligations are likewise maintained. However, once judges are suspended, they are no longer legal judges, hence if they for example take part in trials, their court organisations are acting illegally. The punishment of suspension includes the scenario in which the court presiding board (*Präsidium*) neither assigns a judge to a judicial court in its distribution of work nor permit the judge to take part in trials.[650] Suspension is different from provisionally prohibiting the execution of official duties (*vorläufige Untersagung der Führung der Amtsgeschäfte*)[651] and temporary suspension from duty (*vorläufige Dienstenthebung*).[652] In the latter two scenarios, judges still maintain their concrete and actual judgeship in the original courts and are merely temporarily prohibited from taking part in court trials.[653]

#### *(b) The Subject of Relocation and Suspension (Paragraph 1 of Article 30 of the German Judges Act)*

##### (i) In Implementing the Procedure of Impeaching Judges

If a federal judge infringes the principles of the Basic Law or the constitutional order of a *Land* in his or her official capacity or unofficially, the Federal Constitutional Court, upon application by the *Bundestag*, may by a two-thirds majority order that the judge be transferred or retired. If the breach was deliberate, they shall be dismissed. *Länder* can apply this provision to *Land* judges (Paragraphs 2 and 5 of Article 98 of the Basic Law). This is referred to as the impeachment of judges, although there has not yet been a case of impeachment of judges in German history.[654]

---

650 Decision of 25th March 1964 by the Federal Constitutional Court, BVerfGE 17, 252; Engelbert Niebler, Die Stellung des Richters in der Bundesrepublik Deutschland, DRiZ 1981, pp. 281 ff

651 Article 35 of DRiG

652 Paragraph 2 of Article 63 of DRiG und Article 83 of DRiG in conjunction with the *Land* disciplinary laws

653 Günter Schmidt-Räntsch, Jürgen Schmidt-Räntsch, Deutsches Richtergesetz (DRiG), Kommentar, 6th edition, Munich 2008, Article 30, margin number 9

654 Willi Giger, Die Unabhängigkeit des Richters, DRiZ 1979, pp. 65 ff

(ii) In Formal Disciplinary Procedures

(iii) Due to Judicial Interests

Due to judicial interests, judges may not only be relocated or suspended but also retired or temporarily retired. The basic concept of this provision is that not relocating a judge in no way guarantees the individual wishes of the judge but does protect the interests of judicial independence. If a judge gets into a situation where they cannot adjudicate convincingly, no longer able to ensure that they are executing their post as judge lawfully, and do not have the confidence of others, then not relocating judges lose its significance. Thus, it can be seen that considerations of not relocating must give way to considerations of judicial interests. Therefore, the provisions of this article are in line with the provisions of the first sentence in Paragraph 2 of Article 97 of the Basic Law.[655]

Paragraph 1 of Article 30 of the German Judges Act guarantees that the scenario of being relocated or suspended due to judicial interests is only applied to judges appointed for life and judges appointed for a fixed term. However, the facts of judicial interests should remain outside the facts of adjudication,[656] since irrespective of the nature of said facts and whether it was the judge's intent that the facts should arise, this would otherwise do serious damage.[657]

(iv) Due to a Change in Court Organisation

This provision is derived from the third sentence in Paragraph 2 of Article 97 of the Basic Law. Because this affects the independence of judges' status, there is a need to further limit the interpretation of what is and is not relocation or suspension due to a change in court organisation, i.e. because the organisation or area of jurisdiction of a court has changed, this change impacts on the court's workforce, and the reduction in the courts' organisation is directed at all the judges working for said court rather than against particular individuals.[658]

If a court's organisation or area of jurisdiction changes, judges may be transferred to other courts within three months of this change. If there is no post which bears the same final basic salary (*Endgrundgehalt*), judges may be sus-

---

655 Günter Schmidt-Räntsch, Jürgen Schmidt-Räntsch, Deutsches Richtergesetz (DRiG), Kommentar, 6th edition, Munich 2008, Article 31, margin number 3

656 The action of adjudicating does not pertain to this article, because judges must not be disadvantaged because of their adjudications unless they have abused the law in their judgements (Article 339 of the German Penal Code); Paragraph 1 of Article 97 of the Basic Law).

657 Günter Schmidt-Räntsch, Jürgen Schmidt-Räntsch, Deutsches Richtergesetz (DRiG), Kommentar, 6th edition, Munich 2008, Article 31, margin numbers 7 and 8

658 Günter Schmidt-Räntsch, Jürgen Schmidt-Räntsch, Deutsches Richtergesetz (DRiG), Kommentar, 6th edition, Munich 2008, Article 32, margin numbers 4 and 5

pended. But they can also be transferred to new posts or to posts which bear a lower final basic salary at any time, but must always then receive their original salary.

*(c) The Procedure of Relocation and Suspension*

Guaranteeing the status of judges is as important in procedural law as it is in substantive law.[659] Unless permitted in writing, the relocation or suspension of judges appointed for life or judges appointed for a fixed term is limited to the four situations mentioned above, and except for changes in court organisation, can only be carried out in accordance with a specific court decision. Nevertheless, this does not mean that judges can be relocated or suspended without a court decision as long as they permit it. If relocation or suspension of judges is decided beyond the causes in Article 30 of the German Judges Act, and the judges permit it in writing, then there is no need for a court decision. If relocation or suspension is based on the first or second situation in Paragraph 1 of Article 30 (i.e. in an impeachment procedure or a disciplinary procedure), then there is a need for a court decision, even if a judge has permitted it in writing. This is because an impeachment procedure or a disciplinary procedure is a disciplinary measure imposed by courts with legal effect. Although relocation or suspension due to judicial interests is not a disciplinary measure, it still concerns judicial interests and thus has to be confirmed by courts.[660]

In principle, relocation or suspension is to be decided by courts in advance. Paragraph 2 of Article 30 of the German Judges Act stipulates that except for a change in court organisation, the relocation or suspension of judges can only be declared by a legally valid court decision in order to permit the supreme competent authority to impose the disciplinary measure, or is decided directly by courts.[661] In the case of a change in court organisation, service courts shall investigate after the event.[662]

---

659 See Hu Fangxin, On the Development of the Personnel System of Judges in China in View of the German Judges Act, master's thesis at Taiwan Fu Jen Catholic University, June 1988, p. 48

660 Judges can be not only relocated or suspended but also retired or temporarily retired due to judicial interests (Article 31 of DRiG). In the latter situation, it is not possible for the judges themselves to permit this (see the provisions of Articles 30 and 31 of DRiG).

661 For example, the Federal Constitutional Court passes a decision directly in an impeachment procedure, and service courts passes a decision directly in the procedure for disciplining judges.

662 Günter Schmidt-Räntsch, Jürgen Schmidt-Räntsch, Deutsches Richtergesetz (DRiG), Kommentar, 6th edition, Munich 2008, Article 32, margin number 12

## (5) Retirement

### *(a) Types of Retirement and Grounds for Retirement*

#### (i) Voluntary Retirement

In principle, there are restrictions on the retirement age of German judges, and the time of retirement is not allowed to be deferred, so as to prevent judges from pandering to their superiors by postponing their retirement, which would damage their judicial independence.[663] Federal judges appointed for life may apply for retirement at the earliest when they are 63 years old.[664] The disable may apply to retire when they are 60 years old.[665] The purpose of the restricting provisions on retirement age is to prevent judges from applying for retirement early due to the interference of outside pressure, which would also affect judicial independence.[666]

In addition, the original Article 116 of the German Judges Act stipulated the circumstances of retirement which applied in particular cases, such as that judges who had served and participated in criminal justice proceedings during the Nazi period from 1st September 1939 to 9th May 1945 had to apply for retirement. However, the final date for applying for retirement under the provisions of this article was 30th June 1962, hence it has since lost its function and has thus been removed.

#### (ii) Retirement due to Reaching a Certain Age (Retirement by Order)

Federal judges appointed for life may apply for retirement once they are over 65 years old. But the retirement age for judges of the Federal Constitutional Court, as judges appointed for a fixed term, is different and currently stipulated as beginning at 68 years of age. The retirement age of judges of the various *Länder* is

663 Weng Yuesheng, Appointment Qualifications, Appointment Methods and Status Guarantees for German Judges, in his work: Administrative Law and the Modern State under the Rule of Law, p. 518

664 The normal retirement age for federal judges is 67 years old, see Paragraph 1 of Article 48 of DRiG.

665 Formerly, judges shall apply to retire due to disability when they are 65 years old. Since 1st January 1980, the age restriction has been relaxed to 60 years old (see Paragraph 3 of Article 48 of DRiG).

666 Liao Yinan, Report on Issues Regarding Whether Judges Appointed for Life Can Enjoy Retirement Benefits, in: Taiwan University Legal Review, June 1987, Volume 16, Issue 2, p. 33

stipulated by the *Länder* themselves. Presently, the *Land* Judges Laws of the various *Länder* uniformly stipulate a retirement age of 65.[667]

(iii) Retirement due to Incapacity

Judges appointed for life or judges appointed for a fixed term who are incompetent in the judgeships can be ordered to retire by a court decision, without their permission. There is no specific interpretation in the German Judges Act as to what does and does not constitute incompetence. In accordance with the provisions of Articles 46 and 71 of the German Judges Act, the interpretation of "incompetent" employs the provisions of the Federal Civil Servants Act and the Civil Servants Status Act, to mean that judges are continuously or permanently unable to carry out their obligations of duty due to their physically state or for reasons of health.[668] In accordance with the provisions in the second sentence of Paragraph 1 of Article 42 of the Federal Civil Servants Act, federal judges can also be regarded as incompetent in their post if they have failed to carry out their duties for more than three months in a six-month period because of illness and there is no sign that they will be able to return to their post within the following six months.[669]

(iv) Retirement Due to Judicial Interests

In order to avoid severe obstructions in the course of justice, judges who have been formally appointed and encounter difficulties in their judgeship can, in addition to being relocated or suspended, also be ordered to retire (Article 31 of DRiG).

(v) Temporary Retirement Due to Judicial Interests (*einstweiliger Ruhestand*)

Judges can only be temporarily retired due to judicial interests.[670] The difference between temporary retirement and permanent retirement is not limited to judges' benefits and income. Judges who are temporarily retired may be obliged to be reappointed as judges appointed for life. If they fail to comply with a reappointment order from the competent authority, they are in neglect of their duties by having violated their obligations. However, the new post to which they are appointed must carry the same final basic salary as their original post. When decid-

---

667 Günter Schmidt-Räntsch, Jürgen Schmidt-Räntsch, Deutsches Richtergesetz (DRiG), Kommentar, 6th edition, Munich 2008, Article 48, margin number 5

668 Paragraph 1 of Article 44 of BBG; first sentence in Paragraph 1 of Article 26 of BeamtStG

669 Günter Schmidt-Räntsch, Jürgen Schmidt-Räntsch, Deutsches Richtergesetz (DRiG), Kommentar, 6th edition, Munich 2008, Article 34, margin number 3

670 Günter Schmidt-Räntsch, Jürgen Schmidt-Räntsch, Deutsches Richtergesetz (DRiG), Kommentar, 6th edition, Munich 2008, Article 34, margin number 2

ing whether relocation, suspension, retirement or temporary retirement is to be imposed on a particular judge, it should also be taken into account whether or not said judge could be reappointed, and how many years the judge still has before retirement.[671]

*(b) Procedure for Retirement*

(i) Voluntary Retirement

Those who wish to retire voluntarily and are over 63 years old may apply in writing. Judges can apply up to three years before reaching retirement age. Those who wish to retire because of disability may apply as soon as they are over 60 years old.

(ii) Retirement by Order

The German Judges Act does not make any further provisions on retirement due to reaching the age of retirement. In accordance with Articles 46 and 71 of the German Judges Act, the relevant provisions of the Federal Civil Servants Act and the Civil Servants Status Act can be applied. When general civil servants retire at the retirement age, their employment status terminates naturally and immediately,[672] with immediate effect based on the provisions of law and not requiring separate dismissal. Therefore, although actual retirees still go through the process of retirement and leaving office, this process only involves the formality of declaration and does not affect the retiree's actual retirement benefits,[673] which is the same for the retirement of judges. It is worth noting that German civil servants who wish to begin retirement must have held their office for at least five years, in addition to having reached the retirement age.[674] If they have reached retirement age but have not held office for at least five years, then their employment status is terminated by dismissal rather than by retirement.[675] The above also applies if they have reached retirement age when they are appointed.[676] Sections 3 and 5 in Paragraph 2 of Article 21 of the German Judges

671 Günter Schmidt-Räntsch, Jürgen Schmidt-Räntsch, Deutsches Richtergesetz (DRiG), Kommentar, 6th edition, Munich 2008, Article 31, margin number 13

672 Paragraph 2 of Article 21 of BeamtStG

673 Liao Yinan, Report on Issues Regarding Whether Judges Appointed for Life Can Enjoy Retirement Benefits, in: Taiwan University Legal Review, June 1987, Volume 16, Issue 2, p. 38

674 Paragraph 1 of Article 4 of BeamtVG

675 Article 35 of BBG

676 Paragraph 3 of Article 41 of BBG, cf. Günter Schmidt-Räntsch, Jürgen Schmidt-Räntsch, Deutsches Richtergesetz (DRiG), Kommentar, 6th edition, Munich 2008: an appointment after having reached the age limit is not null and void but in fact fully

Act make similar provisions to those above, but in accordance with the guarantee of the status of judges which protects them from being dismissed, such dismissal has to be decided by service courts.[677]

(iii) Retirement due to Incapacity

Whether judges are incompetent in their posts is confirmed by their direct superiors (*unmittelbare Dienstvorgesetzte*) and dependent on confirmation by official doctors. If superiors have confirmed that a judge is incompetent in his infrared her post, they shall firstly notify the judge in question.[678] If such judges or their custodians agree to retire in writing, the competent authority orders them to retire by dismissal. The written declaration by judges must be explicit and without conditions or reservation of rights. If a judge does not agree to retire and refuses to submit a written agreement, and the supreme competent authority believes there is no reason for them to refuse to retire, then the supreme competent authority can apply to the service courts to initiate an appraisal procedure in accordance with Paragraph 3 of Article 66 and Section 3d of Paragraph 1 of Article 62 of the German Judges Act. If, after appraisal, the service court believes that the judge is competent for the post, it shall reject the application by the supreme competent authority, and if it believes that the judge is indeed incompetent for the post, it shall decide that the sanction of retirement is legal.[679] Such judges are then retired as of the last day of the month in which the competent authority notifies them of their retirement. Probationary judges and judges on commission are directly ordered to retire by the competent authority. If they refuse to obey, they may apply to the service courts to have this disciplinary measure revoked.[680] The provisions on this procedure in the various *Länder* are approximately the same,[681] although judges who do not accept the decision of a *Land* service court can appeal the decision at the Federal Service Court; the Federal Service court then makes the final decision.

General civil servants who have been retired because of incompetence can be reappointed as civil servants if they meet the specific conditions.[682] In accord-

valid, but the judge has to be dismissed, since it is assumed that once the age limit has been reached, the judge is no longer completely competent to serve and Section 2 of Paragraph 1 of Article 41 of BBG applies.

677 See the content under (2) Dismissal in this Section.

678 Article 46 of DRiG; Paragraph 1 of Article 44 of BBG

679 Paragraph 2 of Article 67 of DRiG

680 Paragraph 1 of Article 62 of DRiG

681 Article 77 of DRiG; Paragraphs 3 and 4 of Article 78 of DRiG

682 Article 39 in conjunction with the first sentence in Paragraph 1 of Article 46 of BBG; Paragraph 1 of Article 29 of BeamtStG

ance with Articles 46 and 71 of the German Judges Act, this also applies to judges.

(iv) Retirement or Temporary Retirement Due to Judicial Interests

The provisions on the grounds for retirement or temporary retirement due to judicial interests are the same as for the procedure of relocation, and the procedure is essentially the same as the appraisal procedure for incompetence.

#### *(c) Benefits to Retired Judges*

The German Judges Act does not make specific provisions on the benefits to retired judges. Articles 46 and 71 of the German Judges Act merely stipulate that the relevant provisions of the Federal Civil Servants Act and the Civil Service Pensions Act, respectively, shall be applied. After judges retire, they shall enjoy a pension for life. The level of pension is to be calculated on the basis of the pensionable emoluments (*ruhegehaltsfähige Dienstbezüge*) and pensionable period of service (*ruhegehaltfähige Dienstzeit*).[683] Pensionable emoluments include the basic salary (*Grundgehalt*), family allowance (*Familienzuschlag*) and other emoluments which can be counted towards the pension, as stipulated in the Civil Service Pensions Act.[684] The pensionable period of service means the period of service in public office from the time they are appointed to office. Retired judges cannot request exactly the same income as those who are holding office, since the Basic Law only stipulates[685] that judges who are dismissed due to change in court organisation shall be paid their full salary. There is no provision in the Constitution that full salaries shall be maintained in any other instances.[686]

### (6) Secondment (*Abordnung*)

#### *(a) The Meaning of Secondment*

Secondment means that a judge's employment status does not change and his or her status as judge is maintained and that the judge is temporarily transferred to another public organ to do judicial or non-judicial work, whether or not the place of work changes.[687]

683 Article 14 of BeamtVG, cf. Josef König, Beamtenversorgungsgesetz, Munich 1982, pp. 56 ff

684 Paragraph 1 of Article 5 of BeamtVG

685 The second sentence in Paragraph 2 of Article 97 of GG

686 Günter Schmidt-Räntsch, Jürgen Schmidt-Räntsch, Deutsches Richtergesetz (DRiG), Kommentar, 6th edition, Munich 2008, Article 31, margin number 14

687 Günter Schmidt-Räntsch, Jürgen Schmidt-Räntsch, Deutsches Richtergesetz (DRiG), Kommentar, 6th edition, Munich 2008, Article 37, margin number 3

The difference between secondment and relocation is that in the case of secondment, judges do not serve under a new post, their status as judge is retained, and they are merely transferred to another organ temporarily, whereas in the case of relocation, judges are transferred to another organ permanently. Judges still work in courts after relocation, whereas this is uncertain with secondment. With their agreement, judges may be temporarily transferred by and to any public organs. If they temporarily work for a private institution, then they are merely on leave and this is not regarded as secondment.[688]

### *(b) Procedure and Consequences of Secondment*

Paragraph 2 of Article 97 of the Basic Law does not stipulate any provisions on the secondment of judges, but based on the Constitution's aim of guaranteeing the status of judges, judges may not be prevented from serving as judges against their will. Therefore, secondment must be agreed to by the judge. Paragraph 1 of Article 37 of the German Judges Act stipulates that judges appointed for life and judges appointed for a fixed term can only be seconded with their agreement.

Those who agree to be seconded must declare their agreement and the time of their secondment, without attaching conditions or reservation of rights. Although Paragraph 1 of Article 37 of the German Judges Act does not stipulate that the agreement be in writing, based on the invariability of laws, agreements in writing are preferred.[689]

In accordance with Paragraph 2 of Article 37 of the German Judges Act, secondment shall be for a declared period of time, however long this happens to be. Secondment is however only a temporary transfer to another organ, hence it should not continue for an overly extended period of time.[690] With regard to interpreting the first sentence in Paragraph 1 of Article 27 of the Federal Civil Servants Act, legislators appear to regard "temporary" here as meaning anything under five years.[691]

The rights and obligations of judges who are seconded to another organ shall be determined by the nature of the organ where they will then be working. Once the period of secondment expires, the secondment shall be terminated and the

---

688 Günter Schmidt-Räntsch, Jürgen Schmidt-Räntsch, Deutsches Richtergesetz (DRiG), Kommentar, 6th edition, Munich 2008, Article 37, margin number 5

689 Günter Schmidt-Räntsch, Jürgen Schmidt-Räntsch, Deutsches Richtergesetz (DRiG), Kommentar, 6th edition, Munich 2008, Article 37, margin number 9

690 Paragraph 1 of Article 27 of BBG; Paragraph 1 of Article 14 of BeamtStG

691 In accordance with the provisions of Paragraph 3 of Article 14 of BeamtStG, the agreement of the civil servant is not required if the period of secondment does not exceed five years.

judge returned to the court where he or she originally served. The period of secondment is not in principle allowed to be extended or shortened, but can be terminated in advance or extended with the agreement of the judge. If the secondment is extended, the period of extension must also be clarified and declared.[692]

Secondment shall be ordered by the supreme competent authority of the organ of secondment. If there is a change of employer, it shall be ordered by the original employer in agreement with the new employer.[693]

#### *(c) Secondment under Special Circumstances*

The secondment of judges in principle requires their agreement; however, if they are seconded to another court within the same judicial system to serve at another judgeship for not more than three months in one judicial year, this exceptionally does not require their agreement.[694] Nevertheless, this provision is also restrained by the Constitution which limits the grounds for such secondment, and such secondment also has to be examined by service courts after the event,[695] to reduce the danger of judges being manipulated by their competent authority.[696]

### (7) Effects of the Independence of Status on Court Organisation

The independence of judges includes the principles of jurisdiction (*Gerichtsbarkeit*) and judicial power (*rechtsprechende Gewalt*) enshrined in the Constitution. Therefore, the organisation of courts is charged with making every adjudicative institution upon which the task of adjudication is conferred into an independent court of law.

If all the adjudicative institutions are composed of judges appointed for life or judges appointed for a fixed term who have completely independent status, then they can be guaranteed as being independent courts of law. However, there are some dangers for the judges appointed for a fixed term as compared to the judges appointed for life. If the judges appointed for a fixed term wish to be reelected, their judgements may be influenced by the will of the organs of selection. At present, only judges of the Federal Constitutional Court are judges ap-

---

692 Günter Schmidt-Räntsch, Jürgen Schmidt-Räntsch, Deutsches Richtergesetz (DRiG), Kommentar, 6th edition, Munich 2008, Article 37, margin number 13

693 Günter Schmidt-Räntsch, Jürgen Schmidt-Räntsch, Deutsches Richtergesetz (DRiG), Kommentar, 6th edition, Munich 2008, Article 37, margin number 20

694 Paragraph 3 of Article 37 of DRiG

695 Section 4b of Paragraph 1 of Article 62 and Section 4b of Article 78 of DRiG

696 Günter Schmidt-Räntsch, Jürgen Schmidt-Räntsch, Deutsches Richtergesetz (DRiG), Kommentar, 6th edition, Munich 2008, Article 37, margin number 14

pointed for a fixed term. Their term of service is 12 years and cannot be renewed.[697] Although the Constitution does not recognise any such danger to the independence of judges appointed for a fixed term, Paragraph 1 of Article 28 of the German Judges Act still stipulates that, without the permission of other federal laws, only judges appointed for life can adjudicate trials in courts. This ensures that all courts, as adjudicative institutions, are independent under all circumstances.[698]

### (8) The Independence and Promotion (*Beförderung*) of Judges

The promotion of judges means that judges are granted a new post and receive a higher basic salary. In most cases, they are also granted a new title (*Amtsbezeichnung*), but in some cases may be granted a higher level of salary without a change in title.[699]

When judges are promoted, their independence is protected and bereft of damage, since all judges wish to gain higher positions and salaries. Nonetheless, there are also some potential dangers for the independence of judges caused by promotion. Even though the Basic Law does not explicitly stipulate that the independence of judges must be ensured in the event of promotion, it may be said in accordance with the general definition of the independence of judges in the Basic Law that the Basic Law requires that the possibility of damage being caused to the independence of judges by promotion be closely scrutinised and as far as possible avoided.

In particular, administrative powers are also involved in promotion, which is likely to endanger the independence of the status of judges, since the institutions in charge of promotion are most likely to simply promote judges whom they are satisfied with, whereby the standard of promotion becomes "satisfactory judgement" and "political ideas". In order to obtain the information necessary to decide promotions, it is usual to evaluate judges. The evaluation should consider a judge's inherent intelligence, personality, level of education, achievements, social behaviour and capability in handling cases. The evaluation shall be performed by the leadership within the court (also called senior post officials), which is usually the presiding judge. Probationary judges will want to be promoted to judges appointed for life, and judges appointed for life will want to be promoted to higher positions, so such dangers will exist. Judges will adapt themselves to the standards which senior post officials desire, in order to please the

---

697 Paragraphs 1 and 2 of Article 4 of BVerGG

698 Manfred Wolf, Eduard Kern, Gerichtsverfassungsrecht, Beck, 5th edition, Munich 1975, p.138

699 Carl Creifelds, Rechtswörterbuch, 16th edition, Munich 2000, p. 172

senior post officials and achieve their aim of promotion. As a result, the internal independence of judges can no longer be ensured solely by the legal restraints. In addition, ordinary judges have to assess cases together with the presiding judge and are usually afraid to insist on their own opinion but rather conform to the opinion of the presiding judge in order to prevent resentment. Thus, in order to guarantee the independence of judges to the maximum degree, all the dangers stemming from the breach of laws and legal force as mentioned above have to be entirely avoided.[700]

## (9) Salaries

### *(a) Summary*

It is also possible for judges to be endangered in the discharge of their duties because of insufficient salaries, since if judges do not have sufficient salaries to cover their living costs, they will be forced to earn their livelihood in other ways, thus influencing their thoroughness in the post of judge. Therefore, the content of the guarantees on the independence of status in Paragraph 2 of Article 97 of the Basic Law also includes the provisions that judges shall receive an appropriate salary and be guaranteed financial remuneration. If the salaries of judges fail to cover the living costs of the judges and their families, they are insufficient salaries such as may endanger the independence of judges in the sense of Paragraph 2 of Article 97 of the Basic Law.[701]

### *(b) The Opinions of the Federal Constitutional Court*

The Federal Constitutional Court addressed the principle issues of the status of judges and salaries of judges in a number of judgements in 1969, but it is still open as to whether it declared a particular Constitutional mandate (*Verfassungsauftrag*) for the Judges Remuneration Act (now the Federal Remuneration Act) in accordance with Paragraphs 1 and 3 of Article 98[702] of the Basic Law.[703]

700 Manfred Wolf, Eduard Kern, Gerichtsverfassungsrecht, Beck, 5th edition, Munich 1975, p. 139

701 BVerfGE 26, 157

702 Paragraph 1 of Article 98 of the Basic Law stipulates that the legal status of federal judges shall be regulated by a special federal law; Paragraph 3 stipulates that the legal status of judges in the various *Länder* shall be regulated by special *Land* laws if Clause 27 of Paragraph 1 of Article 74 of the Basic Law does not provide otherwise; Clause 27 of Paragraph 1 of Article 74 of the Basic Law stipulates that matters under concurrent legislative powers (i.e. federal and *Land*) include the statutory rights and duties of civil servants of the *Länder*, the municipalities and other corporations of public law as well

Nonetheless, the Federal Constitutional Court did state that there was no fixed relationship between the salary of the councillors of the higher *Land* courts (*Oberlandesgerichtsräte*) and the salary of the presiding judge. All judges at the various higher *Land* courts (higher *Land* courts, higher *Land* administrative courts, higher *Land* social courts) are on the same level of salary, with no differences between different jurisdictions.

The Federal Constitutional Court has also declared in judgements that the salary paid to the president of *Land* labour courts should follow the example set by the presiding judges of higher *Land* courts and *Land* social courts, providing this does not damage the system of labour courts.

These judgements by the Federal Constitutional Court essentially mean that the salaries of judges shall be the same when they begin to execute the duties of their status as judge, without differentiation, and that salaries begin to differ when some judges begin to serve in positions which combine their duties as judges with certain additional administrative tasks due to promotion (for example from a councillor of a district court (*Amtsgerichtsrat*) to a higher district judge (*Oberamtsrichter*), then a councillor of a social court (*Sozialgerichtsrat*), and finally a councillor of a higher social court (*Obersozialgerichtsrat*)).

The Federal Constitutional Court has also affirmed that the level of salaries of councillors of finance courts is lower than that of the higher *Land* courts and *Land* administrative courts. Although the finance courts rank alongside the higher *Land* courts, they are only established for a short time. At present, however, this division has been abolished.

The essential principles of the judgements of the federal courts only restrict judges appointed for life. Those who have not been appointed as judges for life may be subject to different provisions with respect to their salaries.

### *(c) Latest Developments in Judges' Salaries in Germany*

The essential principles mentioned above were incorporated into the Federal Remuneration Act (Revised) of 14th December 1969 and 5th August 1971, leading to the Remuneration Act of 23rd May 1975 which centralised and newly regulated the provisions for judges at both federal and *Land* level and introduced a special salary group "R" for them which is broken down as follows:

---

as of the judges in the *Länder*, except for their career regulations, remuneration and pensions.

703 Günter Schmidt-Räntsch, Jürgen Schmidt-Räntsch, Deutsches Richtergesetz (DRiG), Kommentar, 6th edition, Munich 2008, before Article 8, margin number 20 ff.

- judges of district courts, *Land* courts and administrative courts fall within the salary group R1;
- presiding judges of *Land* courts and administrative courts and judges of higher *Land* courts and higher administrative courts fall within the salary group R2;
- presiding judges of higher *Land* courts and higher administrative courts fall within the salary group R3;
- judges of the ordinary Federal Court of Justice and the Federal Administrative Court fall within the salary group R6;
- presiding judges of the ordinary Federal Court of Justice and the Federal Administrative Court fall within the salary group R8;
- presidents of the ordinary Federal Court of Justice fall within the salary group R10.

The salaries of the judges of judicial branches (*Gerichtszweige*) of other courts are determined analogously with the above. In comparison with the salaries of civil servants, the initial salaries of judges in the salary group R1 are a little higher than those of civil servants in the salary group A16 (some senior government officials). The final basic salaries (*Endgrundgehalte*) for judges are also slightly higher than those of civil servants in the salary group A15. For judges in the salary group R2, their initial salaries are much higher than those of civil servants in the salary group A16, and their final basic salaries are also higher than those of civil servants in the salary group A16.

However, in comparing the salaries of judges and civil servants, the Federal Constitutional Court did not conclude that the salaries of judges are unconstitutional. In addition, the Basic Law does not require retired judges to be featured in the list of salaries groups.

## Section II The System of Guaranteeing the Status of Judges in China

In China, the Judges Law of the PRC specifies three aspects within the system of guaranteeing the status of judges: the first is that judges shall not be removed or demoted from their post or dismissed, and shall not be given a sanction, without statutory basis and without going through statutory procedures,[704] in order to ensure that judges are not treated unjustly in their posts for enforcing the law impartially; the second aspect concerns the salaries, allowances and benefits

704 Paragraph 3 of Article 8 of the Judges Law of the PRC

paid to judges;[705] and the third aspect concerns the retirement system for judges.[706] However, the Judges Law of the PRC merely provides guiding principles, and a concrete system has yet to be established.

## (1) Removal

### *(a) Grounds for Removal*

The grounds for removal of judges include any of the circumstances specified in Article 13 of the Judges Law of the PRC, namely:

(i) Having Forfeited the Nationality of the People's Republic of China

In accordance with Article 9 of the Judges Law of the PRC, the first necessary qualification of a judge is that they be a national of the People's Republic of China. Therefore, if judges lose their nationality of the People's Republic of China, they cannot meet the requirements for Chinese judges.

In accordance with the Nationality Law of the People's Republic of China, those "having forfeited the nationality of the People's Republic of China" include any Chinese national who has settled abroad and who has been naturalised as a foreign national or has acquired foreign nationality of his own free will"[707] and any Chinese nationals who apply to renounce their Chinese nationality on the grounds that they are near relatives of foreign nationals or have settled abroad or have other legitimate reasons, and have their application approved.[708] There are thus two scenarios, one of losing one's Chinese nationality automatically and one of renouncing one's Chinese nationality, but both result in the loss of nationality of the PRC.

(ii) Having been Transferred out of the Court

Because the Chinese Constitution and the Organic Law of the People's Courts[709] stipulate that the presidents of courts at various levels are elected by the People's Congress at various levels and that the judges of the courts at various levels are nominated by the presidents and appointed by the Standing Committee of the People's Congress at various levels, court president or judges who have been transferred out of the court where they work to another court must first be removed by law from their post as judge at the original court. If they are to con-

705 Articles 34 to 36 of the Judges Law of the PRC

706 Articles 40 and 41 of the Judges Law of the PRC

707 Article 9 of the Nationality Law of the People's Republic of China

708 Articles 10 and 11 of the Nationality Law of the People's Republic of China

709 See Paragraph 7 of Article 62, Paragraph 4 of Article 63, Paragraph 11 of Article 67 and the second paragraph in Article 101 of the Chinese Constitution; Article 35 of the Organic Law of the People's Courts

tinue serving as a judge at the new court, they shall be re-elected or re-appointed by law by the corresponding People's Congress and its Standing Committee in accordance with the provisions of the Constitution and the Organic Law of the People's Courts.

(iii) Having No Need to Maintain His or Her Original Post After a Change of Post

Judges are members of the judiciary who exercise judicial power. If they cease to exercise judicial responsibility, either because they are transferred outside the court system or because they go on to serve in a different, administrative post within the court system, then they shall be removed from their post as judge.

(iv) Being Determined to be Incompetent in the Post Through Appraisal

As public servants, judges in China are both workers who perform official duties according to law and members of the administrative establishment of the State.[710] The Law of the People's Republic of China on Public Servants stipu-

---

710 See Article 2 of the Law of the People's Republic of China on Public Servants. In accordance with the explanation of the draft of the Law of the People's Republic of China on Public Servants and the report of the legal committee of the NPC on the results of consideration of the draft of the Law of the People's Republic of China on Public Servants, there are seven classes of government staff within the sphere of Chinese civil servants: 1. the staff of the organs of the Communist Party of China, including full-time leading members of the central and local party committees and commissions for disciplinary inspection at various levels, the staff of the central and local party committee departments and disciplinary inspection bodies at various levels, and the staff of the organs of the party committees at street and town(ship) level; 2. the staff of the People's Congresses, including the full-time chairman and vice-chairman, the secretary-general and the full-time members of the Standing Committee of the National People's Congress, the full-time director and deputy director, the secretary-general and the full-time members of the Standing Committee of the local People's Congresses at various levels, the full-time director and deputy director of the Standing Committee of the People's Congress at town(ship) level, the staff of the Standing Committee of the People's Congresses at various levels, the full-time members of the Special Committee of the People's Congresses at various levels and the staff of their administrative offices; 3. the staff of administrative institutions, including the members of the People's Governments at various levels and the staff of the departments and agencies of the People's Governments at various levels; 4. the staff of the organs of the CPPCC (Chinese People's Political Consultative Conference), including the chairman, full-time vice-chairman and secretary-general of the committees of the CPPCC at various levels, the staff of the departments of the committees of the CPPCC at various levels and the staff of the offices of the Special Committees of the CPPCC; 5. the staff of judicial organs, including judges, assistant judges and administrative staff at the Supreme People's Court and the local People's Courts at various levels; 6. the staff of the procuratorial organs, including

lates that judges shall be appraised every year and stipulates the corresponding procedures and circumstances of appraisal.[711] The results of regular assessment are divided into four grades: excellent, competent, basically competent and incompetent.[712] Judges who are confirmed by annual appraisal as being incompetent for two successive years shall be removed in accordance with Article 38 of the Judges Law of the PRC. Those who are removed shall also be dismissed (see the below discussion on dismissal).

(v) Being Unable to Perform the Functions and Duties of a Judge for a Long Period of Time Due to Poor Health

Those who are unable to perform the functions and duties of a judge for a long period of time due to poor health shall be removed from their post as judge in accordance with the Judges Law of the PRC. However, the Judges Law of the PRC does not explain in any greater detail what is meant by "being unable to perform the functions and duties of a judge for a long period of time".

(vi) Having Retired from the Post

Referring to the provisions of the Law of the People's Republic of China on Public Servants, the "retirement" of judges includes two situations: one is mandatory retirement,[713] which applies to males who reach the age of 60 and females who reach the age of 55 and to those who have completely lost their ability to work; and the other is voluntary retirement,[714] which applies to males who reach the age of 55 and females who reach the age of 50 and have worked completely for twenty years or to those of any age who have worked completely for thirty years and by which they may retire before reaching retirement age if they apply of their own free will and their application is approved by the department in charge of appointment and removal.

---

public prosecutors, assistant public prosecutors and administrative staff at the Supreme People's Procuratorate and the local People's Procuratorates at various levels; 7. the staff of the organs of the democratic parties, including the chairman, full-time vice-chairman and secretary-general of the central and local committees of the eight democratic parties at various levels and the staff of the functional divisions and offices of the central and local committees at various levels.

711 Articles 34 and 35 of the Law of the People's Republic of China on Public Servants

712 Article 36 of the Law of the People's Republic of China on Public Servants

713 Article 87 of the Law of the People's Republic of China on Public Servants

714 Article 88 of the Law of the People's Republic of China on Public Servants

(vii) Having Resigned the Pose or Having Been Dismissed

1. Resignation

Resignation by judges means that judges resign from their post as judge by applying to resign of their own free will and their application is approved by the department in charge of appointment and removal. Resignation by judges is a matter for the individual and based on the premise that it is voluntary. Judges have the right to apply to resign and this is also an important part of the system of personnel management. All judges have the right to apply to resign in accordance with their wishes and situation in life and to choose a more suitable post or occupation for themselves. There are two senses of "resignation" in this respect: one is the resignation of a leading position at court, such as that of court presidents at various levels, vice-presidents, members of the adjudicative committee, presiding judges, deputy presiding judges, and so on; the other is the resignation of public office, such that the individual never again serves as a judge at court.[715]

2. Dismissal

The dismissal of judges means that judges who are incapable of executing their judicial work are dismissed from their post as judge and their employment status with the respective organ is revoked by the People's Courts at various levels, within their managerial jurisdiction and after examination and approval by the department in charge of appointment and removal, in accordance with the provisions of the law and regulations. With respect to the grounds for dismissing judges, Article 38 of the Judges Law of the PRC stipulates that judges may be dismissed if they are found to fulfil any of the following five criteria:

(1)to be confirmed by annual appraisal as being incompetent for two successive years;
(2)to be unqualified for the present post and decline to accept other assignments;
(3)to refuse to accept reasonable transfer, which is necessitated by restructuring of the judicial organ or reduction of the size of the staff;
(4)to have stayed away from work without leave or to have overstayed his or her leave for more than fifteen days in succession, or for more than thirty days in a year aggregated; or
(5)to fail to perform a judge's duty, and make no rectification after criticism.

These five criteria in the Judges Law of the PRC are practically identical to the five criteria cited as conditions for dismissal in the Law of the People's Republic

715 See the explanation on the official website of the NPC: http://www.npc.gov.cn/npc/flsyywd/xianfa/2002-07/11/content_297398.htm

of China on Public Servants.[716] If any one of these five is fulfilled, the work unit (单位dānwèi) where the judge works shall dismiss the judge.

Where the first criterion reads "to be confirmed by annual appraisal as being incompetent for two successive years", this refers to the end-of-year appraisal of civil servants in state government which is conducted every year and is also referred to as "regular assessment" in the Law of the People's Republic of China on Public Servants.[717] "Two successive years" means two consecutive years such as for example the two successive years of 1999 and 2000. If there are gaps between the two respective years, such as for example 1999 and 2001, then these do not count as two successive years. There are four possible results of the appraisal, i.e. "excellent", "competent", "basically competent" and "incompetent".[718] "Incompetent" means the appraisal made by other civil servants of the standard of a certain individual's ideas, work, etc. over the preceding year by way of joint assessment.

"Unqualified" in the wording "to be unqualified for the present post and decline to accept other assignments" in (2) above means that an individual's level of working capability and professional competence does not equal the various capabilities which he or she must have in the present post. It can also be understood to mean that there is a large difference between the individual's actual capabilities and the various capabilities required in the present post. The "present post" means the post of presidents, vice-presidents, members of the adjudicative committee, presiding judges, deputy presiding judges, judges and assistant judges of People's Courts at various levels. With respect to this provision, if a judge cannot competently serve in his present post, and does not accept another post offered by his work unit, even one in which he could competently serve, then he shall be dismissed.

With respect to "restructuring of the judicial organ" in (3) above, the wording "to refuse to accept reasonable transfer, which is necessitated by restructuring of the judicial organ or reduction of the size of the staff" refers to when courts restructure their internal judicial departments in accordance with the law, including any judicial courts, juvenile courts, executive offices and other departments relating to judicial affairs. "Restructuring" includes increasing, reducing, changing or combining institutions, among other things. "Reduction of the size of the staff" means that the number of staff who deal with judicial affairs shall be reduced on the basis of a program of reforming state organs and the organisational arrangement of court staff. When restructuring a judicial organ or

716 Article 83 of the Law of the People's Republic of China on Public Servants

717 Articles 34 and 35 of the Law of the People's Republic of China on Public Servants

718 Article 36 of the Law of the People's Republic of China on Public Servants

reducing the size of the staff, there will be problems caused by the need to provide work to those who have been shed in the reduction of the size of the staff. In this situation, if the shed staffs refuse to accept a reasonable transfer offer by their work units, then the work units have the power to dismiss them in accordance with this provision. "Reasonable transfer" means that the work units shall offer shed staff a transfer based on the nature of their previous work, to a post which they are suitable for in view of their material or factual working abilities and professional competence, so as to continue to make the best possible use of them within the reasonable bounds of circumstance.[719]

The fourth criterion above specifies four circumstances under which judges would have violated the rules of discipline and could be dismissed. The first is if they have stayed away from work without leave for more than fifteen days in succession; the second is if they have overstayed their leave without good reason for more than fifteen days in succession ("more than" here excludes the exact figure given itself); the third is to have stayed away from work without leave for more than thirty days in a year; and the fourth is to have overstayed their leave without good reason for more than thirty days in a year ("more than" here excludes the exact figure given itself). The wording "to have stayed away from work without leave" means to have been absent from work or duty without good reason and without leave. With respect to the wording "to have overstayed one's leave for more than fifteen days in succession", this is to be calculated from the second day as of the last day of proper leave.[720]

A "judge's duty" as referred to in the provision of (5) above in the wording: "to fail to perform a judge's duty, and make no rectification after criticism" means the seven duties which judges must execute in accordance with the provisions of Article 7 of the Judges Law of the PRC.[721]

---

719 See the explanation on the official website of the NPC: http://www.npc.gov.cn/npc/flsyywd/xianfa/2002-07/11/content_297398.htm

720 See Article 83 of the Law of the People's Republic of China on Public Servants.

721 Article 7 of the Judges Law of the PRC stipulates that judges shall perform the following obligations: (1) to strictly observe the Constitution and laws; (2) to take facts as the basis, and laws as the criterion when trying cases, to handle cases impartially, and not to bend the law for personal gain; (3) to protect the litigation rights of the participants in proceedings according to law; (4) to safeguard State interests and public interests, and to safeguard the lawful rights and interests of citizens, legal persons and other organisations; (5) to be honest and fair, faithful in the discharge of their duties, and to abide by the rules of discipline and professional ethics; (6) to keep State secrets and the secrets of judicial work; and (7) to accept legal supervision and supervision by the masses.

### (viii) Being Disqualified from Continuing to Hold the Post Because of Violation of Discipline, the Law or Commission of a Crime

"Violation of discipline, the law or commission of a crime" is intended to have a broad sense here and includes both actions which violate party discipline, government discipline[722] and/or the law and prohibited actions which violate the provisions of the Judges Law of the PRC (Article 30 of the Judges Law of the PRC).[723]

Article 31 of the Judges Law of the PRC stipulates that a judge who has committed any of the acts listed in Article 30 of the Judges Law of the PRC shall be given sanctions; if the case constitutes a crime, he or she shall be investigated for criminal responsibility. Article 32 stipulates that sanctions may include a disciplinary warning, a demerit recorded, a grave demerit recorded, demotion, dismissal from one's post, and discharge from public employment. In accordance with the Disciplinary Measures of the People's Courts on Adjudication promulgated on 7th September 1998 by the Supreme People's Court, if a

---

722 In accordance with the Regulation of the Communist Party of China on Disciplinary Sanctions, actions which violate party discipline and government discipline include the following ten categories: violating political discipline (Articles 45-49); violating organisational and personnel discipline (Articles 60-71); violating the provisions on fairness, honesty and self-discipline (Articles 72-82); submitting to corruption (Articles 83-96); disrupting the socialist economic order (Articles 97-112); violating financial and/or economic discipline (Articles 113-126); neglecting their duties or committing misconduct (Articles 127-139); infringing the rights of party members or citizens (Articles 140-148); seriously violating socialist ethics (Articles 149-154); and interfering with the social order of management (Articles 155-174).

723 Article 30 of the Judges Law of the PRC stipulates that no judges may commit any of the following acts: (1) to spread statements damaging the prestige of the State; to join illegal organisations; to take part in such activities as assembly, procession and demonstration against the State; and to participate in strikes; (2) to embezzle money or accept bribes; (3) to bend the law for personal gain; (4) to extort confessions by torture; (5) to conceal or falsify evidence; (6) to divulge State secrets or secrets of judicial work; (7)to abuse functions and powers, and to infringe upon the legitimate rights and interests of citizens, legal persons or other organisations; (8) to neglect their duty so as to wrongly judge a case or to cause heavy losses to the party concerned; (9) to intentionally delay the handling of a case so as to affect the work adversely; (10) to take advantage of their functions and powers to seek gain for themselves or other people; (11) to engage in profit-making activities; (12) to meet the party concerned or his or her agent without authorisation and attend dinners or accept presents given by the party concerned or his or her agent; or (13) to commit other acts in violation of the law or rules of discipline.

judge has been discharged from public employment due to a sanction, their post and grade shall be automatically revoked.[724]

### *(b) The Procedure of Removal*

Paragraph 3 of Article 8 of the Judges Law of the PRC stipulates that judges have the right not to be removed or demoted from their post or dismissed, and not to be given a sanction, without statutory basis and without going through statutory procedures. The statutory basis is any of the circumstances listed in Article 13 of the Judges Law of the PRC as mentioned above, although the Judges Law of the PRC does not include corresponding provisions on the statutory procedures.

It has been elucidated in conjunction with the section on the supervision of judges' posts that in China, it is possible to be removed from the post of court president merely by removal (for the procedural specifics, see this chapter). Removal is within the authority of the Standing Committee of the People's Congress. The procedure of removal when decided by the Standing Committee of the People's Congress is usually that: (i) the president of the court which made the appointment proposes the removal; (ii) in the proposal for removal, the grounds for removal usually only require a simple explanation; (iii) the Standing Committee of the People's Congress decides by a vote, following a discussion of the proposal for removal.

## (2) Demotion from a Post

Since the Judges Law of the PRC does not include any specific provisions regarding demotion from a post, it is necessary in this respect to refer to the provisions of the Law of the People's Republic of China on Public Servants.

### *(a) Grounds for Demotion from a Post*

Article 47 of the Law of the People's Republic of China on Public Servants stipulates that if a civil servant is determined to be incompetent through regular assessment, he shall be demoted to a post at the next lower level in compliance with the prescribed procedures. Article 33 of the Law of the People's Republic of China on Public Servants stipulates that: "the assessment of public servants shall be conducted in compliance with the limits of authorised administration, comprehensively covering their political integrity, ability, diligence, achievements and incorruptibility." Article 34 stipulates that: "the assessment of public

724 Article 16 of the Disciplinary Measures of the People's Courts on Adjudication

servants shall be divided into routine and regular assessments" and that "regular assessments shall be made on the basis of routine assessment". The first paragraph in Article 36 then stipulates that: "the results of regular assessment are divided into four grades: excellent, competent, basically competent and incompetent." Based on the above provisions, a civil servant who is assessed to be incompetent in the regular assessment shall be demoted to a post at the next lower level.[725] Judges in China are subject to routine assessment and regular assessment in accordance with the methods for assessing civil servants. Those who are assessed to be incompetent in the regular assessment shall be demoted to a post at the next lower level.

It is worth noting that demotion is a form of change in employment status which corresponds to promotion rather than a disciplinary measure. While there are some similarities between demotion and a reduction in rank as a disciplinary measure, such as that both represent a reduction in the level or grade of post, there are also several material differences:

- the causes are different. The cause of a demotion is that a civil servant is assessed to be incompetent in their regular assessment. Such incompetence may relate to any one of or more than one of the criteria of political integrity, ability, diligence, achievements and incorruptibility, whereas a reduction in rank as a disciplinary measure relates to actions by the civil servant which violate the law and/or rules of discipline.
- the aims are different. The aim of demotion is to ensure a high quality of civil servants. Demoting those who are incompetent in their post is a way of employing a competitive mechanism whereby high-level posts are given to the most competent, thus increasing overall work efficiency. By contrast, the aim of a reduction in rank is to discipline a civil servant who has violated the law and/or rules of discipline, in order to make them take the corresponding disciplinary responsibility for their actions and to caution and educate other civil servants to always observe the rules of discipline and to obey the law.

725 A civil servant who currently holds the position of chief of a division and is assessed to be incompetent in the regular annual assessment will be demoted one level, i.e. to deputy chief of a division. It should be noted firstly that the extent of demotion cannot exceed one level; for example, the civil servant in the above example cannot be directly demoted to a section-level post. Secondly, it is not appropriate as a demotion to move a civil servant from a leading position to a non-leading position at the same level; for example, to move the civil servant in the above example from a position as chief of a division to a position as an administrative researcher. Thirdly, if the rank of the demoted civil servant exceeds the highest possible rank in their new post, then their rank shall be reduced to that of the highest possible rank in their new post.

- the duration is different. Demotion is a single, discrete act which once performed, is complete and does not subsequently involve a particular period of time, whereas a reduction in rank as a disciplinary measure has a particular period of effect. In accordance with Article 58 of the Law of the People's Republic of China on Public Servants, the period of effect of a reduction in rank as a disciplinary measure is 24 months, during which time the civil servant cannot be promoted to a higher grade of salary.

*(b) The Procedure of Demotion from a Post*

In accordance with Article 14 of the Interim Regulations on the Promotion and Demotion of Civil Servants formulated by the Ministry of Human Resources in 1996, before civil servants can be demoted from their post, their work unit must first present an opinion on the proposal for demotion, then the grounds for demotion must be examined and verified and the opinion of the civil servant to be demoted must be heard, and finally a negotiated and collective decision on demotion is made in accordance with the law by the leadership of the organ in charge of appointment and removal.

In accordance with Article 90 of the Law of the People's Republic of China on Public Servants, civil servants who disagree with a demotion imposed on them may, within thirty days of being informed of the decision, apply for a review to the department which handled the case; civil servants who are in turn not satisfied with the result of the review may, within fifteen days of receiving the result of the review, appeal to the department in charge of civil servants at the same level or to a department at the next level above the department which handled the case; they may also skip the review stage and appeal the decision directly to said higher department within thirty days of being informed of the decision. If they disagree with an appeal decision made by a department below the provincial level, they may appeal again to a department at a higher level. If a civil servant of an administrative department disagrees with a demotion and appeals to the supervisory administrative department, the provisions of the Law on Administrative Supervision are applied.

### (3) Dismissal

The grounds and procedures for dismissing judges have already been discussed above in the section on dismissal and shall not therefore be discussed again here.

### (4) Disciplinary measures

With respect to the disciplinary measures imposed on judges, please see the discussion on the Service Supervision of Judges in the chapter on the Service Supervision of Judges in this dissertation.

### (5) Judicial Independence and the Retirement of Judges

Article 44 of the Chinese Constitution stipulates that: "The State applies the system of retirement for workers and staff members of enterprises and institutions and for functionaries of organs of State according to law. The livelihood of retired persons is ensured by the State and society." In view of the fact that judges are workers who exercise state judicial power, the nature of their work is different from that of other state institutions. Accordingly, they are subject to different conditions of retirement as compared to the staff of other state institutions. Article 42 of the Judges Law of the PRC stipulates in this respect that: "the retirement system regarding judges shall, in light of the characteristics of judicial work, be formulated separately by the State." However, the retirement system regarding judges has so far not yet been separately formulated. The details of the retirement system for judges continue to be taken from the retirement system for civil servants.

In accordance with the provisions of the Law of the People's Republic of China on Public Servants, retirement is divided into mandatory retirement and early retirement.

#### *(a) Types of Retirement and Grounds for Retirement*

#### (i) Mandatory Retirement

Article 87 of the Law of the People's Republic of China on Public Servants stipulates that civil servants who reach the age for retirement prescribed by the State or completely lose the ability to work shall retire. On the basis of this article, there are two grounds for mandatory retirement: one is reaching the age for retirement; the other is a complete inability to work.

#### 1. Reaching the Age for Retirement Prescribed by the State

In China, there is a developed but still evolving set of provisions regarding the age of retirement for civil servants. The Interim Procedures on Arrangements for Old, Weak, Infirm and Disabled Cadres as promulgated by the State Council in 1978 on the basis of principles approved by the Standing Committee of the National People's Congress stipulates that in the case of cadres of Party and government organisations, organisations of the masses, enterprises and public institutions, males who reach the age of 60 and females who reach the age of 55 and who have participated in the revolution for at least ten years of their working life may retire.[726] A 1978 Notice by the Organisational Department of the CPC Central Committee, the Ministry of Labour and the Ministry of Human Resources on the age of retirement for female cadres stipulates that if a female cadre in a department (at county level) reaches the age of 55 and there are no appropriate replacement candidates and she is able and willing to continue working normally, then her age of retirement may be correspondingly deferred in accordance with her wishes, if examined and approval by her work unit and approved by the organ of appointment and removal.[727] The 1982 Decision of the Chinese Communist Party Central Committee on Establishing a Retirement System for Old Cadres stipulates that the retirement age of ministers and deputy ministers of the central or State organs, senior secretaries and secretaries of the Party Committees in the provinces, municipalities and autonomous regions, governors and lieutenant governors of provincial governments and senior officials of disciplinary inspection committees, courts and procuratorates in the provinces, municipalities and autonomous regions shall be not more than 65 in case of senior staff and not more than 60 in the case of deputy senior staff, although the retirement age of cadres serving as chiefs of divisions or departments shall not generally be more than 60.[728] However, individuals who have reached retirement age may, in view of the demands of their work and if they are willing and able, ask to continue working normally and continue to serve in their leadership post and temporarily defer their retirement within a certain period of time agreed by the organisation in question.[729] The Interim Regulations on Civil Servants formulated by the State Council in 1993 essentially continues to use the provisions of the Interim Procedures on Arrangements for Old, Weak, Infirm and Disabled Cadres, namely that males retire at 60 and females at 55. The Law of the People's Republic of China on Public Servants does not include specific provisions on the age of retirement for civil servants, hence in principle, it likewise continues to use the relevant original provisions.

726 Paragraph 1 of Article 4 of the Interim Procedures on Arrangements for Old, Weak, Infirm and Disabled Cadres

727 Article 3 of the Notice by the Organisational Department of the CPC Central Committee, the Ministry of Labour and the Ministry of Human Resources on the age of retirement for female cadres

728 For example, the current President of the Supreme People's Court, Wang Shengjun, is at the ministerial level of the State organs. He was 60 when he was elected and is now 62, so his retirement age will be 65.

729 Paragraph 3 of Article 3 of the Decision of the Chinese Communist Party Central Committee on Establishing a Retirement System for Old Cadres

## 2. Complete Inability to Work

A civil servant who is completely unable to work shall also be retired. This "complete inability to work" is understood to mean that a person suffers great physical and/or psychological harm due to illness or accident and is consequently unable to work normally. Civil servants who are completely incapacitated shall retire in order to rest and recover. Thus, the retirement of civil servants due to complete incapacity reflects the duty of care on the part of organs towards civil servants. It is worth noting that while the Interim Regulations on Civil Servants of 1993 stipulates that civil servants who are incapacitated shall be retired, the Law of the People's Republic of China on Public Servants actually amends this point to the effect that civil servants who are only partially incapacitated and not completely incapacitated shall not be retired. In cases of partial incapacity, organs shall instead find an appropriate post involving duties which are appropriate to the civil servant's physical and/or psychological status following their partial incapacity.

At present, there is no standard and/or unified definition of complete incapacity in Chinese law. The "Standards on the Degree of Disability at Work due to Illness or Injury (for Trial Implementation)" enumerate 17 instances of complete incapacity.[730]

---

730 The 17 conditions are: 1. various diseases of the central nervous system or surrounding nerve muscle. Once diagnosed, these may fall into one of the following categories: a. monoplegia, with muscle strength at or below grade 2; b. diplegia or triplegia, with muscle strength at or below grade 3; c. paralysis of both hands or feet, with muscle strength at or below grade 2; d. global (sensory or mixed) aphasia; e. non-limb paralysis with moderate dyskinesia. 2. Long-term serious breathing difficulty. 3. Long-term cardiac function above III, with left ventricular ejection fraction of 50% or less. 4. Untreatable malignant ventricular tachycardia. 5. Various forms of severe anaemia which are difficult to cure, with post-treatment long-term haemoglobin levels at or below 6g/dl. 6. Total gastrectomy or total colectomy or 3/4 small intestine resection. 7. Acute and/or chronic liver dysfunction. 8. Irreversible chronic renal failure. 9. Various metabolic or endocrine diseases, connective tissue disease or serious complications of decompensated dysfunction in more than one of the organs including the heart, brain, kidneys, lungs, liver and other organs caused by autoimmune diseases. 10. Various malignant tumours (including blood tumours) which are incurable or postoperatively recurrent despite radiotherapy, chemotherapy and/or combined treatment. 11. Light perception or no light perception in one eye, with a corrected visual acuity of less than 0.2 or a radius of field of vision of 20° or less in the other eye. 12. A corrected visual acuity of less than 0.1 or a radius of field of vision of 20° or less in both eyes. 13. Chronic organic mental disorders, with retention of any one of the following symptoms after two years' treatment in a way seriously impairing occupational function: dementia (moderate cognitive decline); continuous or recurrent delusions and hallucinations, persistent or recur-

(ii) Early Retirement

In accordance with the provisions of the Law of the People's Republic of China on Public Servants,[731] the conditions for early retirement for civil servants are as follows. Firstly, that the civil servant has worked completely for 30 years, which means at least 30 years have passed in which the civil servant has worked for State organs, counting from the first year in which the civil servant began to work for State organs to the year in which the civil servant applied for retirement. Secondly, that the civil servant is less than five years away from the retirement age prescribed by the State and has worked for over 20 years. Thus, in accordance with the relevant provisions,[732] male civil servants who are over 55 years of age and have worked in State organs for at least 20 years and female civil servants who are over 50 years of age and have worked in State organs for at least 20 years can retire early. Thirdly, other conditions for early retirement as prescribed by State provisions.[733] This condition ensures that civil servants operating in certain special fields are permitted to retire early because of the special nature of their field and in order to protect their health. For example, civil servants involved in nuclear tests, field work and toxic and/or hazardous materials may retire early in accordance with these provisions in order to protect their health.

---

ring emotional instability with inability to control urge to attack. 14. Schizophrenia proving irreversible even after five years' treatment; paranoid disorders and/or concrete paranoia which cannot be alleviated for a continuous period of five years and seriously impairs occupational function. 15. Refractory affective disorder which cannot be reversed over five years of treatment in males of 50 or older or females of 45 or over and which seriously impairs occupational function. 16. Refractory obsessive-compulsive disorders exhibiting a clear compulsive personality and which cannot be reversed over five years of treatment and seriously impairs occupational function. 17. Those qualifying for Standards 1 to 4 of the "Standards on the Degree of Disability at Work due to Illness or Injury".

731 Article 88 of the Law of the People's Republic of China on Public Servants

732 Paragraph 1 of Article 78 and Paragraph 2 of Article 78 of the Interim Regulations on Civil Servants

733 For example, in accordance with Paragraph 2 of Article 1 of the Interim Procedures of the State Council on the Retirement of Workers, retirement shall also be granted to the following staff: those who have been engaged in high altitude work and/or especially heavy physical work for a total of 10 years; those who have been engaged in work down shafts and/or exposed to high temperature for a total of 9 years; and those who have been engaged in other work which is damaging to health for a total of 8 years.

### (b) *The Procedure of Retirement*

Neither the Law of the People's Republic of China on Public Servants nor the Judges Law of the PRC include specific provisions regarding the procedure for the retirement of civil servants, especially mandatory retirement. As long as civil servants fulfil the conditions for mandatory retirement, they may automatically retire and enjoy their retirement benefits with regard to other circumstances. In practice, the procedure of early retirement is as follows. Firstly, civil servants who fulfil the conditions apply voluntarily. The voluntary application by the civil servant initiates the procedure of early retirement. Only civil servants who fulfil the conditions and apply voluntarily can be permitted to retire early; even civil servants who fulfil the conditions for early retirement will not otherwise be ordered to retire early by individuals or work units. Secondly, the organs in charge of appointment and removal approve the civil servant's early retirement. Once the organs in charge of appointment and removal have received an application for early retirement from a civil servant, they shall examine whether the civil servant fulfils the conditions for early retirement. If the civil servant does not fulfil the conditions for early retirement, the application shall not be approved; if the civil servant does fulfil the conditions for early retirement, the application shall be approved.[734]

### (c) *Retirement Benefits*

In accordance with the provisions of the Judges Law of the PRC and the Law of the People's Republic of China on Public Servants,[735] judges shall enjoy retirement benefits after they retire. Retirement benefits for civil servants means the rights which civil servants shall enjoy after they retire, which mainly relate to economic benefits such as the pension and other living and welfare allowances enjoyed by retirees. The pension is the principal economic benefit awarded to civil servants after they retire.

---

734 See Chapter 14 of the Law of the People's Republic of China on Public Servants, on the website of the NPC, http://www.npc.gov.cn/npc/flsyywd/xingzheng/200508/05/content_353269.htm

735 Article 41 of the Judges Law of the PRC stipulates that after retirement, judges shall enjoy the insurance of an old-age pension and other benefits as prescribed by the State. Article 89 of the Law of the People's Republic of China on Public Servants stipulates that after retirement, civil servants shall enjoy a retirement pension and other benefits as prescribed by the State, and that the State shall provide the necessary services and assistance for their everyday life and health and encourage them to participate in social development by bringing their specialities into play.

In China, pensions for civil servants are allocated and paid by the State financial committee and are calculated on the basis of the civil servant's standard monthly wage before retirement multiplied by a certain percentage which is usually decided by the length of service. Pensions are paid monthly and their minimal level should suffice to maintain ordinary social living standards and their maximum level should not exceed the salaries of civil servants working in the same post and at the same grade. In addition to their pension, civil servants may also enjoy other welfare benefits provided by the government upon their retirement, some of which are received while they are still working and are maintained after retirement, and the rest of which are provided by the State especially for retirees, such as public health services, air-conditioning and heating subsidies, travel expenses, funeral allowances, pensions for next-of-kin, etc.

In accordance with the provisions of the Law of the People's Republic of China on Public Servants of China,[736] the retirement benefits for civil servants belong to the welfare and insurance rights of civil servants. In addition, the funds required to allow civil servants to receive retirement benefits when they retire are ensured by State financing. When the State draws up its budget, it must take the retirement benefits of civil servants into account. The competent organs shall earmark budgetary funds for the specific purpose of civil servants' retirement benefits, which may not be diverted.

### (6) Guarantee of the Status of Judges and Their Wages and Benefits

The wages and benefits of judges in China accordingly include the two individual aspects of judges' wages and judges' benefits. Wages are the salaries which judges shall receive for the duration of their employ, and benefits means the material benefits which judges enjoy in addition to their wage, such as medical treatment, housing benefits and travelling expenses.[737]

At present, the Judges Law of the PRC only includes very general provisions on judges' wages and benefits in Articles 34, 35 and 36 and does not in-

736 The first paragraph in Article 77 of the Law of the People's Republic of China on Public Servants stipulates that the State establishes an insurance system for civil servants to guarantee them access to assistance and compensation when they are retired, fall ill, are injured at work, give birth, become unemployed, etc. Article 79 stipulates that the expenditures required for payment of salaries, welfare benefits, insurance premiums and retirement pensions to civil servants and for the recruitment and employment, training, reward and dismissal of civil servants shall be guaranteed by having them listed in the financial budget.

737 Zhao Xiaosuo, Structure of the Chinese System of Judges, People's Court Press, Beijing, April 2003, p. 175

clude any explicit and/or concrete provisions regarding the wages and benefits which judges shall enjoy. In accordance with the Scheme to Regulate Staff Wages at State Organs and Institutions established by the State Ministry of Human Resources, the State Development Planning Commission and the State Ministry of Finance on 19th December 1989 and the Notice on Regulating the Standard of Wages for Staff of State Organs and Institutions implemented by the State Ministry of Human Resources and the State Ministry of Finance on 1st October 1997, the wages of judges in China are in fact the same as those of staff at other State organs, and their medical treatment and housing benefits are almost the same as those of other civil servants and do not receive particular consideration. Moreover, the standard of wages and benefits enjoyed by judges and other civil servants in China is in practice even lower than that of civil servants of other State organs such as political and law committees, public security bureaux and justice departments.[738]

## Section III Comparison

In Germany, there are neither explicit legal grounds for the dismissal, relocation, suspension and retirement of judges nor a comprehensive procedure for guarantees. All these matters are decided by the service courts. In China, there are neither comprehensive provisions on the grounds for dismissal nor provisions on guarantees for the procedures. In addition, the Judges Law of the PRC does not mention the suspension or relocation of judges, leading to judges being transferred to other sites arbitrarily and in practice excessively. It is clear that arbitrarily transferring judges does not conform to the requirements for guaranteeing the status of judges. Once judges are appointed, this should mean that they cannot be arbitrarily transferred from one court to another. If there are no legal provisions on the grounds or procedures for such transfers, it is easy for this to be-

738 For example, the President of the Yuhang District People's Court in Hangzhou pointed out in his survey and study report that of the nearly 500 judges who took part in the investigation, 69% believed their incomes were disproportionately low. His court employed five bachelors of law and one master of law in 2001, but by 2006, only one remained while the others had transferred to other government organs or institutions because of the superior benefits. See Fu Zhangxuan et al., Difficulties and Ways Out: an Investigation and Consideration of the Brain Drain Problem at the Basic People's Courts in Developed Economic Areas, Taking the Basic People's Court of Hangzhou as an Example, in: Guidance and Research on Establishing the Professionalisation of Judges, edited by the Political Department of the Supreme People's Court, 2007, Volume 1, p. 49

come a means for superiors, who hold the power of relocation over judges, to influence the adjudicative independence of judges.

In addition, the retirement system for judges in China merely draws on the retirement system for civil servants, as there are no special provisions on the retirement system for judges. In accordance with the Law of the People's Republic of China on Public Servants, there are differences between the retirement ages of males and females, which has no scientific basis and violates the fundamental principle of equality between the sexes. With the enhancement of living standards and the development of medical health services, people's average life span has been extended and the onset of old age has been delayed. Thus, the retirement age for judges in China is relatively early and should also be extended somewhat. Society at large has to make a significant outlay in order to cultivate qualified and gifted judges, and a wealth of judicial experience is an important resource in adjudication, hence the early retirement of judges represents a huge waste of social resources.[739] For this reason, it is necessary to refer to current international practice and to consider an appropriate extension of the retirement age of judges when amending the Judges Law of the PRC.

Finally, the problem of judges' salaries shall be discussed. Although in Germany, judges' salaries do relate to those of civil servants, there are some differences in the salaries of judges as compared to those of civil servants due to their special status.[740] The salaries of judges are governed by the law.[741] The level of salary is decided by the *Bundestag*. Generally, before legislating, the *Bundestag* negotiates contracts with the various trade unions who represent civil servants.[742] In both Germany and China, the level of salary is decided by the

739 See Song Jianchao (Deputy Director of the Political Department of the Supreme People's Court), Chen Haiguang (Director of the Administrative Office for Judges at the Political Department of the Supreme People's Court), Research on Countering the Shortage of Judges, in: Guidance and Research on Establishing the Professionalisation of Judges, edited by the Political Department of the Supreme People's Court, 2007, Volume 1, p. 37

740 Because of the particularities of the functions of judges, different salary groups should be established. The salaries of judges should not be determined, like those of civil servants, by their grades of post and administrative functions. In order to guarantee the independence of judges, a special salary system which is different from that of general civil servants needs to be devised and established, cf. BVerfGE 32, 199 (213 f)

741 The Federal Remuneration Act and the Civil Service Pensions Act stipulate that this provision is also applied to judges, see Paragraph 1 of Article 1 of BBesG and Paragraph 2 of Article 1 of BeamtVG

742 For example with the Public Service, Transport and Communications Union (*Gewerkschaft Öffentliche Dienste, Transport und Verkehr = ÖTV*), now part of the United Service Union (*Vereinte Dienstleistungsgewerkschaft = ver.di*)

judge's post.[743] The salary system for judges in Germany comprises different grades of salary depending on the various posts of judge. There are different initial salaries and allowances at each grade, which are paid in accordance with the employment history and family status of judges.[744] With respect to the salaries of judges, the Federal Constitutional Court allows legislators a certain degree of leeway,[745] but the fundamental principle cannot be violated, which is that judges at the same grade shall receive the same salary irrespective of their employment history, individual contributions and achievements or appraisal results.[746] Fixed salaries can prevent courts from influencing the judicial activities of judges by establishing different salaries in their administration.[747] In a European context, the salaries of judges in Germany, particularly in terms of their purchasing power, are below average.[748] The salaries of judges at the highest specialised courts are almost the same as those of members of parliament; the salaries of other judges are more like those of civil servants.[749] Nevertheless, as compared to judges in China, the salaries of German judges are at least enough to ensure a better standard of living for themselves and their family and are sufficient to curtail the temptation to engage in illegal actions for economic ends. Although German judges do not receive an especially high level of pay, their incomes are stable and guaranteed for life, and they enjoy better retirement benefits than in other

743 A judge who is 35 years old and has just started working as a judge shall generally receive € 35,316 before tax, increasing to € 52,584 for those who reach 45 years of age and are still in their original post. If promoted to the Appeal Court, the salary becomes € 57,627, and if promoted to the Supreme Special Court, it becomes € 80,724.

744 Increases in salary also depend on their period of service and promotions.

745 See the decisions of 12th February 2003 (2 BvL 3/00 and 2 BvR 709/99) by the Federal Constitutional Court; BVerfGE 107, 257

746 The Federal Constitutional Court has repeatedly emphasised that in order to guarantee the independence of judges, the executive must be prevented by law from influencing the judiciary, and in particular prevented from applying higher or lower salaries to the same post, see BVerfGE 26, 79 (93 ff); 32, 199 (213 f). Even against this background, there are currently still some differences between the salaries of judges in the East and West Germany, but in the view of the Constitution, this does not breach the principle of equality. Currently, courts simply pay the cost of the economic, financial and living standards in the new federal states in the interim, see in this respect the decisions of 12th February 2003 (2 BvL 3/00 and 2 BvR 709/99) by the Federal Constitutional Court; BVerfGE 107, 218; 107, 257

747 See BVerfGE 26, 79 (93)

748 See the European Union Investigation of Judges: Comparison of the Incomes of European Judges, in: DRiZ 2002, pp. 277 ff; Angelika Peters, Deutschland – arme Richter, in: DRiZ 2002, p. 278

749 See the European Union Investigation of Judges: Comparison of the Incomes of European Judges, in: DRiZ 2002, p. 277 (279)

occupations. But in China, the salaries and benefits for judges are even lower than those of civil servants. In order to attain a better standard of living, judges often and repeatedly engage in judicial corruption, risking violations of the law and rules of discipline. It is unclear whether a high level of salary would ensure that every judge acted fairly in this regard, but if the salary is too low, judges are certainly likely to accept additional benefits from interested parties and to pass illegal judgements regardless of the rues of judicial discipline. Judges are ultimately still flesh and blood. Therefore, there have been many calls for the salaries of judges in China to be increased,[750] but there are also objectors who believe that the quality of judges in China is currently still very low, hence it is not possible to compare them with judges in Western countries who are well versed in law and order, and they are not qualified to receive higher salaries.[751]

In this author's opinion, China should follow Germany's lead in recognising the special nature of judges' work and aiming to separately provide a special social status and salary system for judges so as to guarantee the independence of judges. As a country in which regional economics, culture and politics are often significantly disparate, it is very difficult for China to establish a unified standard for judges across the whole country. But it is unrealistic to talk about a unified salary system for judges across the whole country which completely eliminates regional variations. As mentioned, some differences still exist even among German judges. In the opinion of this author, and in view of the current graded system of finance, the most effective approach at this time would be to determine an enforceable compulsory minimum standard for the appropriations of judges' salaries by local governments. This standard could take into account regio-

750 For example, one vice-president of a court points out: "Because judges at Basic People's Courts are under a huge workload pressure, have an unequal status and no prospect of a rise in salary, the prospect of working as a judge at a Basic People's Court is not very attractive; those who pass the judicial examination do not want to enter these courts, and the court staff who pass the judicial examination want to get out of the courts. Moreover, middle-aged judges want to be transferred to posts involving logistics." Hence, "there is now the greatest need to resolve the problems of conditions and benefits. The Judges Law of the PRC needs to stipulate concrete provisions regarding salaries, welfare benefits and job security for judges as soon as possible, in order to change the discrepancy between the rights and obligations of judges which has existed for so many years." See Deng Jiaming, Yao Yuemei, Concerns Regarding the Shortage of Judges at the Basic People's Courts and Approaches to the Professionalisation of Judges, in: Guidance and Research on Establishing the Professionalisation of Judges, edited by the Political Department of the Supreme People's Court, 2007, Volume 1, pp. 73-79

751 Tang Zhongmin, High Salaries Promote Incorruptibility, in: Hebei Law, January 2003, Volume 21, Issue 1

nal variations at least to a certain extent and would mean that salaries for public service by judges would depend as little as possible on the respective local government. In Germany, for example, the Federal Remuneration Act determines the grades of salary and the standard of judges' allowances, which each *Land* then increases as it sees fit. Some scholars posit that judges' salaries could be made to maintain a certain minimum percentage of the average salaries at the supreme posts, as established by the government. This would also go some way towards guaranteeing the independence of each judge. This has already been attempted in some areas of China: Changde, for example, stipulates that the salaries for judges of the Intermediate People's Courts shall not be less than 45,000 Yuan, and those of the Basic People's Courts not less than 35,000 Yuan.[752] The effective salary standards for judges shall be the same as those of higher-earning professions at the present time in the area where the courts are located, as announced by the State, or shall be multiplied by a certain factor (5–8), using as a base the average annual income of local citizens as announced by the State Department of Statistics,[753] which would place judges among the higher earners in their locality and help to make it a more attractive profession among groups in their area of jurisdiction.

Judges are the professional group most seeking equality of employment conditions, so the salaries of judges should reflect a certain natural equality and fairness. Artificial influences on the differences between judges' salaries should be reduced as far as possible. The extent of increase in salaries should also be kept slight, because the initial salary of judges is high enough, and increases will only invite comparison and possible resentment between judges. The salaries may be increased organically. When judges reach a certain period of service, their salaries will automatically increase to a higher grade, so they can concentrate on cases and not on where their next increase in salary will come from. At present, most scholars believe that the budget of courts should be centralised and

---

752 See Zhu Mei'an, Wang Qingquan: Changde Municipal Party Committee (Both Chambers) Decides Not to Participate in the Deliberation and Evaluation of Trends, People's Court Paper, 1st June 2004, front page

753 Some scholars have different ideas on the factor by which this base value should be multiplied, but that does not detract from the basic aim of increasing the salaries of judges to a higher level. In addition, some scholars consider that the level of salary for judges should be set at roughly twice the average income of those with a master's degree or doctorate, so that even if a judge's spouse does not have a job, an average standard of living for judges will still be guaranteed. See Yao Li, Analysis of the Current State of the System of Chinese Judges, and Restructuring the System, in: Jurisprudence, 2003, Volume 9, p. 27

paid centrally so that judges' salaries are essentially guaranteed.[754] But in the longer term, there are two other problems which need to be gradually resolved in order to realise the aim of higher salaries for judges: one is how the State finances would bear the burden of the higher salaries for judges; and the other is how to promote the quality of judges so that they deserve these higher salaries. These two aspects complement each other. Only once the State provides higher salaries to judges will talented, more highly qualified candidates be inclined to apply to serve as court judges; and once the workforce of judges consists of such talented individuals, it will be able to handle the huge number of trial cases without having too many judges, hence the State finances will be able to bear the cost of the higher salaries given to this lower number of judges.

According to statistics, there were almost 300,000 court employees in China by 2007, around 220,000 of whom were judges. The proportion of the total court workforce serving as judges was thus 73.3%.[755] But in Germany, the number of judges only accounts for 22.6% of the total court staff.[756] Some scholars believe

---

754 Wang Liming, All Court Funding Should be Incorporated into the Central Budget, in: Legal Daily, 8th March 2007

755 Jiang Bixin, Practical Background and Ideal Method of Reforming the Classification of Court Staff, in: Guidance and Research on Establishing the Professionalisation of Judges, edited by the Political Department of the Supreme People's Court, 2007, Volume 1, p. 10

756 According to the statistics of the Federal Office of Justice, Department III 3 (dated 28th July 2008), there were – by the end of 2007 – 46,734.1 person-time staff and 7,957.64 person-time judges in district courts in Germany (Bundesamt für Justiz, Referat III 3, Personalbestand der Amtsgerichte, Stand: 24. September 2008 – *Federal Office of Justice, Department III 3, Staff Complement of the District Courts, dated 24th September 2008*), 4,914.16 person-time staff and 12,752.16 person-time judges in *Land* courts (Bundesamt für Justiz, Referat III 3, Personalbestand der Landgerichte, Stand: 28. Juli 2008 – *Federal Office of Justice, Department III 3, Staff Complement of the* Land *Courts, dated 28th July 2008*), and 5,499.72 person-time staff and 1,800.90 person-time judges in the higher *Land* courts (Bundesamt für Justiz, Referat III 3, Personalbestand der Oberlandesgerichte, Stand: 28. Juli 2008 – *Federal Office of Justice, Department III 3, Staff Complement of the Higher* Land *Courts, dated 28th July 2008*). Therefore, there are 14,672.7 judges in total and 64,985.98 person-time staff in the *Länder*, hence judges account for 22.6% of court staff (excluding the various Federal Special Courts, since there are no statistics on them in the Federal Department of Statistics of Germany but only data for ordinary federal courts at the level of Federal Courts. On the basis of the statistics for the ordinary Federal Courts, there is no great difference in the proportion of judges within the overall court staff as compared to the *Länder*, since the number of judges at the Federal Court of Justice is 126 and the total staff complement is 408, hence the proportion of judges is about 31%. See the Bundesamt für Justiz, Referat III 3, Bundesgerichtshof Zusammenstellung des Personalbestandes, Stand: 4. März 2009 –

that there are currently too many judges in China,[757] but other scholars believe that there are not in fact too many.[758] In most courts in China, the total number of judges is very high, but the highly professional core within these is small,[759] hence overall staffing levels in the organisation of judges are high, but the staff who truly bear responsibility as judges are in fact few. If those judges who have no capacity for judging are excised from the pool of judges and only those with good profession skills and a high quality of work remain, State finances would be entirely capable of providing higher salaries to these judges. This is doubtless a slow and difficult process, because the interests of so many judges are involved, but it must be embarked upon, otherwise the overall quality of judges in China cannot increase in the future.

Because the effects of such a process of shedding judges are so far-reaching, this process needs to be planned and implemented carefully and effectively. Some scholars feel that the number of judges in China should be drastically reduced, for example to about 20,000,[760] while others feel that this is too radical, because the procedure of litigation in China is multifaceted, and judges have

---

*Federal Office of Justice, Department III 3, Composition of the Staff Complement, dated 4th March 2009*)).

757 Some scholars point out that because the overall quality of judges is low and their efficiency in handling cases is therefore low, the number of Chinese judges is consequently high, and the heavy judicial workload currently merely relies on increasing numbers. See Chen Wenxing, Comparative Analysis of the System of Prescribed Numbers of Judges, in: Journal of Tianjin University (Social Sciences Edition), July 2008, Volume 10, Issue 4, p. 353

758 See also Xu Qianfei, Further Discussion of the Qualities of Judges, in: People's Judicature, 2002, Volume 1, p. 34. He believes that in China, the number of judges is not high compared to the total population. The number of Chinese judges for every 10,000 citizens is 1.1. If the nearly 20% of those who are executive staff are excluded, this goes down to just 0.88. In Germany, the ratio is 2.46. In December 2006, the total number of judges in the German Federation and *Ländern* was 20,138.31 (excluding prosecutors) and the population was 82,315,000. For the former figures, see Bundesamt für Justiz, Referat III 3, Zahl der Richter, Staatsanwälte und Vertreter des öffentlichen Interesses in der Rechtspflege der Bundesrepublik Deutschland am 31. Dezember 2006, Stand: 7. Februar 2008 (*Federal Office of Justice, Department III 3, Numbers of Judges, Public Prosecutors and Public Representatives in the Judicature of the Federal Republic of Germany on 31st December 2006, dated 7th February 2008*); for the latter figures, see Auszug aus dem Datenreport 2008 vom Statistischen Bundesamt Deutschland, p. 12, Tab. 1: Bevölkerung am 31. Dezember 2006 (*Extract from the 2008 Data Report by the German Office of Statistics, page 12, Table 1: Population on 31st December 2006*)

759 Wang Limin, Research on Judicial Reform, Legal Press, 2000, p. 421

760 He Weifang, The Judicial Concept and System, China University of Political Science and Law Press, 1998, p. 101

non-adjudicative duties in addition to their professional work as judges. Because this is different than in other countries, they suggest the number of judges should be cut to around 50,000.[761] This author concurs with the former school of thought: within ten years, the total number of judges should be cut to around 80,000. Given the current economic development and increasing awareness about litigation in China, there is potential for a significant increase in the number of cases in future, which also needs to be considered when setting the number of judges in order to avoid a situation where there are too many cases and too few judges. The specific planned approach is by strict examination and appraisal by assessment committees every year, which shall eliminate 10% of existing judges each year, and also keep the number of retirees and replacements balanced. There would thus be around 80,000 judges after ten years. Assuming that the rate of increase in the number of cases is 10% each year, there will be approximately 16,000,000 cases of the first instance in China in ten years' time, hence each judge will on average deal with about 200 cases a year. This would be far less than in Germany,[762] but in view of other factors such as the state of the judicial system in China, it would be fairly reasonable.[763] Additionally, if judges' salaries are increased 15% each year, they will be about four times their current level in ten years. It can be said the salaries of judges would be increased in real terms (based on the premise that the prices of commodities changes small and the salaries of other administrative officials increase as the existing salary

761 Zhang Wusheng, Research on the Regrouping and Re-assignment of Chinese Judges, in Legal Science, 2004, Volume 3, p. 46

762 Taking the district courts in Germany as an example, there were 3,040,657 cases in all handled by the district courts of the various *Länder* in 2007, which distributed among 7,957.64 judges means each judge handles on average about 382 cases a year, see Bundesamt für Justiz, Referat III 3, Geschäftsentwicklung bei Gerichten und Staatsanwaltschaften, Stand: 5. Februar 2009 (*Federal Office of Justice, Department III 3, Workload Development at Courts and Public Prosecutors' Offices, dated 5th February 2009*)

763 For example, there are no provisions on the pre-emptive procedure of pre-trial settlement and disclosure in Chinese law. A pre-trial procedure could reduce the workload for judges and enhance trial efficiency. Due to the lack of a pre-trial procedure, most cases heard by Chinese courts have to be go through comprehensive and complicated litigation procedures before being concluded. It is thus clear that the judicial system is inefficient and why the workload which Chinese judges bear is so heavy. See also Xu Qianfei, The System of Rating Chinese Judges and Reform of the System of People's Courts, in: Applied Law, December 2002, Issue 201, p. 15

system).[764] Such a plan considers both the State's financial capacity and its capacity for acceptance by courts and judges, so it is feasible.

Once judges' incomes are guaranteed by the State salary system, self-discipline by judges be confidently ensured. The economic reality for judges will realise their independence. Therefore, judges may become genuinely dedicated legal practitioners, study judicial skills diligently and with focus and ultimately realise social justice.[765]

# C Internal Independence

## Chapter VI The Internal Independence of Judges

The above chapters have looked into the protection of the Constitution and the framework of a system of substantive independence and independence of status for judges. The other necessary independence of judges is internal independence. Countries under the rule of law require the judiciary to be neutral, objective and impartial, as is also expected by the public.[766] Parties defer to judges to adjudicate disputes because judges embody the concept of justice.[767] Therefore, judges must be free of personal bias. Internal independence is a basic premise in order to guarantee that judges adjudicate fairly and objectively, free from external influences.

Based on the essential principle of procedural justice, judges shall treat the two parties in litigation equally.[768] If judges fail to remain morally independent, they can neither recognise threats to their independence nor draw support from measures of protection designed to defend it. The legal procedure of litigation also then loses its prerequisites. With respect to the interference and influence which intangible laws cannot control, it is necessary to rely in particular on re-

---

764 Pan Jianfeng, A Higher-Salary System: the Basic Guarantee of a Fair Judiciary, Incorruptibility and a High Quality of Judges, in: Politics and Law Forum, 2001, Volume 6, p.19

765 See Zhou Jianjie, Du Kailin, Restructuring the System of Salaries for Chinese Judges, Applied Law, 2005, Volume 7, p. 16

766 Otto-Rudolf Kissel, Justiz zwischen Anspruch und Wirklichkeit, DRiZ 1987, p. 301 (303)

767 Ralf Bernhard, Rechtspfleger, Richter- und Rechtsprechungsbegriff, DRiZ 1981, p. 368

768 In British law, this derives from the principle of natural justice; see Peter Rädler, The Independence and Impartiality of Judges, in: David Weissbrodt, Rüdiger Wolfrum (ed.), The Right to a Fair Trial, Berlin 1997, p. 727

sistance from judges' internal sense of independence.[769] The reliability and acceptability of judicial decisions rests not only on the adequacy of the grounds of the decision but also rests on the trust placed by the public in the fairness and independence of judges. If judges practise favouritism or show individual prejudice in their adjudications, the public trust will be damaged.[770]

The fairness of judges comprises subjective and objective aspects:[771] on the one hand, individual actions or specific opinions by judges may cause their fairness to fall under suspicion; on the other hand, objective situations will show if judges fail to keep the necessary distance in order to judge cases fairly. It is possible for a conflict of interests in the judge's decision to arise because the judge and one of the parties are relatives, because the judge participated in an earlier trial procedure in the same case, or because of action by the judge outside the court.

In Germany, Paragraph 3 of Article 20 and Articles 92 and 97 of the Basic Law may be viewed as the legal basis[772] on which judges maintain internal independence.[773] Therefore, the neutrality of judges is determined as another characteristic and duty in addition to the substantive independence and independence of status of judges. Based on decisions by the Federal Constitutional Court, the nature of judicial activities demands that they be performed by a third party who has substantive independence and independence of status.[774] In addition, the documents show that the duties of judges as stipulated by the Constitution in-

---

769 See Hans-Jürgen Papier, Die richterliche Unabhängigkeit und ihre Schranken, in: NJW 15/2001, p. 1089

770 Hilke Thiedemann, Judicial Independence – Eine rechtsvergleichende Untersuchung der Sicherung unabhängiger Rechtsprechung in Südafrika und Deutschland, Baden-Baden 2007, p. 366

771 As above. The European Court of Human Rights also draws this distinction. See Olivier Jacot-Guillarmod, Rights Related to Good Administration of Justice (Article 6), in Macdonald/Ronald St. J. et al., The European System for the Protection of Human Rights, pp. 397 f

772 For a basic analysis of these aspects, see Konrad Zweigert, Zur inneren Unabhängigkeit des Richters, Festschrift für Fritz von Hippel zum 70. Geburtstag (edited by Josef Esser and Hans Thieme), pp. 711-723

773 Wolfgang Heyde, Rechtsprechung, in: Ernst Benda, Werner Mainhofer, Hans-Jochen Vogel (eds.), Handbuch des Verfassungsrechts, 2nd edition, Berlin 1994, Article 33, margin number 101

774 BVerfGE 26, 186 (198); BVerfGE 27, 312 (322); BVerfGE 60, 175 (203)

clude that judges shall treat parties neutrally (fairness) and resolve disputes objectively (objectivity).[775]

Some scholars consider internal independence to be the most essential form of judicial independence among the various factors.[776] Internal independence makes judges fair and objective.[777] Judges should morally, ethically and conscientiously seek out internal independence.[778] Internal independence will guarantee that judges maintain self-determination, self-restraint and self-criticism in all matters, especially political matters.[779] Nevertheless, some other scholars believe that there is no obligation in law for judges to maintain internal independence. They regard Article 97 of the Basic Law as an article which protects judges rather than defining their duties.[780]

German laws have not stipulated on internal independence in law, because internal independence is a matter of individual attitude.[781] Internal independence can neither be governed by rules nor enforced by the judiciary. Therefore, some scholars suggest that when selecting judges, the internal independence of judges can best be guaranteed by strengthening the examination of judges' characters and choosing those who exhibit a strong personality, independence and confidence, i.e. it is necessary to take greater stock of appointees' characters and to more formally survey this aspect.[782]

In China, regulations on the internal independence of judges are contained mainly in the Code of Judicial Ethics for Judges issued by the Supreme People's Court on 18th October 2001. Article 7 in the first section "Guaranteeing Judicial Fairness" stipulates that judges must deliberate independently, decide autonomously and be emboldened to insist on their correct opinions. Article 9 stipulates that judges must avoid subjective bias. Article 10 stipulates that judges must treat parties equally. Article 11 stipulates that judges must maintain neu-

---

775 Wilhelm Dütz, Richterliche Unabhängigkeit und Politik, JuS 1985, 745 (747); Peter Gilles, Richterliche Unabhängigkeit und parteipolitische Bindung von Richtern, DRiZ 1983, 41 (44)

776 Schmidt-Jortzig, Richteramt und politische Betätigung, NJW 1984, p. 2057

777 Wilhelm Dütz, Richterliche Unabhängigkeit und Politik, JuS 1985, 745 (749)

778 Willi Geiger, Die Unabhängigkeit des Richters, DRiZ 1979, p. 65 (66)

779 Peter Gilles, Richterliche Unabhängigkeit und parteipolitische Bindung von Richtern, DRiZ 1983, p. 41 (48)

780 Helmut Fangmann, Richterverhältnis und Meinungsfreiheit, in: Labour and Law (*Arbeit und Recht* = *AuR*) 1985, p. 7 (9)

781 Ernst Benda, Eckart Klein, Bemerkungen zur richterlichen Unabhängigkeit, in: DRiZ 1975, p. 166

782 Frank Lansnicker, Richteramt in Deutschland. Im Spannungsfeld zwischen Recht und Politik – Darstellung und Analyse anhand von ausgewählten Fallbeispielen, Frankfurt on the Main 1996, p. 98

trality. In addition, the Judges Law of the PRC also stipulates that judges must be honest and fair, faithful in the discharge of their duties and must abide by the rules of discipline.[783] However, compliance with this code of judicial ethics is largely unenforceable in practice, and there are no measures for corresponding supervision, hence it is in practice just a document.

Some scholars believe that in order to realise the internal independence of judges,[784] the legislature must perform a legislative survey and study in order to establish feasible rules of operation and to establish a specific organisational framework for examination and punishment,[785] causing judges to consciously improve their morality and self-cultivation. But some other scholars believe that due to the particular practical conditions in China,[786] judges have to remain politically aware and incisive, and make political decisions in any case. But political insight, decision-making and consideration are not tantamount to the complete imitation of the guiding principles and politics of the governing party. In

---

783 Paragraph 5 of Article 7 of the Judges Law of the PRC

784 Chen Weidong, Judicial Fairness is Grounded in the Professional Ethics of Judges, in: Journal of Nantong Teacher Training College, December 2001, Volume 17, Issue 4, p. 28

785 With respect to the prospective idea of organising morality and punishment and the associated discussion, see also Geng Yuji, Queries and Demonstrative Analysis of the Code of Judicial Ethics for Judges, from the Point of View of the Basic People's Courts, in: Analects of the Sino-Dutch Seminar "Behaviour and Professional Ethics of Judges", edited by the State Judges College, May 2002

786 Some survey papers on judges point out that in China, most peasants have only a vague legal awareness. They favour traditional ethics and standards. In the eyes of peasants, there is no authority in the law, but rather judges have absolute authority. Therefore, when there is a dispute, parties expect more from the judges than from the law. The common saying "the case has not come to court, the plaintiff has come" also illustrates this aspect. For the related discussion, see Geng Yuji, Queries and Demonstrative Analysis of the Code of Judicial Ethics for Judges, from the Point of View of the Basic People's Courts, in: Analects of the Sino-Dutch Seminar "Behaviour and Professional Ethics of Judges", edited by the State Judges College, May 2002

some circumstances,[787] judges and courts have to accept political responsibility that cannot shirked using the governing rules.[788]

More specifically, the internal independence of judges in China is influenced only by society and the political Party, whereas in Germany, the system of judges' involvement in political activities is, by comparison, multifaceted. In the following, this dissertation will discuss the major aspects which influence the internal independence of judges.

## Section I Social Influences

Judicial activities have to be judged on merit, because this procedure does not simply enable a judgement to be made automatically after looking up a series of rules. Due to their abstract nature, laws cannot provide a single, inflexible plan for judges to apply in order to resolve disputes.[789] Therefore, judicial activities are a complicated procedure of interpreting and applying rules in accordance with a certain method. Whether consciously or unconsciously, judges always apply their own predispositions and values when deciding on facts and applying laws.

Judges' social background, party allegiance, religious or other social affiliation, the environment in which they grew up, their individual lifestyle, form of education and relationship with the media may all factor in their internal independence, influencing judges in specific ways when faced with specific facts and legal problems.[790] All the social environmental factors mentioned above may lead judges to harbour a certain bias and to make incorrect decisions when hear-

787 Such circumstances may include those where: there is no law which can be applied directly, and the dispute can only be resolved by the court interpreting the nearest applicable laws; there are applicable laws, but if these laws were applied, publicly recognised boundaries of justice and fairness as formed over the course of history would be directly infringed; any decision will cause social unrest in many areas of society. See Su Li, Understanding the Thoughts and Behaviour of Judges, in: Northern Law, 2009 Volume 1, p. 111

788 Su Li, Understanding the Thoughts and Behaviour of Judges, in: Northern Law, 2009 Volume 1, p. 111

789 Hilke Thiedemann, Judicial Independence – Eine rechtsvergleichende Untersuchung der Sicherung unabhängiger Rechtsprechung in Südafrika und Deutschland, Baden-Baden 2007, p. 368

790 The influence on the judiciary of judges' social background and form of education was discussed in the 1960s and 1970s in Germany, which centred on judges' social characteristics. Some scholars consider that judges' decisions are determined primarily by their social background, but this point cannot be proven. See Ernst Benda, Eckart Klein, Bemerkungen zur richterlichen Unabhängigkeit, in: DRiZ 1975, p. 166

ing cases. Therefore, judges must keep their personal opinions to themselves and maintain a necessary distance when hearing cases and respect the different opinions of others.[791] The duty to maintain neutrality also requires judges to keep their personal opinions to themselves and to maintain a critical distance at all times.[792]

Nevertheless, it is impossible for judges to completely divorce themselves from social influence. The decisions by courts are to be made in accordance with rules which are established on the basis of underlying social values. Therefore, when judges execute their duties, they are also doing their duty in the name of society and must have a constant and clear sense of social development and values.[793] This is because as the individuals behind such decisions, judges do not apply laws inflexibly but strive to realise the intention of the legislature within the legal framework. It is most important that judges have a sense of this requirement, so that when they hear cases, they are not prevented from making correct decisions of value due to some external influence. Judges should also take note of and deliberate over any criticisms. Restricting judges through the law can reduce the possibility of too many different values being applied, and any extreme individual values held by judges in their interpretation of the law can ultimately be controlled by the system of different instances of court.[794]

In China, the influence on judges of their individual predispositions and social environment have a vivid typicality. The great commotion and debate generated by the "Concubine Inheritance Case"[795] and the cases of Liu Yong[796]

---

791 Manfred-Carl Schinkel, Bindung an das Gesetz und richterliche Unabhängigkeit – ein Spannungsfeld?, in: Jürgen Goydke, Dietrich Rauschning, Rainer Robra, Hans-Ludwig Schreiber, Christian Wulff (ed.), Vertrauen in den Rechtsstaat: Beiträge zur deutschen Einheit im Recht, Festschrift für Walter Remmers, Munich 1995, p. 297

792 Max Rheinstein, Wer wacht über die Wächter?, in: Jus 1974, p. 409

793 Wolfgang Heyde, Rechtsprechung, in Ernst Benda, Werner Mainhofer, Hans-Jochen Vogel (eds.), Handbuch des Verfassungsrechts, 2nd edition, Berlin 1994, Article 33, margin number 101

794 Hilke Thiedemann, Judicial Independence – Eine rechtsvergleichende Untersuchung der Sicherung unabhängiger Rechtsprechung in Südafrika und Deutschland, Baden-Baden 2007, p. 369

795 In this case, the plaintiff Ms. Zhang was a so-called concubine of Mr. Huang, the husband of the defendant Ms. Jiang. Mr. Huang and Ms. Jiang had been married for many years but had no children. In 1994, Mr. Huang met Ms. Zhang and they subsequently began to live together. In the period from February to April 2001, Mr. Huang suffered the effects of liver cancer and Ms. Zhang took care of him much in the manner of a wife. Before Mr. Huang died, he made a will, in which he left his estate to Ms. Zhang, and had it notarised. This lead to extensive debate throughout the country when in 2001, a court decided that, although there were corresponding provisions in the Inheritance

and Xu Ting[797] mentioned above show that Chinese judges still have great difficulty in both faithfully applying the law and maintaining internal independence when assessing the facts of a case and making reasoned decisions. In the concubine inheritance case, for example, the various pertinent social values and the limited information reaching the public meant that no matter what the court decided, there was likely to be a lot of debate. But the court can only make a political decision based on core values of society.

In China, "concubines" are generally frowned on as going against the moral standards of society and committing an offence against common decency. In this case, one such "concubine" had unusually dared to take her lover's original wife to court, present the deceased's will and claim his estate, which undoubtedly touched a tender spot with many in the population at large. In strictly legal terms, a will had been legally made and was thus valid and effective, but in order to respect public opinion and balance the moral considerations, the judge ultimately decided to invalidate the bequest. When the decision was announced, more than 1,000 of those assembled broke into thunderous applause to show their approval of the judge's decision to put accepted social mores before a strictly legal interpretation, although most jurists objected to the flagrant breach of the individual's right to dispose of their own property.

The huge influence of society on Chinese judges is due in part to the fact that the functions performed by Chinese judges are different from those of German judges. In addition to the basic function of adjudication, Chinese judges also fulfil a multitude of social functions. When German judges deal with disputes, they demonstrate their professional strength by only considering the beneficial relationships in a specific case, selecting the rules which govern it, pursuing justice in accordance with the letter of the law in the specific case, and responding passively to any social issues raised by the case, whereas in Chinese society, the standards by which adjudicative decisions by judges are assessed are diverse. Chinese judges cannot just knock their gavel and call the next case, but rather have to take many elements outside the law into consideration and complete a lot of non-judicial work both within and outside their division in order to

---

Law and the will was genuine, Mr. Huang's attempt to leave his estate to the "other woman" violated Article 7 of the General Rules of Civil Law which stipulates that "Civil activities shall have respect for social ethics and shall not harm the public interest, undermine State economic plans or disrupt the social economic order." On the basis of this provision, the court overruled the plaintiff's request for litigation. For related reports, see Record of the First National Case in Which a Concubine Fights for Inheritance by Presenting a Will, Legal Daily, 5th November 2001

796 See Footnote 370

797 See Footnote 371

achieve the maximum possible degree of substantive justice and satisfactory settlements to disputes.

For this reason, mediation has to be emphasised in litigation procedures, and a lot of energies are expended in the cause of mediation.[798] For example, most cases accepted by the Basic People's Courts concern marriage, death, food, clothing, housing and transportation, production and operation and other matters closely related to the daily life of the masses. Although the legal awareness of parties is small, their conflicts are heated and their influence is often extensive, such that it is possible to cause unrest if cases are handled carelessly. In order to conclusively resolve disputes and avoid the same parties in dispute repeatedly returning to court over the same issue, judges always mediate throughout the entire adjudicative procedure.[799] Moreover, Chinese parties have no notion of evidence in the modern litigious sense but rather adhere to a deep-rooted understanding that judges shall take the parties' issue into their own hands and conduct a thorough investigation of the facts, hence when judges deal with cases, they have to investigate and collect evidence themselves, trying as far as possible to get past the stories and accounts to the actual original facts, which is very different from German judges, who passively examine the evidence provided by the parties, determine which evidence is admissible, and decide between the two parties on this basis. In addition, because most Chinese court attendees do not understand such modern legal requirements as due and proper procedure and merely want the court to tell them the what, why and how[800] in

798 For example, in the second meeting of the Eleventh National People's Congress on 10th March 2009, the Supreme People's Court highlighted in its work report that in the previous year, the Supreme People's Court had "paid close attention to the use of mediation to resolve disputes, with a view to improving social harmony, and changed the approach to adjudication, insisting on the principles that mediation take priority and that mediation and judgement be combined", and that mediation was promoted throughout all the procedure of accepting cases, hearing cases and deciding cases. See the website of the Supreme People's Court:
http://www.court.gov.cn/news/bulletin/activity/200903180015.htm

799 For the relevant discussion, see Li Hong, Ye Lei, The System of Judges at Basic People's Courts: Between What Ought to Be and What Actually Is, from the Point of View of the Duties Undertaken by the Judges of Basic People's Courts, in: Guidance and Research on Establishing the Professionalisation of Judges, edited by the Political Department of the Supreme People's Court, 2007, Volume 2, p. 127

800 This concept of "telling them what, why and how" comes from the 1992 film "Qiu Ju Goes to Court" directed by the famous Chinese director Zhang Yimou. This film tells the story of a dispute in a countryside village in the northwest. Qiu Ju, a stoic peasant woman, demands an apology when the village chief kicks her husband in the groin, as she believes that the village chief might have the right to hit her husband but not to

order to resolve the dispute, judges consciously or unconsciously pay close attention to the matter of settling substantive problems in the course of judicial activities. For example, judges do not generally force the plaintiff to give evidence or provide proof of ownership, but actively search for said proof and personally find and provide the evidence needed to reach a decision. Outside of adjudication, judges often need to actively go out into society, even venturing into the field of economics, such as promoting the institutions of law before pupils of primary and secondary schools, serving as vice-presidents, directing People's Mediation Commissions, supporting economic construction, and so on.[801]

Sixty years ago, a famous Chinese sociologist, Mr. Fei Xiaotong, said: "From the grassroots level, Chinese society has the characteristic of natives";

---

"kick him where it counts". Qiu Ju wants justice and demands that the authorities criticise the village chief and that the village chief admits his transgression. Because such disputes often happen in the countryside, and the damage was not serious, the judge does not formally punish the village chief but tries to mediate. Qiu Ju refuses mediation and goes to the county court and then the provincial capital, asking them to tell her the "what, why and how". By various efforts, and helped by an attorney, Qiu Ju finally convinces the higher authorities to send some policemen to investigate, who determine that the husband was slightly injured but not permanently damaged in the groin region, so the village chief is lightly punished by being led away by the Public Security Bureau officers and incarcerated for 15 days. When Qiu Ju – who merely wanted a personal apology from the village chief – is informed of this outcome, she is confused and asks "why was he arrested? I just wanted justice". She did not understand why the law operated in this way. See Su Li, Qiu Ju's Confusion and Shan Gangye's Tragedy, in his work: Bringing the Law to the Countryside (edited version), University Press of China University of Political Science and Law, March 2004, p. 25

801 On 10th March 2009, the Supreme People's Court highlighted in its work report that the principle work of the Supreme People's Court is firstly "to make efforts to serve the overall situation and to provide judicial guarantees for smooth and steady economic development", see the website of the Supreme People's Court: http://www.court.gov.cn/news/bulletin/activity/200903180015.htm. For example, the research report by the associate director of the Political Department of the Yanting Court in Beijing showed that from January to December of 2006, the judges of the court made a total of more than 120 visits to the countryside and alleviated poverty, took part in the establishment of a government service year and joined in efforts to build sanitation facilities in the county national-wide, wherein each judge dedicated about 290 hours of their work time to these activities. See Dong Xiaojun, Research on the Mental Pressure on Judges at Basic People's Courts, Taking the Yanqing People's Court as an example, in: Guidance and Research on Establishing the Professionalisation of Judges, edited by the Political Department of the Supreme People's Court, 2007, Volume 1, p. 95

"this is an "acquaintance" society, there are no strangers".[802] Today, sixty years on, the reality of Chinese society is that the country has seen rapid industrial development, but folk culture, religious belief and traditional social organisation have not disappeared but have in fact provided a significant level of continuity in people's lives.[803] Such social control means that laws have only a weak effect. The social order is really based on social mores, ethics, habits, customs and even rural rules and civil agreements, which Hayek calls internal rules.[804] In the context of Chinese tradition, the substantive intention of these internal rules is a "common sense" which is rich in meaning and can include human kindness,[805] natural justice[806] and the interaction between human kindness and natural justice.

---

802 Fei Xiaotong, The Generational System in Rural China, Beijing University Press, 1998, p. 6

803 Wang Liming, Research on Social Anthropology in China, Triad Bookshop Press, 1997, quoted from Yao Danqi, Dilemmas and Ways Out: Research on the Practical Judicial Capability of Young Judges at the Basic People's Courts – Beginning to Unscramble a Social Text, in: Guidance and Research on Establishing the Professionalisation of Judges, edited by the Political Department of the Supreme People's Court, 2007, Volume 2, p. 80

804 Such "internal rules" as referred to by Hayek are rules spontaneously formed in the extended progress of a culture. See Deng Zhenglai, The Duality Opinion of the Regulation of Social Order, Research on the Legal Theory of Hayek, in: Legal Commentary of Beijing University, Volume 2, Issue 2, Legal Press 2000, p. 419

805 In the opinion of Chinese scholars of the social sciences, human kindness means the behaviour of exchange through associations in China, including the ties of blood and ethics. It is a sense of the condition of interpersonal friendship, which is also called friendship or personal friendship. Generally, there are three types of exchange of human kindness. The first is receiving help from others in a time of need, which comes under the category of "debt of gratitude" in the associations of human kindness. The one providing help is then called the "benefactor". The second is the investment of human kindness with some purpose, usually called "gift-giving". "Gift-giving" causes the recipient to be ashamed and uneasy (to "feel embarrassed", as it is usually called by Chinese peasants). The two parties then have a "debt of gratitude" relationship, hence the recipient will have to reciprocate when the opposite party makes a request. The third is general courtesy demanding reciprocity, which means behaviour such as visiting each other regularly, treating someone to a meal or giving presents at festivals in order to strengthen mutual feelings of kinship and realise an exchange of the scenario of showing due respect for someone's feelings. See Zhai Xuewei, The Reproduction of Human Kindness, Reputation and Power, and the Method of Social Exchange in a Common Sense Society, in: Social Sciences Research, 2004, Volume 5, pp. 50, 52

806 Natural justice is the natural rules which people cannot change and which are considered to be "right" or "wrong" by the customs and etiquette of a population. As an incarnation of nature, natural justice has a hint of universality, whereas human kindness has various individual differences and more the character of particularity. Chinese soci-

In an acquaintance society, common sense directly establishes the mode of behaviour of villagers under the pressure of public opinion. It is also the determining standard for social events rooted in the mind of villagers. Consequently, some scholars believe that it is currently merely a beautiful illusion – divorced from the reality of the Chinese countryside – that Chinese judges who are rooted in native society apply regulations strictly.[807]

## Section II Influence of the Party

When judges adjudicate cases, they should be clearly conscious of the relationship between themselves and the particular social groups involved, in order to maintain enough distance from political influence or other benefits.[808] They shall be conscious of their bias and dependence and anticipate the potential influence of these on their decisions in cases.[809] Active political behaviour includes having some political belief or belonging to a political party, which may clash with the fairness of judges.[810] Political influence has existed long before judges were appointed, whether in the Chinese system or the German system. Therefore, it has to be decreed in the legal system that judges cannot continue to be loyal to their political party when they are adjudicating.[811]

There are many differences in the provisions of the legal systems of different countries with respect to the political activities of judges. Some countries

---

ety does not divide universal natural justice and particular human kindness into two opposing parts, but does expect people to emphasise the two in their dealings. Thus, Chinese stress the combination of human kindness and natural justice in interpersonal association and consider that real human kindness cannot be separated from justice which is "fair and reasonable". See Zhai Xuewei, The Reproduction of Human Kindness, Reputation and Power, and the Method of Social Exchange in a Common Sense Society, in: Social Sciences Research, 2004, Volume 5, p. 49

807 See Su Li, Bringing the Law to the Countryside, University Press of China University of Political Science and Law, 2000, p. 6

808 Wolfgang Heyde, Rechtsprechung, in: Ernst Benda, Werner Mainhofer, Hans-Jochen Vogel (eds.), Handbuch des Verfassungsrechts, 2nd edition, Berlin 1994, Article 33, margin number 77

809 Arthur Kaufmann, Richterpersönlichkeit und richterliche Unabhängigkeit, in: Einheit und Vielfalt des Strafrechts, Festschrift für Karl Peters zum 70. Geburstag, Tübingen 1974, p. 295

810 Ernst Benda, Eckart Klein, Bemerkungen zur richterlichen Unabhängigkeit, in: DRiZ 1975, p. 166

811 Hilke Thiedemann, Judicial Independence – Eine rechtsvergleichende Untersuchung der Sicherung unabhängiger Rechtsprechung in Südafrika und Deutschland, Baden-Baden 2007, p. 393

strictly limit the participation of judges in the activities of political parties.[812] One direct method for preventing judges' decisions from being politically influenced is to require judges to end their relationship with any political organisations, political parties, economic associations or other social groups. In the system of common law, judges usually give up their relationship with a political party.[813]

In Germany, the provisions on such aspects are relatively broad. The integrity of judges (*Mäßigungsgebot*) (Article 39 of the German Judges Act) does not prohibit judges from continuing their relationship with a political party during their tenure, but merely requires that the fairness and independence of judges be relied on,[814] as also with the commercial activities of judges.[815] If a judge is merely a member of a political party and does not actively take part in the activities of the political party, then the public may trust that the judge's independence is not endangered.[816] But judges still control their political activities and bear responsibility for maintaining the neutrality required by their posts.[817] German law only requires judges to govern their political activities and not to give them up completely.[818] In this respect, German law regards judges as ordinary citizens and encourages them to take part in the democratic process and so advance the internal democratisation of the judiciary.[819] The other reason that judges are

812 For the comparative research on this aspect, see Christiane Niethammer-Vonberg, Parteipolitische Betätigung des Richters – deutsches Recht und rechtsvergleichender Überblick, Berlin 1969. See also Ingo von Münch, Unabhängigkeit und Abhängigkeit des Richters mit besonderer Berücksichtigung der Richter des Bundesverfassungsgerichts, Tbilisi 2003, p. 22

813 In England, for example, judges are prohibited from taking part in the political activities of any political parties. The traditional principle that they do not take part in the political activities of any political parties and do not issue opinions on political problems under debate is also defined among the professional ethics of judges in the Belize Code of Judicial Conduct & Etiquette, see Section 1.8 of these principles.

814 See also Peter Gilles, Richterliche Unabhängigkeit und parteipolitische Bindung von Richtern, in: DRiZ 1983, pp. 41 ff; Erich Heimeshoff, Parteipolitische Betätigung von Richtern, in: DRiZ 1975, pp. 261 ff

815 See the Federal Constitutional Court in DRiZ 1984, p. 241; Kissel/Mayer, Gerichtsverfassungsgesetz (GVG): Kommentar, 4th edition, Munich 2005, Article 1, margin number 161

816 BVerfGE 78, pp. 216 ff

817 The provisions for federal judges can be seen in Paragraph 2 of Article 60 of BBG; the provisions for *Land* judges can be seen in Paragraph 2 of Article 33 of BeamtStG

818 Kissel/Mayer, Gerichtsverfassungsgesetz (GVG): Kommentar, 4th edition, Munich 2005, Article 1, margin number 161

819 Hans Klein, Gedanken zur Verfassungsgerichtsbarkeit, in: Verfassungsstaatlichkeit, Festschrift für Klaus Stern zum 65. Geburtstag, Munich 1997, p. 1135

permitted to engage in political activities is that political influence is likely to only be realised when they are appointed and promoted.[820] In an international comparison, these provisions of German law are unusual.[821] Germany also once attempted to pass legislation to prohibit judges from being members of political parties, but the legislation was ultimately not approved.[822] Most of the judges at the Federal Supreme Court are even members of some political party.[823]

The Code of Judicial Ethics for Judges of the People's Republic of China includes the following stipulations: judges are not allowed to participate in commercial or other economic activities which may lead the public to doubt their honesty or integrity;[824] judges cannot act as lawyers or legal consultants for enterprises, organisations or individuals at the same time as serving as judges;[825] judges should not join any organisation centred around a satanic religion;[826] judges should not join any profit-making organisation or any organisation which could profit from influencing the judge.[827] In addition, Article 17 of the Judges Law of the PRC also stipulates activities which judges should avoid, namely: "former judges may not act as legal agents or defence lawyers within two years of leaving their post at a People's Court; former judges may not act as legal agents or defence lawyers in cases handled by the court to which they previously belonged; spouses or children of judges may not act as legal agents or defence lawyers in cases handled by the court to which the judge previously belonged."

However, there are no specific provisions in the Judges Law of the PRC or the Code of Judicial Ethics for Judges of the People's Republic of China which

---

820 This situation is usually considered as a shortcoming of the public democratic system, but in the political and legal discussion, it is considered a basic reconciliation within the system, see Münch/Kunig, Grundgesetz-Kommentar, Volume 2, Article 33, margin number 17

821 The International Bar Association Minimum Standards of Judicial Independence stipulate that judges shall not hold positions in political parties, see Article 37 of said code of standards

822 One draft of the German Judges Act also stipulated that judges were prohibited from taking part in political activities, but this provision was not adopted in the final Act. The historical development of this problem can be seen in Kissel/Mayer, Gerichtsverfassungsgesetz (GVG): Kommentar, 4th edition, Munich 2005, Article 1, margin number 161

823 About 65% to 75% of judges at the Federal Finance Court and Federal Labour Court belong to the same Party groupings. See Münch/Kunig, Grundgesetz-Kommentar, 3rd edition, Volume 2, Article 33, margin number 17

824 Article 25 of the Code of Judicial Ethics for Judges of the People's Republic of China

825 Article 28 of the Code of Judicial Ethics for Judges of the People's Republic of China

826 Article 41 of the Code of Judicial Ethics for Judges of the People's Republic of China

827 Article 43 of the Code of Judicial Ethics for Judges of the People's Republic of China

prohibit judges from joining a political party or taking part in political activities. In fact, for particular reasons of Chinese history, the organisations of the party in power and the government are combined, forming the basis of a system whereby the party in power leads national affairs, including judicial organisations. This is mainly shown by the fact that: the organisation system of judicial organisations and the organisation system of the Party almost overlap; important judicial posts such as the president and presiding judge are also Party leaders (usually, the president or vice-president concurrently serves in the Secretariat). The majority of judicial staff is Party members.[828] "Maintaining the unified leadership of the Party in the judicial reform of the People's Courts at all times" is the basic principle which, as repeatedly emphasised by the Supreme People's Court, all courts should observe.[829] By contrast, German law stresses that judges shall govern their own political activities, whereas Chinese law stresses that the augmented influence of judges as Party members should be employed in judicial practice. Chinese courts also frequently have to arrange for their judges, as Party members, to learn various ideas and policies of the Party.[830] Moreover, the Party leads the judiciary by two main methods. The first is by political leadership, i.e. so-

828 For example, the President of the Intermediate People's Court of one city has stated that: "the People's Courts are the judiciary led by the Party, and the People's Judges are a judicial group composed mainly of members of the Party." See Yuan Xingman, Demonstrating the Advantages of Party Members in Judicial Practice, http://ch.ahxf.gov.cn/ONEWS.asp?id=719

829 See the Work Report of the Supreme People's Court of 10th March 2008, on the website of the Supreme People's Court: http://www.court.gov.cn/news/bulletin/activity/200903180015.htm

830 On 19th September 2008, the Central Committee of the CPC convened a meeting to mobilise the whole of the Party to learn in depth the "sustainable development plan". The General Secretary of the Communist Party of China, Hu Jintao, emphasised the engagement in activities for learning the sustainable development plan in depth. Subsequently, in all party and government organisations, enterprises and institutions, schools, and even in the countryside and in street communities, these activities for learning the sustainable development plan in depth were engaged in with great effort, including in all Chinese courts. For example, the Party organisations at various levels of the First Intermediate People's Court of Beijing, "in its activities for learning the sustainable development plan in depth, arranged for the Party members to go out of court, into society, in order to experience personally the huge achievements accomplished in the economic and social structure of China since the process of reform and opening up and to make efforts to strengthen the confidence and identification of judges as party members within the system of socialism with Chinese characteristics, as guided by the sustainable development plan, and also in order to decide the correct direction of their jurisdiction." See the website of the First Intermediate People's Court of Beijing: http://bj1zy.chinacourt.org/public/detail.php?id=559

called routes, guiding principles and policies. In a specific judicial procedure, this is shown by the leading effect of the Party ideology. The second is by organisational leadership which leads by controlling the powers to select and appoint judges, which is the core method by which the Party leads the judiciary.[831] In recent years, courts have not stated when recruiting judges that those who apply for examination have to be Party members.[832] However, the Organisational Department of the Party Committee always plays an active role and has significant influence in the procedure of recruitment.[833]

In the Chinese Constitution, the phrase "the CPC leadership" appears four times. It may be said that the leadership status of the CPC is confirmed by the Constitution, and given the fundamental status of the Constitution, there can therefore be no doubt that the CPC has absolute powers of leadership over the various national affairs. "The modern Chinese revolution is a revolution of various purposes including national independence, national unification, economic development, cultural innovation and changes to the political system, which necessitate the centralisation of judicial power and prominence of judicial leader-

---

831 For the details of this discussion, see Tan Shigui, Research on Issues of Judicial Independence, p. 123

832 From this author's own experience: In 2003, when I graduated and received my master of law degree, the Supreme People's Court and the courts of all provinces and cities still stressed that only Party members could be recruited. After looking in the recruitment plan of the Supreme People's Court in 2008 and the recruitment plan of all the courts in 2009, I found that at present, the Supreme People's Court and all the other courts do not require applicants to have a political affiliation. The Recruitment Plan of the Supreme People's Court in 2008 can be accessed at:
http://learning.sohu.com/s2007/0576/s252643823/index.shtml

833 For example, the Announcement for Recruiting Civil Servants in Hunan in 2009 clearly states that appointments to courts and procuratorates are uniformly delegated by the Organisational Department of the Provincial Party Committee, the Provincial Higher People's Court and the Provincial People's Procuratorate, and carried out by the Organisational Departments of the provincial, city and prefecture party committees, the People's Courts and the People's Procuratorates at corresponding levels. The designated number of recruits are examined and accepted by the Organisational Department of the Provincial Party Committee. Interviews are organised and held by the Organisational Departments of the provincial, city and prefecture party committees, the People's Courts and the People's Procuratorates. The groups of interview officials are separately composed by the Organisational Departments of the Party Committee above the level of cities and prefectures, the People's Courts and the People's Procuratorates and relative experts and scholars. There are usually nine interview officials in each group, of whom the officials from the Organisational Departments of the Party Committee, the People's Courts and the People's Procuratorates each form one third of the total. The specific content can be viewed at: http://edu.rednet.cn/c/2009/04/09/1741315.htm

ship".[834] This is the logical premise and basic framework which form the basis for various kinds of theoretical discussion and practical reform (including the reform of the economic system and the reform of the political system) in China. "Such a principle cannot be flexible at any time. It is the essential guarantee that the judiciary insists on the correct political direction and accomplishes its mission".[835] Clearly, in China, the structure of the system of independent judges cannot disobey the basic principle of the "leadership of the CPC". Indeed, many people currently accept that the execution of judicial reform and realisation of the independence of judges need to be overseen by the Party and the necessary guarantees ensured by the Party.[836] In China today, no forces except the ruling Party which has the position of leadership can help the judiciary to escape the various kinds of illegal or improper intervention, because "the Party not only leads the people in making laws but also in executing laws."[837]

The American Chief Justice Richard Persina believes that the laws of a country reflect the political common consensus or compromise in this country and address its specific social problems. Therefore, the judiciary is political.[838] Within the present framework of the Chinese political system, it is legal for the CPC to lead the judiciary. However, in this author's opinion, party politics will then nonetheless influence the internal independence of judges slightly. As Persina points out, the ideal of impartiality can be realised, but the neutrality of ideology cannot.[839] Because the CPC's ideas, routes, guiding principles and policies have permeated deeply into the different aspects of society, it is difficult and unlikely for judges to have any extreme political views, or it may be said that those who have opinions differ widely from the mainstream of social ideology

---

834 Xu Xianming, Twenty Topics on Judicial Reform, in: Jurisprudence, 1999, Volume 5, p. 5

835 Kong Xiancui, A Legal System for Guaranteeing Independent Judgements at the People's Courts Needs to be Established, in: Modern Law, 1995, Volume 5, p. 69

836 See Wang Youzhang (Vice-President of the Zhejiang Higher People's Court and Assistant Secretary of the Party Committee), Brief Discussion of the Leadership of the Party and Judicial Independence, in: Forefront of Theory, 2005, Volume 1, p. 13; Zhu Xiangdong, Xiao Guilin, On the Dialectical Integration of Judicial Independence and Party Leadership, in: Journal of Southeast University, September 2005, Volume 7, Issue 5, pp. 11–12; Han Yong, Zhou Xiaojun, Research on a New Model for the Relationship between the Ruling Party and Judicial Organs, in: Journal of the Ningxia Party School, September 2006, Volume 8, Issue 5, p. 29

837 Selected Works of Peng Zhen, People's Press, Beijing 1991, p. 389

838 Richard Persina, translated by Su Li, How Judges Deliberate, Beijing University Press, 2009, pp. 245–266

839 Richard Persina, translated by Su Li, How Judges Deliberate, Beijing University Press, 2009, p. 279

cannot become judges. Thus, judges rarely have to consider whether they may have some political bias which would render their decision partial towards a particular party when hearing a case. At this time, loyalty to the CPC is equivalent to loyalty to the law, and loyalty to the law means loyalty to the CPC. The rules of the CPC regulate how the Party ensures that the legislature, judiciary, administrative organisations, economic and cultural organisations and civil groups work actively, independently and harmoniously. The Party also emphasises justice and fairness. Only if judges are loyal to the law and maintain justice can the people believe in the law and defend the leadership status of the CPC. If the people do not trust judges or are dissatisfied with the courts, they will be dissatisfied with the law and with the ruling party, thus endangering the leadership status of the CPC. However, it is also stressed that the Party does not have to actively lead in all judicial matters, and the Party cannot interfere in the decisions of specific cases.

As mentioned above, the influence of the party can only be exercised in the procedure of appointing and promoting judges. Referring to the content of the section of this dissertation dealing with the selection of judges, it may be seen that the Party Committees at various levels have wide-ranging powers in deciding which judges are selected, and the court presidents at various levels are selected by the local Party Committees at various levels. The court presidents examined and selected by the local Party Committee have to be candidates with perfect "political characteristics" and loyalty to the Party, and the judges selected to work under the president are nominated or appointed by the president, which guarantee the "purity" of the judges in terms of politics and hierarchy. Therefore, in order to prevent judges from being influenced by the Party, it is time to improve the procedure of selecting judges, establish independent selection organs and abandon the procedure whereby Party Committees have the final decision on selecting judges.

## Section III Brief Summary

It is a fundamental principle of the state under the rule of law that judges maintain internal independence when hearing cases. But this is essentially a matter of judges' personal qualities and cannot be regulated by rules. It has to be admitted that it is impossible for judges to maintain neutrality under all circumstances. Judges' personal predispositions as moulded by their social background are a greater or lesser part of their personal qualities and cause them to make certain evaluations in the course of adjudication. This is most obvious in China, where the legal tradition is different from that of Germany. In Germany, even judges' intuitions based on internal beliefs have to be dependent on the law. But in traditional Chinese culture, internal independence is not like this. The social system of human kindness and natural justice derived from the traditional Chinese culture is passed on from generation to generation by a process of socialisation and is still in force today.[840] Certainly, Chinese judges see themselves within such a "field of human kindness and natural justice". The conflicts between laws and society mean that Chinese judges frequently have to make political decisions according to the circumstances. It may be said that while the internal independence of German judges is based on the law, the internal independence of Chinese judges is based on morality.

With regard to whether judges can join political parties and take part in party-political activities, the restrictions in German law are generally very relaxed as compared to those in other countries. By contrast, the particular present situation in China is such that there are no limitations or at least such that it may be said that there is no need for limitations. In the scenario in which the CPC's ideas and policies form the mainstream of social ideology, judges who enforce the law and exercise their jurisdiction are automatically enforcing the laws formulated under the guidance of the mainstream of social ideology, hence it becomes unimportant whether or not they are members of the CPC. Accordingly, German law still stresses that judges should restrain their political activities, whereas Chinese judges are encouraged to actively take part in various Party activities and strengthen their political education. Although a political influence on judges is exerted both in Germany and China in the procedure of appointing and promoting judges, the fact there are many political parties in Germany means that this procedure is contained and restricted by the different parties among each other, thus reaching a balance. But in China, the supreme power to select judges is held almost exclusively by the Party Committee, so from the outset, judges cannot be independent either of the Party or of the court leadership. Hence in order to truly realise the independence of judges in China, it is necessary to begin with the appointment of judges, by establishing independent selection organs and preventing the Party from influencing and monopolising this power.

840 Liu Zhisong, Difficult Analysis and the Internal Independence of Judges – Orientation Differences in the Internal Independence of Chinese and Western Judges, in: Northern Law, 2008, Volume 2, p. 115

# Outlook

In modern Western society, the independence of judges is a principle of judicial independence which as a component of the Constitution is universally acknowledged by all classes of society. The background and circumstances of the emergence of this demonstrate its main particularities which are closely associated with the specific structure of Western society and the tradition of the rule of law. When Berman summarises the traditional characteristics of Western law, he notes that the self-government of the law has been established since the 12th or 13th century, when laws were separated from politics and morality. "The historic significance of the law is associated with the concept that laws have supremacy over political authority. Since the 12th century, in all Western countries – even those ruled by an absolute monarchy – the idea that laws are above politics is extensively reiterated and constantly conceded."[841]

However, judicial independence also has its relative and complex aspects. In any society, there is an interactive relationship between the judiciary on the one hand and politics and other social phenomena on the other. Judicial independence does not mean that the judiciary is above the influence of social forces. "It is important when providing a robust institutional environment for judicial independence to try to make judges into a group which can exert a counter-influence upon political society. Its homogeneity will ensure its unity, but good vocational morality and moderate superceding of popular social customs will strengthen its decision-making authority and effect. Only through this normal interactive relationship with society can the judiciary be an effective regulator of social relationships and a propelling force for social development."[842] Therefore, judicial independence is superficially a design of the system, but at a deeper level, it is merely a consequence of a balance of forces. Modifications in the make-up of society, especially the rise of civil society and the separation of the state and society have resulted in the rise of a judicial class pursuing independent values and the emergence of a system of judicial independence which is independent of foreign influences. As the result of an institutionalised legal culture, judicial independence was gradually formed in the course of the interaction between the advancement of Western society and the development of laws. This system has the twin values of history and reality in relation to contemporary China and the process of localisation to China.

---

841 Harold J. Berman, Law and Revolution: The Formation of the Western Legal Tradition, translated by He Weifang, Gao Hongjun, Zhang Zhiming, Xia Yong, Chinese Encyclopedic Press, 1993, p. 11

842 Mu Huai, Exerting Influence on Judges, in: Legal Research, 1994, Volume 3, p. 72

As to the value in history, if it is said that in modern China, the mission of judicial independence in Chinese society is that of exploration and construction, then at present, whether judicial independence is understood as being driven by the notion of rule-by-law constructivism or guided by the principle of rule-by-law experimentalism, the mission of judicial independence has been sufficiently accomplished to fulfil both requirements, since whether learning from history or employing a theoretical construct, the ultimate purpose is to inspect and verify the practical value of the theory, so as not to repeat tragedies of history. Thus, having gone through more than a hundred years of a difficult and arduous process of development, it may be said that judicial independence is not a matter of choice, but that it is time that the traditional legal systems and institutions in China should genuinely learn from the community of more outstanding legal cultures at higher levels. If it may be said that in the next hundred years, the persistence in contemporary China of those with lofty ideals in their aim of a fair and equitable mechanism of judicial independence will be coupled from the start with that of a powerful and prosperous nation and national development, then today's legal practitioners can say that this aim for which certain hardships and efforts are to be suffered today must become the motivating force in contemporary China to develop the rule of law.

As to the value in reality, the Chinese have through the ages always been an honest people. As a large developing country, and as a founding member of the international cause of human rights, China aims to fulfil all its obligations as established by any international conventions within the bounds of its current state of social and economic development, on which depends its international image as a large and conscientious country. More important still is how, against a background of economic globalisation, China's entry into the WTO will cause China to change from the "factory of the world" to a major international market, with a "passport to the world" replacing the current "distinct Chinese characteristics". Whether in economic activities or judicial behaviours, if China blindly emphasises its own particularities and quibbles over its obligations, this will directly influence the international image of the country. All these factors will inevitably drive Chinese society at large towards change in the areas of politics, the economy, society and culture. Reform of legal system will therefore be an essential aspect in establishing and developing the rule of law in China well into the future.

China's pursuit of the ideal of the state under the rule of law is an active, voluntary and gradual process. In 1978, after a period of lawless and anarchic upheaval, China put forward the essential principles for developing a socialist democracy and perfecting a socialist legal system, and for the first time formally drew up a national political strategy for establishing democracy and a legal system. Soon after, with reform of the economic system as the fundamental motivating force, the reform and development of the legal system were gradually accelerated. From 1982, when the planned economy was given priority and the market economy assisted in economic policy, to 1992 when a clear proposal was made to establish a socialist market economy system, the planned economy which had occupied a leading position was substantially transformed to a market economy in the time since the founding of the state. This transition of the economic system brought with it huge changes in the state and in social and economic activities, and these changes propelled the original basic reforms to the legal system. Then, the proposal for "a state under the rule of law and the development of a socialist state under the rule of law" was advanced in 1996 and written into the Constitution in 1999, thus establishing the socialist state under the rule of law as a basic national policy. Looking back on this process of development over the last 30 years, the basic conclusion may be drawn that China has implemented a process of transition towards the rule of law and has already taken a substantial step on the long journey towards realising the ideal of the rule of law. This substantial step is both the result of 30 years of economic development and the starting point for further development in the country's economy following its entry into the WTO and merging into international economic circles. Thus, there can be no doubt as to the following conclusion, namely that over the last 30 years, the cause of establishing a legal system in China has accompanied the progressive path of standardisation, and that all the conditions for establishing a state under the rule of law have matured gradually following the process of reform and opening up to the outside world and above all the rapid economic expansion. We may thus have reason to believe that as the basic strategy for managing state affairs in accordance with the law is comprehensively implemented and judicial reform is continuously advanced, the principle and system of judicial independence can ultimately be established and effectively implemented, and the Chinese people's dream of a century will inevitably be realised. We look forward to this and of course must continue to work towards it.

# Bibliography


*Arndt, Claus*, Der Richter im demokratischen Staat; in: DRiZ 1972, pp. 41-42

*Arndt, Herbert*, Die Dienstaufsicht über Richter in der Rechtsprechung des Bundesgerichtshofes; in: DRiZ 1978, p. 299

*Arntz, Herbert*, Über die Notwendigkeit, die Richterbeurteilung abzuschaffen, in: DRiZ 1972, p. 199

*Bai Shanyun*, Thoughts on Strengthening the Authority of Collegial Panels, http://www.law-lib.com/LW/lw_view.asp?no=498

*Baur, Fritz*, Die Beurteilung des Richters und seine Unabhängigkeit, in: DRiZ 1973, p. 6

*Benda, Ernst / Klein, Eckart*, Bemerkungen zur richterlichen Unabhängigkeit, in: DRiZ 1975, p. 166

*Berman, Harold J.*, Law and Revolution: The Formation of the Western Legal Tradition, translated by He Weifang / Gao Hongjun / Zhang Zhiming / Xia Yong, China Encyclopedia Press, Beijing 1993

*Bernhard, Ralf*, Rechtspfleger, Richter- und Rechtsprechungsbegriff. Verfassungsrechtliche Überlegungen zum Verständnis von Richter und Rechtspfleger, in: DRiZ 1981, p. 368

*Bettermann, Karl August*, Die Unabhängigkeit der Gerichte und der gesetzliche Richter, in: Bettermann, Karl August / Nipperdey, Hans Carl / Scheuner,Ulrich, Die Grundrechte, Handbuch der Theorie und Praxis der Grundrechte, Volume 3, 2nd semi-volume – Rechtspflege und Grundrechtsschutz, Berlin 1959, p. 523-529

*Billing, Werner*, Das Problem der Richterwahl zum Bundesverfassungsgericht, Ordo Politicus, Volume 11 (1969), pp. 121 ff, p. 124

*Bluhm, Gerhard*, Die Beurteilung des Richters und seine Unabhängigkeit, in: DRiZ (1971), p. 330

*Bornkamm, Joachim*, Pressefreiheit und Fairneß des Strafverfahrens: die Grenzen der Berichterstattung über schwebende Strafverfahen im englischen, amerikanischen und deutschen Recht, Baden-Baden 1980, p. 224

*Brugger, Winfried*, Kampf um die Verfassungsgerichtsbarkeit: 200 Jahre Marbury v. Madison, in: JuS 2003, pp. 320-325

*Cai Dingjian*, History and Reform, the Course of Establishing a Legal System in New China, Beijing, China University of Political Science and Law Press, March 1999, Volume 1, p. 390

*Calamendrei, Piero*, Procedure and Democracy, translated by John Clarke Adams and Helen Adams, New York University Press, Washington Square 1956, pp. 35, 36

*Chen Weidong*, Judicial Fairness is Grounded in the Professional Ethics of Judges, in: Journal of Nantong Teacher Training College, December 2001, Volume 17, Issue 4, p. 28

*Chen Weidong / Liu Jihua*, Thoughts on the Current Situation and the Preservation or Abolition of the Procedure of Judicial Review of Death Sentences, in: Chinese Legal Science, 1998, Volume 5, p. 98

*Chen Weidong / Han Dongxing*, Research on the Election of Judges, in: Legal Forum, 5th May 2002, p. 110

*Chen Wenxing*, Comparative Analysis of the System of Prescribed Numbers of Judges, in: Journal of Tianjin University (Social Sciences Edition), July 2008, Volume 10, Issue 4, p. 353

*Chen Xiaofeng*, Research on Chinese Legal Culture, Henan People's Press, p. 491

*Chen Xinmin*, The Principle of the State under the Rule of Law, the Concept of the Rule of Law in Britain and the State under the Rule of Law in Germany, Taiwan University Essays, Volume 28, October 1998, p. 93

*Cheng Chunyi*, The Independence of Judges and the Service Supervision, master's thesis at Taiwan National University Politics Department, June 1988, p. 127

*Chlosta, Christiane*, Nur dem Gesetz unterworfen? Eine rechtsgeschichtliche Untersuchung zu Idee und Wirklichkeit richterlicher Gesetzestreue unter besonderer Berücksichtigung der Aufwertungsrechtsprechung und des richterlichen Prüfungsrechts, Frankfurt on the Main 2005, p. 205

*Creifelds, Carl*, Rechtswörterbuch, 16th edition, Munich 2000, p. 172

*Debusmann, Gero*, Zum Berufsbild des Richters: Vortrag anlässlich der Informations- und Bewerbungsmesse „JurStart" am 19. Mai 2005 in Münster (*paper delivered at the "JurStart" information and advertising trade fair on 19th May 2005 in Münster*)

*Degenhart, Christoph*, Staatsrecht 1, Staatsorganisationsrecht, 19th revised edition, Heidelberg 2003, margin number 620, pp. 249, 288

*Deng Chukai*, An analysis of reference to rules and regulations, in: People's Court Gazette, 25th December 2009

*Deng Jiaming/Yao Yuemei*, Concerns Regarding the Shortage of Judges at the Basic People's Courts and Approaches to the Professionalisation of Judges, in: Guidance and Research on Establishing the Professionalisation of Judges, edited by the Political Department of the Supreme People's Court, 2007, Volume 1, pp. 73-79

*Deng Zhenglai*, The Duality Opinion of the Regulation of Social Order, Research on the Legal Theory of Hayek, in: Legal Commentary of Beijing University, Volume 2, Issue 2, Legal Press 2000, p. 419

*Dietrich, Thorsten Erwin*, Richterwahlausschüsse und demokratische Legitimation, Frankfurt on the Main 2007

*Dinslage, Karl-Heinz*, Richterliche Unabhängigkeit und Dienstaufsicht, in: DRiZ 1960, p. 201

*Dong Xiaojun*, Research on the Mental Pressure on Judges at Basic People's Courts, Taking the Yanqing People's Court as an example, in: Guidance and Research on the Establishment of the Professionalisation of Judges, edited by the Political Department of the Supreme People's Court, 2007, Volume 1, p. 95

*Dütz, Wilhelm*, Richterliche Unabhängigkeit und Politik, in: JuS 1985, pp. 745-749

*Eichenberger, Kurt*, Die richterliche Unabhängigkeit als staatsrechtliches Problem, Bern 1960, pp. 54, 219

*Fang Baoguo*, Supervision of Specific Cases by the National People's Congress Must be Approached with Caution, in: New Beijing News, 27th April 2004

*Fang Liufang*, Observations on Legal Education in China, in: Research on Comparative Law, 1996, Volume 2

*Fangmann, Helmut*, Richterverhältnis und Meinungsfreiheit, in: Labour and Law (*Arbeit und Recht = AuR*) 1985, pp. 7-9

*Fei Xiaotong*, The Generational System in Rural China, Beijing University Press, 1998, p. 6

*Foster, Nigel G. / Sule, Satish*, German Legal System & Laws, 3rd edition, Oxford University Press, 2003, pp. 67-68

*Frauendorf, Lutz*, Zur richterlichen Selbstverwaltung im demokratischen Rechtsstaat, in: Public Administration (*die öffentliche Verwaltung = DÖV*) 1980, pp. 553 ff

*Freckmann, Anke / Wegerich, Thomas*, The German Legal System, Sweet & Maxwell, 1999, pp. 129-131

*Fu Dalin*, Proposed Amendment to the Administrative Procedure Law – a Breakthrough in the Adjudicative Administration "Bottleneck", in: China Youth News, 9th November 2005

*Fu Zhangxuan et al.*, Difficulties and Ways Out: an Investigation and Consideration of the Brain Drain Problem at the Basic People's Courts in Developed Economic Areas, Taking the Basic People's Court of Hangzhou as an Example, in: Guidance and Research on Establishing the Professionalisation of Judges, edited by the Political Department of the Supreme People's Court, 2007, Volume 1, p. 49

*Gao Quanxi*, Legal Order and Liberalism: Hayek's Law and Constitutionalist Thought, and On the Mutual Recognition of Legal Rights: Research on the Phenomenology of Mind, Beijing University Press, 2003 and 2004 editions

*Gao Quanxi*, On Constitutional Politics. Presented at the "Theory Seminar to Commemorate the Semi-Centennial of the "May Fourth" Promulgation of the Constitution and Founding of the National People's Congress" hosted by the Chinese Academy of Social Sciences Research Institute on 5th September 2004; also the introductory section to the short document "Essay on Constitutional Politics".

*Gao Yifei*, The President Who Was Not a Judge, in: Illuminated Research, 7th November 2007

*Geiger, Willi*, Die Unabhängigkeit des Richters, in: DRiZ 1979, pp. 65-69

*Geng Yuji*, Queries and Demonstrative Analysis of the Code of Judicial Ethics for Judges, from the Point of View of the Basic People's Courts, in: Analects of the Sino-Dutch Seminar "Behaviour and Professional Ethics of Judges", edited by the State Judges College, May 2002

German Judges Association (*Deutscher Richterbund = DRB*), in: DRiZ 1996, pp. 246, 248

*Gilles, Peter*, Richterliche Unabhängigkeit und parteipolitische Bindung von Richtern, in: DRiZ 1983, pp. 41-48

*Gilles, Peter / Fischer, Nikolaj*, Juristenausbildung 2003: Anmerkungen zur neuesten Ausbildungsreform, in: NJW 2003, pp. 707-711

*Grimm, Helmut*, Richterliche Unabhängigkeit und Dienstaufsicht in der Rechtsprechung des Bundesgerichtshofs, Cologne 1972, p. 56

*Grimm, Dieter*, Die Verfassung und die Politik: Einsprüche in Störfällen, Munich 2001, pp. 23-26

*Grünhut, Max,* Die Unabhängigkeit der richterlichen Entscheidung, Monatszeitschrift für Kriminalpsychologie und Strafrechtsreform, Supplement No. 3, Heidelberg 1930, p. 1

*Guarnieri, Carlo*, Appointment and Career of Judges in Continental Europe: The Rise of Judicial Self-Government, in: Legal Studies, 2004, Volume 24, Issue 1-2, pp. 169-187

*Guarnieri, Carlo*, Judicial Independence in Latin Countries of Western Europe, in: Peter H. Russel and David M. O'Brien (eds.), Judicial Independence in the Age of Democracy, Critical Perspectives from Around the World, University Press of Virginia, Charlottesville 2001, p. 111

*Guo Zegao*, On the System of Judicial Selection, http://hngf.gov.cn/theory/artilce_list.asp?id=1704&l_class=3

*Haberland, Stephan*, Problemfelder für die richterliche Unabhängigkeit, in: DRiZ 2002, p. 301

*Han Bo*, Research on Reform of the Court System, People's Court Press, Beijing, May 2003, Volume 1, pp. 240-277

*Han Xu*, New Ideas on Chinese Judges in the 21st Century, in: Yunnan University Journal of Jurisprudence, 2001, Volume 1, pp. 19-24

*Han Yong / Zhou Xiaojun*, Research on a New Model for the Relationship between the Ruling Party and Judicial Organs, in: Journal of the Ningxia Party School, September 2006, Volume 8, Issue 5, p. 29

*Hassemer, Winfried*, Vorverurteilung durch die Medien?, in: New Judicial Weekly (*Neue Juristische Wochenschrift = NJW*) 1985, pp. 1921-1929

*Hayek, Friedrich A.*, translated by Deng Zhenglai, The Constitution of Liberty, Beijing Joint Publishing Press, 1997, Part 2, Freedom and the Law, Chapter 13, Liberalism and Administration: The State Under the Rule of Law

*He Derong / Song Jian*, Establishing a Judicial Court System with Chinese Characteristics, in: Application of Law, 2000, Volume 1

*He Huahui*, Theory and Practice of the System of the People's Congress, Wuhan University Press, 1992, p. 55

*He Qinhua*, Choosing the Western Model and Modernisation of the Chinese Judiciary, in: Huadong Law Issues, Beijing Legal Press, 2002, Volume 1, p. 3-28

*He Qinhua*, A History of Western Jurisprudence, China University of Political Science and Law Press, Beijing 1996, p. 191

*He Weifang*, Amendments to the Organic Law of the People's Courts of the People's Republic of China and Judicial Independence, a speech given at the "Seminar on the Rule of Law in China" at the Carnegie Foundation

*He Weifang*, The Course of Chinese Legal Education, China University of Political Science and Law Press, Beijing, 1997 edition, pp. 9-30

*He Weifang*, Two Problems of the System of Judicial Management in China, in: Social Sciences of China, 1997, Volume 6, p. 123-128

*He Weifang*, The Judicial Concept and System, China University of Political Science and Law Press, 1998, p. 101

*He Weifang*, Judicial Reform Begins Again: the Funding for Basic People's Courts is to be Incorporated into the Central Budget, in: 21st Century Economic Report of 5th December 2008

*He Weifang*, Eight Major Issues of Judicial Reform in China, from a speech by He Weifang delivered at the Intermediate People's Court of Haikou on 21st December 2001, entitled "Talk on the Length and Breadth of Judicial Reform", http://www.tecn.cn/data/2885.html

*He Weifang*, Amendments to the Organic Law of the Courts Should Emphasise the Independence of Judges, in answer to a question from the Beijing News, http://article.chinalawinfo.com/Article_Detail.asp?ArticleId=33872

*Heimeshoff, Erich*, Parteipolitische Betätigung von Richtern, in: DRiZ 1975, pp. 261-65

*Hesse, Konrad*, Grundzüge des Verfassungsrechts der Bundesrepublik Deutschland, 15th edition, Heidelberg 1985, p. 212, margin number 689, pp. 256 ff

*Heyde, Wolfgang*, Rechtsprechung, in: Benda, Ernst / Mainhofer, Werner / Vogel, Hans-Jochen (eds.), Handbuch des Verfassungsrechts, 2nd edition, Berlin 1994, Article 33, margin numbers 76, 77, 101

*Heydte, Friedrich August*, Richterfunktion und "Richtergesetz", in: Forschungen und Berichte aus dem öffentlichen Recht, Gedächtnisschrift für Walter Jellinek, edited by Bachof, Otto / Drath, Martin / Gönnenwein, Otto / Walz, Ernst, Munich 1955, p. 493

*Hodenberg, Christian von*, Die Partei der Unparteiischen, Der Liberalismus der preussischen Richterschaft 1815-1848/49, Göttingen 1996, pp. 163 ff

*Hoffmann-Riem, Wolfgang*, Gewaltenteilung – mehr Eigenverantwortung für die Justiz?, in: DRiZ 2000, pp.18-19

*Hoffmann-Riem, Wolfgang*, Das Ringen um die verfassungsgerichtliche Normkontrolle in den USA und Europa, in: Law Practitioner's Gazette (*JuristenZeitung = JZ*) 2003, pp. 269-275

*Hou Yilin*, Perfecting the System of Collegial Panels with Respect to the System of Selecting and Appointing Presiding Judges, in: Legal Systems and Society, 2008, Volume 11 (No. 2 of 2), p. 148

*Hu Fangxin*, On the Development of the Personnel System of Judges in China in View of the German Judges Act, master's thesis at Taiwan Fu Jen Catholic University, June 1988, p. 48

*Hu Jinguang*, On the Void of Judicial Review in China, in: Henan Social Sciences, September 2006, Volume 5, pp. 72-73

*Hu Jinguang*, Research on the Judicial Review of Abstract Behaviour in China, in: Xiamen University Legal Review, Volume 13, Xiamen University Press, June 2007 edition, pp. 37-39

*Hu Jinguang*, On the Review of the Constitutionality of Laws, in: Northern Law, 2007, Volume 2, p. 65

*Hu Xiabing / Feng Rengqiang* (ed.), Summary of Research on Judicial Fairness and Judicial Reform, Tsinghua University Press, Beijing 2001, pp. 164-167

*Huang Yan*, Review and Structure of the System of Judicial Selection, http://www.lawbook.com.cn/lw/lw_view.asp?no=6367

*Huber, Ernst Rudolf*, Die Verfassungsgeschichte seit 1789, Band VI: Die Weimarer Reichsverfassung, Stuttgart/Berlin/Cologne 1993, p. 90

*Immisch, Lars*, Der sozialistische Richter in der DDR und seine Unabhängigkeit, Frankfurt on the Main 1997, p. 20

*Jacot-Guillarmod, Olivier*, Rights Related to Good Administration of Justice (Article 6), in: Macdonald / Matscher / Petzold (eds.), The European System for the Protection of Human Rights, pp. 381-404

*Jarass, Hans / Pieroth, Bodo*, Grundgesetz für die Bundesrepublik Deutschland, 7th edition, Munich, Article 97, margin number 6

*Jiang Bixin*, Practical Background and Ideal Method of Reforming the Classification of Court Staff, in: Guidance and Research on Establishing the Professionalisation of Judges, edited by the Political Department of the Supreme People's Court, 2007, Volume 1, p. 10

*Jiao Hongchang*, From the Localisation of Courts to the Two-Track System of Establishing Courts, in: Journal of the National School of Administration, 2000, Volume 1

*Kang Youwei*, Comment on Politics, in: The Kang Youwei Collection, Volume 1, Shanghai Chinese Classics Publishing House, 1987

*Kang Youwei*, Sixth Letter to the Qing Emperor, Wu Hsu Reforms, in: The Kang Youwei Collection, Volume 2, Shanghai Chinese Classics Publishing House, 1990

*Kaufmann, Arthur*, Richterpersönlichkeit und richterliche Unabhängigkeit, in: Bauman/Tiedemann (ed.), Einheit und Vielfalt des Strafrechts, Festschrift für Karl Peters zum 70. Geburtstag, Tübingen 1974, p. 295

*Kern, Eduard von / Wolf, Manfred von*, Gerichtsverfassungsrecht, 5th edition, Munich 1975, pp. 134-139

*Khorrami, Saltanat*, Das Einstellungs- und Beförderungsverfahren englischer und deutscher Richter, Hamburg 2005, pp. 23, 119-115

*Kissel, Otto Rudolf*, Justiz zwischen Anspruch und Wirklichkeit, in: DRiZ 1987, pp. 301-312

*Kissel, Otto Rudolf / Mayer, Herbert*, Gerichtsverfassungsgesetz (GVG): Kommentar (*Commentary on the Court Constitution Act)*, 4th edition, Munich 2005, Article 1, margin numbers 39 f, 109, 110, 161; p. 142, margin number 34; Article 12, margin number 85; Introduction, margin number 170

*Klein, Hans H.*, Gedanken zur Verfassungsgerichtsbarkeit, in: Burmeister, Joachim (ed.), Verfassungsstaatlichkeit, Festschrift für Klaus Stern zum 65. Geburtstag, Munich 1997, p. 1135

*Kommers, Donald P.*, Autonomy versus Accountability: The German Judiciary, in: Peter H. Russell / David M. O'Brien (eds.), Judicial Independence in the Age of Democracy, University Press of Virginia, 2001, pp. 140-141

*Kong Qingyu*, How Ancient Judges "Rivalled" the Emperor, in: People's Court Weekly, 28th July 2006

*Kong Xiancui*, A Legal System for Guaranteeing Independent Judgements at the People's Courts Needs to be Established, in: Modern Law, 1995, Volume 5, p. 69

*Kopp, Ferdinand O. / Schenke, Wolf-Rüdiger*, Verwaltungsgerichtsordnung, 11th edition, Munich, Article 55, margin number 14

*Krützmann, Karl*, Zur richterlichen Unabhängigkeit im verfaßten Gemeinwesen des Grundgesetzes, in: DRiZ 1985, pp. 201-206

*Lamprecht, Rolf*, Richter contra Richter, Baden-Baden 1992, p.28

*Lansnicker, Frank*, Richteramt in Deutschland. Im Spannungsfeld zwischen Recht und Politik – Darstellung und Analyse anhand von ausgewählten Fallbeispielen, Frankfurt on the Main 1996, p. 98

*Liang Huixing,* Judicial Corruption at an Unacceptable Level, in: Southern Metropolis Daily, 13th March 2009

*Li Jianliang*, Introduction to Administrative Law, Yue Dan Express, Taiwan, January 1988, pp. 168-169

*Li Hong / Ye Lei*, The System of Judges at Basic People's Courts: Between What Ought to Be and What Actually Is, from the Point of View of the Duties Undertaken by the Judges of Basic People's Courts, in: Guidance and Research on Establishing the Professionalisation of Judges, edited by the Political Department of the Supreme People's Court, 2007, Volume 2, p. 127

*Li Hongxi*, Constitutionalism and the Judicial System, in: China Forum, Volume 5, October 1977, p. 22

*Li Yunlong / Shen Deyong*, Comparative Study of the System of Death Sentences, China People's Public Security University Press, Beijing 1992, p. 248

*Li Zhenshan*, Independent Adjudication by Judges According to the Law, in: Law and Justice, Wunan Press, Taiwan 2000, p. 74

*Liao Shunjiang / Zhang Weirong*, Thoughts on the Authority of Railway Transport Courts and on Reform of the Railway Transport Court System, in: Contemporary Legal Forum, Volume 2, 2006

*Liao Yinan*, Report on Issues Regarding Whether Judges Appointed for Life Can Enjoy Retirement Benefits, in: Taiwan University Legal Review, June 1987, Volume 16, Issue 2, pp. 33-38

*Lin Chaorong*, Research on Democratisation of the Prosecution System, doctorial dissertation in the legal research institute of the political science university, June 1993, p. 303

*Lin Jingsong*, Reflections on the System of Deliberation in Chinese Collegial Panels, in: Jurisprudence, 2005, Volume 10, p. 17

*Liu Jiachen*, Litigation and its Axiology, Beijing Normal University Press, 1993, p.46

*Liu Songshan*, Development Zone Courts Represent the Unconstitutional and Illegal Establishment of Judicial Authorities, in: Jurisprudence, 2005, Volume 5, p. 29

*Liu Zhisong*, Difficult Analysis and the Internal Independence of Judges – Orientation Differences in the Internal Independence of Chinese and Western Judges, in: Northern Law, 2008, Volume 2, p. 115

*Liu Zuoxiang*, Legal Culture Theory, Commercial Press, Beijing, 1999 edition, p. 301

*Louven, Klaus*, Inhalt und Grenzen richterlicher Unabhängigkeit, in: DRiZ 1981, pp. 299-300

*Lübbe-Wolf, Gertrude*, Unabhängige Richter im Interesse der Demokratie – Mut zu unbequemen Entscheidungen, in: Neue Zürcher Zeitung of 16th February 2005, p. 11

*Ma Jianhua*, Research on the Professionalisation of Judges, pp. 33, 44-45, 69, 95 ff, 109

*Maunz, Theodor / Dürig, Günter*, Grundgesetz: Kommentar, Munich 2009, Article 97, margin numbers 23, 40, 63 ff; Article 100, margin number 2

*Maunz, Theodor / Dürig, Günter / Herzog, Roman*, Grundgesetz: Kommentar, Munich 1980, Article 97, margin numbers 56, 57

*Meador, Daniel J.*, German Appellate Judges: Career Patterns and Anglo-American Comparisons, in: 67 Judicature No. 1, June-July 1983, pp. 27-30

*Merryman, John Henry*, Judicial Responsibility in the United States, in: The Rabel Journal of Comparative and International Private Law (*Rabelszeitschrift für Ausländisches und Internationales Privatrecht = RabelsZ*) 41, pp. 332-337

*Meyer, Wolfgang*, Dienstaufsicht, richterliche Unabhängigkeit und Zusatzgutachten ohne richterliche Ernennung, in: German Judges Journal (*Deutsche Richterzeitung = DRiZ*) 1981, pp. 22-24

*Mo Jihong*, New Theories on Constitutional Government IV: On the System of Judicial Review in China, http://article.chinalawinfo.com/article/user/article_display.asp?ArticleID=24838 (retrieved on 16th October 2008)

*Mu Huai*, Exerting Influence on Judges, in: Legal Research, 1994, Volume 3, p. 72

*Münch, Ingo von / Kunig, Philip* (eds.): Grundgesetz-Kommentar, Volume 2, 5th edition, Munich 2001; Volume 3, 3rd edition, Munich 1996

*Münch, Ingo von*, Staatsrecht 1, 6th edition, Stuttgart 2000, margin number 89

*Münch, Ingo von*, Unabhängigkeit und Abhängigkeit des Richters mit besonderer Berücksichtigung der Richter des Bundesverfassungsgerichts, Tiblisi 2003, p. 22

*Münch, Joachim* (ed.), Die neue Juristenausbildung: Chancen, Perspektiven und Risiken, Boorberg, Stuttgart 2004, p. 94

*Nie Yongqing / Liu Yanming*, Thoughts on Constitutional Amendment – An Interview with the Constitutional Expert Professor Xu Qing, in: Law and Society, 1999, Volume 3

*Niebler, Engelbert*, Die Stellung des Richters in der Bundesrepublik Deutschland, in: DRiZ 1981, pp. 281 ff

*Niethammer-Vonberg, Christiane*, Parteipolitische Betätigung des Richters – deutsches Recht und rechtsvergleichender Überblick, Berlin 1969

*Oberto, Giacomo*, Richterliche Unabhängigkeit – rechtsvergleichende Betrachtung ihrer institutionellen Ausgestaltung in den Ländern Europas, in: ZRP 2004, pp. 207 ff

*Oppermann, Diethard*, Richterberufung und richterliche Unabhängigkeit, Marburg 1966, pp. 46 ff, pp. 147-148

*Pan Jiaming*, The System and Chosen Method of Judicial Review of Constitutionality, in: Journal of Literature, History and Philosophy, March 2004, pp. 144-149

*Pan Jianfeng*, A Higher-Salary System: the Basic Guarantee of a Fair Judiciary, Incorruptibility and a High Quality of Judges, in: Politics and Law Forum, 2001, Volume 6, p.19

*Papier, Hans-Jürgen*, Die richterliche Unabhängigkeit und ihre Schranken, in: NJW 15/2001, p. 1089

*Peng Dongfang*, On the Feasibility of Abolishing the System of Judicial Committees, in: Western Legal Review, 2009, Volume 1, p. 118

*Peng Zhen*, Selected Works of Peng Zhen, People's Press, Beijing 1991, p. 389

*Persina, Richard*, translated by Su Li, How Judges Deliberate, Beijing University Press, 2009, pp. 245–266, 279

*Peters, Angelika*, Deutschland – arme Richter, in: DRiZ 2002, p. 278

*Qu Tongzu*, Essays on Law by Qu Tongzu, China University of Political Science and Law Press, Beijing 1998, p. 413

*Rädler, Peter*, The Independence and Impartiality of Judges, in: Weissbrodt, David / Wolfrum, Rüdiger (ed.), The Right to a Fair Trial, Berlin 1997, p. 727

*Rheinstein, Max*, Wer wacht über die Wächter?, in: JuS 1974, p. 409

*Sachs, Michael*, Grundgesetz, Kommentar, 5th edition, Munich 2009, Article 97, margin numbers 11 and 38

*Scharpf, Fritz,* Die politischen Kosten des Rechtsstaats, Tübingen 1970, p. 56

*Schinkel, Manfred-Carl*, Bindung an das Gesetz und richterliche Unabhängigkeit – ein Spannungsfeld?, in: Goydke, Jürgen / Rauschning, Dietrich / Robra, Rainer / Schreiber, Hans-Ludwig / Wulff, Christian (ed.), Vertrauen in den Rechtsstaat: Beiträge zur deutschen Einheit im Recht, Festschrift für Walter Remmers, Munich 1995, p. 297

*Rudolf, Kurt*, Die Unabhängigkeit des Richters, in: DRiZ 1984, pp. 135-143

*Schlosser, Peter*, Zivilprozeßrecht I: Erkenntnisverfahren, Munich 1991, p. 56

*Schmid, Gerhard*, Richterauswahl und Richterwahl im Kanton Basel-Landschaft: Auslegeordnung des Status quo und der Reformvorschläge, in: Aspekte der richterlichen Unabhängigkeit und Richter(aus)wahl, Liestahl 2000, p. 111

*Schmidt-Jortzig, Edzard*, Richteramt und politische Betätigung, in: NJW 1984, p. 2057

*Schmidt-Räntsch, Günter / Schmidt-Räntsch, Jürgen*, Deutsches Richtergesetz, Kommentar, 6th edition, Munich 2008: Article 12, margin number 4, p. 321; Article 21, margin numbers 2, 3, 4, 6, 9, 9a, 11, 12, 16, 20, 23, 24, 29, 31; Article 24, margin numbers 3, 8, 9; Article 25, margin number 18, p. 353; Article 26, margin number 19; Article 30, margin numbers 7, 9; Article 31, margin numbers 3, 7, 8, 13, 14; Article 32, margin numbers 4, 5, 12; Article 34, margin numbers 2, 3; Article 36, margin number 2, p. 513; Article 37, margin numbers 3, 5, 9, 13, 14, 20; Article 43, margin number 3; Article 48, margin number 5; pp. 231, 237, 238, 242, 359, 423 ff, 677.

*Schmidt-Räntsch, Günther*, Deutsches Richtergesetz, 3rd edition, Munich: Introduction, margin number 3; Article 25, margin numbers 3, 4; Article 26, margin numbers 30 ff; Article 28, margin numbers 3, 6 ff; pp. 228-229

*Schmidt-Räntsch, Ruth*, Dienstaufsicht über Richter: zugleich eine Auseinandersetzung mit der Rechtsprechung des BGH als Dienstgericht des Bundes, Bielefeld 1985, p. 14

*Schulze-Fielitz, Dr. Helmuth / Dreier, Horst* (ed.), Grundgesetz. Kommentar, Volume 3, Tübingen 2000, Article 97, margin number 37

*Schunck, Egon / De Clerck, Hans*, Allgemeines Staatsrecht und Staatsrecht des Bundes und der Länder, 3rd edition, Siegburg 1970, p. 264

*Seif, Ulrike*, Recht und Justizhoheit, Historische Grundlagen des gesetzlichen Richters in Deutschland, England und Frankreich, Berlin 2003

*Seif, Ulrike*, Recht und Gerechtigkeit: die Garantie des gesetzlichen Richters und die Gewaltenteilungskonzeptionen des 17.-19. Jahrhunderts, in: Der Staat, 2003, pp. 110 ff

*Seifert, Karl-Heinz / Hömig, Dieter* (ed.), Grundgesetz für die Bundesrepublik Deutschland, Kommentar, 8th edition, Nomos, Baden-Baden 2007, Article 98, margin number 2, p. 464

*Shapiro, Martin*, Courts, paperback edition, University of Chicago Press, 1986, p. 65

*Shapiro, Martin*, The European Court of Justice, in: Peter H. Russel / David M. O'Brien (eds.), Judicial Independence in the Age of Democracy: Critical Perspectives from Around the World, London 2001, pp. 273, 279

*Shen Deyong*, A System of Courts Adapted to the Market Economy Should be Established, in: People's Court Paper, 6th June 1994

*Shetreet, Shimon*, Judicial Independence: New Conceptual Dimensions and Contemporary Challenges, in: Shetreet, Shimon / Jules Deschênes, Judicial Independence: The Contemporary Debate, Dordrecht 1985, Chapter 52, pp. 393 f, 646 f

*Simon, Dieter*, Die Unabhängigkeit des Richters, Darmstadt 1975, pp. 2 ff

*Song Jianchao* (Deputy Director of the Political Department of the Supreme People's Court) / *Chen Haiguang* (Director of the Administrative Office for Judges at the Political Department of the Supreme People's Court), Research on Countering the Shortage of Judges, in: Guidance and Research on Establishing the Professionalisation of Judges, edited by the Political Department of the Supreme People's Court, 2007, Volume 1, p. 37

*Stanicki, Henning*, Die Dienstnachschau – Ein Eingriff in die richterliche Unabhängigkeit?, in: DRiZ 1986, pp. 329, 330

*Steinlechner, Wolfgang*, Der Richter im dritten Reich, Mainz 1974, pp. 111-114

*Su Li*, Bringing the Law to the Countryside, China University of Political Science and Law Press, Beijing 2000, pp. 6, 77

*Su Li*, Qiu Ju's Confusion and Shan Gangye's Tragedy, in his work: Bringing the Law to the Countryside (edited version), China University of Political Science and Law Press, March 2004, p. 25

*Su Li*, Understanding the Thoughts and Behaviour of Judges, in: Northern Law, 2009, Volume 1, p. 111

*Su Yanxin*, Influence of Roman Law in Mediaeval Western Europe, in: CASS Journal of Foreign Law, 1997, Volume 4, pp. 35-51

*Tan Shigui*, Research on Issues of Judicial Independence, pp. 17, 106, 116, 121-127

*Tang Zhongmin*, High Salaries Promote Incorruptibility, in: Hebei Law, January 2003, Volume 21, Issue 1

*Teetzmann, Hanspeter*, Selbstverwaltung der Justiz in Europa: Nachholbedarf für Deutschland?, in: DRiZ 2002, p. 394

*Teetzmann, Hanspeter*, Selbstverwaltung der Justiz: Rechtsvergleichender Überblick, in: DRiZ 2003, pp. 44 f

*Teubner, Ernst*, Die Bestellung zum Berufsrichter in Bund und Ländern, Entwicklung, Modelle, Analysen, Köln 1984, pp. 34 f, 91

*Tian Yu / Li Shufeng*, A View on the Professionalisation of Chinese Judges, People's Court Gazette, 21st December 2002

*Thiedemann, Hilke*, Judicial Independence – Eine rechtsvergleichende Untersuchung der Sicherung unabhängiger Rechtsprechung in Südafrika und Deutschland, Baden-Baden 2007, pp. 238, 241, 245, 366, 368, 369, 393

*To Van-Hoa*, Judicial Independence: Legal Research on its Theoretical Aspects, Practices from Germany, the United States of America, France, Vietnam, and Recommendations for Vietnam, Lund 2006, p. 179

*Träger, Ernst*, Der gesetzliche Richter–aktuelle Fragen aus Verfassung und internationalem Recht, in: Fürst, Walther, Festschrift für Wolfgang Zeidler, Volume 1, Berlin 1987, pp. 123 ff

*Wagner, Albrecht*, Der Richter: Geschichte, aktuelle Fragen, Reformprobleme, Karlsruhe 1959, pp. 51 ff, 134, 138

*Wang Guochun / Wu Yugong*, Existing Problems and Countermeasures in the Chinese Judicial System, in: Journal of Changde Normal School (Social Sciences Edition), September 2000, Volume 25, Issue 5

*Wang Liming*, Research on Judicial Reform, Legal Press, Beijing 2000, pp. 98, 100, 102, 104, 421

*Wang Liming*, All Court Funding Should be Incorporated into the Central Budget, in: Legal Daily, 8th March 2007

*Wang Liming*, Research on Social Anthropology in China, Triad Bookshop Press, Beijing 1997

*Wang Pan / Cheng Zhengju*, Judicial Independence and Impartiality, China People's Public Security University Press, Beijing 2002, p. 541

*Wang Qiguo / Zhang Diqiu*, On the Dual Nature of Adjudicative Independence, in: Legal Science, 1989, Volume 3, pp. 67-69

*Wang Renbo*, On the Rule of Law, People's Press, Shandong 1989, pp. 325, 340

*Wang Shuwen*, On Safeguarding Constitutional Implementation, in: China Legal Science, 1992, Volume 6

*Wang Shuwen / Zhou Yanrui*: New Developments in the System of the People's Congress, in: Zhang Youyu, Essays on the Constitution (Forum on Law and Order in China), Social Sciences Literature 2003, p. 164

*Wang Youzhang* (Vice-President of the Zhejiang Higher People's Court and Assistant Secretary of the Party Committee), Brief Discussion of the Leadership of the Party and Judicial Independence, in: Forefront of Theory, 2005, Volume 1, p. 13

*Wang Zhenmin*, The System of Constitutional Review in China, China University of Political Science and Law Press, Beijing 2004, p. 267

*Wassermann, Rudolf*, Alternative Commentary on the Basic Law (*Grundgesetz-Alternativkommentar = GG-AK*), Luchterhand, Neuwied 1984, Article 97, margin numbers 21 ff, 43, 60 ff, 67 ff, 85, 89

*Weng Yuesheng*, Administrative Law and the Modern State under the Rule of Law, Yuedan Press, Taiwan 1990, pp. 513, 515, 518

*Wolf, Manfred / Kern, Eduard*, Gerichtsverfassungsrecht, Beck, Munich 1975, pp. 134-136, 138, 139, 205 f, 213, 215

*Wu Jialin,* On the Necessity and Feasibility of Establishing Constitutional Supervision, in: Law Review, 1991, Volume 2

*Xiao Jianguo / Xiao Jianguang*, Examining the System of Judicial Committee and the Factual Basis for Abolishing the System of Judicial Committee, in: Journal of Beijing University of Science and Technology (Social Sciences Edition), 2002, Volume 3

*Xie Weiyan*, On the Autonomous Development of Constitutional Law, http://www.gongfa.com/xiewyxianfazizhuxing.htm (retrieved on 15th October 2008)

*Xie Youping,* Construction of Justice, China Procuratorate Press, Beijing 2005, pp. 280-281

*Xiong Xianjue*, The Judicial System and Judicial Reform, pp. 67, 68 ff, 73

*Xu Chunzhi*, Judicial Fairness and the Qualities of Judges, http://www.lawlib.com/lw/lw_view.asp?no=3824

*Xu Qianfei*, Further Discussion of the Qualities of Judges, in: People's Judicature, 2002, Volume 1, p. 34

*Xu Qianfei*, The System of Rating Chinese Judges and Reform of the System of People's Courts, in: Applied Law, December 2002, Issue 201, p. 15

*Xu Xianming*, Twenty Topics on Judicial Reform, in: Jurisprudence, 1999, Volume 5, p. 5

*Xu Yang*, Research on Issues within the Subject of Criminal Adjudication, master's thesis at Renmin University of China, June 2004, p. 27

*Yan Fu*, The Essence of the Law, Volume 19, Chapter 26, authors' comments, Commercial Press, Shanghai 1909

*Yan Yang*, Railway Courts Should Be Allowed to Die a Natural Death, Kaidi Weekly of 7th October 2007

*Yao Danqi*, Dilemmas and Ways Out: Research on the Practical Judicial Capability of Young Judges at the Basic People's Courts – Beginning to Unscramble a Social Text, in: Guidance and Research on the Establishment of the Professionalisation of Judges, edited by the Political Department of the Supreme People's Court, 2007, Volume 2, p. 80

*Yao Li*, Analysis of the Current State of the System of Chinese Judges, and Restructuring the System, in: Jurisprudence, 2003, Volume 9, p. 27

*Yu Weiqing*, It is Time to Abolish Judicial Committees, in: Journal of Fuyang Normal College (Social Sciences Edition), 2002, Volume 2

*Yuan Xingman*, Demonstrating the Advantages of Party Members in Judicial Practice, http://ch.ahxf.gov.cn/ONEWS.asp?id=719

*Zätzsch, Jörg*, Richterliche Unabhängigkeit und Richterauswahl in den USA und Deutschland, Baden-Baden 2000, pp. 36, 49, 63, 80

*Zeng Jinsheng*, Reinvestigating the Case of Li Huijuan, in: Trends of the Times, People's Daily 2004, Volume 9

*Zhai Xuewei*, The Reproduction of Human Kindness, Reputation and Power, and the Method of Social Exchange in a Common Sense Society, in: Social Sciences Research, 2004, Volume 5, pp. 49, 50, 52

*Zhang Chunhe*, On the Presidents of Courts, in: Jurisprudence Magazine, 1997, Volume 3, pp. 37-38

*Zhang Jinfan*, China's Legal Tradition and its Modern Transformation, Legal Press, Beijing 1997, pp. 42, 427

*Zhang Jinfan*, Summary of a Hundred Years of Law and China under the Rule of Law, in: China Legal Science, 2005, Volume 5, pp. 185-192

*Zhang Qianfan*, From a Constitution to Constitutional Government, in: Research on Comparative Law, 2008, Volume 1, p. 75

*Zhang Qianfan*, From a Constitution to Constitutional Government, in: Developments in the Law in Mainland China, Taiwan, Hong Kong and Macau in 2006 (Book One), edited by Tang Dezong / Wang Pengxiang, Xin Xuelin Publishing House, Taiwan 2007, p. 59

*Zhang Qianfan*, Dealing with the Constitution Conscientiously: On the Necessity and Feasibility of Constitutional Government Review, in: Chinese and Foreign Jurisprudence, 2003, Volume 5, p. 560

*Zhang Taiyan*, Criminal Officer, in: Zhang Clan Series, Volume 7, People's Press, Shanghai 1980

*Zhang Wenyu*, Evaluating Judges and the Independence of Judges, Constitutional Government Times, Volume 26, July 2000, p. 5

*Zhang Wusheng*, Research on the Regrouping and Re-assignment of Chinese Judges, in Legal Science, 2004, Volume 3, p. 46

*Zhang Yongquan*, On the System of Collegial Panels, http://www.dffy.com/faxuejieti/ss/200404/20040405212454-3.htm

*Zhang Zhaokai*, A History of the Judiciary in Ancient China, Yuelu Press, Changsha 2005, p. 3-4

*Zhang Zhongqiu*, Comparative Research on Chinese and Western Legal Culture, Nanjing University Press, 1999, Volume 2, p. 348

*Zhao Junru*, The Current Situation of the Judicial Court System and Prospects for its Reform, in: Modern Law, October 1999, Volume 21, Issue 5

*Zhao Xiaosuo*, Structure of the Chinese System of Judges, People's Court Press, Beijing, April 2003, pp. 175, 178

*Zhou Anping / Liu Huigui*, Criticisms of the System of Supervision of Individual Cases by the National People's Congress, Chinese Justice, 2006, No. 11, pp. 31-32

*Zhou Jianjie / Du Kailin*, Restructuring the System of Salaries for Chinese Judges, in: Applied Law, 2005, Volume 7, p. 16

*Zou Ju*, The Role of the News Media in the Balance and Guiding of Social and Public Opinion in the Case of Liu Yong, from: the Death of Socrates Speeches, News Knowledge, 2004, No. 4

*Zhu Fuhui / Shao Zihong*, Comparison of the Court Systems in the USA and Germany, in: Modern Jurisprudence, December 2001, Volume 23, Issue 6, p. 16

*Zhu Mei'an / Wang Qingquan*, Changde Municipal Party Committee (Both Chambers) Decides Not to Participate in the Deliberation and Evaluation of Trends, in: People's Court Paper, 1st June 2004, front page

*Zhu Xiangdong / Xiao Guilin*, On the Dialectical Integration of Judicial Independence and Party Leadership, in: Journal of Southeast University, September 2005, Volume 7, Issue 5, pp. 11-12

*Zhuo Zeyuan*, The State under the Rule of Law, Legal Press, Beijing 2001, p. 64

*Zuleeg, Manfred*, Der Wandel der deutschen Judikative in Zeiten knapper Mittel, in: Zeitschrift für Rechtspolitik (ZRP), Volume 33 (2000), Issue 11, pp. 483-489

*Zweigert, Konrad*, Zur inneren Unabhängigkeit des Richters, in: Esser, Josef / Thieme, Hans (eds.), Festschrift für Fritz von Hippel zum 70. Geburtstag, pp. 711-723

# Reports / Documents / Interviews

Historical Records of the Preparations for Constitutionality in the late Qing dynasty, Volume 2, in Archival Documents Concerning Late Qing Dynasty, Zhonghua Book Company 1979

International Bar Association Code of Minimum Standards of Judicial Independence

Discussion with judge Li Qing of the First Court of Beijing, held on 29th March 2007

Section 6 of the Second Five-year Reform Plan of the People's Courts (2004-2006), Reform and Perfection of the Court Personnel Management System, http://www.dffy.com/faguixiazai/xf/200512/20051214221735-2.htm

White paper of 19th October 2005 on Building of Political Democracy in China

Speech by Xiao Yang, President of the Supreme People's Court: Course and Outlook of Reform of the People's Courts, http://www.hflib.gov.cn/law/law/falvfagui2/CXF/LWJ/1019.htm

21st Century Economic Report of 14th June 2004, the Logic of Central Enterprises Breaking Away From Public Security Organisations, Prosecutorial Organisations and People's Courts

Joint Notice of the Supreme People's Court, the Supreme People's Prosecutors' Office, the Ministry of Public Security, the Ministry of Justice and the Railway Department on relevant issues in the adjudication by Railway Transport Courts and the Prosecutors' Office

Regulation on the Jurisdiction of Railway Transport Courts with respect to Economic Disputes issued by the Supreme People's Court on 16th June 1990

Document No. 9 of the Central Committee of the Chinese Communist Party

Second 5-year Reform Program of the People's Courts by the Supreme People's Court, October 2005

"Looking Back at 27 Years of Devolved Competence to Examine and Approve Death Sentences to Lower Courts: From the Rule of Man to the Rule of Law", China Newsweek, 29th December 2006

Special topic in the Prosecutors' Daily, "Focus on the Withdrawal by the Supreme People's Court of the Devolved Competence to Examine and Approve Death Sentences", http://www.jcrb.com/zyw/sxfh/index.htm

"Supreme People's Court Wishes to Establish a System of Authority for Collegial Panels", reported on Xinhua Net on 6th January 2007, http://news.xinhuanet.com/legal/2007-01/06/content_5573359.htm

Bundesamt für Justiz, Referat III 3, 2224 III - B7 221/2007 Ausbildungsstatistik, Stand: 6. Februar 2008 (*Federal Office of Justice, Department III 3, 2224 III - B7 221/2007 Statistics on Education, dated 6th February 2008*)

Bundesamt für Justiz, Referat III 3, 3110/6 - B7 17/2007, Stand: 7. Februar 2008 (*Federal Office of Justice, Department III 3, 3110/6 - B7 17/2007, dated 7th February 2008*)

Regulation of the Presidents of the Higher People's Courts and Provincial Chief Procurators, Xinhua website, 25th December 2007, http://news.xinhuanet.com/legal/2007-12/25/content_7310406.htm

Paragraph 1 of Article 4 and Articles 16, 20 and 44 of the "Party and Government Administration Leadership Cadre's Working Regulations on Selection and Appointment" as printed and distributed by the Chinese Communist Party Central Committee on 9th July 2002, http://news.xinhuanet.com/ziliao/2003-01/18/content_695422_1.htm

Verordnung über die Errichtung von Truppendienstgerichten vom 16. Mai 2006 (BGBl. I S. 1262)

Official website of the Bavarian State Ministry of Justice: http://www.justiz.bayern.de/ministerium/berufe/rista/00042/

Article "Many Judges at Shenzhen Intermediate People's Court being Investigated according to the 'Two-fold Directive'" of 7th November 2006, http://www.gmw.cn/content/2006-11/07/content_504081.htm

Judgement of 17th October 1977 by the German Federal Court of Justice (the service court of the German Federation), NJW 1978, p. 825

How to Execute When Local Regulations Conflict with State Laws (17th November 1989), by the Legal Work Committee of the Standing Committee of the National People's Congress (I) 18

Preliminary Investigation on Reform of the System of Guaranteeing Funds for the Court of Yangpu, in: Legal Forum of the Special Economic Zones, 2003, Volume 77

Judgement of 3rd November 2004 by the German Federal Court of Justice (Bundesgerichtshof = BGH, the service court of the German Federation) in: DRiZ 2005, pp. 83 f

Report in the First Finance and Economics Daily, 14th November 2005: Judicial Reform Shoulders Heavy Responsibilities, Funding for Courts Looking Up

Report in the People's Court Paper, 7th May 1993: Serious Deficiencies in Funding for Basic People's Courts in Poverty-Stricken Areas

Report in the Legal Daily of 8th May 2007: One Month after the Implementation of the New Method of Court Costs and Some Courts are Faced with Strains on their Funding

Report in the People's Daily, 19th September 2007, Central Financing Committee Establishes a System of Special Funds to Subsidise Courts in their Handling of Cases

Report in the Procuratorial Daily, 10th March 2008, Government Work Report Orders a Strengthening of the Guarantees on Judicial Funding

Stellungnahme Hamburger Verwaltungsrichter in dem Abschlussbericht der Arbeitsgruppe II, p. 114

Bulletin of the Supreme People's Court, 1993, Volume 1, p. 34
Bulletin of the Supreme People's Court, 1993, Volume 2, p. 71

Press report, Mit Ost-Erfahrung an ein Bundesgericht, in the *Frankfurter Allgemeine Zeitung (FAZ)* of 9th September 2004, p. 10

Website of the Supreme People's Court:
http://www.court.gov.cn/about/200302130028.htm

Explanation on the official website of the NPC: http://www.npc.gov.cn/npc/flsyywd/xianfa/2002-07/11/content_297398.htm

Article 3 of the Notice by the Organisational Department of the CPC Central Committee, the Ministry of Labour and the Ministry of Human Resources on the age of retirement for female cadres

Paragraph 3 of Article 3 of the Decision of the Chinese Communist Party Central Committee on Establishing a Retirement System for Old Cadres

Chapter 14 of the Law of the People's Republic of China on Public Servants, on the website of the NPC, http://www.npc.gov.cn/npc/flsyywd/xingzheng/2005-08/05/content_353269.htm

European Union Investigation of Judges: Comparison of the Incomes of European Judges, in: DRiZ 2002, pp. 277 ff

Statistisches Bundesamt, Ausgewählte Zahlen für die Rechtspflege - Fachserie 10, Reihe 1–2009, Stand: 22.12.2009 (*Federal Office of Statistics, Selected Figures for the Judicature - specialist series 10, set 1–2009, dated 22nd December 2009*)

Bundesamt für Justiz, Referat III 3, Bundesgerichtshof Zusammenstellung des Personalbestandes, Stand: 4. März 2009 (*Federal Office of Justice, Department III 3, Composition of the Staff Complement of the Federal Court of Justice, dated 4th March 2009*)

Bundesamt für Justiz, Referat III 3, Zahl der Richter, Staatsanwälte und Vertreter des öffentlichen Interesses in der Rechtspflege der Bundesrepublik Deutschland am 31. Dezember 2006, Stand: 7. Februar 2008 (*Federal Office of Justice, Department III 3, Numbers of Judges, Public Prosecutors and Public Representatives in the judicature of the Federal Republic of Germany on 31st December 2006, dated 7th February 2008*)

Auszug aus dem Datenreport 2008 vom Statistischen Bundesamt Deutschland, p. 12, Tab. 1: Bevölkerung am 31. Dezember 2006 (*Extract from the 2008 Data Report by the German Office of Statistics, page 12, Table 1: Population on 31st Decemeber 2006*)

Bundesamt für Justiz, Referat III 3, Geschäftsentwicklung bei Gerichten und Staatsanwaltschaften, Stand: 5. Februar 2009 (*Federal Office of Justice, De-*

*partment III 3, Workload Development at Courts and Public Prosecutors' Offices, dated 5th February 2009*)

Press report, Record of the First National Case in Which a Concubine Fights for Inheritance by Presenting a Will, in: Legal Daily, 5th November 2001

Website of the Supreme People's Court: http://www.court.gov.cn/news/bulletin/activity/200903180015.htm

Work report of the Supreme People's Court on 10th March 2009, on the website of the Supreme People's Court: http://www.court.gov.cn/news/bulletin/activity/200903180015.htm

Work Report of the Supreme People's Court of 10th March 2008, on the website of the Supreme People's Court: http://www.court.gov.cn/news/bulletin/activity/200903180015.htm

Website of the First Intermediate People's Court of Beijing: http://bj1zy.chinacourt.org/public/detail.php?id=559

Recruitment plan of the Supreme People's Court in 2008, accessed at: http://learning.sohu.com/s2007/0576/s252643823/index.shtml

Elena Torreguitar

# National Liberation Movement in Office

## Forging Democracy with African Adjectives in Namibia

Frankfurt am Main, Berlin, Bern, Bruxelles, New York, Oxford, Wien, 2009.
504 pp.
Europäische Hochschulschriften. Reihe 31: Politikwissenschaft. Vol. 567
ISBN 978-3-631-57995-4 · pb. € 74,50*

How does a liberation movement transform itself into a political party? What are the burdens and liabilities that come about when these movements integrate in the democratic process? The author tries to answer these questions analyzing SWAPO's war of independence against the South African apartheid regime and the changes it went through once the party won the first free elections in 1989. The authoritarian regime that emerged was the outcome of thirty years of exile in neighboring Zambia and Angola. The latter and the consequences of the earlier destruction of the African traditions, following the colonial intervention, gave way to a specific African version of democracy. Is this democracy going to develop into a full, all embracing system or it is going to end in democratic failure? The author looks deeply into the historical and political past of the Namibian process and gives an optimistic, upbeat account of an African democracy.

*Content:* Democracy · African Democracy · Namibia, South Africa and the UN · The formation of SWAPO · Liberation Movements · Liberation War · Repression and the Detainees Issue · Inside Namibia and Abroad · Independence, Peace Accords, Elections and the Role of the UN · Namibia in its Regional Context: Zimbabwe, Angola, Mozambique and South Africa